Sentencing and the Legitimacy of Trial Justice

This book discusses the under-researched relationship between sentencing and the legitimacy of punishment. It argues that there is an increasing gap between what is perceived as legitimate punishment and the sentencing decisions of the criminal courts.

Drawing on a wide variety of empirical research evidence, the book explores how sentencing could be developed within a more socially inclusive framework for the delivery of trial justice. In the international context, such developments are directly relevant to the future role of the International Criminal Court, especially its ability to deliver more coherent and inclusive trial outcomes that contribute to social reconstruction. Similarly, in the national context, these issues have a vital role to play in helping to reposition trial justice as a credible cornerstone of criminal justice governance where social diversity persists. In so doing the book should help policy-makers in appreciating the likely implications for criminal trials of 'mainstreaming' restorative forms of justice.

Sentencing and the Legitimacy of Trial Justice firmly ties the issue of legitimacy to the relevant context for delivering 'justice'. It suggests a need to develop the tools and methods for achieving this and offers some novel solutions to this complex problem.

This book will be a valuable resource for graduate students, academics, practitioners and policy-makers in the field of criminal justice, as well as scholars interested in socio-legal and cross-disciplinary approaches to the analysis of criminal process and sentencing and the development of theory and comparative methodology in this area.

Ralph Henham is Professor of Criminal Justice at Nottingham Law School, Nottingham Trent University. Recent publications include *Sentence Discounts and the Criminal Process* (2001); *Punishment and Process in International Criminal Trials* (2005); *Transforming International Criminal Justice: Retributive and Restorative Justice in the Trial Process* (2005) and *Beyond Punishment: Achieving International Criminal Justice* (2010) (with Mark Findlay), in addition to numerous articles on theoretical, comparative and policy-related aspects of sentencing. He has held visiting positions at the Universities of Cambridge, Oxford, Sydney and the European University Institute, Florence.

Sentencing and the Legitimacy of Trial Justice

Ralph Henham

Routledge
Taylor & Francis Group

LONDON AND NEW YORK

First published 2012
by Routledge
2 Park Square, Milton Park, Abingdon, Oxon, OX14 4RN

Simultaneously published in the USA and Canada
by Routledge
711 Third Avenue, New York, NY 10017

Routledge is an imprint of the Taylor & Francis Group, an informa business

© 2012 Ralph Henham

The right of Ralph Henham to be identified as author of this work has been
asserted by him in accordance with sections 77 and 78 of the Copyright,
Designs and Patents Act 1988.

British Library Cataloguing in Publication Data
A catalogue record for this book is available from the British Library

Library of Congress Cataloging in Publication Data
Henham, Ralph J., 1949-
Sentencing and the legitimacy of trial justice / Ralph Henham.
p. cm.
1. Criminal justice, Administration of--Philosophy. 2. Punishment--
Philosophy. 3. Sentences (Criminal procedure)--Philosophy. I. Title.
K5001.H46 2011
345'.0772--dc22
2011004645

ISBN13: 978-0-415-67141-5 hbk
ISBN13: 978-0-203-80673-9 ebook

Typeset in Times New Roman
by Integra Software Services Pvt. Ltd., Pondicherry

Printed and bound in Great Britain by
CPI Antony Rowe, Chippenham, Wiltshire

For Anne Marie, as always

Humanly speaking, in default of natural sanctions, the laws of justice are ineffective among men: they merely make for the good of the wicked and the undoing of the just, when the just man observes them towards everybody and nobody observes them towards him

(Jean Jacques Rousseau, 1762)

Contents

List of figures

Table of cases

England and Wales

R v Billam (1986) 8 Cr App R (S) 48
Attorney-General's Reference (No. 4 of 1989) [1990] 1 WLR 41
R v Secretary of State for the Home Department, Ex parte Venables and R v Secretary of State for the Home Department, Ex parte Thompson [1997] UKHL 25
R v Perks (2001) 1 Cr App R (S) 19
R v Kefford (2002) 2 Cr App R (S) 106
R v Mills (2002) 2 Cr App R (S) 229
A and Ors v Secretary of State for the Home Department [2004] UKHL 56
Attorney-General's Reference Nos 31, 42, 43, 45, 50 and 51 [2004] EWCA Crim 1934
R v Cain & Ors (2006), *The Times*, 26 December
R v Saw & Ors [2009] EWCA Crim 1

France

Conseil Constitutionnel, n 93–325 DC, 13 August 1993
Conseil Constitutionnel, n 95–360 DC, 2 February 1995

Italy

Corte Constituzionale, judgment n 107/1980
Corte Constituzionale, judgment n 313/1990

European cases

X v United Kingdom (1972) 40 CD 64
Deweer v Belgium (1979–80) 2 EHRR 439
Funke v France (Case A/256-A) ECHR [1993]; 1 CMLR 897
Thynne, Wilson and Gunnell v United Kingdom (1991) 13 EHRR 666

International cases

ICC

Decision on the Applications for Participation in the Proceedings of VPRS 1, VPRS 2, VPRS 3, VPRS 4, VPRS 5 and VPRS 6, Situation in the Democratic Republic of Congo, Case No ICC 01/04, Pre-Trial Chamber I, 17 January 2006.

ICTR

Prosecutor v Akayesu (Case No ICTR–96–4-T) 2 September 1998.
Prosecutor v Kambanda (Case No. ICTR-97-23-S), Judgement and Sentence, 4 September 1998.
Prosecutor v Niyitegeka (ICTR-96-14-T), Judgement and Sentence, 16 May 2003.

ICTY

Prosecutor v Delalić et al (Case No. IT-96-21-T), Judgement, 16 November 1998, (the '*Čelebići*' case).
Prosecutor v Delalić (Case No. IT-96-21), Appeals Judgement, 20 February 2001
Prosecutor v Deronjić (Case No IT-02-61-S), Dissenting Opinion of Judge Wolfgang Schomburg, 30 March 2004.
Prosecutor v Deronjić (Case No IT-02-61-S), Sentencing Judgement, 30 March 2004.
Prosecutor v Furundžija (Case No. IT-95-17/1-T), Judgement, 10 December 1998.
Prosecutor v Krstić (Case No. IT-98-33-T), Judgement, 2 August 2001.
Prosecutor v Krstić (Case No. IT-98-33-A), Appeals Chamber Judgement, 19 April 2004.
Prosecutor v Kunarac et al. (Case No IT-96-23-T & IT-96-23/1-T) 22 February 2001.
Prosecutor v Momir Nikolić (Case No. IT-02-60/1-S), Trial Chamber, Sentencing Judgement, 2 December 2003.
Prosecutor v Momir Nikolić (Case No. IT-02-60/1-A), Judgement on Sentencing Appeal, 8 March 2006.
Prosecutor v Plavšić (Case No. IT-00-30&40/1-S), Trial Chamber, Judgement, 27 February 2003.
Prosecutor v Tadić (Case No. IT-94-1-S), Sentencing Judgement, 14 July 1997.
Prosecutor v Todorović (Case No. IT-95-9/1), Sentencing Judgement, 31 July 2001.

Table of legislation

United Nations

Universal Declaration of Human Rights 1948
International Covenant on Civil and Political Rights 1976

European legislation

European Convention on Human Rights 1950

England and Wales

Criminal Justice Act 1988
Criminal Justice Act 1991
Anti-Terrorism, Crime and Security Act 2001
Criminal Justice Act 2003
Constitutional Reform Act 2005
Criminal Justice Act 1988 (Review of Sentencing) Order
  2006
Criminal Justice and Immigration Act 2008
Coroners and Justice Act 2009

France

French Criminal Code 1994
French Criminal Procedure Code 1808
French Criminal Procedure Code
The French Constitution 1958
Livres des Procédures Fiscales
Code de Santé Publique
Law n 81–908, 9 October 1981
Law n 99–515, 23 June 1999

Italy

Other National Legislation

International Legislation

ICC

ICTR

ICTY

Acknowledgements

Sentencing is pivotal to the credibility of the criminal process. It is through sentencing that the legitimacy of punishment is declared and justified. However, punishment is increasingly portrayed as something that should be more responsive to the pluralistic values and needs of individuals and communities in contemporary society. They may have very different perceptions of what justice should consist of and how it should be delivered. Despite this, the relationship between sentencing and legitimacy is something which has received scant attention in recent analyses of the role of the criminal trial. Such accounts generally fail to explain how the trial process might be implicated in delivering more inclusive forms of sentencing by tying the issue of legitimacy more firmly to the relevant contexts for delivering 'justice'. This book sees the ability of the trial to produce more socially responsive sentences as key to the effectiveness of criminal justice governance and directly connected to issues of social welfare and the cohesion of communities. The volume builds on the author's previous work on developing more inclusive forms of trial justice and its implications for the future of 'legitimate' governance in criminal justice at both the international and domestic level.

The research and writing of this book were greatly facilitated as a result of time spent as a Visiting Scholar at the Institute of Criminology and Pembroke College, Cambridge during the Easter Term of 2010. In particular, the author wishes to thank Professor Loraine Gelsthorpe of Cambridge University for her most helpful and constructive comments on the manuscript. My thanks also to Dr Caroline Fournet of the University of Exeter and Professor Grazia Mannozzi of the University of Insubria, Como for their invaluable assistance with the French and Italian materials, and to Professor Roger Cotterrell of Queen Mary, University of London, and Dr Jonathan Doak of Nottingham Trent University for helping me to clarify my thinking in the early stages. Needless to say, the views expressed herein, and any errors that remain, are mine alone.

Finally, the constant support and encouragement of my wife, Anne Marie, is also acknowledged. Without it, this book would never have been written.

Ralph Henham
Nottingham, October 2010

List of abbreviations

CC	Criminal Code
CPP	Code of Criminal Procedure (codice di procedura penale)
ECHR	European Convention on Human Rights
ICC	International Criminal Court
ICCPR	International Covenant on Civil and Political Rights
ICTR	United Nations International Criminal Tribunal for Rwanda
ICTY	United Nations International Criminal Tribunal for the Former Yugoslavia
RPE	Rules of Procedure and Evidence
SAP	Sentencing Advisory Panel
SC	Sentencing Council
SFRY	Socialist Federal Republic of Yugoslavia
SGC	Sentencing Guidelines Council
VAS	Victims' Advocate Scheme
VFS	Victim Focus Scheme
VIS	Victim Impact Statement
VPS	Victim Personal Statement

Introduction

This book discusses the relationship between sentencing and the legitimacy of punishment. By 'legitimacy' the book refers to the public perception of punishment, rather than offering a moral critique of the sentencing process. Sentencing is crucial because it is the point in the trial where the aims of punishment are given concrete and public expression in specific cases. Therefore, the process of sentence decision-making provides a crucial link between the ideology[1] which informs punishment and the context against which the legitimacy of punishment is judged.

The book argues that there is an increasing gap between what is perceived as legitimate punishment and the sentencing decisions of the criminal courts. The book contends that this argument holds good for sentencing in both international and national contexts, and has significant implications for the future role of trial justice. The book suggests that the aims of punishment and their realisation through sentencing are becoming increasingly divorced from what individuals and communities perceive as 'justice' for certain types of behaviour and offender. This perceived 'failure' is invariably blamed on the judiciary and their wide discretionary powers in sentencing, in addition to the legal framework, structures and procedures that shape the sentencing process.

The book argues that there are important similarities, as well as differences, between international and domestic sentencing practices. The most important similarities are the ideological and normative constraints placed upon sentencing by the predominantly retributive sentencing philosophy and adversarial model of trial justice prevalent in common law based systems of criminal justice, such as the United States and England and Wales.

In developing its argument, the book draws on a wide range of international and national sentencing sources. The main international focus is the sentencing practices of the United Nations International Criminal Tribunals for the Former Yugoslavia (ICTY) and Rwanda (ICTR), and the International Criminal Court (ICC), although the analysis also draws on the experiences of

---

1 'Ideology' here refers to penal ideology, which is a matter of political reality.

internationalised and hybrid courts and tribunals, such as those of Kosovo, Sierra Leone and East Timor.

The domestic focus is on the sentencing practices and criminal justice systems of Western Europe; more particularly, England and Wales, France and Italy. England and Wales provides an excellent example of a common-law jurisdiction which combines adversarial trial with a sentencing philosophy based on just deserts. The influence of the latter has gradually diminished over the last twenty years or so, this being accompanied by a slow erosion of judicial discretionary power in sentencing. On the other hand, other countries in Western Europe, such as Italy, have become more hybridised, with the dominant civil law, inquisitorial mode of trial being infiltrated by adversarial trial practices that have often not been fully integrated into pre-existing penal ideology and processes. This phenomenon has caused significant conceptual and practical difficulties in the area of sentencing.[2]

In addition, the book draws on a wide variety of empirical research evidence. For example, in the international context, such evidence ranges from victim surveys examining perceptions of punishment in Rwanda and the Former Yugoslavia to the evaluation of recent initiatives, such as the ICC's Outreach programme and its impact on the delivery of trial justice. In the domestic context, evidence from England and Wales draws on recent developments such as the victims' advocate scheme,[3] as well as the Sentencing Advisory Panel's research report on the perception of sentences for driving-related deaths.[4]

The book suggests two reasons why the role of sentencing in shaping perceptions of punishment has major significance for the future of criminal justice and its credibility:

1. Contemporary societies increasingly contain individuals and groups with very different perceptions of what justice should consist of and how it should be delivered. Consequently, conflicting views as to the legitimacy of punishment delivered through the sentencing decisions of criminal trials are likely to increase for the foreseeable future.
2. The question of legitimacy is directly related to that of effective governance in criminal justice, because loss of faith, or lack of moral empathy by citizens with the ideologies, processes and outcomes of punishment suggests that the ability of criminal justice to function effectively (for example, by maintaining the 'rule of law') is gradually being undermined.

This book does not pretend to provide the solution to what is a very complex problem. Rather, by focusing on the theory, principles and practice of sentencing it seeks to illuminate one aspect of the debate and so offers a positive way forward.

---

2 Henham and Mannozzi (2003).
3 The Victims' Advocate Scheme was replaced by the Victim Focus Scheme in 2007.
4 Hough *et al.* (2008).

One of the book's core objectives is to develop the analytical tools to help us comprehend more accurately what such a crisis in legitimacy might mean in practical terms for the future role of criminal justice. Consequently, the book argues that existing theories and methods for explaining sentencing fail to provide an effective framework for understanding its relationship to questions of legitimacy. Sentencing theory is generally weak in helping us to explain the normative effect of sentencing; namely, how people's expectations about punishment relate to what *actually* transpires when a sentencing decision is made, and the impact the sentence itself has on values and behaviour beyond the courtroom.

In conceptualising the notion of legitimacy, the book takes a broad and inclusive view of the role of the trial in delivering 'just' punishment. In other words, it does not simply focus on the issue of individual criminal responsibility, and the trial's traditional purpose of punishing individuals found guilty of alleged crimes. Instead, it supports the view that notions of criminal responsibility should be delineated by their social context, so linking them inextricably to social and community concerns.[5] Such a perspective not only recognises that social conditions contribute to criminality, but also that the harmful consequences of crime and their effective punishment are directly connected to issues of social welfare and the cohesion of communities.[6] This is based on the view that responsibility for both the causes and consequences of criminality should be shared between individuals and communities. Internationally, for example, the notion of individual responsibility appears inadequate when much of the violence is collective in nature and rooted in cultural history.[7] Hence, the book argues strongly that a major focus for the trial should be to reflect the justice expectations of both individuals and communities in the practice of sentencing.

The book examines how far these justice expectations are currently reflected in the theory and practice of sentencing. An important aspect of this, and essential to extending the ability of the trial to produce more socially responsive sentences, is the extent to which values about punishment are shared in any particular social context. For example, in national systems, this sharing may reflect commonly held views about how courts should deal with particular types of crime, or criminal. These may vary in their intensity according to community or culture.[8] In the international context, universally shared values

---

5 Shared responsibility, restoration and community reintegration are also key concerns of restorative justice.

6 See, further, Hudson (1993), Lacey (1988).

7 At the domestic level, there may be wide differences between offences such as burglary and fraud in terms of perceived gravity, notions of responsibility and appropriate sentencing levels that are the result of cultural history; see Slapper and Tombs (1999).

8 In England and Wales, for example, the jury or magistrates personify the concept of lay participation, although, of course, the deliberations of the former are restricted solely to matters of innocence or guilt.

might include the widespread condemnation of crimes such as genocide and crimes against humanity. However, there may be less agreement about how to achieve peace and reconciliation, and the extent to which trial justice might be expected to contribute to this. Therefore, such a perspective recognises the importance of reflecting the diversity of justice expectations in trial processes and outcomes.

The book aims to advance knowledge in a number of key areas:

- It proposes a more normative perspective for analysing the social reality of sentencing which focuses on the relationship between sentence decision-making and social context and aims to extend our capacity for understanding the impact of trial justice.
- Its detailed analysis of the structures and processes of sentencing seeks to enhance our understanding of the relationship between the ideology of punishment and sentencing practice in criminal trials and its implications for criminal justice policy.
- The book's methodological focus on deconstructing the social context of sentencing is aimed at increasing our understanding of how trial justice is perceived in different jurisdictions. It is hoped this will assist those policy-makers who wish to consider more effective ways of making sentencing more inclusive and socially responsive.
- The book should help provide clearer insights into the relationship between values and process on the international platform and those on the domestic platform, and the extent to which they cross-fertilise each other.

In summary, the book discusses how sentencing could be developed within a more socially inclusive framework for the delivery of trial justice.[9] In the international context, such developments are directly relevant to the future role of the ICC, especially its capacity for delivering more coherent and inclusive trial outcomes that contribute to social reconstruction. Similarly, in the national context, these issues have a vital role to play in helping to reposition trial justice as a credible cornerstone of criminal justice governance where social diversity persists. In so doing, the book should assist policy-makers in appreciating the likely implications for criminal trials of 'mainstreaming' restorative forms of justice.

---

9 The expression 'trial justice' refers to the significance of the sentence in terms of its perception by 'relevant audiences'. It should not therefore be taken as referring to the perceived 'justice' of the overall trial. Consequently, when referring to sentencing in the context (or as part) of the trial, my object is to draw attention to the importance of conceptualising it as something which is part of a continuous process of structured social interaction (the criminal trial process), rather than, as has often been the case hitherto, explaining sentencing as if it were a self-contained entity, detached from both what has gone before and what is to come. This approach is consistent with my view that a holistic appreciation of the trial, and the place of sentencing within it, is necessary in order to facilitate the kind of comparative contextual analysis of sentence decision-making that is necessary when making cross-cultural and jurisdictional comparisons and inferences.

Structure of the book

The aim of the first chapter is to illustrate why the issue of legitimacy has become so important in criminal justice. Accordingly, it reflects on the increasingly isolated position of the judiciary in England and Wales in matters of punishment and sentencing, drawing out significant broader themes about the relationship between punishment and criminal justice governance which are developed during the course of the book. It argues that recent sustained criticism of judicial sentencing in England and Wales reflects a much deeper malaise afflicting the legitimacy of punishment which not only threatens the liberal consensus view of the judiciary as pivotal to the rule of law, but also undermines the rationality which underpins conventional paradigms of criminal justice more generally.

The chapter goes on to argue that there are important lessons to be learned from engaging with the debates about punishment and sentencing which are taking place on the international stage, suggesting that the crisis in domestic sentencing is really symptomatic of a more fundamental crisis in penal legitimacy that affects the whole of civil society; one that touches upon the role of punishment in the governance of so-called democratic states. It concludes that the time may have come to modify the predominant neo-liberal paradigm of punishment and sentencing prevalent in western criminal justice by making it more responsive to the needs of communities.

The second chapter focuses on issues of theory and method and looks at different theoretical approaches for conceptualising the relationship between legitimacy and sentencing from a cross-disciplinary perspective. One of the core objectives of the book is to draw together legal, criminological and sociological ideas to engage with current debates. For example, it challenges those approaches which emphasise the 'closed' nature of legal rules and the distorting tendencies of sociological theorising about law.[10] It argues that theoretical engagement with criminal justice and punishment, in particular, must proceed from a basis which involves asking questions about the social functions of law, and that these questions can only be answered if social theory is capable of providing explanations of how the outcomes of penal justice are perceived in moral terms.

The discussion also evaluates current models of criminal justice and their relevance to the comparative analysis of trial justice at both the global and local levels. It focuses particularly on the extent to which such modelling is

---

10 An illustration of this approach is Wandell's recent application of autopoiesis theory to the analysis of sentencing. Following Luhmann, Wandell argues for the self-referential and reciprocal character of legal systems, emphasising the capacity of law to synthesise those communications which are essentially legal through its operational structures. However, it is argued that this theoretical approach fails to provide a convincing conceptualisation of sentence decision-making because it does so from a perspective which maintains a false conceptual duality between legal closure and contextual openness; Wandall (2008).

capable of engaging with the normative aspects of sentencing and suggests alternative approaches to understanding.

The chapter also identifies key methodological issues raised by the comparative analysis of trial justice.[11] This analysis describes different methodologies and their justifications; identifies weaknesses and suggests solutions. Again, the emphasis is on making connections between theory and method with the aim of improving our capacity to appreciate the relationship between the perception and the social reality of trial justice.

Chapter 3 explores some inherent problems in the comparative contextual analysis of punishment rationales and suggests why and how normative questions about punishment could be addressed more effectively by criminal justice theory. In this context it focuses on the purposes for attributing responsibility, both individual and collective, and their expression through punishment and sentencing. The chapter also discusses why the meanings and relevance attributed to penal aims and the principles of distributive justice need to be understood contextually. It explores theoretical and methodological difficulties of comprehending the meanings attached to different punishment rationales and studies the relationship between values, norms and the legitimacy of punishment in different social contexts.

Chapter 4 considers the relationship between judicial discretionary power and sentencing from both theoretical and contextual perspectives. More particularly, it evaluates different models of judicial sentencing with the object of assessing how universal factors in decision-making and particular contextual influences on sentencing practice are balanced. The analysis considers the nature of sentencing norms and whether existing models of sentence decision-making are capable of engaging with the relevant normative aspects of sentencing. These concerns are addressed from both a local and global perspective, focusing particularly on their implications for governance in criminal justice.

The chapter then explores the difficulties of conceptualising the notion of 'context' for the purposes of modelling. It explains the approach of comparative contextual modelling[12] and its use as a tool for understanding sentencing as a process of discretionary decision-making. The chapter further suggests how sentencing modelling could be improved to better reflect normative considerations such as legitimacy in different contexts. The discussion concludes by assessing the broader implications of this approach for criminal justice governance.

---

11 For example, it is suggested that, in order to make sense of sentencing comparatively, it is necessary to comprehend the meaning and significance of 'penality' in different contexts, and how international and domestic systems cross-fertilise each other.

12 Contextual modelling is an approach which relies on an initial evaluation of a particular context to determine its theoretical orientation and methodological prescription. It is a conceptual vehicle for testing various (possibly competing) versions of what might constitute the process of sentence decision-making in any particular context. Therefore, it typically reflects a combination of methodologies designed to serve the interests of both inductive and deductive theory. For a detailed description of this approach, see Findlay and Henham (2007).

The main focus of Chapter 5 is on issues of procedural justice and due process. The chapter's principal aim is to discuss the extent to which the structures and processes of criminal process tend to militate against any principled engagement with notions of justice, at the global and local level. It illustrates this by examining the theory and practice of plea bargaining in the context of different models of criminal justice, both global and local. The chapter focuses particularly on the extent to which the rhetoric and symbolism of criminal process are related to criminal justice governance. It concludes by suggesting that structural processes such as plea bargaining might be re-conceptualised as forms of relational justice[13] whose values are aimed at providing communities with socially 'relevant' solutions to crime problems.

Chapter 6 is concerned with the issue of deconstructing evidence for sentencing and describing the factual basis for sentence in global and local forms of trial justice. It explores the likely impact on this process of adopting alternative punishment rationales and trial models, and also examines the significance of relevant sentencing norms and practice within different jurisdictional contexts and trial traditions. The emphasis is on exploring the broader context in which information is attributed the status of fact and 'truth' for the purposes of sentence.

The chapter focuses particularly on problems associated with conventional procedures for establishing the factual basis for sentence. It considers differences between adversarial, inquisitorial and hybridised forms of trial justice; the relevance of substantive law issues and their impact on sentence determination; the significance of the verdict; the relevance of previous convictions; and the adequacy of mechanisms for resolving disputes about evidential status.

Chapter 7 addresses questions of access to justice, rights and accountability in relation to sentencing. It begins by examining the relationship between victimisation and sentencing, exploring how the needs of victims and communities can be more effectively accommodated within existing paradigms of trial justice. The primary focus is to emphasise the links between victimisation and the legitimacy of punishment from a sociological perspective.

The chapter continues by examining the extent and effectiveness of the normative frameworks which regulate and protect the rights of offenders and victims from a comparative perspective. More specifically, it argues that trial justice as presently conceived is a partial form of accountability that fails to engage with substantive and procedural rights. An example of this is the extent to which the ideological framework of retributive justice works against

---

13 Norrie suggests that a relational model of justice is concerned to examine the connections between responsible individuals and communities, so that punishment is envisaged as part of that shared experience. Rights conceived in these terms imply a sharing of the justice process, so they are no longer conceived as a distinct set of normative constraints on process, but rather as an integral and inseparable component of relational justice; Norrie (2000).

victim participation in sentencing at the international and domestic level. This may be conceived in terms of: restricting access to sentencing (pre-sentence factors which affect sentence determination, such as plea bargains); access to sentencing by those within the trial (victim participation in sentence determination); and access to the community through sentencing (factors which identify or connect sentences to victims and communities). The chapter goes on to suggest ways in which sociological accounts of access to sentencing and reciprocal notions of rights and accountability could more readily reflect their normative significance.

Chapter 8 explores the relationship between sentencing and legitimacy in France and Italy.[14] The purpose of this analysis is to give the reader an overview of the socio-political and historical influences that have shaped the sentencing systems of these two countries and to draw comparisons where appropriate regarding the impact of adversarial, inquisitorial and hybridised trial justice on sentencing practice and its public perception. Consistent with the theme of the book, the analytical approach taken is to consider the relationship between social factors and the normative framework that underpins sentencing and evaluate the extent to which existing theories and concepts of criminal justice can assist us in exploring these issues. A significant example is the extent to which perceptions about the role of the victim have influenced how victims are treated for the purpose of sentencing and structural reforms designed to increase victim participation in the sentencing process.

The final chapter draws conclusions about the role of punishment and sentencing as elements of criminal justice governance. It suggests how cross-disciplinary theorising could be improved to achieve a greater understanding of the normative aspects of sentence decision-making and outcomes, and what this might signify for individuals and communities. More particularly, it suggests why such an approach may make it easier for analysts to speculate, in any given context, about how the framework of punishment and sentencing could respond more effectively to community expectations of the 'justice' process. These conclusions support the book's main thesis that reflecting public perceptions of punishment more effectively through sentencing will enhance the legitimacy of criminal justice as a whole.

Concluding comments

The relationship between sentencing and legitimacy is something which has received scant attention in recent analyses of the role of the criminal trial.[15] This lacuna is especially significant given the developing discourse about the

---

14 The alternative approach of integrating these comparative observations into the themed chapters was not pursued on the grounds that it would tend to obscure rather than clarify the complex influences on sentencing within these two countries.
15 See, for example; Duff, Farmer, Marshall and Tadros (2004, 2006, 2007).

future for international criminal justice and, more particularly, the ICC. Although the legitimacy of punishment has received significant attention in theoretical writings and empirical research across a variety of disciplines,[16] these generally fail to explain how the trial process might be implicated in delivering more inclusive forms of sentencing.[17]

This book builds on the author's previous work in two distinct ways. Firstly, it develops previous writing on the transformation of international trial justice.[18] One of the cornerstones of these arguments is the need for the outcomes of international trials to engage more fully with the justice aspirations of victims and communities following social conflict. This book seeks to explain more fully the role of sentencing in delivering a more inclusive form of trial justice and argues that this agenda is critical for the growth of 'legitimate' governance in criminal justice at both the global and local level. Secondly, it builds on earlier work[19] dealing with the sociological interpretation of moral issues in the sentencing context, particularly that which seeks to understand how sentencing is implicated in linking penal ideology and trial outcomes, and the significance of this beyond the trial. Therefore, a major purpose for this book is to develop a more normative framework for explaining sentencing; particularly through theorising the engagement of victims and communitarian 'interests' in the delivery of trial justice. In short, the book firmly ties the issue of legitimacy to the relevant contexts for delivering 'justice'. It suggests a need to develop the tools and methods for achieving this end and offers some novel solutions to this complex problem.

---

16 In the present context, see Tyler (ed.) (2008).
17 For important contributions, see Indemaur (2008) and Hutton (2008).
18 Findlay and Henham (2005). The practical implications are developed in Findlay and Henham (2010).
19 Henham (2001), Henham (2007b).

1 Challenging Existing Paradigms

A core argument of this book is that the role of sentencing in criminal justice governance depends to a large extent on its perceived legitimacy.[1] More specifically, it is concerned with the relationship between sentencing outcomes and how they are perceived.[2] It therefore focuses on those factors that may determine whether sentences are perceived as 'just' by individuals or groups and, more importantly, whether and how sentencing changes their perceptions of justice, and perhaps influences their behaviour. It is argued[3] that criminal justice theory is currently inadequate in explaining the significance of these issues because it does not give sufficient attention to the complex relationship that exists between the normative[4] and social contexts of sentencing.

The concept of legitimacy

The chapter is prefaced with a preliminary section whose purpose is to elaborate the use of the concept of legitimacy as it is employed in this book.

Legitimacy and the relationship between international and domestic legal settings

The approach taken here is based on the view that there are important parallels to be drawn between the legitimacy of sentencing in international and domestic contexts. However, it may be argued that this unjustifiably conflates:

---

1 'Legitimacy' in the present context refers to the moral attachment of individuals and social groups to the penal ideologies, processes and outcomes of criminal trials. The book makes an analytical distinction between the notion of 'Punishment' as being concerned with debates about values, justifications and norms, and 'Sentencing' as referring to the practical everyday processes of discretionary decision-making.
2 The book is equally concerned with the individual and collective aspects of legitimacy, so that the significance of the individual as part of a social group is as important as the significance of that group within any particular social context. Thus, notions of individual and group are treated as both universal and particular depending upon context.
3 See chapters 2 and 4.
4 The expression 'normative' is used here to signify the fact that sentence decision-making produces outcomes that impact on perceptions and conduct.

- the criminality of collective international crime with that of individual ordinary crime;
- the legitimacy of sentencing in settled domestic legal orders with those in unsettled international orders; and
- experiences of sentencing in advanced industrial democracies with those of transitional societies that constitute the locus of the bulk of atrocity crimes.

This book does not seek to draw parallels between international and domestic forms of criminality. The primary focus for the thesis is the concept of 'legitimacy' and its connection to punishment and sentencing, which, it is argued, is a phenomenon common to both international and domestic forms of legal order, settled or otherwise. It is not therefore seeking to make comparisons between different forms of legal order and criminality by simply juxtaposing accounts of legitimacy and its relationship to trial justice.

What is being argued is that the legitimacy of trial justice is a feature common to all legal settings that raises similar problems. However, in order to understand what it signifies in any legal setting requires profound and theoretically informed contextual analysis. Thus, the point of such analyses is not to make comparisons but to permit the discourse about legitimacy to be conducted from a position of accuracy in terms of its historical and cultural context. The only generalised assumption made about the nature of legitimacy is that its understanding in any context depends upon comprehending the complex relationship between moral and social experience, whether that perspective is individual or collective.

The reason for drawing lessons from international criminal trials in particular is that sentencing research[5] has raised the issue of legitimacy in a very vivid and direct manner. I am not arguing that the way legitimacy has manifested itself is common to different legal settings and forms of criminality, rather that questions about legitimacy and different responses to it have highlighted the need for a greater normative awareness about the relationship between shared experience and perceptions of trial justice. For this reason, it is considered valid to consider how sentencing responds to this challenge in different settings and the extent to which it appears capable of reflecting the shared interests of different communities, whether global or local.

Hence, the juxtaposition of settled democracies against transitional societies following mass atrocity is designed to highlight that the notion of transition is in a very real sense common to both. By this I mean that the role of trial justice in transitional societies depends upon the extent to which it draws legitimacy in the eyes of local communities of interest. In this situation, trial justice is operating against a background of conflicting interests. However,

---

5 See, for example, *Articles*: Alvarez (1998), Alvarez (1999), Amann (2002), Keller (2001), Beresford (2002), Carcano (2002), Dana (2004), Gaynor (2007); *Books*: Olusanya (2005), Henham (2005b), Drumbl (2007a).

to achieve credibility,[6] in the sense that trial justice can make a positive contribution to governance, depends upon the extent to which it *actually* responds to shared interests, since these reflect shared moral values that impact critically upon the norms of social life. The fact that interests are diverse is common to both global and local legal settings, where the value of pluralism characteristic of post-modern societies has increased significantly in recent years.

Legitimacy and authority

Alison Liebling has recently considered the relationship between authority and legitimacy in examining the role of prison officers.[7] Drawing on Richard Sennet's work on authority,[8] Liebling stresses the importance of competency and the fact that authority is normally evaluated against its capacity to achieve some higher ideal, such as fairness or justice. The shifting nature of authority, especially Sennet's description of it as a contingent and 'interpretative process', is consistent with the notion that the 'appropriate' balance between those who exercise authority and those who are subject to it is constantly changing.

Liebling links this dialogic conception of authority to unpublished work by Bottoms and Tankebe on legitimacy in which they define legitimacy as authority used rightfully, or 'power exercised in accordance with established rules' and values.[9] Liebling elaborates this as follows:

> Their argument, following Weber and others, is that power holders do not 'sit back and wait' for the subjects of power to obey them. In addition to any material, emotional or religious motives those subjected to power may have for obedience, power holders make claims to legitimacy: that is, they attempt to 'establish and cultivate' legitimacy on an ongoing basis ... These claims solicit a response, which may influence the form or basis for the next claim. In other words, legitimacy is not a fixed phenomenon, but constitutes 'a perpetual discussion', a continuing dialogue between those who hold power and the recipients. The acceptability of the power holder's claim requires appropriate attitudes as well as conduct on the part of the power holder

This notion of legitimacy as 'dialogic',[10] dynamic or conditional resonates with the relative and contingent nature of justice. More particularly, it

---

6 Meaning that the exercise of power is accepted as broadly legitimate.

7 Liebling (2010).

8 Sennett (1980).

9 'Any given exercise of power must be derived from a valid source of legitimate authority in that society ... it should be exercised in a manner that is considered appropriate, and it must serve a recognisable general interest, rather than simply the interests of the power holder' (cited in Liebling 2010).

10 For further elaboration of this concept in the context of Constitutional Law, see Poole (2005), Allan (2006).

supports the approach taken in this book, especially the need for careful analysis of the underlying contextual influences on structured social interactions such as sentencing. The argument suggests that for legitimacy to be accorded to trial justice depends upon its being perceived as reflecting the 'appropriate' balance between the power holders and its recipients. I argue that several factors have combined to suggest that this balance is no longer perceived as fair or just, in the sense that trial justice fails to reflect the shared interests of diverse communities within western industrialised societies.

The nature of communitarian morality and its normative impact on the perception of trial justice need to be understood as aspects of social experience. The interests of such morally diverse communities on penal ideology and practice are little recognised at present, especially in terms of contingency and change. This book argues the need for enhancing the legitimacy of sentencing and draws a clear link between this and greater engagement with socially diverse communities that do not regard their interests as either represented or served by current manifestations of trial justice.

Legitimacy and morality

Anthony Bottoms[11] has usefully drawn on the distinction between positive and critical morality made by Hart[12] in considering the relationship between penal ideology and morality in criminal justice. Positive morality is shared by a given social group, whereas critical morality consists of general moral principles used to critique social institutions. As an example, Bottoms examines the interesting question of how the critical morality of the Enlightenment became the positive morality of many eighteenth-century European states.

Bottoms relates positive morality to the question of rule formation and the maintenance of social order. He justifies the analysis of moral principles with social analysis and discusses the importance of distinguishing different kinds of compliance, especially normative. This he defines as relating to the actor's response to a 'principle' or 'standard' that serves to regulate action and judgement and is supposed to reflect peoples' expectations of behaviour.[13] Bottoms's discussion of normative compliance is based on legitimacy, referring to the degree of moral assent to the right of the person in power to hold that power.

On the relationship between positive and critical morality, Bottoms suggests we are now in an era of developing a new positive morality, the core of which may be seen in gradually changing public attitudes: for example, drink driving. These notions are consistent with the discussion of driving-related deaths in this chapter, but also more generally, in drawing attention to the issues of contingency and change and the need for trial justice to play its part in helping to develop a coherent and publicly accepted interpretation of morality that is

---

11 Bottoms (2002) 23–42.
12 Hart (1963).
13 *Ibid.* 31.

sensitive to criticism and able to respond positively to the justice needs of different communities of interest.

By reference to the principle of respect for others Boutellier[14] goes some way towards elaborating the criteria upon which to base the development of a coherent and socially responsive positive morality in 'moralising our culture' by reference to the principle of respect for others. He argues that there are broadly shared common values that abhor personally harmful actions, involving cruelty, undeserved suffering, humiliation, harm infliction and exclusion, and that crime and criminal justice provide a 'basal negative point of reference for a pluralistic morality'. Boutellier explains how the criminal law becomes a mechanism for manifesting shared values.

Again, these themes resonate with those advanced here, in the sense that this book argues for 'moralising' the foundations for penal ideology by reflecting shared moral values. However, I agree with Boutellier that the point of reference for recognising a pluralistic morality needs to move away from Durkheim's authority model of social solidarity. Hence, in terms of enhancing the legitimacy of trial justice, this means remoralising penal ideology and practice to ensure that it has the capacity to respond to the 'legitimate' justice needs of diverse moral communities, whether these are global or local.

Legitimacy and social structure

From a practical perspective, penal legitimacy often depends upon what is politically expedient. However, this is not necessarily a function of the degree of political control of the criminal process. Delmas-Marty[15] argues that external relationships of dependence and independence from the political process, or relationships of the criminal process to society depend on the degree to which the process is open or closed. This issue and the response depend on each country's context. However, particularly interesting is Delmas-Marty's point that if relationships with political powers are widely diversified, then other variables come into play. The degree of access and participation is one aspect so affected, especially the notion of 'who are the parties'.

Correspondingly, in discussing the legitimacy of trial justice it may be argued that the degree to which the structural aspects of the criminal process are distanced from political interference is critical to how it can respond to the 'legitimate' interests of diverse communities and social groups, whether within or beyond state boundaries. Crucially, this determines the ability of trial justice to contribute to the 'appropriate' balancing of interests, and is especially germane in times of economic stringency. As Delmas-Marty argues,[16] in France the demand of 'security and liberty' is contradictory, since

---

14 Boutellier (2000) 156–57. See Daems (2008) 134 for discussion of Boutellier (2004).
15 Delmas-Marty (1995) 194.
16 *Ibid.* 195.

liberty is at risk, so the difficult balance is combining efficiency without disarming the state, whilst respecting individual rights and therefore the rule of law. Accordingly, I would argue that political imperatives to increase control over the recognition of 'legitimate' interests can only be countered by ensuring that the moral foundations of 'rule of law' structures such as the criminal process allow penal practices to be more socially responsive. This does not 'disarm the state' because it contributes to the state's ability to govern democratically.

Legitimacy and the concept of 'balance'

Notwithstanding, it may be argued that to reconceptualise penality so that its norms and structures are more responsive to the moralities and expectations of diverse communities of interest is potentially catastrophic for the development of principled and coherent criminal justice governance. Whatever the 'truth' of this assertion, its resolution ultimately depends on political decisions that identify 'legitimate' interests and determine the 'appropriate' balance between those 'interests' and conceptions of the public interest, and the rights that should be accorded to them. For example, Ashworth[17] argues that victims' interests should not be prioritised over those of others when considering 'in whose interests' the criminal justice process is being carried out.

As Ashworth suggests, defining the nature of the public interest raises some difficult questions, such as whether public-interest arguments are contrary to the intrinsic nature of fundamental rights; or how conflicts between fundamental rights and the public interest (or conflicting public interests) might be resolved. Furthermore, Douzinas[18] argues that there is no rational basis for reconciling public interests and fundamental rights. Therefore, it may be argued that there is no rational basis upon which to explore the relational basis for trial justice beyond reasoning that it should be perceived as 'legitimate' in the eyes of citizens. Although the assertion of fundamental human rights for citizens may be seen as a rational way to 'balance' the interests of criminal justice, this ignores the political realities that determine penal policies and practices in western industrialised democracies.

Cavadino and Dignan[19] counter Ashworth's objections to extending victims' participatory rights in sentencing by suggesting that, as long as there is some sort of officially administered 'state veto' of the behaviour, what judges choose to do to satisfy any reparative requirements of the victim should be accommodated. Whilst recognising that victim satisfaction and empowerment constitute an aspect of the 'public interest', Cavadino and Dignan[20] advocate

---

17 Ashworth (1993), Ashworth (2000d) 185–204, Ashworth (2002b).
18 Douzinas (1996) 115, 128.
19 Cavadino and Dignan (1997) 233, 237.
20 *Ibid.* 238.

that restorative themes are more likely to be maximised through the adoption of an 'integrated restorative justice' model which allows for a principled compromise between retributive and reparative/restorative justice themes. Nevertheless, the fact remains that 'rebalancing' the penal equation towards the pursuit of restorative themes in sentencing, and hence increasing its legitimacy, is destined to remain severely constrained by the limited scope for victim participation offered by conventional retributive-based models of punishment.

Context and conjecture in sentencing

The judiciary is crucially implicated in defining the parameters of 'legitimacy' because it is through its exercise of discretionary power in sentencing that trial outcomes are formulated. Hence, this book begins by describing how the notion of legitimacy relates directly to the exercise of judicial discretionary power in sentencing, and its legal and moral foundations. It is argued that the notion of judicial independence in England and Wales, with its roots in the liberal consensus model of punishment and adherence to the rule of law, provides an excellent illustration of why legitimacy is relevant, and of its implications for criminal justice governance.[21]

In recent years several high-profile cases have left members of the English judiciary looking vulnerable and isolated.[22] These have generally been accompanied by highly personalised and concerted media attacks on their approach to sentencing.[23] In addition, the increasing drive by the executive to manage and control the discretionary basis for sentence decision-making,[24] and the willingness of some government ministers to openly criticise particular sentencing outcomes,[25] poses a distinct challenge to the judiciary's

---

21 This book conceptualises 'governance' in purely descriptive and functional terms. For example, the United Nations describes governance as 'the exercise of political, economic and administrative authority to manage a nation's affairs. It is the complex mechanisms, processes, relationships and institutions through which citizens and groups articulate their interests, exercise their rights and obligations and mediate their differences. Governance embraces all of the methods – good and bad – that societies use to distribute power and manage public resources and problems'; United Nations (1997).

22 A typical example is the life sentence imposed in the case of paedophile Craig Sweeney; for commentary, see Gillespie (2006).

23 For examples of press coverage in the Sweeney case, see Pascoe-Watson and Coles (2006), Freedland (2006). For the government's response, see the consultation paper Home Office (2006). For analysis, see Allen and Hough (2008) 224, 232.

24 This has been achieved incrementally since the Criminal Justice Act of 1991 through the introduction of statutory criteria for sentencing and its increased regulation through sentencing guidelines promulgated by statutory bodies, namely the Sentencing Advisory Panel, The Sentencing Guidelines Council and, more recently, the Sentencing Council.

25 Attorney-General, Lord Goldsmith's attack on the judiciary in 2006 over apparent leniency in the sentencing of sex offenders is a case in point. This was prompted by the release of figures from his own office to the media under the Freedom of Information Act, revealing over 200 referrals to the Court of Appeal in such cases.

conventional constitutional position,[26] calling into question its role in sentencing and the principle of judicial independence.[27]

This chapter argues that several complex and inter-related issues are relevant to understanding the nature and significance of these events for the legitimacy of sentencing. These go beyond simple consideration of whether structural improvements could be made to the existing framework for sentencing.[28] More significantly, they challenge established notions about the respective roles of the state and the judiciary with regard to matters of sentencing policy and practice, and prompt broader speculation as to the future role of sentencing in reflecting the aspirations for justice of citizens and communities in an increasingly pluralistic[29] society.

My thesis is that members of the judiciary are effectively locked into inappropriate and dysfunctional sentencing arrangements, leaving them unable to respond effectively to public perceptions of justice,[30] and increasingly vulnerable

---

26 The English retributive-based sentencing model has its roots in the classical liberalism of the Enlightenment, but the nature and development of constitutional convention, and the absence of any Constitutional Court or other effective regulatory mechanisms, have all contributed to the continued reinforcement of the centrality of the judicial role and judicial discretion as the key variables in the development of sentencing jurisprudence. The principle of judicial independence has therefore placed the judiciary in the vanguard of determining the ambit of substantive and procedural sentencing law and the parameters of policy. Furthermore, the context in which this judicial discretion has been exercised is one which supports and sustains the concept of individualisation of sentences. Within this conceptual framework retributive considerations are balanced against utilitarian concerns such as deterrence, rehabilitation and reparation; see, further, Radzinowicz and Hood (1990).

27 See Ashworth (1983), ch. 2. More generally, Stevens (1999). This tension between the executive and the judiciary was particularly evident in the House of Lords judgement in *R v Secretary of State for the Home Department, Ex parte Venables and R v Secretary of State for the Home Department, Ex parte Thompson* [1997] UKHL 25. In this case their Lordships upheld challenges against the Home Secretary's fixing of the tariff for murder on the basis of procedural unfairness, but more particularly on the basis that the Home Secretary's decision had been unduly influenced by considerations of public opinion, to the extent that, in the words of Lord Goff, the Home Secretary had in fact gone so far as to assume the sentencing function of the courts. The European Court of Justice subsequently held there had been a violation of Article 5(4) of the ECHR because Venables and Thompson were unable to have the continuing lawfulness of their detention reviewed by a judicial body, and Article 6(1) in respect of the trial and the fixing of the sentence, especially on the point that tariff fixing by the Home Secretary (who was a politician and therefore not independent of the executive) amounted to sentencing. For further discussion see Haydon and Scraton (2000).

28 Further significant constraints on the exercise of sentencing discretion were recently introduced by the Coroners and Justice Act (2009).

29 This expression here refers to value pluralism and its implications for the perceived legitimacy of sentencing.

30 See Roberts and Hough (eds) (2005); Indermaur and Hough (2002), ch. 11. Public opinion may also be media-driven and susceptible to politically-motivated manipulation; see, for example, Young (1972). However, paradoxically, it is the political ideology which underpins penal policy that ultimately determines the nature and extent of 'legitimate' public interests requiring a judicial response.

to the partisan, and often media-driven, political responses which characterise contemporary penal policy-making.[31] It is further argued that the malaise afflicting sentencing is symptomatic of a failure to address those social factors that influence perceptions of justice, and which have hitherto failed to make any significant impact on the way in which punishment is conceptualised and the everyday practice of sentencing.

Rather than seeking to advocate further measures to curtail sentencing discretion, I would argue that these difficulties provide an important opportunity for instigating a wider debate about the future direction of sentencing – especially in thinking about ways in which the undoubted discretionary power bestowed upon sentencers might be utilised more constructively to promote outcomes that are more readily perceived as legitimate by citizens. Undoubtedly, the alternative strategy of merely reacting to events[32] may eventually result in the gradual and imperceptible elimination of individualised sentencing, thus provoking further unwarranted encroachment by the state in matters of punishment and sentencing.[33]

Such progressive alienation of citizens and increasing penal repression by the state is potentially critical,[34] not simply because it represents a disintegration of the liberal consensus model of punishment but, more significantly, because it symbolises the gradual breakdown of criminal justice governance more generally.[35] This is reflected in this book's broader message; that there are important lessons to be learned from engaging with debates about the legitimacy of punishment and sentencing in all contexts of criminal justice, whether international,

---

31 For an attempt by the Lord Chief Justice, Lord Phillips to publicly defuse matters by seeking greater co-operation between the executive and the judiciary, see http://www.judiciary.gov.uk/publications_media/speeches/index.htm (accessed 2008).

32 The two most significant factors that have influenced moves to restrict sentencing discretion in England and Wales since 2003 have been the rapid rise in the prison population and increasing pressure on the probation services during a period of shrinking resources and falling public confidence in the effectiveness of the criminal justice system.

33 Zedner has recently argued that articulating a principled approach, through judicial oversight and unremitting defence of due process, is likely to provide a better defence against the unwarranted erosion of liberty so far deemed necessary as a response to the terrorist threat to collective security that the debate on the appropriate balance between international and constitutional lawyers has produced; Zedner (2005).

34 Nevertheless, there are signs of greater citizen involvement in England and Wales through such things as local police and public consultative meetings, youth offender panels, and the gradual development of victim participatory rights in sentencing. Notwithstanding, the potential of the last of these is circumscribed by the adversarial and retributive context of sentencing praxis.

35 As Loader argues, there have been significant changes in the notion of what constitutes 'good governance' since the Liberal elitism of the mid-twentieth century. Most importantly, the management of public emotion towards crime and punishment is no longer considered desirable or possible in the late post-modern era. This phenomenon has had a corrosive effect on the idea that the judiciary has the capacity to reflect popular sentiment through sentencing. The previously unquestioned liberal notion of moral paternalism has long since given way to the politicisation of penal policy. Loader (2006) 569 and 582.

regional or domestic. It is argued that the credibility and effectiveness of criminal justice as a crucial pillar of the governance framework depends on developing moral foundations and outcomes for punishment that are perceived as legitimate by those who are affected by them.

In summary, the argument in this chapter is developed as follows:

(1) It begins by examining the rationale of the liberal consensus model and assesses its contemporary significance in defining the role of judicial sentencing.

(2) The chapter then considers how the prevailing retributive dynamic of western criminal justice has facilitated this process and consequently constrained the judicial discretionary power of individualisation in sentencing. It is argued that the political ideologies which inform the structure and practice of retributive-based sentencing have resulted in a paradox whereby penal law and policy often bear little relevance to the experiences of many citizens and their perceptions of the morality of trial justice.[36] This weakening of the moral bond which has traditionally underpinned the liberal consensus model has left the judiciary dangerously exposed to the vagaries of executive manipulation and populist criticism.

The discussion explores why the isolated position of the judiciary reflects the increasing inability of governments to pursue penal policies which are perceived as morally legitimate by individuals. It is argued that the ideologies and normative structures of criminal justice as currently conceived are unable to deliver outcomes which engage with the relative expectations and aspirations for justice of individuals, groups and communities within our increasingly complex and pluralistic societies. It is suggested that this kind of moral engagement is vital for all forms of criminal justice governance, whether international, regional or domestic.

(3) The third strand of the argument suggests the need for another kind of moral framework to underpin punishment and sentencing: one which might sustain the legitimacy of trial outcomes and therefore ensure that criminal justice functions more effectively as a pillar of governance. The chapter argues for a form of moral engagement for trial justice that would change the way we think about the values that underpin notions of responsibility. Here the emphasis is on suggesting how aspirations for justice should be reflected through access and rights for all citizens who claim a 'legitimate' interest, whatever the context of criminal justice. It is suggested

---

36 In this respect, Durkheim's assertions about the 'normality of crime' and the nature of 'collective sentiments' appear especially pertinent, and might lead to us to reflect upon the proposition that the function of punishment as expressed by sentencing praxis is to promote social solidarity through the recursive re-affirmation of societal values – in particular, to reflect and re-affirm society's moral opprobrium regarding particular acts or omissions defined as crime or deviance; see Durkheim (1982), Durkheim (1984) 101–32.

that realising the potential of judicial discretionary power to develop more inclusive and individualised forms of sentencing is vital in ensuring that the struggle to relegitimate the moral foundations of criminal justice becomes a reality.

(4) The chapter concludes that the instrumental capacity of judicial discretion to engage with different contexts in a relational sense is presently inhibited by the retributive dynamic prevalent in penal ideology. Consequently, instead of judges being free to utilise their discretionary powers to develop a more inclusive and socially sensitive sentencing jurisprudence, individualised sentencing is increasingly constrained by the adversarial focus on establishing individual criminal responsibility and the retributive need for proportionality. Instead, it is argued that the concept of individual responsibility and its association with the allocation of blame and guilt should be replaced with a more instrumental notion of fact-finding for sentencing; one which promotes the emergence of truth from a process of compromise; one that is driven by the desire to regulate relationships of community, rather than a celebration of the subjugation of the offender and the vindication of the victim as part of the apparatus of social control.

However, such a mobilisation of judicial discretion will only be possible if the normative structures put in place are developed from a strong ideological foundation to which judges are formally committed. Without this ideological commitment, moving from a situation of judicial diversity to one of coherence remains problematic. Once at liberty to look beyond retributive justice alone, judges can become a driving force for developing other aspects of the new normative framework: aspects such as lay and professional interaction, victim participatory rights, or distinctions in the type and function of 'facts' within the trial. In this sense, therefore, it is argued that discretion can help to bring about a developing normative framework that derives its moral authority from different penal purposes for the trial.

Deconstructing the prevailing paradigm

Questioning the liberal consensus

The starting point for this chapter is the paradigm for conceptualising punishment described by Alan Norrie in his seminal book *Crime, Reason and History*.[37] Norrie envisages the exercise of judicial discretionary power at the sentencing stage as a vital arm of state instrumentality.[38] In other words, inherently partisan:

> What counts for good or bad motive is not left at large in the community:
> it is kept politically safe with the judges, far away from the noise and

---

37 Norrie (1995), Norrie (2001) ch. 10.
38 Norrie (2001) 47.

conflict of the world outside. The social mores of the 'common people' are mediated, for good or ill, by the judges' perception of them.[39]

Additionally, as Norrie reminds us,[40] the impartiality of the judiciary is also questionable, because the power of judges to individualise sentences is exercised outside the general constraints of the rule of law or a 'legal conception of justice'. This not only undermines the principle that all citizens are equal before the law, but also introduces the idea that there exists a particular aspect of the judicial function that is exercised completely independently of it.[41] Whilst agreeing with Lacey[42] that tensions at the sentencing stage reflect fundamental disagreements about the core values which underpin the criminal law, Norrie[43] goes on to suggest that these may be attributable to ongoing tensions within our prevailing liberal model of justice.

Nevertheless, as suggested, evidence of an impending crisis in the perceived legitimacy of trial justice, both in the post-modern state and internationally, now threatens the validity of this approach. Therefore, it may be argued that the time has come to consider modifying the dominant neo-liberal paradigm of punishment and sentencing in western criminal justice by suggesting more effective ways of engaging with the problem of legitimacy, both conceptually and practically, in an increasingly pluralistic and ambivalent penal environment.

The immediate context

Much has changed since Norrie first elaborated his critique of the liberal model of justice in the early 1990s. Subsequently, English criminal justice endured the ramifications of persistent political failure on the part of governments in the late post-modern era to address the social causes of crime. In consequence, the credibility of penal policy was severely tested, especially by the media. In common with many other areas of state governance, criminal justice had to cope with the consequences of family and social breakdown, and the moral fragmentation which increasingly came to symbolise western 'civil' society. The latter was typified by a seemingly relentless questioning of accepted 'truths' and rationales, by apparent political paralysis, and by an

---

39 *Ibid.* 46.
40 *Ibid.*
41 Dworkin argues that judges do not derive their authority democratically, as does the legislature, and their task is not therefore directly concerned with implementing the will of the majority. Instead, he sees the authority of the judiciary as deriving from within the law itself, so denying the possibility of uncontrolled judicial discretion, since the capacity for judges to decide hard cases comes from within the legal rules and principles. So the judiciary's capacity to be creative comes from its capacity to make decisions within the framework provided by existing legal resources. Dworkin (1977).
42 Lacey (1987) 222–23.
43 Norrie (2001) 200.

almost serial inability of democratically-elected governments to formulate policy which engaged with the aspirations of citizens.

As a result, it may be argued that there has been a gradual drift away from Dicey's much revered 'rule of law' as the primary justification for punishment.[44] This served to undermine a functional dichotomy between the executive and the judiciary in matters of sentencing that has developed by convention through the operation of the separation of powers doctrine since the late nineteenth century.[45] Over the last twenty years penal ideology has frequently been undermined,[46] with the result that the principles which underpin penal policy have become increasingly obfuscated.[47] Judges have appeared progressively more isolated, thereby threatening their integrity and so weakening the rationale that gave rise to the principle of judicial independence and allowed it to develop and flourish virtually unhindered until the late twentieth century.

Consequently, in matters of sentencing, members of the higher judiciary have occasionally been portrayed as no longer appearing to know why they are there, or what their proper role should be.[48] A typical caricature might depict the popular media as openly vilifying the judiciary with impunity, against a backdrop of short-term, populist penal policy-making that progressively undermines the rationale for punishment and the legitimacy of trial justice in the eyes of citizens.[49] Thus, it is not unreasonable to argue that the diminished credibility of judicial sentencing is implicated in an increasingly felt lack of legitimacy in the entire penal apparatus which undermines the rationale of criminal justice more generally.

It has been argued that these events pose a consummate threat to the rule of law. Nevertheless, the social reality of sentencing is recursively constituted through the criminal trial process. This re-enforces maintenance of the rule of law as the primary rationale for retributive justice and so hinders the development of alternative penal rationales. Hence, if we argue that the legitimacy of trial justice is gradually being eroded, this implies that the disjunction between retributive punishment and its perceived legitimacy is consistently compounded.

The judicial contortions provoked by the imposition of a just deserts framework for sentencing in the Criminal Justice Act of 1991 in England and Wales is surely adequate testimony to this. It clearly illustrated judicial

---

44 A rationale for penal retribution attributable to Kant.
45 For a summary, see Ashworth (2010) 51–55.
46 The retributive rationale which implicitly informs penal policy and sentencing legislation has often been undermined by the judiciary where it has been perceived as encroaching too far on the discretionary power of individualisation. The clearest example of this followed the passing of the Criminal Justice Act 1991, discussed below; see, further, Ashworth (2000c).
47 As reflected in, and often exacerbated by, a continuing process of review
48 An example of such obfuscation is Lord Woolf's incursions into penal policy-making during his time as Lord Chief Justice; see BBC News (2003).
49 As mentioned, the typical government response to this has been to increase the constraints on judicial discretion through legislative and regulatory control.

sensitivity to the need for a principled accommodation between the state's drive for consistency, and the broader requirements of what was regarded as achieving 'justice' in individual cases. Similarly, the fervent judicial reaction against the introduction of mandatory minimum sentences for serious offenders contained in the Crime (Sentences) Act of 1997 was prompted by a strongly held view on the part of certain members of the higher judiciary that the Act represented a fundamental incursion into the principle of judicial independence and, as such, set a dangerous precedent.[50]

I would argue that failure to move beyond the conceptual straightjacket of the retributive dynamic has exacerbated the perceived alienation of the judiciary and contributed to the inability of modern penal policy to deliver sentencing outcomes that resonate with the justice aspirations of citizens. Despite its apparent erosion, and the increasing political allure of restorative themes and practices, retributive justice in the form of just deserts has remained the conceptual cornerstone of penal ideology well into the twenty-first century. The continuing debate about the merits or demerits of integrating retributive and restorative forms of justice is in danger of leading to paralysis and to the progressive distancing of institutional rationales for punishment from the moral expectations of citizens.

The instrumentality of retributivism

It may be argued that, in common with international punishment,[51] the rationality of retributive justice has increasingly been exposed as partial. As Garland suggests,[52] this has proved an instrumental factor in sustaining the prevailing culture of hegemony and control, so fundamental to the continued existence of capitalism and its structures in the post-industrial world. Taking this further, it may be argued that the politics of penal control, whether in relation to global or local forms of criminal justice, share common characteristics of isolation, stigmatization, exclusion and repression. Such characteristics are systemically promoted through the penality of retributive justice that informs the structures of criminal trial processes in western industrialised democracies.

In this respect Mathiesen's[53] writings on the social functions of imprisonment are insightful, and merit further discussion in the context of post-modern penality.[54] Mathiesen postulates expurgatory, power-draining, symbolic, diverting and action functions for imprisonment, which have equal resonance and utility for all forms of criminal justice, whether local or global, although particular emphasis may differ. For instance, in the context of international criminal

---

50 See Henham (1998).
51 See Henham (2003b).
52 Garland (2001).
53 Mathiesen (1990).
54 This reflects the contested nature of penal values and how penal institutions in post-modernity are implicated in maintaining the conditions of differentiation that militate against social cohesion.

justice, those interests deemed worthy of protection by the institutions of criminal justice might be conceived as humanitarian, economic or political. However, in removing individuals or groups who are deemed to threaten political hegemony from positions of responsibility, international trial justice may be perceived as supporting the interests of nations or groups of states outside the conflict. Such interests may have perhaps instigated (or encouraged) conflict for economic reasons (for example, to satisfy the demand for cheap energy, or to expand the market for the supply of weapons). Alternatively, they may profess a political justification for intervention (for example, under the pretext of advancing democracy or the fight against terrorism) when economic interests are really paramount. In this context, international criminal justice might also be deployed to disguise support for particular regimes within post-conflict and transitional states.

The symbolism of punishment is widely acknowledged;[55] those who are stigmatised and publicly labelled through conviction and imprisonment are symbolically distanced in terms of the perceived morality of their actions. Furthermore, individuals judged as socially dangerous, or as a threat to the prevailing social (moral) order may be subjected to selective forms of incapacitation, designed to divert attention away from greater social harms being perpetrated by those in control.[56] The latter are seen as inappropriate targets because they are implicated in supporting ideals which are perceived as morally just (for example, the political economy, democratic principles). Finally, the use of punishment provides tangible reassurance that something is being done about 'the problem' and the threat to humanity it poses; in the case of international criminal justice, it implies that steps are being taken to bring the culture of impunity to an end.

It may be argued that retributive justice is repressive, discriminatory and lacking in credibility because it fails to connect in any meaningful way with the 'interests' of victims and communities. Both internationally and domestically, criminal justice tends to give symbolic attention to victims, with rights of access to, and participation in, *actual* decision-making, especially in relation to sentencing, being effectively denied.[57] On the international stage, as Mark Findlay and I suggest,[58] retributive penality has been unable to move much beyond such symbolism and rhetoric to produce outcomes which resonate

---

55 See, for example, King (1978).
56 See, Hall, S. *et al.* (1978).
57 Arguably, alternative structures and processes, such as Truth and Reconciliation Commissions, in their various guises, provide alternative and more relative interpretations of truth and justice that are drawn from (and rooted in) context, and, international trial justice may be seen as having a more enduring impact on victims, because trials contribute more directly to the deconstruction of myths that surround notions of collective responsibility. International criminal trials also provide a symbolic and historically definitive version of truth with legal consequences which assists in achieving closure and a refocusing of efforts on the reconstruction of broken communities.
58 Findlay and Henham (2005).

clearly with the demands for justice of victims and communities in post-conflict states. Similarly, at the domestic level, within England and Wales, successive governments since the early 1980s have progressively abandoned what was once the holy grail of relating penal policy to crime causation in favour of more reactive penal policies based on populism.

In addition, as Garland describes,[59] the demise of welfarism has been characterised by massive increases in covert surveillance and major incursions into individual liberty.[60] The resulting lack of autonomy for individual citizens is further reinforced by the shifting contexts of criminal justice governance in post-modernity[61] at both the state and interstate level, which is seen as intimately connected to the management of political and economic risk. Since criminal justice is a lynchpin of governance, and therefore pivotal in managing such risks, it follows that sentencing is fundamentally implicated in supporting these rationales for control.[62]

The paradox of justice delivery

Paradoxically, this has also been the era of human rights and individual autonomy. Regrettably, as Sanders suggests,[63] in terms of integrating victims into the criminal process these aspirations appear to be little more than symbolic and rhetorical, since meaningful participative rights for victims have proved to be largely illusory. More broadly, the reality of the apparent surrender of individual autonomy to citizens by the state has in reality been accompanied by a diminution in the state's acceptance of responsibility for criminal justice which has resulted from the adoption of bifurcation as a guiding principle for criminal justice policy-making.[64] This has produced the opposite effect. As

---

59 Garland (2001).
60 Zedner (2005).
61 See Sheating (2001) 203, 207.
62 However, there are notable exceptions in cases where the higher judiciary perceive a threat to fundamental freedoms and liberties. For example, in considering the possible indefinite detention of suspected 'terrorists' under section 21 of the Anti-terrorism, Crime and Security Act 2001, the House of Lords was trenchant in its defence of the principles of individual freedom and the threat of arbitrary detention without trial, and especially concerned to uphold the democratic principle that respect should always be accorded to those who have equal rights regardless of their minority status. *Per* Baroness Hale: ' ... neither the common law, from which so much of the European Convention is derived, nor international human rights law allows indefinite detention at the behest of the executive, however well-intentioned. It is not for the executive to decide who should be locked up for any length of time, let alone indefinitely. Only the courts can do that and, except as a preliminary step before trial, only after the grounds for detaining someone have been proved. Executive detention is the antithesis of the right to liberty and security of the person.' (para 222); *A and Ors v Secretary of State for the Home Department* [2004] UKHL 56. For further discussion; see, Feldman (2005).
63 See, for example, Sanders (2002b).
64 As Garland suggests, via the process of 'responsibilization', the state/citizen relationship is reconfigured through policy objectives designed to shift accountability where certain state functions such as crime control have become unattainable; Garland (1996).

a consequence, responsibility by the state for criminal justice governance has centred upon an increasingly diminishing terrain.[65]

Consequently, it may be argued that alienation and suspicion between citizen and state in matters of criminal justice is not caused simply by the state's failure in those areas where it claims responsibility; it is also a function of the state's duplicity. By falsely claiming control for certain types of crime and criminality, but effectively relinquishing accountability, the credibility of criminal justice policy (and that of its structures and human agents) has been gradually eroded.[66] Furthermore, asserting the autonomy and rights of citizens without promoting responsibility in the exercise of those rights has created a 'responsibility vacuum' in the sphere of criminal justice. Rationalising what to do about the consequences is further obfuscated by the need for criminal justice policies to reflect increasingly fragmented and pluralistic values.[67]

The paradox of justice delivery may be illustrated by taking two examples from England and Wales:

Victims' participatory rights

The historical development of victims' rights to participate in the sentencing process of England and Wales reflects very accurately the gap between the rhetoric and the reality of access to justice. The two principal reasons for this paradox stem from the fact that increasingly in recent years the normative framework of sentencing has had to conform to the adversarial model and ensure that it delivers outcomes constrained by retributive ideology.

The debate has focused on the desirability and effect of adopting victim impact statements (VIS), and this has intensified over the last twenty or so years. More recently, Ashworth[68] repeated his reservations, suggesting that the use of VIS in the context of adversarial criminal justice processes tends to increase sentencing severity and also that they are a cynical political ploy used to appease victims' concerns whilst, in reality, such statements tend to corrupt substantive and procedural justice goals. Erez[69] on the other hand, has consistently championed the use of VIS, stressing particularly their cathartic and therapeutic aspects, and suggesting that they empower victims, helping them cope with victimisation and the criminal justice experience. Erez also suggests

---

65 Since executive policymaking over this shrinking terrain has become increasingly politicised, the higher judiciary has increasingly found itself in the position of having to defend itself against the use of the penal law which encroaches upon the fundamental rights and freedoms of citizens.
66 See Sparks (1996).
67 This is exacerbated by the limited extent to which post-modern criminology has engaged with theorising the 'causes' of crime.
68 Ashworth (2000d).
69 See, particularly, Erez and Tontodonato (1990), Erez (1994), Erez *et al.* (1994), Erez and Roeger (1995), Rogers and Erez (1999), Erez and Rogers (1999), Erez (1999).

that the incorporation of victim statements tends to enhance proportionality rather than increase penal severity, as Ashworth maintains.

Sanders *et al.*[70] take issue with Ashworth's assertion that substantive (i.e. service) rights are as effective as procedural rights in satisfying victims, but without the disadvantages of procedural rights. They assert that victim information schemes are ineffective in promoting victim satisfaction with the criminal justice process without interaction and discussion with victims, and they maintain that, 'were victims helped to understand the process of VIS-appraisal and decision-making in general, and if these processes were fair, it is likely that dissatisfaction regarding unpalatable outcomes would be greatly reduced.' Ultimately, Sanders *et al.* regard a reconceptualisation of victim participation as essential, especially in recognising that it serves entirely different purposes for victims and the court process. In particular, they view participation along continental or restorative justice lines as inappropriate mechanisms for assisting the English courts, and suggest further specific procedural reforms are vital to ensure that victims have a 'genuinely participative system' This accords with Edwards,[71] who asserts that what may be needed is a reconceptualisation of the role of the victim and provision made for the integration of victims into the sentence decision-making process.

Despite this background of controversy and confusion regarding the proper purpose and effectiveness of VIS, a victim personal statement scheme (VPS) was introduced on the 1st October 2001. The scheme essentially enables victims to provide such a statement when making their initial witness statement to the police, but it may be provided or updated at any time prior to sentence. Although the police are charged with the function of informing victims of the scheme, and facilitating the statement's completion,[72] the decision whether or not to make a VPS is entirely one for the victim. Once presented with a VPS the court is expected to take it, and any evidence presented in support, into consideration prior to passing sentence.

The Home Office Circular[73] addressed to those agencies charged with administering the scheme appeared to compound the ambiguous status of the VPS stating that, 'it is important to remember that the scheme is not primarily a sentencing tool', emphasising that, whilst it is not a VIS in the conventional sense, where a VPS had been made, it could prove helpful to sentencers. Although stressing the policy objective of greater involvement for victims in the criminal justice process, the circular cautioned that the police should provide victims with a realistic appraisal of the potential for the VPS to affect sentencing decisions: more specifically, that judges and magistrates are unlikely

---

70 Sanders *et al.* (2001), Sanders (2002b).
71 Edwards (2001), Edwards (2004).
72 However, from 2005 the Victims' Code of Practice ceased to require the police to inform victims of this right other than in cases of murder and manslaughter: Home Office (2005).
73 Home Office (2001).

to take victims' views on the appropriate punishment into account, although they will have regard to the effect the crime has had on the victim.

The correct approach for the court was elaborated in a Practice Direction issued by the LCJ on 16 October 2001 to coincide with the introduction of the scheme. It made clear that the court must pass what it considers the appropriate sentence having regard to the circumstances of the offence and of the offender, taking into account, so far as the court considers it appropriate, the consequences to the victim. The opinions of the victim or the victim's close relatives *as to what the sentence should be* are therefore not relevant, unlike the consequences of the offence on them. Victims should be advised of this. If, despite the advice, opinions as to sentence are included in a statement, the court should pay no attention to them. The court also has to consider whether it is desirable in its sentencing remarks to refer to the evidence provided on behalf of the victim.

The position as summarised in the Practice Direction of 2001 was, in any event, merely a restatement of existing sentencing principles, developed by the Court of Appeal over several years, dealing with the relevance of victim impact evidence on sentence. These principles were reconsidered in detail by the Court of Appeal in *R v Perks.*[74] The issue in *Perks* which prompted this restatement of relevant principles concerned the appropriate sentence following the defendant's guilty plea to robbery on a woman who was walking home after a shopping trip. Despite substantial mitigation, the first-instance court had been particularly concerned to find a document prepared by the husband of the victim included amongst the court papers detailing the traumatic effects of the attack upon his wife, and urging the court in the strongest possible terms to impose a custodial sentence on the defendant. The Court of Appeal, in reviewing the authorities, confirmed the long held principle that, where there is evidence of particularly damaging or distressing physical or psychological effects on the victim, this should be taken into account by the court in passing sentence.

Sanders *et al.*[75] suggest that the VPS is no more participative than other victim statement schemes and fails to deal with the problems of false expectations and victim dissatisfaction previously identified, resulting in the continued 'marginalisation' of the victim. The absence of any coherent rationale and strategic guidance is evidenced by the fact that the procedure remains essentially expressive, with limited instrumental or procedural impact for victims. In these circumstances, Ashworth's[76] conclusions remain pertinent:

> In the context of a sentencing system whose primary aim is not restorative …
> there must be grave doubts about allowing a victim to voice an opinion as

---

74 [2001] 1 Cr App R (S) 19.
75 Sanders *et al.* (2001).
76 Ashworth (2010) 385.

to sentence. It is unfair and wrong that an offender's sentence should depend on whether the victim is vindictive or forgiving: in principle, the sentence should be determined according to the normal effects of a given type of crime, without regard to the disposition of the particular victim. *If it is then said that allowing the victim to make a statement on sentence is not the same thing as allowing the victim to determine the sentence, one wonders about the point of the exercise.* Victims' expectations might be unfairly raised and then dashed if a court declines to follow the suggestions made, and the whole process might appear to victims as a cruel pretence. [Emphasis added.]

Arguably, the VPS represents the worst of both worlds: neither providing for actual participation in the sentencing outcome, nor guaranteeing that victim impact will have some measured and principled effect on sentence, in circumstances where full information and transparency are not mandatory requirements. It serves to illustrate the limited focus of the contemporary legal and policy debate regarding victim participation in English sentencing. This debate appears to ignore the constructive influence of restorative justice, which, in addition to victim participation, concentrates on the humanitarian treatment of trial participants; elements of compensation, restitution, reparation and reintegration; and, diversionary and mediatory processes.[77]

Significantly, neither the Auld Review[78] nor the Halliday Report[79] into sentencing made detailed recommendations on the issue of victim participation in the sentencing process. Auld acknowledged that improvements in service rights for victims were desirable, and that there should be a role for victims in the monitoring and enforcement of diversion schemes, whilst the Halliday Report somewhat obliquely referred to the fact that 'victim statements once available would be considered as part of the judgement of seriousness', exactly how this proposal would be implemented being left to the imagination.

However, in September 2005 the Government was persuaded that it should take the concept of victim allocution one step forward and decided to pilot the use of 'family impact statements' in court. This was to allow the families of victims of murder or manslaughter to make an oral statement on the impact of the offence post-conviction, but before sentence was passed. Thus, the Victims' Advocates Scheme (VAS) was established in five Crown court centres, and ran from April 2006 to April 2008.[80] Regrettably, many of the original problems

---

77 For a full discussion of the issues; see Doak (2008), Hall (2009), Bottoms and Roberts (2009). See also Zedner (1994), Dignan and Cavadino (1996).
78 Auld (2001).
79 Halliday (2001).
80 The pilot centres were the Central Criminal Court (the Old Bailey), and the Crown Courts at Birmingham, Cardiff, Manchester and Winchester. The VAS was superseded by the Victim Focus Scheme (VFS) (originally announced by the Attorney-General in October 2007), which continued to enable the families of murder and manslaughter victims to work with prosecutors on the

remain. The main lesson to be learned is that the tensions and obfuscation caused by trying to accommodate victims' 'interests' through such mechanisms as the VAS, particularly in the sentencing context, will not be dissipated unless there is greater clarity about what the purposes of victim engagement are and what it is meant to achieve. Arguably, the key lies in ensuring that:

- The rights given to victims are 'real', in the sense that their 'interests'[81] are *actually* factored into sentencing decisions.
- Sentencing judges are given the normative flexibility to achieve this.
- A positive duty is placed upon the Court to ensure that victims' rights do not jeopardise the rights of the accused or threaten a fair and impartial trial process.[82]
- An ideological shift takes place to underpin penal policy, thereby empowering trials (and sentencing in particular) to capitalise on the normative flexibility to pursue more restorative outcomes for victims. Such an approach will make it easier for courts to reach beyond the immediate families of victims to take account of 'interests' within the wider community when sentencing for serious crimes.

As Edwards[83] points out, in reality the debate about victim participation in the English sentencing system is firmly trapped between advocates of proportionality and those promoting principles of restorative or reparative principles. This dichotomy is fundamental, since proportionalists generally regard victims as marginal because they threaten commensurability and the achievement of 'just deserts', whilst restorative advocates see victims as the primary focus of sentencing, and instrumental to achieving wider re-integrative purposes.

The willingness of the Court of Appeal to recognise the emotional effects of victim harm when sentencing offenders convicted of crimes against property, such as domestic burglary, was recently re-emphasised by Lord Phillips LCJ in *R v Saw & Ors.*[84] The focus of his remarks was very much directed towards the nature of the risk and the adverse consequences that an offender may run when committing burglary, whether these are intentional or not. These effects relate not only to the emotional consequences of material loss, but also to the

---

preparation of an impact statement subsequently read out in court. In 2010 a National Victims Service was established, and it was announced that the scheme would in future be administered by Victims Support; see http://www.justice.gov.uk/news/speech270110a.htm (accessed 2010).

81 Clearly, the nature and scope of such 'interests' and the purpose of victim participation need to be very carefully defined. One of the most important issues to be resolved is how these purposes might be linked to other sentencing aims and their achievement in concrete cases.

82 In this the State should assume a greater responsibility for ensuring that the trial fulfils the legitimate expectations of its citizens for 'justice'.

83 Edwards (2001).

84 [2009] EWCA Crim 1.

aggravating impact, and aftermath, of the severe shock that victims (especially the elderly) often experience when intruders are known to be present.

In particular, the Court thought it unhelpful to compartmentalize the aggravating features of the offence in such cases as high or medium risk, or proceed on the basis that the appropriate sentence was a matter of aggregating such factors by 'some kind of hypothetical, quasi-mathematical calculation'. Although specific guidance was clearly necessary on the 'objective' impact of high and low risk factors for reasons of consistency of approach, sentencers needed to be free to address the realities of each case before them. In this, the Court appeared to accept the need for some adjustment in the balance of the penal equation reflecting retributive demands for consistency and proportionality, the culpability of the offender, and the harmful consequences for the victim.

It may be argued that, by rejecting a formulaic approach to calculating victim impact, the Court was implicitly recognizing the need for sentencing discretion to take greater account of the state's obligation to the victim, and to the wider community, in reflecting the harmful consequences of burglary. Taken alone, cases such as *Saw* cannot be presumed to suggest a trend towards the sentencing process engaging with the issue of victim harm in a more participative sense. However, together with cases of murder and personal violence, its emphasis on victim harm as an important indicator of the gravity of an offence, and the need to take more effective account of it when sentencing, should be seen as an important move in the right direction.

Sentencing for driving-related deaths

It is difficult to find a better illustration of a 'legitimacy' gap than that which exists between the justice expectations of citizens and the reality of the punishment administered by the state in England and Wales for driving-related deaths. This disjunction between perceived harm and the legitimacy of so-called proportionate sentencing as an adequate penal response in such cases was recently the subject of a detailed report drawn up for the Sentencing Advisory Panel as the basis for guidance prepared for the judiciary by the Sentencing Guidelines Council.[85]

It is clear from the SAP's research, and other independent studies, that the public underestimates, and has no clear understanding of, the way in which the sentences imposed by the courts in such cases are arrived at, or the nature of the legal constraints placed upon sentence decision-makers. However, there were some interesting variations, especially as between the new offences of causing death by driving while unlicensed, disqualified or uninsured, where the public perception was that the maximum sentence of two years imprisonment was too low, and that of causing death by careless driving, where the

---

85 Hough *et al.* (2008).

maximum sentence of five years was regarded as too high because the offence itself was perceived as less serious than the former offence.

The views of the relatives of victims appear consistent with victims' experiences of the criminal justice process in general, as reflected in the discussion in the previous section dealing with victims' perceptions of the Victim Advocates' scheme. For example, issues of lack of transparency and engagement with victims, such as failure to explain the sentence properly to the bereaved, were especially significant. There was a distinct perception that the criminal justice process responded inadequately to the devastating impact of bereavement and its inevitable emotional and practical consequences, and that what appeared to be an important opportunity for meaningful involvement on the part of victims often proved to be little more than symbolic. In many respects, society's response appeared to reflect the low moral priority attached to death caused by those forms of driving which are defined as legally culpable.

In terms of sentence perception the SAP report tended to confirm the findings of previous studies, illustrating a significant divergence between citizens' perceptions of the custody rate and actual practice. However, despite public concern about sentence proportionality, noted in earlier studies,[86] the notion that this concern can be reflected against clearly identifiable purposes for sentencing in death-by-driving cases is probably misplaced. For example, respondents in the SAP study were asked to identify the 'main objective' for sentencing an offender who has committed a death-by-driving offence from the statutorily defined list of purposes for sentencing provided in S143(1) of the Criminal Justice Act (2003). Not surprisingly, no clear pattern emerged from this exercise. Not only does this reflect the findings of previous research,[87] but it also highlights the problem of demonstrating how sentencers draw links between the purposes of sentencing and their application in individual cases, or as Morris and Tonry put it,[88] the purposes *for* sentencing and the purposes *at* sentencing. In a sense, generalizing about proportionality and its relationship to the relative perception of the seriousness of different categories of death-by-driving offence, whilst giving a general indication of harm perception, fails to provide a proper understanding of how purposes and outcomes are perceived as related in concrete cases.

Thus, it may be argued that such studies need to engage more with the phenomenology of sentencing in individual cases, since it is within this subjective context that connections are made between the penal ideology that underpins the norms of sentencing and the perceived morality of sentencing outcomes. This phenomenon occurs at two distinct levels – the first relates to the perceptions of immediate participants, and the second to the trial's wider

---

86 Roberts and Hough (2005).
87 Research indicates that sentencers generally find it difficult to discriminate between penal aims in individual cases; see Henham (1990) chs 8 and 9.
88 Morris and Tonry (1990).

moral audience, from which it may be possible to draw tentative generalized conclusions explaining how such shared sentiments are constructed.

The perceived detachment of the structures and processes of criminal justice from the needs of lay participants, and the perception that they exist instead to serve those of the professional players in the adversarial trial contest, has been widely noted.[89] These observations were mirrored in the SAP report, especially in terms of how procedural devices, such as the guilty plea discount, appeared to operate almost autonomously, without reference to the perceived need for remorse on the part of victims' relatives. Understandably, many found guilty plea discounts wholly inappropriate where the evidence against the offender was overwhelming, or in any case where death had been caused. The SAP report concluded that there was a significant discrepancy between expectations and preferences regarding the punishment of the two more serious death-by-driving offences.

More generally, the attention given to the offender's rights was perceived as disproportionate to the harm caused in death-by-driving cases and its consequences. In particular, the impersonal and disruptive nature of the process at a time of great stress for victims' relatives, the relative failure of the victim impact statement to meet their perceived needs, and the apparent lack of sensitivity by court officials, all contributed to a deep sense of detachment and frustration with the trial and its sentencing outcome.

Ultimately, the moral legitimacy attached to the manner of assessing harm in death-by-driving cases, particularly the weight attached to harm as opposed to individual culpability, has to be reflected against a set of objectively identified principles.[90] However, the social relevance of these normative principles may be minimal because the underlying purposes they are designed to facilitate may themselves reflect a weak moral consensus about the role of punishment in such cases. Hence, even if a more restorative approach to sentencing in death-by-driving cases were to be adopted, it would have limited social impact within the existing retributive justice framework, despite increasing rights of access and participation for victims or community representatives, because the moral value attached to those rights would be circumscribed by the dominant penal ideology.

To objectify any identifiable shared morality through the framing of substantive offences for death-by-driving cases, as Clarkson and Keating suggest,[91] seems fraught with difficulty, since these can at best only provide a contested and inflexible reflection of moral values. They are also likely to exclude from consideration many of the factual situations which go towards constructing our perceptions of the morality of a particular manner of driving

---

89 Such a view is consistent with notions of legal closure and the self-referential and recursive nature of legal structures shaping the parameters of human interaction.
90 Such as the human rights principles embodied in the ECHR; see Ashworth (1994).
91 Clarkson and Keating (1994) 814.

in any particular situation. An example of the potential difficulties caused by the contested nature of such judgments may be found in the Sentencing Guidelines Council's Definitive Guideline on Causing Death by Driving issued in July 2008, especially in the variety and suggested emphasis given to the factors which may be used to distinguish between different degrees of risk in death by dangerous driving cases,[92] or in the fact that the standard of driving is completely ignored in cases causing death where the driver is unlicensed, disqualified or uninsured, as the SAP report bears out.

If sentencing is the best place to send out the correct moral message in such cases, what arguments ought we to consider when deciding how to objectify different moral positions? A number of points having general relevance to questions concerning the objectification of risk have been discussed by Anthony Duff.[93] To begin with, Duff points out that there are different levels of risk awareness. These are a matter of subjective fact and may range from risk-taking where death is a virtual or moral certainty to inadvertent risk-taking. In sentencing terms, the degree of subjective awareness could simply be taken into account as mitigation or aggravation, yet if penalty levels are to be predicated on risk assessment (as opposed to harm) some standardised objective measure is necessary.[94]

It may be argued that risk-taking should be measured by some objective criterion, because it is necessary to decide the extent to which the risk-taking was unjustified. This is to judge the reasonableness of the risk of which the defendant was aware. The reasonableness or unreasonableness of a risk may also depend upon its relative disvalue. In the context of death by driving there is clearly some disagreement between subjective and objective perceptions of the balance between social utility and action. This makes the development of objective criteria for risk assessment more problematic.

It is also difficult for objective criteria to reflect the difference between choice and indifference in risk-taking. The debate in criminal law as to whether recklessness should involve only conscious risk-taking illustrates a significant problem in sentencing motoring offenders where penalty levels are determined by assessing culpability predominantly on the basis of advertent or inadvertent risk-taking. One answer to this dilemma, as Duff recognises,[95] is to stress the subjective component in any objective standard adopted, so that, for example, the ability of a driver convicted of causing death by careless driving is judged primarily against the objective standard of the reasonable person, the subjective element in that accused's culpability being determined by whether he *could* have taken the care which he failed to take and the extent of his failure.

---

92 Sentencing Guidelines Council (2008) 10.
93 Duff (1990) 142.
94 Equally, the perception of harm has both objective and subjective aspects; see, for example, Mathiesen's description of how the subjective dimension of 'time' as measured by desert-based sentencing systems is largely ignored in custodial sentencing; Mathiesen (1990) 132.
95 Duff (1990) 156.

If any such subjectivisation is ruled out, and the legal test is unequivocal in stating that drivers are to be judged by reference to the objective standard of a competent and careful driver, there is greater scope for moral conjecture, not only about defining how the requisite standard might be arrived at, but also as to how, for the purposes of sentencing, subjective factors are to be treated in terms of determining their factual basis and the weight to be attached to them.

Early research by Corbett and Simon[96] reinforced suspicion about the general public's ambivalent view of the perceived criminality of motoring offences. A typical example of the problem concerns the public's perception of the relationship between alcohol consumption and driving ability, and how this affects the rules of evidence. For instance, in *R v Woodward*[97] the English Court of Appeal held that, on a prosecution for causing death by dangerous driving, evidence that the motorist had been drinking before driving was admissible, but mere consumption of alcohol in itself was insufficient to establish that he had consumed such a quantity as might adversely affect a driver. In other words, the issue was whether a jury would have been satisfied that the appellant had consumed enough alcohol to adversely affect a driver. In such circumstances it was incumbent on the trial judge to warn the jury against taking the appellant's drinking into account because, if they did so, they could only be speculating. This is despite the fact that in this case the estimates as to the appellant's drinking ranged from two to six pints of lager, although there was conjecture as to its effects. Notwithstanding that social attitudes against drinking and driving may have since hardened, the fact remains that the objectification of a moral standard for judging behaviour which possesses such a large subjective component in its assessment remains problematic.

For sentencing, such dilemmas mirror those of desert-based sentencing schemes and their ability to achieve proportionate penal justice, since, increasingly, moral discord characterises the condemnation of many areas of human behaviour, some of which are criminalised. As suggested, research evidence indicates a high degree of moral ambivalence regarding many aspects of motoring behaviour, with only the more serious and blatant behaviours drawing widespread condemnation. Nonetheless, a high degree of conjecture persists about how penal law and sentencing should reflect such moral condemnation.

Law's authority rests on a presumed moral consensus[98] which is objectified in the form of penal norms,[99] despite the fact that in reality the presumed consensus may often, as with the perceived appropriateness of sentence levels for cases of death by driving, have fragile moral foundations. As regards risk assessment, it may be argued that objective evidential assessment necessarily

---

96 Corbett and Simon (1991).
97 *The Times*, 7 December 1994.
98 Unless one argues that law consists of a closed system of norms from which it derives its own authority; see Raz (1999).
99 As characterised by Durkheim's notion of the collective sentiments.

imposes a value judgement,[100] which may hamper the court's evaluation in individual cases.

An alternative argument is that by concentrating more on harm assessment rather than culpability it is possible to develop the basis for a hierarchy of offences which could be linked directly to penalty levels and would not need to be re-interpreted to form desert-based principles. However, this wrongly assumes that the concept of harm assessment is essentially value-neutral, except for the initial decision as to which harms should be included,[101] since the objective existence of physical harm is incontrovertible.

Arguably, however, understandings of the legitimacy attached to penal measures in any social context should focus on the balance between harm perception and penal responses. More particularly, such legitimacy reflects the morality that underpins shared perceptions of what is 'appropriate' within any penal context. As revealed in the criminalising and punishing of death-by-driving cases, there is an urgent need to consider both individual and communitarian dimensions of these value systems and their impact.

Establishing new boundaries

Redefining contested terrain

It may be suggested that, since the role of the judiciary in enforcing the rule of law through sentencing has increasingly been challenged, and the judiciary itself has become symbolically detached from its perception as an 'arm of the state' in the minds of many, its future penal role might be considered as open for renegotiation. This suggestion implies that the long-running consensus between the executive and judicial organs of state in matters of criminal justice is in greater danger of breaking down than at any other time in recent history. More significant, however, is the fact that the nature of this breakdown extends beyond arguments about the separation of powers, the weakening of the rule of law, or the value of individualisation in sentencing. It is an argument about the legitimacy of what passes for criminal justice more generally, and a realisation of the fact that there must be a *real* assumption of responsibility by the state for criminal justice. This 'relational'[102] responsibility should inform penal ideology and practice and reach beyond the symbolism of retributive justice and deterrence. Such a principle holds true for both international and domestic systems of criminal justice.

In short, the notion of responsibility should not only be recognised as a core value which informs criminal justice governance, it should also be seen as effective in practice. As argued, recognising that citizens have perceptions

---

100 See McBarnet (1981a).

101 For examples of different approaches to this issue, see Gross (1979), Packer (1969), Walker (1972).

102 'Relational' here means that penal ideology and practice should be linked much more effectively than at present to the moral expectations of communities and their social needs.

about the legitimacy of sentencing suggests that there is some kind of moral consensus which underpins the meaning of responsibility. At the domestic level, this might imply moral convergence regarding the nature of responsibility as between citizen and state. On the international plane, it ought to be reflected in some identifiable moral attachment to penal ideology and practice, whether by humanity as a whole or by citizens of post-conflict transitional states.

What this suggests is that penal accountability cannot be seen simply in abstract terms which recognise and define the limits of behaviour, prescribing what are considered to be appropriate penalties for individual or collective failure to fulfil obligations. Penal accountability needs to be morally grounded, and its social function fully articulated. In other words, the rationales and principles by which individuals are held responsible for criminalised behaviour should be perceived as legitimate by relevant social actors, so that there is 'real' accountability, in the sense of moral significance, in particular social contexts.

It has been argued that the moral bases for holding individuals or groups criminally responsible for particular types of behaviour may appear partial and often uncertain for those victims and communities who have been 'harmed'[103] by that behaviour. In addition, the contentious nature of much recent domestic penal policy-making has obfuscated conventionally accepted demarcations of responsibility for particular forms of human activity and its control through the criminal justice process. Hence, the state is often perceived as claiming responsibility, but failing to exercise it, whilst citizens seem unaware that responsibility is theirs, or unwilling to accept the fact that responsibility for certain behaviours has been effectively transferred to them because the moral parameters which underpin the governance role of criminal justice have become blurred, deliberately or otherwise.

Penal governance and judicial responsibility

The difficulties chronicled above are being played out against the shifting terrain of judicial responsibility. However, it may be argued that the gradual alienation of the judiciary from the executive in matters of sentencing policy, increasingly evident in England and Wales, should not necessarily be regarded as a negative development. The seemingly relentless erosion of judicial discretion through successive policy initiatives and legislative interference has done little to clarify the role of the judiciary in sentencing. It has merely created a situation where the normative parameters governing the operation of the principle of judicial independence have effectively been increased. Arguably,

---

103 The exact scope and significance of this expression should be carefully defined within a communitarian context.

the impact has been to weaken the conventional ties that bind the judiciary and the executive together, so that the common purpose of penal policy has been eroded, perhaps irrevocably.[104]

In the English context, Lord Woolf CJ's remarks in *R v Kefford*[105] illustrate clearly the uncertainty that now surrounds the judiciary's role in the implementation of penal policy.[106] In this case, Lord Woolf appeared to mirror comments by the then Home Secretary, David Blunkett, urging judges and magistrates to refrain from custodial sentencing unless strictly necessary, in order to ease prison overcrowding. In so doing, he referred to the fact that the prison population was the highest ever recorded at 69,892,[107] as compared with a prison population of 45,000 recorded at the time of the Strangeways prison riots in 1990.[108] Lord Woolf intimated that, although not responsible for the provision of prison places, the courts had to accept the realities of the situation, so that a prison sentence should only be imposed when absolutely necessary, and for no longer than necessary. However, his Lordship went on to emphasise that nothing should deter courts from imprisoning those offenders who committed violence and intimidation or similar grave crimes for the appropriate period. Particularly where such offences involved vulnerable members of the community, this understandably undermined the public's sense of safety, and the courts consequently had to respond by playing their part in protecting the public.

Furthermore, Lord Woolf suggested that there were other categories of offences where a community punishment or a fine may be suitable, rather than imprisonment. In the case of economic crimes, for instance, a first-time offender

---

104 This view is not shared by all scholars. Michael Tonry, for example, has argued in favour of more rigorous control of judicial sentencing discretion for England and Wales. Writing in the wake of the Halliday report of 2001, Tonry sees the introduction of guidelines as an opportunity to bring the rule of law into English sentencing. He suggests that, whilst there are a large variety of evidentiary, procedural and processual standards aimed at assuring justice in adjudication, few are aimed at ensuring it in punishment. Tonry sees statutory guidelines, if successful, as making English sentencing more consistent, transparent and predictable; reducing the scale of racial, ethnic and gender disparities; providing a management tool for the control of state penal resources; and ensuring that judges are more accountable for their decisions about citizens' liberties. However, making judges part of the solution, as Tonry suggests, does not tackle the underlying problem of penal legitimacy discussed in this book; see Tonry (2004), ch. 5.

105 *R v Kefford* [2002] 2 Cr App R (S) 106. See also *R v Mills* (2002) 2 Cr App R (S) 229 for similar comments by Lord Woolf in connection with the rising female prison population.

106 See Ashworth (2005) 40, 50–54.

107 The designated 'overcrowded capacity' of the prison system was 70,834. The current prison population is nearer to 90,000 inmates. For prison populations updates, see http://www.hmprisonservice.gov.uk/resourcecentre/publicationsdocuments/index.asp?cat=85 (accessed 2010).

108 Lord Woolf's influential report on the disturbances at Strangeways prison concluded that a careful balance needed to be maintained between security, control and justice in managing the prison population of England and Wales; Woolf (1990).

convicted of obtaining credit by fraud might regard a court appearance as a significant punishment *per se*.[109] His Lordship also commented on the retributive aspects of sentencing in such cases, which could be achieved, for example, by combining a community punishment and a curfew and on the potential for deterrence, suggesting that the performance of useful community work might provide an effective form of atonement.

Although relatively infrequent, these kinds of pronouncements on sentencing policy by the higher judiciary are by no means unique.[110] Nevertheless, it may be argued that in *Kefford* the Lord Chief Justice was complicit in driving home a sensitive political message concerning the appropriateness of the executive's penal policy of bifurcation, which had been a constant source of tension between the executive and the judiciary since the Criminal Justice Act of 1991.[111] In a sense, therefore, there were conflicting political agendas at work. First, there was that of the judiciary, in asserting its need for control over the parameters for the exercise of judicial discretion in custodial sentencing by making a very public statement of its apparent sensitivity to issues of prison overcrowding. Secondly, there was that of the executive, in wishing to publicly reinforce the case for bifurcated sentencing, with its implicit agenda of resource management and diminished reach for criminal justice governance.

Hence, the thrust of Lord Woolf's remarks may be seen as primarily directed towards clarifying the role of the judiciary in asserting clear parameters for the exercise of judicial discretionary power in custodial sentencing,[112] whereas the Home Secretary was more concerned with addressing the pragmatic realities of political accountability. Paradoxically, not only did these agendas appear contradictory, but the judiciary itself, in its concerted opposition to crucial aspects of the 1991 Act, had previously indicated its lack of support for bifurcation as a pivotal component of sentencing policy.

Numerous other examples may be cited from the 1990s where tension between the judiciary and the executive about the appropriateness of controls over sentencing discretion precipitated a public distancing of the judiciary

---

109 This is consistent with the so-called 'clang of the prison gates' principle which had previously been widely advocated for such offenders.

110 For example, Lord Phillips of Worth Matravers LCJ's comments in 2007 that judges should consider prison costs before imposing a custodial sentence.

111 Easton and Piper (2005), ch. 2.

112 Ashworth (2010) 61. It has been suggested that judges already regard themselves as imprisoning only when necessary, and for no longer than necessary; see Taylor, Wasik and Leng (2004) 186. In fact, the research by Hough, Jacobson and Millie, to which Taylor *et al.* refer, suggests that the issue is far more complex than may initially be thought. The research concluded that harsher sentencing resulted from the interplay of a politicised climate about punishment fuelled by the media, legislative change and increasing control of sentencing discretion, in addition to sentencers' perceptions of changes in the pattern of offending behaviour; Hough, Jacobson and Millie (2003).

from particular aspects of sentencing policy.[113] Such tension reached its zenith when mandatory minimum sentences were introduced for certain types of repeat offending in the Crime (Sentences) Act of 1997.[114] This prompted Lord Woolf, during the Second Reading of the Bill in the House of Lords,[115] to suggest that the proposals prevented judges from doing what they felt to be necessary in the interests of justice, that they upset the constitutional balance, and that they involved the judiciary surrendering what had hitherto always been accepted as its traditional role. However, Ashworth[116] was quick to point out that the formulation of sentencing policy is an entirely appropriate Parliamentary function, and that the function of the principle of judicial independence is essentially confined to promoting impartiality in the administration of justice.

There is no doubt that the higher judiciary regarded the 1997 Crime (Sentences) Act as symbolic of the increasingly partisan politicisation of penal policy. Such pandering to populism, or reflection of 'populist punitiveness' as Bottoms[117] preferred to call it, had the effect of driving a wedge between the judiciary and the executive over matters of penal policy, since the former felt it was increasingly being taken to task and made to account publicly[118] for policies which it appeared to regard as threatening the liberty of individual citizens.[119] Regrettably, this tense relationship between the judiciary and the executive has persisted.[120]

---

113 For a discussion of the policy implications in the aftermath of the Criminal Justice Act (1991), see Henham (1996), ch. 7.

114 See Henham (1998).

115 HL Deb vol 577, col 997, 27 January 1997.

116 Ashworth (1996b). For further discussion, see Ashworth (2000b).

117 Bottoms (1995) 17–49.

118 Through the affirmation of sentencing, and paradoxically, through its apparent public acquiescence outside the courtroom (since, at that time, the judiciary was by convention forbidden to defend or explain sentencing decisions to the media, or any other 'audience' beyond the courtroom).

119 Arguably, this may be seen as a thinly disguised attempt to conceal the judiciary's perception that it was entitled to override the legislature where sentencing policy encroached on its discretionary power. As Ashworth (2000b) 303 suggests; 'In brief, Parliament has pursued a mixture of well-conceived and ill-conceived policies, often in a poorly drafted form, and the courts have attempted to pursue their own policies with as little regard for the legislature as possible.' For further discussion, see Ashworth (2001).

120 Notable examples have included the setting of tariffs where a life sentence is imposed for murder and the appropriateness of custodial sentences for first-time burglars; for summary and context, see Ashworth and Player (2005). The modern judiciary now routinely defends its position on sentencing in the public media, and comments openly on government penal policy as deemed appropriate; see, for example, the media statement from the Judicial Communications Office given to the *Sunday Times* regarding criticism of judges' sentences, 11 June 2006, and the attack by Lord Phillips CJ on government penal policy and its impact on prison overcrowding; Phillips of Worth Matravers (2007).

Tightening the grip

This section summarises the increasingly political role played by the executive over recent years in controlling the exercise of judicial discretionary power through legislative means.[121]

The Court of Appeal has traditionally provided sentencing guidance for sentencers in the lower courts through its decisions on sentencing appeals.[122] This guidance has developed into a fully-fledged sentencing jurisprudence establishing numerous sentencing principles for different categories of offence.[123] In recent years there has been an increasing trend by the Court of Appeal to deliver guideline judgements which provide indications to sentencers of the sort of sentences that may be appropriate to reflect differing degrees of gravity in particular types of cases.[124] This has been done in order to maintain proportionality and consistency. Their significance increased following the Criminal Justice Act of 1991.[125]

Section 80 of the Crime and Disorder Act 1998 placed a duty on the Court of Appeal to produce sentencing guidelines. However, S81 of the 1998 Act also created a Sentencing Advisory Panel (SAP) to act as an advisory body to the Court of Appeal on the framing of sentencing guidelines. The Panel proved to be a successful innovation and formulated advice recommending sentencing guidelines for many kinds of offence.[126]

However, an important distinction could be drawn between guideline judgements and sentencing guidelines. The former, as suggested, were concerned with developing the Court of Appeal's general advice to sentencers and were aimed at influencing the exercise of judicial discretionary power by encouraging principled and consistent sentencing. However, the important point is that this process was entirely controlled by the judges themselves. An alternative meaning for the expression 'sentencing guidelines' was to suggest (for various reasons) that greater control be advocated over what the judges did in sentencing, and some extra-judicial means suggested to provide the guidelines. Many alternative schemes were mooted over the years: for instance, normal or presumptive sentences indicated by statutory principles; sentencing standards set by a Sentencing Commission; or sentencing guidelines developed for

---

121 For a comprehensive discussion; see Ashworth (2010) 24–70. Ashworth draws attention to the absence of any empirical evaluation of the impact of sentencing guidelines on sentencing practice. This information would be of considerable value when discussing the legitimacy of sentencing.

122 However, it is important to note the different grounds for appeal from the magistrates and the Crown Court; the generally limited relevance of Court of Appeal decisions to magistrates' sentencing, and the fact that the Magistrates' Association issue sentencing guidelines specifically for magistrates.

123 This work was pioneered by David Thomas; see Thomas (1970).

124 See, for example, *R v Billam* (1986) 8 Cr App R (S) 48 (rape).

125 For further discussion, see Ashworth (2000c) 72.

126 See, further, Wasik (1998), ch. 12.

a particular jurisdiction. All the above had weaknesses and were judged inappropriate for use in England and Wales.[127]

The undoubted tension between the judiciary and the executive over sentencing discretion that developed during the 1990s has continued and precipitated calls for greater external regulation.[128] The Criminal Justice Bill of 2002 proposed much tighter executive control over the powers of the Court of Appeal to issue sentencing guidance. The resulting S167 of the Criminal Justice Act of 2003 established a Sentencing Guidelines Council (SGC) consisting of the Lord Chief Justice as chairman, seven judicial members and five non-judicial members. Politically, this move was especially significant since, as well as for the first time introducing a statutory mechanism to regulate the exercise of sentencing discretion, the legislation provided that non-judicial members of the SGC would be appointed by the Secretary of State, albeit after consultation with the senior judiciary.

However, the potential for executive influence went further than this. Section 170 of the 2003 Act made the SGC responsible for the formulation of sentencing guidelines; defined as meaning guidelines relating to the sentencing of offenders which could be general in nature or limited to a particular category of offence or offenders.[129] Notably, the Secretary of State was given considerable power to influence those areas where guidelines were felt to be necessary; clearly this was a politically sensitive decision, since S163(2) allowed the Home Secretary to propose to the SGC at any time that sentencing guidelines be revised or framed by it in respect of offences or offenders of a particular category, or as regards any particular matter affecting sentencing. On the other hand, the SGC could act on its own initiative in considering whether it should frame sentencing (or allocation) guidelines, but was mandated to do so if a proposal was received from either the SAP or the Secretary of State.

Any guidelines issued as definitive by the SGC had to be kept under review and regard had to several matters when deciding to frame or revise sentencing guidelines. These included the cost of different sentences, which many argue is

---

127 Many different schemes operate in the United States with varying degrees of success. For a useful overview, see Tonry (1996).

128 The Government instituted a Review of the Sentencing Framework (The Halliday Review) in 2000 principally on the basis that it was felt there was a narrow sense of purpose underlying the Criminal Justice Act of 1991 and that its objectives had become diluted following the many changes since its implementation; see Halliday (2001). Detailed suggestions were also included in Lord Justice Auld's comprehensive review of the criminal courts; see Auld (2001), and the general theme was developed by the Government in its White Paper setting out its priorities for the criminal justice system in 2002; see Home Office (2002), in particular, chapter 5. Accordingly, a Criminal Justice Bill was introduced into the House of Commons on 21st November 2002, eventually receiving the Royal Assent on the 20th November 2003. For commentary on the background to the changes, see Baker and Clarkson (2002), Roberts (2002). See, generally, Rex and Tonry (2002). For commentary on the changes themselves, see Taylor, Wasik and Leng (2004), Ashworth (2004).

129 It was also made responsible for formulating so-called allocation guidelines, which concern decisions made by magistrates' courts as to whether an offence is more suitable for summary trial, or trial on indictment.

not a relevant issue when fixing what should be the 'appropriate' punishment for a particular offence. Other factors – such as the need to promote consistency in sentencing; have regard to sentences imposed by courts in England and Wales for offences to which the guidelines relate; the relative effectiveness of particular sentences in preventing re-offending; and the need to promote public confidence in the criminal justice system – were included. Arguably, such factors would be borne in mind by most judges in any event when sentencing in individual cases and did not merit inclusion in a statutory scheme.

Public confidence may be seen as a two-edged sword, however. A politician may equate what promotes public confidence with what promotes electoral advantage. Consequently, it may be argued that the possibility for increasing executive control over sentencing discretion that these provisions permitted required greater scrutiny and accountability.[130]

The degree of statutory control increased further with the introduction in Part 4 of the Coroners and Justice Act 2009[131] of a more rigid regulatory framework for promulgating sentencing guidelines.[132] The Act created a new body called the Sentencing Council (SC), amalgamating the functions of the SAP and the SGC, to formulate sentencing guidelines and monitor their use. The general remit of the SC also requires it to assess the impact of sentencing practice and promote awareness of sentencing matters, and it may also be required to consider the impact of policy and legislative proposals relating to sentencing.[133] An important example of the widening of accountability required of the SC is its duty under S131 to consider the implications of 'non-sentencing factors' as well as 'sentencing factors' on the resources available for sentencing. The former include: recalling persons to prison, breaches of community orders, patterns of reoffending, early release recommendations

---

130 The SGC had to publish and consult on any draft guidelines, and the consultees had to include the Secretary of State. Only after completing this process and making any amendments it considered appropriate could the SGC issue the guidelines as definitive.

131 The relevant provisions came into force on the 15 March 2010. See Ashworth (2010) 424–29, for a summary. The controlling effect of the provisions is mitigated to the extent that S125 of the Act requires every sentencing court to follow any sentencing guidelines which are relevant to the offender's case, and to follow any sentencing guidelines which are relevant to the exercise of the function, *unless the court is satisfied that it would be contrary to the interests of justice to do so* (emphasis added).

132 A Sentencing Commission Working Group chaired by Lord Justice Gage was set up by the Lord Chancellor and Lord Chief Justice in response to the Carter review on the use of custody *Securing the Future* (2007). The Working Group issued a consultation document 'A Structured Sentencing Framework and Sentencing Commission' in 2008 http://www.judiciary.gov.uk/publications_media/general/sentencing_consultation310308.htm (accessed 2008), wherein it recommended building on the existing processes for issuing guidelines and merging the Sentencing Advisory Panel (SAP) and Sentencing Guidelines Council (SGC) into one body; http://www.justice.gov.uk/publications/sentencing-commission.htm (accessed 2008).

133 An illustration of this is the requirement for any draft or definitive guideline to be accompanied by a resource assessment indicating the likely effect of the guidelines on the provision of prison places, probation provision and youth justice services (S127(3)).

made by the Parole Board, and custodial remands. Not only is the potential for executive influence sustained through the Lord Chancellor's[134] powers of recommendation and intervention,[135] but the explicit expansion of the SCs remit into broader issues of criminal justice policy paradoxically increases the vulnerability of the judiciary to external criticism should it be perceived as failing to respond to these 'internal' regulatory pressures on sentencing practice.

Additional pressures and debates

Several other disparate but nevertheless fundamental concerns threaten the primacy of trial justice and the significance of judicial sentencing discretion in shaping perceptions of its legitimacy.

Diversion from sentencing

Pre-trial mechanisms such as diversion and mediation fall into this category. A recent English example of the exponential growth of out-of-court disposals is the use of cautioning by the police.[136] Although originally intended to respond to behaviour not previously subject to prosecution, increased police cautioning has been heavily criticised as ineffective[137] and an unnecessary encroachment on civil liberties. In addition, inconsistencies have been revealed in police practice, with some forces apparently using conditional cautions to deal with altogether more serious offences.[138]

This phenomenon obscures the purposes of punishment and the role of trial justice. On the one hand, it typifies what Cohen[139] terms 'widening the net': the process whereby alternative programmes tend to capture those who would not formerly have been at risk, or would not otherwise have been informally dealt with. The end result is to increase the total number drawn into the criminal justice system. By 'thinning the mesh', not only are more individuals brought into the system, but the amount of intervention they are then subjected to is greater

---

134 The judicial functions of the Lord Chancellor were removed by the Constitutional Reform Act 2005, and in 2007 the Lord Chancellor was appointed the Secretary of State for Justice.

135 S124(1) Coroners and Justice Act (2009).

136 A caution may take the form of either a simple caution or a conditional caution, which has specific conditions attached that the offender must satisfy; see Part 3, Criminal Justice Act (2003). Other examples include Fixed Penalty Tickets, Penalty Notices for Disorder and various forms of administrative fine.

137 For example, Slack (2009).

138 For example, it was reported that offenders committing actual bodily harm had been conditionally cautioned, whereas the guidelines specifically state that no offence above the level of common assault should be included; see, BBC *Panorama* (2009).

The potential damage of these inconsistencies to penal legitimacy prompted the then Labour government to instigate an immediate review of out-of-court disposals in November 2009; see http://www.justice.gov.uk/news/newsrelease141209b.htm (accessed 2009).

139 Cohen (1985).

than they would have received under one of the more traditional alternatives to custody, such as fines, community sentences or conditional discharges.

However, there appears to be a double paradox. The first, identified by Cohen,[140] is that diversion was originally heralded as a more radical form of destructuring, short of complete non-intervention or decriminalization. This has clearly not been the case. The second paradox is police practice in diverting serious offenders away from trial justice. Consequently, the possibility of sustaining a holistic purpose for the criminal process is systematically undermined by sub-system rationales and objectives.[141] This serves to obfuscate penal ideology and destabilise trial praxis such as sentencing. More broadly, it weakens the legitimacy attached to the governance role of criminal justice.

The rise of the prosecutor

The issue of public confidence has also been important in delineating the scope of the prosecutorial role in sentencing matters. Again, the position in England and Wales provides a useful starting point for describing the adversarial context. A significant expansion of the prosecutor's sentencing role took place in 1988 when S36 of the Criminal Justice Act created a new system for the review of sentences which appear unduly lenient to the Attorney-General.[142] The latter has power to refer such sentences to the Court of Appeal (Criminal Division), but the power only applies to persons convicted of an offence triable on indictment (or an offence of the kind specified in S1 under regulations made by the Home Secretary). The Attorney-General must get leave from the Court of Appeal before the case is reviewed. If leave is granted the court may quash any sentence imposed by the trial court and substitute such sentence as they consider appropriate for the case and as the court below had power to pass. Where the offender is convicted of two or more offences in the same proceedings the whole of the sentence may be reviewed. Existing restrictions on the power of the court to increase a sentence on an appeal by an offender were not removed by S36. There may be further reference by either the Attorney General or the offender to the Supreme Court on points of law.

Writing at the time, David Thomas[143] expressed the view that some of the benefits S36 might produce, such as badly needed case law on the use of non-custodial measures, were unlikely to be achieved. He also felt that its restriction to indictable offences probably prevented the Court of Appeal from being presented with the chance to examine principles which should be applied on the most critical borderline in sentencing, that between immediate custody and other disposals, which is relatively rarely exposed

---

140 *Ibid.*, 51.
141 See Cicourel (1968).
142 See Henham (1994), Shute (1999).
143 Thomas (1989).

in the most serious cases. However, the procedure was gradually extended[144] following an amendment made by Schedule 9, paragraph 34 of the Criminal Justice and Public Order Act of 1994 which enabled the Home Secretary to add cases involving sentences of any specified description to those which the Attorney-General may refer to the Court of Appeal for a review. This extension of executive control has proved to be a significant political tool.[145]

However, the greatest potential source of conflict between public and judicial perceptions of justice in this area stems from the nature and meaning of the test used to determine 'undue leniency'. This ambivalence has been exacerbated by the more sensationalist media.[146] Public misunderstanding appears rooted in its failure to comprehend the mechanics of sentencing,[147] and the particular legal constraints under which judges operate in the Crown Court. Neither is the remit of the Court of Appeal and the constraints on its ability to remedy perceived deficiencies in penal policy appreciated.

Guidance as to the correct approach for dealing with references under S36 was originally given by the Court of Appeal in *Attorney-General's Reference (No. 4 of 1989)*,[148] which further indicated that it would not intervene unless it was clear that there was some error of principle in the judge's sentence.[149] It was in this more restricted sense that the Court of Appeal sought to assess the extent to which public confidence would be damaged if the sentence was not altered. This is clearly at odds with what might be considered a lay understanding of the meaning of 'undue leniency'. This would normally refer to a

---

144 The Criminal Justice Act 1988 (Review of Sentencing) Order 2006 extended coverage to include:
- making threats to kill;
- child cruelty;
- certain serious and complex frauds;
- certain sexual offences;
- certain offences in relation to the illegal importation of controlled drugs or indecent material;
- production, supply or possession with intent to supply of controlled drugs or the cultivation of cannabis;
- racially or religiously aggravated forms of assault, criminal damage, public order offences or aggravated harassment.

Attempting to commit or inciting the commission of all of these offences are also included.

145 The reason for this is that it allows the executive indirectly, through the Attorney-General's office, to signal its disapproval of sentencing practices that attract adverse media attention. See BBC News (2006b).

146 For example, see 'Judge refused to jail the thug who left me with brain damage ... because he's a doctor' *The Sun*, 17 June 2008, http://www.thesun.co.uk/sol/homepage/woman/real_life/2484987/How-can-we-fix-broken-Britain-with-these-soft-sentencing-scandals.html (accessed 2010).

147 This relates principally to how sentencing decisions are reached and the normative constraints placed upon decision-makers; see Roberts and Hough (2005).

148 [1990] 1 WLR 41.

149 Namely that 'it falls outside the range of sentences which the judge, applying his mind to all the relevant factors, could reasonably consider appropriate'. In Attorney-General's Reference Nos 31, 42, 43, 45, 50 and 51 [2004] EWCA Crim 1934 it was emphasised that the sentence must be not simply low but 'manifestly not sufficiently severe'.

discernible moral consensus about the severity of the sentence as having failed to reflect the gravity of the crime and/or the culpability of the offender. Attempts to 'objectify' the test, so that it takes greater account of what public opinion might reasonably expect, have yet to materialise.

However, a greater sentencing role for the prosecutor is envisaged by some scholars. For instance, in his recent analysis of the prosecutor's role in sentencing in England and Wales, Rogers[150] raises some important issues that resonate far beyond their immediate domestic context. His most controversial suggestion is that the prosecutor should take a much more proactive stance in giving effect to the 'public interest' through justifying the decision to prosecute against the likelihood of achieving particular purposes for punishment in individual cases. Rogers is not advocating usurping judicial responsibility for decisions about punishment; rather he sees the role of the prosecutor as identifying a putative justification for punishment in any particular case which the judge *could* potentially validate by selecting an appropriate punishment.[151] He expands this point by further suggesting that prosecutors should be able to override judges where they 'appear to disagree', substituting instead their assessment of what might be a 'valid' rationale for punishment,[152] again qualifying this only by providing that the judge should possess the power to impose a sentence capable of satisfying the prosecutor's chosen aim.

While Rogers's ideas for greater prosecutorial involvement in sentencing may appear superficially attractive, arguably they illustrate an analytical approach lacking a broader appreciation of context and the crucial need to examine penal law and process as something which is embedded in the fabric of a particular society. For example, a salutary lesson learned from international criminal justice is that the question of legitimacy should be approached from a perspective which regards international criminal law and the structures and processes for its enforcement as essential tools for governance. Accordingly, this should be evidenced through its responses to those who commit gross breaches of international humanitarian law. Such an approach takes into account the significance of international criminal justice as a force for influencing beneficially both international and state forms of governance.

Consequently, as argued hitherto, the ideology of the trial should be conceived as a litmus test for determining what purposes may be regarded as appropriate in specific cases. Unless this synergy of purpose exists there is little prospect of prosecutorial (or judicial) discretion becoming instrumental in shaping the exercise of discretion in international or domestic forms of criminal trial. Instead, trial outcomes will simply come to represent the discrete agendas of trial participants, whether dictated by particular professional system interests, or purely personal in nature.

---

150 Rogers (2006) 775, 778.
151 *Ibid.*, 779.
152 *Ibid.*, 780.

Which ideological concerns might inform prosecutorial decision-making may be illustrated by referring more closely to Rogers's observation that the courts are 'not the only agency ... which accepts *responsibility* for making sentencing-related decisions',[153] and his later comment that:

> ... distinguishing between the harms of punishment and prosecution not only helps us to restructure the exercise of prosecutorial discretion; it also helps us to define the *responsibilities* owed by prosecutors to others.[154]

The key word in each case is 'responsibility', and Rogers goes on to give us some idea of what this might mean in terms of balancing the requirements of the criminal process against participants' needs and those of the wider community by including the possible effects upon victims, relatives and 'close intimates' of proceeding with a prosecution.[155]

Unfortunately, the narrow processual focus on system interests that Rogers's proposes does not give a sufficiently holistic conceptual shape to the notion of 'responsibility' for it to become integral to defining the ideology of the trial. Such an essential connection between the constituent elements of trial ideology and the role of the prosecutor is absent. Accordingly, were restorative justice to become an essential component of penal ideology for international or domestic forms of trial, a clear understanding of what was meant by restorative notions of 'responsibility' would carry through to the trial's normative framework. Hence, trial outcomes would be capable of delivering appropriate forms of restorative 'accountability'.

Coherent and principled purposes for punishment based on this ideology would therefore inform the functions of both prosecution *and* sentencing, and each would be articulated. Hence, concepts such as 'responsibility' could be made more socially relevant, if these broader purposes were acknowledged as crucial to the achievement of trial justice. In short, the rationales which inform the prosecutor's role should be compatible with those that drive the system of justice as a whole.

The adoption of a proactive approach along the lines of the English model would appear to provide a constructive way forward.[156] Nevertheless,

---

153 *Ibid.*, 781 (emphasis added).
154 *Ibid.*, 792 (emphasis added).
155 *Ibid.*, 796.
156 The English Code for Crown Prosecutors provides that they should draw the court's attention to:
 a) any aggravating or mitigating factors disclosed by the prosecution case;
 b) any Victim Personal Statement;
 c) where appropriate, evidence of the impact of the offending on a community;
 d) any statutory provisions, sentencing guidelines or guideline cases which may assist; and
 e) any relevant statutory provisions relating to ancillary orders (such as anti-social behaviour orders) (para, 11.1).

 Prosecutors should challenge any assertion made by the defence in mitigation that is inaccurate, misleading or derogatory. If the defence persist in the assertion, and it appears

although the prosecution is under a positive duty to assist the Court, including an obligation to intervene to ensure that adequate information is available,[157] this approach is inadequate as a means of adding greater legitimacy to trial justice, since it is constrained by the narrow remit of the English prosecutorial function and the limited constitutional independence of the Crown Prosecution Service. As Ashworth argues,[158] a more integrated conceptualisation of the prosecutorial function would allow greater engagement with principles of fairness and social justice.

Towards a new paradigm

The ongoing tension between the executive and the judiciary over sentencing policy has exposed the failings of penal policy and, moreover, the failure of the executive to own responsibility for critical areas of criminal justice governance. Paradoxically, however, it has also revealed the true value of judicial discretionary power, especially its potential as a force for protecting the liberties of individual citizens against unwarranted incursions by the state in defending due process and human rights.[159] More significant, however, is the implication that the principled development of judicial discretionary power in sentencing could provide a vehicle for realising the diverse expectations of the justice process held by citizens and communities.

Rather than further stifle this constructive potential of judicial discretionary power with increasingly rigid normative guidance, which may indirectly bolster already discredited penal policies or force judicial acquiescence in the implementation of new ones, the answer may lie in mobilising such discretion as part of an overarching review of the rationales for punishment and the principles of sentencing.[160] Such a review should be set free from short-term

---

relevant to the sentence, the court should be invited to hear evidence to determine the facts and sentence accordingly (para, 11.5). See Crown Prosecution Service (2010).

157 Emphasised by the Lord Chief Justice, Lord Phillips, in the Court of Appeal; see, *R v Cain & Ors* (2006), *The Times*, 26 December.

158 Ashworth (2000a) 281. Such an approach would also help to clarify the relationship between prosecutorial decision-making and the sentencing finction, particularly with regard to the use of diversionary mechanisms such as conditional cautions; see, for example, Brownlee (2007).

159 As Zedner (2005) 525 argues, the impartiality of judicial decision-making is not something that can be taken for granted. However, as discussed later, mobilising judicial discretion as a positive force is something to be achieved within the context of a transformed trial process informed by integrating changes in ideology, policy and practice.

160 However, the relativity of social context, and its effects, is a major concern for commentators who, like Davis, have explored the concept of discretion from a socio-legal perspective. In neo-classical vein, Davis cautions against the unfettered use of discretionary power, arguing that it tends to militate against the liberties of the individual citizen, although such dangers may be reduced by increasing administrative and judicial regulation and review, and ensuring transparency; Davis (1969). Although Dworkin (1997) 39 is similarly circumspect in attributing a wide measure of judicial discretion beyond what is necessary to interpret legal

political agendas. These have remained largely unconcerned with establishing a moral framework for punishment that reflects the diverse expectations of citizens, or the communities in which they live.

It has been argued that sentencing should be conceptualised as a synergy between justification and practice. However, the capacity for it to become more socially reflexive depends upon the normative flexibility of the sentencing framework.[161] To achieve greater social accountability the relationship between penal ideology and sentencing should be conceived as a recursive process that derives its moral authority more directly from the community than through the political process. Hence, the governance potential of penal policy would be realised only if the normative framework for sentencing is empowered to respond directly to public concerns about the legitimacy of punishment.

More specifically, I have suggested elsewhere[162] that, since the procedural norms of sentencing are informed by particular penal ideologies and policies which circumscribe their potential for reconciling competing claims for justice, this limits the capacity for sentencing outcomes to vindicate the moral legitimacy of such claims. Therefore, the capacity for sentencing to reconcile competing moral claims for justice depends upon the degree to which competing groups can exert power to assert what they perceive as morally legitimate objectives for punishment.[163] Hence, although sentencing may be conceptualised as synergising penal ideology and process, its legitimacy in reality depends upon its level of engagement with citizens' expectations. Ultimately, this determines the functional capacity of the criminal process, and the parameters set for the exercise of discretionary power.

The exercise of judicial discretionary power may be conceived as determining sentencing outcomes within the normative framework for rational action permitted by penal ideology. Thus, the practice of sentencing is effectively preprogrammed to merge fact and value in correspondence with such rational objectives for action. For sentencing, the debate about legitimacy focuses on the extent to which this paradigm should have the capacity to attribute value to fact for consequential reasons which may lie beyond the constraints imposed by the ideology that supports it. In England and Wales, for instance, the present penal paradigm is essentially retributive, whilst the paradigm that dictates the style and content of the trial process as a whole is adversarial in nature.

A deeper understanding of what is normatively feasible and of the reality of what can be achieved in practice is particularly important for satisfying

---

rules, his notion of a 'strong' sense of discretion can be related to sentencing in common law jurisdictions, where the legal status of sentencing principles may be ambiguous and the parameters for the exercise of discretionary power unclear.
161 Zedner (2005) 516 rightly points to the crucial balance between rights, values and interests.
162 Henham (2001).
163 See McBarnet (1981a).

the expectations of victims and communities. More particularly, the paradox between the ideology and praxis of sentencing described above could be resolved by adopting a normative approach that is more tolerant of inclusion. The paradox of exclusion currently perpetuated by retributive penal ideology seems incapable of accommodating conflicting interests. It therefore lacks the problem-solving capacity that would allow decision-makers to move more towards a model for reconciling violators and protecting the violated.

Such a pragmatic approach to sentencing requires a significant ideological shift, rather than mere procedural reform.[164] To achieve this, the trial process should become a mediator of 'truth' rather than a forum for adversarial contest and the dispensing of retributive justice. At present sentencing, as a methodology for achieving 'justice', is divorced both conceptually and practically from such a penal ideology at both the international and domestic levels. To redress this deficiency suggests changing penal ideology so that sentencing is seen as an integral part of a strategy for intervention in the social causes of crime and criminality, firmly rooted in the idea of delivering a form of justice that addresses the concerns of citizens and communities.

Accordingly, Mark Findlay and I[165] have argued in favour of utilising the instrumental power of judicial discretion through a transformation in international criminal trial process in order to enhance its legitimacy. In the context of sentencing, we argue that enhanced discretion exercised within the appropriate normative framework could provide the negotiating flexibility needed to mediate between competing moral values. This would permit sentencing judges to go beyond the conventional adversarial framework which presently controls the way in which the purposes of punishment can be realised.

From a socio-legal perspective, such a strategically relational paradigm suggests that law's moral power can be realised through sentencing by developing judicial discretionary power, so that the outcomes produced engage more effectively with their social context. Clearly, the capacity for developing the instrumental power of judicial discretion depends on allowing maximum flexibility for decision-makers. Consequently, discretion needs to be free to determine the morally appropriate linkage between value and fact.

This kind of conceptualisation implies that the outcomes resulting from the recursively organised practice of sentencing should correspond more closely with subjective perceptions of its moral legitimacy held by the relevant social audience. Hence, it follows that the ability of judicial discretionary power to deliver value judgements regarded as morally legitimate may well rest upon the extent to which any identifiable shared moral consensus about the

---

164 The limitations of procedural reform without ideological underpinning is exemplified by the Italian experience; see chapter 8.
165 Findlay and Henham (2005).

purposes of punishment can be said to influence penal ideology and policy, and the consequent exercise of discretion. This will dictate the extent to which criminal trial process is capable of giving practical effect to the different moral values attached to punishment through sentencing.

The notion of a common morality underpinning penal policy and sentencing practice has important dimensions in this context. Such a notion of inclusiveness clearly extends to the morality of punishment as perceived by victims and communities; constituencies that have consistently been excluded from effective participatory rights in sentencing.[166] Therefore, it must be taken as referring to an identifiable shared morality.[167]

To summarise, it has been argued that the need to take account of competing moralities for reasons of inclusiveness should be adopted as a key purpose of trial ideology. So informed, the normative framework for the trial should be conceived as a mechanism possessing the flexibility for reconciling competing moral claims for justice. Judges would therefore be empowered to negotiate these demands within the constraints of this framework through the use of their discretionary power. From a social perspective, human agency rather than structure is seen as the primary means for delivering a more inclusive morality of punishment than currently exists.

Recognising that judicial discretion can be used flexibly and instrumentally to reflect and reinforce common strands between the perceived morality of punishment and its social consequences is fundamental to any project which seeks to reconceptualise penality. In the context of international criminal justice, for example, it may be seen as an important step towards establishing trial justice as a force for promoting peace and reconciliation, so contributing to transitional justice and a return to civil society following social conflict and war.

Such a realisation does not, however, deal with the political realities of operating a fair and just criminal justice system in a society characterised by moral pluralism and diverse expectations of what trial justice should consist of.[168] Nor does it help us to confront the injustices perpetrated where punishment operates as a thinly-disguised form of ideological imperialism, or where hegemonic power appears to support criminal justice processes that

---

166 A vivid example of such an excluded shared morality is that of the relatives of homicide victims discussed earlier. Shared morality in this context is not necessarily concerned with perceived proportionality or any other 'justice' measure of sentencing outcomes; rather, such victims feel collectively excluded from the decision-making process. These shared feelings diminish the moral value attached to the process.

167 Note that this book is not concerned with promoting particular justifications for punishment, nor in suggesting the bases upon which competing moralities might be identified and their interests recognised. The thesis being advanced is that the legitimacy of sentencing depends upon it being perceived as inclusive, in a moral and social sense. Therefore, it should be informed by a penal ideology which resonates with shared moral perceptions about punishment and how these should be reflected in sentencing. The implications of this are developed in chapter 9.

168 Namely, the appropriate penal response in any particular case.

adhere to due process principles and universal human rights, whilst in reality supporting oppressive and discriminatory forms of punishment.

Concluding comments

This chapter has argued that sentencing as an exercise in judicial discretionary power may be 'out of touch' with commonly shared perceptions of trial justice in certain types of cases. Furthermore, it has been suggested that there appears to be a perceptible weakening in the hitherto presumed, although fragile, consensus existing between the executive and the judiciary concerning the role of punishment and sentencing in supporting the rule of law. Arguably, therefore, the principle of judicial independence, which by convention has delineated the judiciary's constitutional role in the implementation of penal policy, should be redefined. Rather than being set against penal policy, or being forced to defend what may be perceived as inappropriate penal law, the instrumental capacity of judicial discretionary power could instead be mobilised in the pursuit of alternative, more inclusive, forms of trial justice.

It has been suggested that, instead of the judiciary being forced to defend itself against accusations of undue leniency, remoteness and abdication of responsibility, its position in sentencing could be re-evaluated. This would only be convincing if a more socially sensitive interpretation of the judiciary's role in enforcing the 'rule of law' is adopted. Since prosecutions are undertaken for victims on the state's behalf, it may be trite, yet nevertheless persuasive, to argue that the state is manifestly failing in its moral duty to citizens if trial outcomes do not correspond effectively with their legitimate expectations for justice.

To draw such a conclusion confirms the post-Enlightenment project's inability to address the social causes of crime, identified by Norrie[169] as the core reason for the failure of successive penal regimes. Surely, what is needed is a more nuanced reading of the social morality underpinning the rule of law, one which recognises that the moral authority of penal law and practice ultimately rest on the perceived legitimacy of its ideology.

In conclusion, changes in trial ideology eventually originate from the political will to rationalise penal law and practice. I have argued that this should form part of a broader agenda which recognises criminal justice as crucial to delivering a system of governance capable of responding effectively to the pluralistic demands of citizens. Such a fundamental principle holds good for all systems of criminal justice, whether international, regional, domestic or transitional, because it recognises the need for criminal justice to connect with the everyday social realities of human experience. In other words, effective criminal justice governance can only be realised through *real* engagement with human feelings and emotions.

---

169 Norrie (2001), ch. 10.

2   Issues of Theory and Method

This aim of this chapter is to examine those problems of theory and method in criminal justice which need to be addressed if we are to explain more effectively what the notion of legitimacy signifies for punishment and sentencing, and assess its implications for criminal justice as a form of governance. It is argued that the issues raised should be explored if progress is to be made towards establishing a more profound normative understanding of the relationship between sentencing and perceptions of trial justice.

However, there are serious epistemological controversies to consider. Not the least of these are arguments about the nature of law itself and its relationship to fundamental moral questions such as the meaning of 'justice'. In addition, conjecture surrounds the capacity of sociological explanations to provide a complete account of the nature of law and legal reasoning. Methodological problems arise largely from hitherto entrenched positions about the appropriate relationship between the theory and methods of social science. These difficulties are epitomised by arguments over the relative merits of inductive or deductive approaches, whilst at the level of modelling scholars of criminal justice have consistently produced one-dimensional or otherwise conceptually incomplete tools for analysis. As for the problem of relativity, commentators continue to argue about the merits of doctrinal versus contextualised or positivist versus interpretative approaches to the comparative analysis of criminal justice and its processes.[1]

These debates need to be considered carefully before we can begin to develop a coherent framework for locating notions of legitimacy within current conceptualisations of punishment and sentencing, or to consider how to go about developing new ones. An additional aspect of such theorising is to consider its implications for explaining the role of criminal justice as a form of governance. The chapter begins by addressing the role of theory.

---

1 For a useful overview see Roberts (2002), Pakes (2010), ch. 2.

Introduction

A major task for criminological theory is to provide the conceptual tools for understanding behaviour in terms of its social reality. These tools not only help us to identify empirically what factors influence behaviour, but also suggest how such a phenomenon might occur. Such a positivist approach deals with so-called observable or 'objectively' verifiable facts. However, other perspectives, such as phenomenology, have claimed to offer insights into the subjective thought processes of individuals in an attempt to explain how meaning is attributed to what may be termed 'objective' reality. Accordingly, methodologies developed from various theories about the nature of social life and the social world have provided valuable insights into those thought processes which are involved in discretionary decision-making. Notwithstanding whether such theories and their associated methods are psychologically or sociologically oriented, they are only able to offer a partial view into the empirical world that constitutes the social reality of sentencing.[2]

Because the issue of what 'ought' to influence the shape of the empirical world remains a question of morality, and its achievement a matter of ethics, particular normative practices are rarely, if ever, analysed in such a way that values and facts, and their interrelationship, are seen as integral aspects of the study of law's social reality.[3]

Disciplinary divisions and internecine debates have therefore contributed to the fragmented nature of our analysis of social life. For example, theorising the nature of law and legal reasoning is preoccupied with debates about whether law is a closed system of rules which cannot be analysed sociologically in any meaningful way.[4] There is a similar difference of opinion between those scholars who advocate that legal reasoning is somehow divorced from moral

---

2 For a summary of the issues see; Gelsthorpe and Padfield (eds) (2003), ch. 1.

3 Raz, for example, argues that the normativity of law depends upon whether it is capable of claiming legitimate authority; Raz (1999) 163–70. Although Raz maintains a clear distinction between the nature of law and morality, he suggests that analysis of the concept of law cannot be seen purely in terms of how successful legal theory is at explaining what goes on in society, but rather in terms of the extent to which legal theory 'helps us to understand how people understand themselves'; Raz (2001) 237, 330. Raz goes on to draw attention to the mediating role of law as part of its claim to authority which involves 'evaluation of law's distinctive character as a method of social organisation.'; *ibid.* 237. However, for Finnis, the significance of such debates is effectively diminished, since the intrinsic goodness of something is self-evident and, therefore, by definition, normative in its effect; Finnis (1980). The attraction of such a position is that it avoids Hume's 'naturalistic fallacy' of deriving 'ought' from 'is', a criticism frequently levelled at the link made by some writers between their observations of socio-legal processes and their moral arguments for reform; Cotterrell (1989).

4 For instance, the debate between Cotterrell and Nelken regarding the extent to which sociological insights should be used in the interpretation of legal ideas. Although there is broad agreement between them on the need for legal sociology to address the socio-legal contexts of legal decision-making, Nelken distances himself from Cotterrell's suggestion that legal contexts should only be interpreted sociologically; see Cotterrell (1998), Nelken (1998).

questions and others who regard the processes of legal reasoning and court decision-making as morally significant exercises, and trial outcomes themselves as having some kind of normative effect.[5]

This book adopts the position that issues of law and morality are irrevocably intertwined in sentencing and that fact and value merge in the process of discretionary decision-making. Consequently, any theorising which purports to 'explain' this social reality needs to explain how moral values are represented in sentencing. In particular, theory should be capable of helping us to conceptualise and explain how the moral values represented in trial ideology find expression in the normative structures and outcomes of the penal process. Hence, concepts need to be developed that address the nature of the relationship between penal ideology and the norms and outcomes of sentencing, especially the role of discretionary decision-making.

Finally, our capacity to appreciate the moral and normative[6] significance of trial outcomes demands greater theoretical clarity than currently exists. Two interconnected observations in particular require more adequate theorisation. The first is that sentencing outcomes express moral values which are related to perceptions about justice. The second is that such perceptions may influence the behaviour of individuals and the social coherence of communities.

In short, this book argues that the nature and function of morality in sentencing, particularly how sentencing is linked to moral reasoning about the nature of justice, are issues which should be of greater concern to criminal justice theory. Theorising the 'social' implies a need for concepts which can help us to appreciate how the 'social' is constructed from a normative perspective. Such explanations should provide meaningful accounts of the interrelationship and function of moral reasoning and social action. Therefore, a major task for this chapter is to illustrate why a more normative perspective for understanding punishment and sentencing is desirable, and how this objective may be advanced, by evaluating existing criminal justice theory and method.

Theorising sentencing and legitimacy

As outlined in the Introduction, this book is concerned with understanding the meaning and significance of 'legitimacy' in the context of punishment and sentencing. For trial justice, the notion of legitimacy is to do with describing and explaining the relationship between the perceived morality of punishment

---

5 See the contrasting views of Hart (1968) and Fuller (1969). In the context of this debate, it is interesting to note that Christodoulidis questions the capacity of legal rules to bring about reconciliatory functions such as 'mercy' through process. He sees law as overdeterministic and incapable of proceeding beyond the categories imposed by the reductive nature of legal rules; he maintains that essentially complex reflexive ethical decisions cannot be reached solely within a legal context; Christodoulidis (2000).

6 The expressions 'value' and 'norm' are given their conventional sociological meaning throughout this text; the former indicating a desired state of affairs and the latter as providing a guide to action.

and sentencing and its significance as a form of social reality. This is a complex conceptual exercise which involves deconstructing the relationship between penal ideology and the normative framework for punishment and sentencing. In effect, for any context this means explaining:

- The aims of punishment – why do they take their present form and how are they represented in penal ideology?
- How does penal ideology find expression in the legal framework for sentencing?[7]
- How does sentencing facilitate the transformation of penal ideology into concrete outcomes?
- The extent to which sentencing outcomes are perceived as 'legitimate' by 'relevant audiences'.
- The relationship between the perceived legitimacy of sentencing and subsequent behaviour.

Relating these ideas theoretically requires the role of punishment and sentencing to be conceptualised in broader terms than is possible using existing forms of social theory. The fact that theory can help to explain how certain structures and processes are functionally implicated in producing particular sentencing outcomes does not mean that we are able to provide contextually valid accounts of the reasons why this should be the case, or of its significance in terms of the legitimacy of trial justice. We can speculate theoretically about the symbolic effects of punishment, or relationships between power and trial ideology, but sociological interpretations of criminal justice, and sentencing in particular, are weak in describing the connections between moral values and punishment, and their social significance.

That being so, there is clearly a normative lacuna in this kind of theorising and a need for social theory to better conceptualise the relationship between values and norms on the one hand, and structure and action on the other. This requires some accommodation in our existing ideas about the relationship between law and morality, and the extent to which legal norms and processes facilitate the transformation of penal ideologies into guides for action through the everyday practice of sentencing.

Before developing these arguments, it is important to emphasise again that this book is not a polemic for a particular morality of justice. Rather, it stresses that more emphasis should be given to the morality of justice as an issue in sociological accounts of the 'reality' of sentence decision-making. Accordingly, it accepts the position that the capacity for punishment and sentencing to contribute to criminal justice governance is a function of social context. Hence, accounts of social reality must reflect how the values and norms of each context impact on that reality.

---

7 Both substantive and procedural.

This is a fundamental point, since it suggests that penal legitimacy should be theorised by developing constructs which are both contextually relevant *and* applicable irrespective of context. This apparent paradox posits a coherent explanatory framework capable of identifying conceptual links between moral and social knowledge, irrespective of context. Such a construct would therefore be prescriptive in an explanatory sense[8] for any particular context.

Accordingly, it is argued that a theoretical framework is required which identifies the most important variables involved in understanding the phenomenon and postulates a heuristic paradigm for explaining the relationship between such variables. Therefore, such an exploratory paradigm should provide the conceptual tools to identify and deconstruct different levels of context relevant to sentencing.

Modelling any particular context will help develop our capacity to deconstruct other contextual settings since the knowledge base informing the design of future models will be enhanced by adding concepts and postulates developed from previous applications.

The conceptual framework for such a heuristic paradigm can be summarised as follows:

The conceptual levels suggested in this paradigm are based on the assumption that there *is* a link between the morality of punishment and sentencing practice. It further posits that there is a recursive relationship between sentencing practice and penal ideology in any particular context upon which the perceived legitimacy of punishment depends. I would argue that the extent to which this relationship reinforces shared moral values about punishment and sentencing in any society is a crucial measure of their legitimacy.

Based on these assumptions, the paradigmatic levels outlined in Figure 2.1 identify those aspects of social context which require description and

MORALITY – reflecting the idea that the legitimacy of punishment depends on a sharing of values

IDEOLOGY – recognising that shared values inform the ideology of punishment

ETHICS – recognising that the norms and structures of criminal justice give concrete form to penal ideology

PRACTICE – the process whereby the norms and values of criminal justice are applied through the human agency of discretionary decision-making to produce sentencing outcomes

PERCEPTIONS – whether sentencing outcomes fulfil the aspirations for justice of the 'relevant' audience

REACTION – recognising that perceptions of justice may influence morality and future behaviour

IMPACT – suggesting that shared perceptions about the legitimacy of trial justice tend to re-enforce underlying moral values and therefore the legitimacy of punishment and sentencing as aspects of criminal justice governance.

Figure 2.1 Conceptualising the legitimacy of trial justice

---

8 In other words, the constructs it contains would be employed to analyse each context.

explanation. Although the chapters which follow focus on discrete issues, they are united by a common objective, which is to explore the links within and between the different levels of this paradigm. It is also important to note that, although the degree of emphasis within each chapter may vary, the overriding aim is to relate what is described to questions of legitimacy.

The analysis for each conceptual level and its relevance for understanding the legitimacy of trial justice will vary according to the context being examined. Accordingly, the book deliberately focuses on a number of broad analytical themes in order to enhance the explanatory potential of each level. Therefore, within each level[9] the analysis focuses on:

- the notion of process as symbolism;
- the relationship between law and morality;
- sentencing as a form of social interaction;
- the relationship between hegemony and punishment.

It is also important to emphasise that the notion of context is not taken as jurisdictionally bound, nor are the conceptual levels for analysis or the themes through which they are interrogated. Instead, as explained below, context is seen as a fluid and dynamic construct, changing over time and space. Therefore, it may include, for example, developing notions of the relationship between international and domestic forms of criminal justice, as well as horizontal dimensions of legitimacy, such as the development of transitional justice strategies following social conflict and war.

An example of the former, which has important ramifications for the legitimacy of trial justice more generally, is the relationship between the risk/security nexus and governance in international criminal justice.

Findlay has argued that,[10] as a consequence of the so-called 'war on terror', the globalisation of risk and security has justified a shift away from more conventional global criminal enterprises as the focus for international criminal justice. This narrow focus on terror and risk tends to equate security with the maintenance of global order. For states perceived by dominant powers as threatening that security, this may precipitate military intervention and regime change. With regard to domestic criminal justice, there is a tendency for this type of threat to be used as an excuse for imposing greater restrictions on the liberty of citizens, so diverting attention away from important social issues, such as the link between poverty and crime. Thus, as Foucault argues,[11] the identification of 'problematic' issues by power elites often provides a convenient smokescreen for oppressive and discriminatory forms of penal policy.

---

9 The interrelationship of these analytical themes across the different conceptual levels of Figure 2.1 should also be examined.
10 Findlay (2008). See also Simon (2007).
11 Foucault (1980).

Without doubt, the most important lesson to be drawn from these observations with respect to penal legitimacy is that globalised threats to peace and security such as the 'war on terror' have the effect of redefining the relationship between punishment and its justification at both the international and national level. Since such global threats automatically translate into domestic threats, domestic and regional forms of criminal justice which appear to dissent from this view, or hamper moves to counter terrorism, may be perceived as resisting the will of the 'global community'. The danger for the legitimacy of trial justice lies in the fact that false notions of 'community' may be invoked by hegemonic powers to justify controlling interventions that facilitate the realisation of their dominant ambitions.[12]

Approaching this issue from the normative perspective of the paradigm suggested in Figure 2.1 focuses specific attention on the question of how the 'legitimacy' of different modalities of punishment and sentencing is established in different contexts, and what this signifies. Considering the problem in purely abstract terms, we can hypothesise that the declared ideologies and structures of international criminal justice do not represent any kind of shared or common view about the legitimacy of punishment and sentencing beyond the appropriateness of retribution and deterrence as justifications for the sentences passed on individual perpetrators where international crimes are proved to have been committed.[13] Arguably, the latter remain purely symbolic, although empirically justifiable 'effects' may be claimed for them. The 'real', and more difficult, question to answer is whether retribution and deterrence are perceived as 'legitimate' justifications for the punishment of those crimes by individuals and groups within specific post-conflict contexts, and whether sentencing outcomes in particular cases meet the demands for justice of these 'relevant audiences'. In the case of international criminal justice 'the relevant audience' may include many different and overlapping constituencies:

- Humanity at large
- The international community – most commonly, political, strategic, or economic alliances of nation states
- Regional alliances

---

12 Note that the jurisdiction of the ICC is limited to 'the most serious crimes of international concern' (Article 1) or 'the most serious crimes of concern to the international community as a whole' (Preamble, and Article 5.1 of the ICC Statute); it does not extend (*inter alia*) to terrorism. The main reason for this exclusion has been the fear of politicising the ICC. Hence, no generally acceptable definition of 'terrorism' has been forthcoming, although general agreement exists regarding the legality of prosecuting states which aid or sponsor state terrorism; see, further, Kittichaisaree (2001). However, opinion seems divided as to whether crimes on the scale of those perpetrated on 9/11 amount to the commission of 'crimes against humanity' within the meaning of Article 7 of the ICC Statute; Dennis (2001). For a more cautious approach, see Cassese (2001).
13 To that extent, punishment fulfils an expressive function; Feinberg (1971).

- Nation states
- Communities or social groups which do not form part of nation states
- Distinct social groups within nation states
- Communities which form part of social groups within nation states
- Individuals who form part of the above

This list highlights the fact that the legitimacy of criminal justice may depend on a wide variety of interrelated audiences and contexts. The paradigm in Figure 2.1 suggests that we should focus on particular levels for analysis within and between contexts, each level being crucial to understanding the relationship between sentencing and the perceived legitimacy of trial justice. As noted, the function of the heuristic paradigm is not to validate the moral claims of any particular constituency. However, it is concerned with exploring whether those constituencies identified as having an 'interest'[14] have their justice demands accurately represented in any process.

Questions of penal legitimacy become increasingly complex when one considers the possibility of prosecuting individuals for so-called 'terrorist' acts[15] before an international court such as the ICC. The nature of this complexity reinforces the case for each social context to be deconstructed against clearly identifiable analytical levels, as suggested in Figure 2.1. Any such analysis will have to confront some difficult issues. One of these is the critical nature of the relationship between the perceived legitimacy of international trial justice for crimes of terrorism and its impact on criminal justice governance at the international and national level. The idea that notions about the legitimacy of punishment and sentencing for 'terrorist' crimes should reflect a sharing of values is clearly problematic. Since 'terrorists' are normally ideologically motivated, this counters the morality of labelling alleged perpetrators as criminals, because there is no universally accepted moral basis for the criminalisation of such acts.[16]

There are evident differences between notions of universal human rights – such as the right to liberty, security and fair trial – and their interpretation in particular contexts. However, differences between individuals and groups in the moral values which inform their attitudes and motivate their actions do not take precedence or diminish the universal moral authority of such norms, or their legal validity. Rather, such tensions should be recognised and accounted for in modelling each social context and the methodologies adopted for its deconstruction. In specific terms, the purpose of a heuristic paradigm should be to ensure that the role of punishment and sentencing and its relationship to criminal justice governance is conceptualised in such a way that we are able to

---

14 The identification of 'interests' is not a value-neutral exercise. For arguments which support a complete reconceptualisation of the moral foundations for international criminal justice and its implications for governance, see Findlay and Henham (2010), ch. 1.

15 Therefore, ignoring for a moment politically motivated reasons for excluding 'terrorist' acts from the ambit of the ICC's jurisdiction.

16 See Wilkinson (1989).

advance our understanding of why and how particular attitudes and motivations have arisen, and what the implications might be for delivering forms of
trial justice.

Affirming the universality of human rights or international legal norms
designed to ensure their enforcement is not an argument for denying the
expressive value of retributive and deterrent punishment. However, for any
understanding of trial justice to move beyond its recognition as merely symbolic or expressive requires a rigorous analytical framework against which to
deconstruct its social context.

One of the most important aspects of social life requiring such profound
contextual analysis is the extent to which the morality underpinning the rule
of law is diminished or weakened through domestic and international forms
of hegemony. The expansion of counter-terrorism laws in many western
countries provides a good illustration of how the discourse of international
hegemony has been transformed in the context of domestic criminal justice.
This process is facilitated by the limitations of universal legal jurisdiction,
leading to the argument that counter-terrorism legislation is best dealt with at
the national or regional level.[17] However, this blurring of the penality of
'terrorism'[18] has tended to increase the domestic focus on the management of
risk and crime prevention/security issues, resulting in measures such as Control
Orders in England and Wales which have serious implications for individual
liberty.[19]

To summarise, the paradigm suggested in Figure 2.1 could be utilised to
interrogate different contexts of criminal justice, international or domestic. Its
purpose is to provide a normative framework which directs and focuses any
analysis on specific areas and themes identified as crucial for understanding
how punishment and sentencing relate to legitimacy, whatever the context.
Consequently, the paradigm is intended to help conceptualise how pluralistic

---

17 Schabas (2007) 60.
18 See, further, Drumbl (2007b), Gaeta and Jessberger (2006). For criminological commentary, see
    Findlay (2007), Mythen and Walklate (2006).
19 Control Orders illustrate how the blurring of the dimensions of risk and security can be
    achieved by political elites through their ability to continually redefine those individuals and
    contexts requiring precautionary legislation. Introduced in England and Wales under the
    Prevention of Terrorism Act 2005, Control Orders subject terror suspects to strict restrictions
    on their activities. Individuals considered to pose the most serious risk to national security can
    be ordered to observe a curfew, and a residential requirement may be imposed. Suspects can
    be electronically tagged, face visiting restrictions, be banned from accessing the internet, and
    face restrictions on their place of religious worship. They can also be ordered to surrender their
    passports and report daily to a monitoring company or to police. Such erosions of civil liberty
    through extending the governance mandate of criminal justice confuse the morality of social
    conflict and war with that of ordinary crime. For minority groups who are disproportionately
    subject to such laws, they may precipitate further alienation. As Young and Lea argue,
    these effects may precipitate militaristic policing, increased social exclusion and greater
    radicalisation, as those who are oppressed gradually withdraw moral legitimacy from the
    organs of state and the structures of governance; Lea and Young (1984).

values may be reflected in relationships between the ideology of punishment and sentencing outcomes at the global and local level.

Thus, the paradigm in Figure 2.1 guides the methodology used to evaluate each conceptual level analysed. This is achieved in each contextual setting because the analysis of each level interrogates a number of specific themes: namely, the notion of process as symbolism, the relationship between law and morality, the concept of sentencing as social interaction, and the relationship between hegemony and punishment. As with any sociological inquiry the empirical analysis of each context will reflect the theory employed to deconstruct it. The extent to which links between law and morality are explained as symbolic or hegemonic, and the extent to which sentencing is portrayed as social interaction, are issues that can be only interrogated against a broad appreciation of the relevant theories and the controversies surrounding them. The most important point to emphasise here is that the levels for analysis and the themes chosen have been identified as fundamental for elucidating the relationship between punishment and sentencing and legitimacy.

Problems of comparative methodology

The kind of modelling described above is also an exercise in comparative methodology because its purpose is to facilitate analysis of the relationship between sentencing and the legitimacy of punishment in different contexts. These contexts may be delineated by jurisdictional, state or other structural boundaries. However, the globalisation of crime and crime problems[20] has correspondingly conflated the international and domestic dimensions of criminal justice and the dynamics which drive it.[21] Consequently, whilst neither international nor domestic forms of criminal justice should be examined in isolation, there is little value in drawing simple comparisons between jurisdictions.[22] Because the legitimacy of punishment is a governance issue common to all forms of criminal justice, it is important to take account of vertical and horizontal relationships between different systems of criminal justice and to explain their significance for sentencing.

These relationships may be portrayed in the following terms:

- **VERTICAL** – concerned with relationships between global and local types of process; or
- **HORIZONTAL** – concerned with process relationships at the same level, such as between nation states.

---

20 See Findlay (2008).
21 As in the case of 'terrorism' and its impact on the risk/security nexus discussed in the previous section.
22 For critical analysis of existing forms of comparative method and their application to criminal justice, see Findlay and Henham (2005) Part 1.

Sentencing may be broken down in terms of legal, organisational and interactive levels for the purpose of analysis,[23] with each level being conceived as fundamental to the recursive reproduction of the process as a whole. Understanding the links between these levels and the purposes served by each should provide insights into the manufacture of trial justice as a structural and organisational reality within any particular context. This should help us to comprehend how trial processes relate to one another both conceptually and practically at the global and local level in terms of similarities and/or differences (for example, how they correspond with particular process styles).

However, as with any social process, the social reality of sentencing mirrors the complexities of human and structural interaction and so cannot be fully comprehended through the partiality of one theoretical lens. Such complex relationships demand evaluation against higher- and lower-order concepts, which may need to be located within a broader theoretical framework for understanding.[24]

Against this background, there is a need to expose and deconstruct propositions conceived at different levels of abstraction that are considered integral to the sentence decision-making process. For example, different levels of theoretical abstraction may be necessary to appreciate the significance and cultural meanings attached to procedural norms for calculating sentence, the symbolic and hegemonic relevance of sentencing decisions, and the procedural and rights implications of victim impact statements upon sentence. The exact purposes and combination of levels chosen for analysis will vary in each case. Hence the importance of developing theoretical constructs which are capable of reflecting these variations.

Such a theoretical approach satisfies the requirement for a culturally specific and sequential analysis of sentencing, so that a deep contextual understanding of those relationships which influence the dynamics of sentencing and the eventual outcome is produced. The sentencing dynamic is therefore envisaged in terms of a series of interrelated decisions and relationships (or pathways of influence) that aggregate into the sentencing decision-making process and thereby shape its contextual reality.[25]

Implications for understanding the legitimacy of trial justice

It is important to bear in mind that the ultimate purpose of the paradigm in Figure 2.1 is to suggest aspects of punishment and sentencing that relate specifically to the legitimacy of trial justice in any context chosen for analysis. The social reality of the governance link will, of course, depend on the dynamics of the relationship between hegemony and punishment. In terms of

---

23 For fuller description, see Henham (2000), Henham (2001) 253.
24 See, for example, Findlay and Henham's elaboration of Giddens's structuration theory in Findlay and Henham (2005) ch. 1.
25 See, further, Henham (2004b).

the paradigm itself, it might be useful to think of this relationship as expressing the morality of the criminal process. More specifically, it may be argued that the criminal process reinforces hegemonic morality, because the relationship between sentencing and penal ideology is recursive. It is therefore vital to appreciate the way in which hegemonic power drives this recursive process, especially why it has arisen and assumed its present form.

The perceived legitimacy of sentencing is a crucial determinant of penal hegemony over time, and therefore of the governance function of criminal justice. In this sense, penal governance may be thought of as a measure of the extent to which the morality that underpins the ideology of punishment coincides with competing moralities within a particular criminal justice context. Therefore, as has been argued, it becomes critical to consider the impact of trial outcomes on those constituencies that claim an interest in criminal justice, especially victims and victim communities. From their perspective, the paradigm in Figure 2.1 can provide a framework for deconstructing what 'legitimacy' actually signifies in any context: more especially, the degree of moral attachment to punishment and sentencing, and how this relates to the hegemony of criminal justice.

The paradigm should therefore help us to investigate the social reality of sentencing. As suggested in chapter 1, this should include the role of hegemony and the impact of 'rule of law' governance in criminal justice; particularly the gradual fragmentation of the liberal consensus in westernised forms of criminal justice. As Findlay points out:[26]

> In the domestic example it is obvious that the justice traditions in theory will sit with the political culture of a particular state. The Western democratic ascription to *separation of powers* for good governance and the supervisory role of the judiciary on which it relies, is a case in point.

As suggested earlier, in the case of England and Wales the integrity of the liberal consensus model has been severely tested against a perceptible erosion of the principle of judicial independence. This has tended to undermine the viability of the separation of powers governance model and tightened the grip of retributive hegemony on the delivery of criminal justice. Accordingly, the capacity of the state to engage with pluralistic interests and the values they represent has diminished. This perception has been consistently reinforced by media representations of the judiciary and reflected in the increased politicisation of penal policy. A heuristic framework for deconstructing such events in terms of their impact on the legitimacy of trial justice should therefore provide a valuable tool for explaining the social significance of this trend by exposing its underlying cultural origins and current manifestations.

Nonetheless, for both global and local forms of trial justice, such deeper contextual understandings can only increase the perceived legitimacy of

---

26 Findlay (2008).

criminal justice governance if future penal policies are directed towards recognising pluralism and diversity rather than sustaining the *status quo* of retributive justice, which, as Hudson argues,[27] serves to perpetuate social division and exclusion. Such a broadening of penal ideology would provide a significant stimulus towards repositioning the focus of criminal justice governance away from the risk/security nexus and its hegemonic morality towards a practical engagement with more pressing governance concerns of social policy.

Addressing broader theoretical concerns

This chapter has so far argued the case for a more normative approach to theorising the relationship between sentencing and the legitimacy of trial justice and outlined the kind of paradigm that could be utilised to advance under-standing in this area.[28] However, there are several important theoretical and methodological issues that continue to provoke controversy and which demand a more considered evaluation before such an aspiration may be realised. Lack of space precludes a profound examination of each of these issues,[29] but the objective here is to alert the reader to some of the complexities, arguments and contingencies that must be confronted, and hopefully to answer some of the criticisms which may be directed against what has been argued for hitherto.

The limitations of existing theory

One of the more intractable issues in legal theory is the debate between scholars who argue that legal rules and legal reasoning are essentially 'closed' in nature, and therefore distorted when subjected to sociological forms of descrip-tion and explanation,[30] and others who advocate the benefits of sociological theorising about law.[31] The latter position supports the view that theoretical engagement with criminal justice and the norms of punishment in particular must proceed from a basis which asks questions about the social functions of law.[32] The argument advanced in this book suggests that this position can only be defended adequately if social theory is deemed capable of providing more convincing accounts of the morality that underpins perceptions of trial jus-tice, in terms of its origins and significance – in other words, of providing contextualised understandings of what the notion of 'legitimacy' actually signifies.

It is clearly beyond the scope of this book to assess the degree to which various types of social theory or perspective may or may not be successful in

---

27 Hudson (1998).
28 The relationship between victimisation and legitimacy is discussed in chapter 6.
29 For further analysis, see Findlay and Henham (2005) chapters 1–2.
30 Nelken (1998).
31 Cotterrell (1998).
32 This is taken as a starting point from which the interplay between penal law and society can be theorised.

accounting for the nature of law and its normativity.[33] Instead, this section focuses on the recent application of autopoiesis theory to sentencing by the Danish scholar Rasmus Wandall[34] to illustrate some of the issues involved.

The importance of this work to the present discussion lies in the fact that Wandall's theoretical approach raises a number of questions about our capacity to explain adequately the relationship between the law of sentencing and the context in which sentence decision-making takes place. Wandall's theoretical stance is developed from the premise that the legal framework establishes only the boundaries and coherence of legal norms. In considering how the relationship between law and other normative systems is reflected in the processes of sentence decision-making, Wandall stresses the self-fulfilling nature of legal process in complex industrial societies, identifying the crux of the problem as understanding how ideological and normative structures are accommodated in 'actual daily decision-making' relating to imprisonment in Danish county courts.

To this end, Wandall criticises so-called 'gap' studies, which emphasise disproportionately the dichotomy between 'law' and 'action', preferring instead an approach which is sensitive to how the practice of sentence decision-making is organised and facilitated in ways which keep it within the boundaries of the formal legal framework. However, in suggesting that 'cases are typically closed as legally valid,' arguably Wandall[35] may be over-generalising from the Danish experience. The identification of what is law, as reflected in the difficulty of distinguishing between law and principle, is significant in the sentencing context, due to the distinctive normative character of sentencing norms. It cannot therefore be assumed that sentencing principles, although essentially legal in character, are equivalent to substantive legal norms. As always, it depends upon the jurisdictional context.[36]

Therefore, when Wandall states[37] that he is concerned with the extent to which court decision-making is organised to allow sentencing to be open to structures beyond its formal legal framework, yet keeping it within the boundaries of law and legal validity, the distinction between the idea of law and legal validity as it relates to sentencing becomes unclear. Wandall appears to argue that the concepts of law and legal validity should be construed similarly, irrespective of whether one is talking about substantive legal norms (offence-creating norms), or sentencing norms (penal norms). In the context of establishing the boundaries of legal closure, law and legal validity are treated as synonymous. Further, in his discussion of so-called 'gap studies', Wandall

---

33 However, this book does argue that valuable insights may be gained from the work of Emile Durkheim and Max Weber.
34 Wandall (2008). See also Henham (2009a) for a review of this work.
35 Wandall (2008) 3.
36 Henham (1990).
37 Wandall (2008).

stresses how these have erroneously conceptualised legality as a behavioural (social) context which can only be fully explained from a sociological perspective.

Wandall utilises Luhmann's theory of law's operational closure which, he suggests, provides a novel way for conceptualising the impact of contexts beyond the law into the operation of processes that are essentially characterised as legal, and must be justified as such. Following Luhmann, Wandell argues for the self-referential and reciprocal character of legal systems, emphasising the capacity of law to synthesise those communications which are essentially legal through its operational structures. In this sense, the theory suggests that law actually creates the conditions for securing its legitimacy and that the influence of human agency is minimised by the way in which the legal system prioritises communication inputs.

Wandell suggests that the key to understanding how the idea of operational closure works lies in appreciating the fact that the legal system is able to balance normative and cognitive expectations. Therefore, to achieve legal validity requires law to interact with its environment and bring about legal closure. Cognitive factors are admitted through organisational structures and interactive contexts of court decision-making. Hence, the system itself provides the opportunities for the law and the environment to interact, and therefore conditions the possibilities for normative and cognitive factors to achieve closure. The possibilities for contextual openness and the influence of social context are consistently tested against the normative requirements of the law. Legal validity is then a function of the capacity of the system to deliver legal closure.

However, it may be misleading to think about the relationship between law and context in these terms. It is clearly correct that law and legal reasoning are identifiable and exist empirically. It is also possible to go beyond this and suggest ways in which functionally law controls the environment necessary to sustain it. However, this is a very narrow conceptualisation of the essence and function of law, particularly sentencing law. Instead, one could argue that deconstructing the social context of sentencing is an essential precursor to understanding its existence as a matter of social reality. This includes its characterisation as law and as something having legal validity. Consequently, sentencing law cannot be conceptually closed off and treated as an entity which merely interacts with different social contexts.

The difficulty with Wandall's approach is that he provides an explanation of what the law is and how it justifies itself through court decision-making in the 'real' world without engaging with the social reality of cognitive expectations, except in so far as they are controlled and selectively admitted through the operational processes of law. Arguably, such a model is significantly deficient in failing to recognise the essential linkage between the internal validity of law and its moral validity.[38] This failure is accentuated in the sentencing context

---

38 See Fuller (1969).

because sentencing law contains normative imperatives. Therefore, it can be regarded as consisting of a combination of legal and moral norms that reflects a conception of 'justice' (a morality of punishment) which is supportive of penal ideology. Sentencing jurisprudence is therefore suggestive of how sentencing law ought to be applied in a social context through the medium of a sentencing decision.

However, the weakness of Wandall's approach extends beyond his failure to recognise the essential moral connections between what is necessary for law to exist and its acceptance as 'valid' law. Accepting this criticism means acknowledging the relative nature of morality and therefore of law as something which has social meaning. This is not to deny that sentencing law can exist as a matter of fact and reason, merely that it is only meaningful for social life if it is analysed from a sociological perspective which takes full account of its normative characteristics. Otherwise, law has no legitimacy beyond its objective existence as written law and legal reasoning. Thus the concept of operational closure does not help us to engage with the legitimacy of law and legal outcomes, because it approaches the issue from a position which only allows the capacity of the legal system to regulate normative expectations. It does not consider the relevance to law of what lies behind cognitive expectations. For sentencing, this means accepting the idea that there is a fundamental link between the ideology which informs law and the outcomes it produces. This relationship between the ideology and outcomes of sentencing is crucial because it is against the outcomes of sentencing that the 'legitimacy' of criminal justice is judged.

These criticisms are not insignificant because they go to the crux of Wandall's theoretical approach to the analysis of sentencing. The implications of this for sentence modelling are profound, in that a satisfactory paradigm should be capable of conceptualising both the nature of legal reasoning in the analytical sense and its sociological significance as process for trial participants and the wider community. Wandall advocates[39] using the theory of operational closure as a tool for modelling sentence decision-making rather than explanation. This is a difficult notion to grasp without further elaboration, since modelling in the positivist sense is conventionally regarded as a precursor to explanation. Wandall's model of decision-making consists of propositions that constrain our ability to recognise the existence of particular states of affairs in the operations of the criminal process. The resulting data are then 'objectively' characterised in terms of the model's taxonomy. Consequently, Wandall's suggestion that the approach can go beyond socially critical perspectives needs to be explained more fully. In suggesting what the theory of conceptual closure is capable of, he neatly side-steps the important issue of whether the actual decision-making which takes place is perceived as 'legitimate', not simply 'legally legitimate'.

---

39 Wandall (2008) 19.

Wandall rightly acknowledges[40] that for law to exist there must be some recognition of law as something distinct from other social rules implicated in controlling human behaviour. However, in so doing he appears to draw a somewhat artificial distinction between law and non-law in less complex societies on the basis that law only becomes a cognitively meaningful system in more complex societies. Arguably, the comparative study of regulatory systems should be approached from a methodological perspective capable of accounting for the ways in which rules come to be culturally accepted as law or not, and the basis upon which the status of rules is ascribed.

This setting-apart or false duality of law and context has a subversive normative effect on the way in which the dynamics of their relationship is portrayed. For example, Wandall suggests that in practice the extent of the environment's subliminal undermining of law's authority is controlled by courtroom participants. Thus, two levels of communication operate in the process of sentence decision-making: one at the legal level, concerned with internal legal validity, and the other at the level of contextual openness, which admits normative considerations beyond the law.

Ultimately, Wandall's theoretical approach does little more than provide us with another way of conceptualising sentence decision-making, but does so from a perspective which maintains a conceptual duality between legal closure and contextual openness. In my view, this is a false dichotomy which fails to address the fundamental issue of legitimacy or, more specifically, explain those contextual factors that determine our perceptions of punishment, and what this signifies.[41] As argued, this is essentially a normative question that needs to be addressed within the context of sociological theory.

Additional conceptual difficulties

Having highlighted the significance of social context for understanding the normative aspects of sentencing, I now propose to advance this argument in more detail by exploring conceptions of the moral and social and suggesting how the relationship between them may be better reflected in sociological accounts of sentencing than at present.

Conceptions of the social

The need to provide contextualised accounts of 'victimisation' has already been alluded to. A similar cautionary note applies when considering the nature

---

40 Wandall (2008) 12.
41 For example, Wandall (2008) 112 concludes that 'actual decision-making reflects a broader normative framework that can be observed from a legal point of view', yet fails to make explicit how the underlying values of sentence decision-making are conceptually related to decisions to imprison, especially the basis upon which the processes of punishment are crucial in sustaining the balance between the reality and the perception of justice.

and significance of other concepts such as community, culture or hegemony, since developing a relevant understanding of these notions ultimately depends on our capacity to engage with the social reality of human experience.

By way of illustration we might take the notion of 'community' and consider its problematic status in the context of international criminal justice. If we accept the idea that increasing the legitimacy of international trial justice has something to do with making it more inclusive and participative for victims and post-conflict communities, it becomes important to consider exactly what we mean when we invoke notions of 'community' for this purpose. For example, Cotterrell[42] questions whether post-conflict societies could be conceptualised as potentially *holistic* communities and, if they could, what might be the responsibilities and expectations of such 'communities' with regard to the trial; more generally, he wonders what might be meant by the expression 'international community'.

In order to answer these questions it may be argued that we need to improve our understanding of how the perceptions of individuals and communities about international trial justice are constructed and how they relate to each other. Moreover, it is particularly important to investigate how subjective factors such as feelings and emotions relate to the ways in which the structures and outcomes of international criminal trials are perceived: in other words, their legitimacy. We do not know, for example, how each 'community' feels about the role of formal punishment rituals, or whether forms of retributive or restorative justice are used, either separately or in combination. Crucially, we do not know whether practices that appear to conform to definitions or understandings[43] derived from other cultures and traditions actually exist at all – in other words, whether actions taken by the community to restore harmony are thought of in retributive, deterrent or restorative terms, or indeed whether the notion of punishment has any significant role in maintaining community coherence. More significantly, there may be no indication of where the line is drawn between resolutions governed by so-called 'law' and those which regulate the infringement of social norms, or of which (if any) have priority, and why.

For example, the social stigma attached to rape and other forms of sexual violence is clearly something culturally specific. Commonplace assumptions about those factors which determine the status of women are also likely to prove incorrect. The observations of the ICTY in the case of *Krstić*[44] provide a useful illustration of this. Here, the Trial Chamber referred to the fact that it was common knowledge that the Muslims of Eastern Bosnia constituted a patriarchal society. Consequently, women were required to have a clear marital

42 Cotterrell (2006).
43 Including the rationales which inform the practices in question and the factors that have shaped them.
44 *Prosecutor v Krstić* (Case No. IT-98-33-T), Judgement, 2 August 2001, para. 592; *Prosecutor v Krstić* (Case No. IT-98-33-A), Appeals Chamber Judgement, 19 April 2004.

status in order to constitute part of that society, and a woman whose husband was missing did not fit within any of these categories: namely married, widowed or divorced. In other words, such a woman was effectively a social outcast.[45]

Similarly, the conflicting aspirations and expectations for justice of particular social groups within any state or jurisdiction must be capable of being accommodated within differing conceptualisations of 'community'. This corresponds to the view taken in this book that the perceived legitimacy of trial justice should be conceived in terms which are sensitive to the idea of 'community' existing in terms of frameworks of commonly-held values within any given context. This implies two things:

1. That there is some *identifiable* consensus about the purposes for which those values are shared. For example, in the case of national systems of criminal justice, this may relate to how individuals should live together as 'civil society', howsoever defined.[46] Alternatively, for international criminal justice, the purpose may be conceived in humanitarian terms as reflecting the need to prevent impunity for international crimes, so giving effect to the common will of the 'international community', or in terms of perceptions about the moral purposes for punishment shared by distinct social groupings within jurisdictional or state boundaries.
2. Such sharing must include a degree of consensus about the *legitimacy* of trial justice and the system of criminal justice necessary to sustain it.

This suggests that understanding the significance of trial justice at either the local or global level requires a profound analysis of the complex relationships existing between the penal ideologies that inform trial outcomes and what is perceived as 'justice', both subjectively by individuals, and in terms of what can be objectively regarded as 'commonly shared' values.

Such an approach suggests that our ability to understand questions about the legitimacy of trial justice depends on our capacity to identify and explain its existence as a shared morality that underpins punishment and sentencing. It takes account of the fact that global and local forms of criminal justice have

---

45 De Londras (2007).
46 The morality of the principles and social arrangements agreed upon will always be a matter for debate. For example, Rawls proposes that the only ones which would be freely entered into by all potential members of society, operating behind the veil of ignorance, would be those ensuring fair distribution of advantages, disadvantages, benefits and burdens, because only in that way could individuals guarantee that they would not be disadvantaged, whatever their social position; Rawls (1973). He therefore insists that social institutions should be evaluated against this notion of *justice as fairness*, arguing that utilitarian theory is not a system that would be agreed to by rational, freely choosing individuals behind the veil of ignorance, because they could not know whether they would be the ones to be disadvantaged. Barbara Hudson disagrees since *actual* society is characterised by inequality rather than fairness, and actual laws promote the interests of certain sections of society, and are imposed on, rather than freely chosen by others. Therefore, Rawl's rationale cannot be imputed to all citizens. Only if society were much more equal could punishment be justified on these terms; Hudson (2003) ch. 1.

different configurations of power and social control, involve crimes of a different magnitude in terms of gravity, and facilitate different punishment objectives. This characterisation therefore envisages that the legitimacy of punishment and sentencing should be judged against contextualised understandings of responsibility and consequential accountability.[47]

Identifying such common understandings and accounting for them also facilitates the development of new theory and methodologies for deconstructing different contexts of sentencing. This approach recognises that only by developing deeper understandings of the reasons why normative frameworks exist and how they operate will we be able to identify points of commonality and difference between different social contexts, and judge their moral significance for particular communities as shared aspects of moral experience.

Asserting that sentencing should reflect different contexts of accountability implies that we have the ability to recognise why particular purposes for punishment or certain trial outcomes may be judged morally indefensible by different communities. The ICTR decision in *Kambanda*,[48] provides a useful illustration of this point in the context of international trial justice. In this case the life sentence imposed on the former prime-minister of Rwanda was upheld on appeal after he had pleaded guilty to offences of genocide. Not only did the sentence fall well short of the retributive expectations of the victim community, but Rwandan law itself advocated the death penalty for those who masterminded such crimes. To make matters worse, it may be argued that the ICTR Trial Chamber compounded this failure for the victim community by not capitalising on the offender's confessions and admissions of guilt in encouraging the process of reconciliation at the local level. This arguably served to undermine the educative and reconciliatory purposes of the trial process, and also its legitimacy.

Since the primary function of the international trial process remains that of allocating blame, it may be argued that more socially constructive sentences depend on the explicit identification of the nature and needs of particular communities. As Cotterrell suggests,[49] these communities may be of shared beliefs or interests which extend beyond the boundaries of the nation state, as well as constituting minorities within them.

---

47 Accountability can be conceptualised and measured in many different ways. For example, in the context of international criminal justice, accountability for practices such as plea bargaining might be measured against purely bureaucratic or economic criteria, as a discrete regulatory context that may be justified as conceptually distinct from the normative framework underpinning the structural arrangements of which it forms part. By contrast, the interpretation adopted here focuses on 'responsibility' as a core concept for governance in a broader, morally inclusive sense, rather than a narrow construct of liberal criminal law or crime control modelling. Hence, this book adopts a more relational and communitarian notion of 'responsibility', reflecting the view that accountability is both individual and collective, so that the legitimacy of trial outcomes must be evaluated against a holistic ('shared') vision of the individual *in the community*.

48 *Prosecutor v Kambanda* (Case No. ICTR-97-23-S), Judgement and Sentence, 4 September 1998.

49 Cotterrell (2002).

This is by no means a straightforward issue. For example, some indigenous communities have no concept of blame. Furthermore, within particular states and regions criminal justice may be portrayed as a key component in the ongoing hegemony of imperialism and colonialism: a crucial element in the ideological and structural apparatus of repression and exclusion, whereby indigenous people are increasingly and disproportionately subject to imprisonment.[50] Such accounts portray customary forms of dispute and conflict resolution as far removed from the confrontation, guilt and accountability associated with adversarial justice. The Navajo Indian culture in Canada provides a good example:

> Our vision of justice is to be based on Aboriginal knowledge about the nature of humans, their society, and our linguistic mode of understanding the ecology. We cannot simply borrow the Eurocentric versions of human nature or psychology or society, since they are not based on our wisdom, knowledge, or language. They have never known who we are.[51]

Consequently, we need to have some idea of how different notions of 'community' might impact upon perceptions of 'justice' and its delivery in different contexts, particularly through alternative interpretations of concepts like 'responsibility' and 'liability' and the implications these might have for developing more inclusive forms of trial outcome.

Conventional criminological concepts pose similar difficulties when employed to deconstruct the social reality of sentencing in different contexts. For example, Hudson's[52] definition of 'penality' as 'the complex of ideas, institutions, rules, practices and relationships pertaining to punishment' invokes a kind of inclusive universe of concrete ideas, relationships, rules and structures centred around punishment and through which particular notions of punishment are promulgated. Garland[53] appears to endorse a similar kind of conceptualisation in referring to 'penality' as 'the networks of laws, processes, discourses, representations and institutions which make up the penal realm'. However, Garland then goes on to elaborate as follows:

> … penality communicates meaning not just about crime and punishment but also about power, authority, legitimacy, normality, morality, personhood, social relations, and a host of other tangential matters.[54]

On the basis of these definitions, one might argue that 'penality' could be conceptualised in terms of either an exclusive or inclusive paradigm.

---

50 Sarre and Wilson (eds) (1998).
51 Henderson (1995).
52 Hudson (2003) 194.
53 Garland (1990) 17.
54 *Ibid.* 252.

Paradoxically, the idea of a more exclusive paradigm for 'penality' tends to correspond more closely with Hudson's implicitly inclusive (i.e. system-bound) universe of ideas, norms, structures and processes through which the dominant ideology of punishment is promulgated. Garland, on the other hand, hints at a more inclusive (i.e. socially reflexive) paradigm for penality; one that invites us to go beyond the semantics of crime and punishment to engage more widely with issues of moral philosophy, psychology and sociology. This distinction is not purely semantic when one begins to think about the relationship between moral and social questions in sentencing, and whether the notion of 'penality' might be an adequate conceptual tool for describing and explaining them.

In this regard, Garland's[55] point about the signifying nature of penality – the idea that it communicates meaning – has special resonance because it suggests that forms of trial justice should be reflective of generally understood cultural meanings about crime and punishment and, consequently, the boundaries of morally acceptable behaviour within specific contexts. In other words, this broader perspective invites us to engage with different contexts in order to understand what the 'legitimacy' of trial justice actually signifies.

Nevertheless, this is a problematic idea for international sentencing, since there is a paradox for trial justice in generalising from the particular to the universal. Because it occurs outside national contexts, it can be argued that international trial justice has the capacity to alter or distort ideas held about the values which conventionally underpin punishment. Conventional definitions of 'penality' appear inadequate in helping us to appreciate the link between punishment administered internationally in the name of humanity and its perception as a legitimate response to alleged criminality by those citizens who inhabit conflict zones and have experienced the horrors of social conflict.

Such weaknesses raise questions about the extent to which sociological concepts such as 'penality' are sufficiently sensitive to the impact of moral questions in accounting for the social reality of sentencing in different contextual settings. Although Garland's focus on its signifying and communicative function points us in the right direction conceptually, it does not suggest paradigms or models for investigating particular contexts. Without these, we are unable to decide whether international trials are capable of reconciling universal and particular truths, or reflecting this in outcomes which have some tangible impact reaching beyond the symbolism of retributive justice.

Failure to address this kind of question makes it difficult to decide on what basis we can attach any underlying or essential meaning to 'penality' and so confirm its utility as a conceptual device, whether in global or local terms. For example, as Alvarez[56] posits for international criminal justice, does 'penality' represent some kind of international consensus about the value of retribution

---

55 *Ibid*, 253.
56 Alvarez (1999).

or deterrence, or is it just another vehicle for giving effect to the hegemonic ambitions of powerful states? This reasoning is equally applicable for analysing domestic forms of trial justice. It returns us to the problem of how to identify those shared values which underpin punishment and sentencing within any particular social context and the 'true' nature of the 'interests' they represent.

Conceptions of the moral

This section is not concerned with making moral judgements, but rather with evaluating the present capacity of criminal justice theory to conceptualise and account for the existence and impact of moral values upon penal ideology and sentencing. As argued above, the notion of 'penality' provides an inadequate conceptual bridge between the ideological foundations of penal law and the normative effects of putting that law into practice through sentencing. This difficulty persists irrespective of state or other boundaries. In the context of international criminal justice, for example, the potential 'audience' is vast, and may range from humanity at large down to particular individuals, groups and communities that have been victimised by social conflict and war.

Therefore, within such a framework, we struggle to appropriate contextualised meanings to concepts such as responsibility, duty and expectation if they are taken to signify something beyond the legal, especially if that raises moral questions. The relationship between law and morality has long been a concern of legal theorists.[57] Whilst some scholars defend the moral integrity of law,[58] others argue that the value-pluralism of contemporary secular society forces us to confront questions about the nature of our legitimate engagement with punishment with a greater degree of urgency. This imperative is portrayed as more acute in the face of the perceived global threat from terrorism and consequent reconfiguration of penality in terms of security and control at both the international and domestic level.

In a recent chapter,[59] Alan Norrie makes some salient observations about the relationship between citizen and state and the way in which notions of individual criminal responsibility have been reconfigured in the post-modern era. Norrie argues that there has been a movement away from a relationship of dependency between human agency and social context towards a more insular form of individual responsibility that is significantly detached from its communitarian roots. In this sense, therefore, the notion of the immutable interdependency of citizen and state typified by liberal theory has mutated, through the neo-liberalism of the paternalistic state,[60] to a point where the concept of individual responsibility that has characterised criminal justice since the demise of welfarism in the early 1970s now fulfils both expressive and

---

57 See the debate between Hart and Fuller, *supra*, note 5.
58 Raz (2001).
59 See Norrie (2009).
60 Loader (2006).

repressive functions. It is expressive in the sense that it appears to endorse the liberal concept of individual freedom of will, whilst paradoxically repressive, in that the state has increasingly curtailed individual liberties through legal intervention as a form of social control.

In distancing itself from its social context, present notions of individual criminal responsibility increasingly stretch the liberal interdependency of social and moral responsibility. The moral synergies which characterised the administration of justice in the liberal state have been replaced by a diminishing moral consensus between citizen and state regarding the social function of punishment. This fragmentation of society's 'moral cement' has weakened the state's capacity to respond strategically to the causes of crime and criminality so that, as Garland observes,[61] the state's diminishing terrain is now concerned with controlling politically defined areas of risk and security which tend to isolate, label and repress individuals and groups in terms of their perceived 'dangerousness'. This may be interpreted as a thinly disguised form of hegemony that increases moral and social division within states, and so alienates citizens from the state's institutions and their official ideologies. As Norrie puts it:

> Criminal law is not just about the moral relations between individuals, it is also the basis for a system of state control over individuals, and as such there is a constant possibility that arguments based upon state necessity will kick in to negate ideas of individual right and responsibility.[62]

Norrie goes on to argue that the fusion of individual and political citizenship, whereby the state assumes total responsibility for upholding the individual rights and freedoms of *all* citizens without favour, reached its post-war zenith with the advent of the socialist welfare state.[63] With the gradual demise of welfarism in criminal justice from the 1970s onwards, the balance between individual and social conceptions of responsibility shifted incrementally towards the individual at the expense of the social.

Norrie sees the increasing authoritarianism of penal law in the late postmodern era as exacerbated through the continued emphasis on retributive punishment[64] and the deliberate recasting of political citizenship in terms of the state legitimising the use of law in authoritarian terms. Retributive punishment is effectively a moral vindication of the state's actions, so that each increase in the 'responsibilisation' of citizens is followed up with increased punitiveness on the part of the state. Consequently, the moral relationship between citizen and state is further reduced, as is the moral terrain over which the state holds sway. Therefore, the prevalent notion of individual responsibility

---

61 Garland (2001).
62 Norrie (2009) 18.
63 The relationship between criminal justice and changing concepts of political accountability is discussed in Lacey (2008) Part I.
64 *Ibid.* 29.

is one where the citizen has effectively been decontextualised and remoralised, rather than one where, as Norrie has argued elsewhere,[65] conceptions of moral and social responsibility merge through relational justice.

However, as Findlay argues,[66] the emergent threat to humanity is now moving beyond the risk/security nexus through a phase of global economic crisis and must now confront the increasingly devastating consequences of climate change resulting from the relentless degradation of the environment. Consequently, pluralistic concerns will more than ever need to engage with the threat and consequences of environmental degradation and the catastrophic impact of climate change.

It may be argued that such concerns extend far beyond the conventional remit of penal law and contemporary notions of penality. However, such a narrow view may be misguided. Contrary to the prevalent exclusory approach, penal law could develop a major role in combating activities which precipitate environmental degradation. However, such a role is currently ill-defined, and many questions remain unanswered. Chief among these are questions about the conceptual parameters of penal ideology, and the utility of existing penal rationales and their conceptual and normative frameworks for dealing with the perpetrators and consequences of catastrophic environmental harm, both internationally and domestically.

This is not the place to elaborate the basis for these assertions, or their practical implications. Nevertheless, the debate is pertinent in the present context, since it provides a further illustration of why the social reality of trial justice is inextricably linked to the shared moral values that underpin penal ideology. In particular, it draws attention to the fact that, whatever measures are taken in the name of humanity to 'penalise', 'punish' or 'deter' perpetrators of global environmental harm, these must draw moral support from both global and local constituencies. For this reason it becomes crucial to explain the moral value of penal law and to consider more deeply the fact that the nature of its role will depend on the legitimacy attached to it in any particular context.

This kind of understanding depends upon the ability of social theory to engage with the moral pluralism of the late post-modern era. The limits set for this engagement in this book are concerned with identifying shared moral values

---

65 Norrie's suggestion that 'liberal theories of subjective right and justice need to be supplanted by premises of a more social or communitarian kind' is important in directing our attention to the existential nature of relations between individuals and communities; Norrie (1996b) 540, 546. Norrie considers that the dialectic connection between notions of formal and popular justice is exclusory, since so-called rational formal law is supportive of selected moral and political norms, whilst 'popular justice' is incorrectly portrayed as representing the social and political interests of abstract individuals and the rule of law. Clearly, it is also necessary for communitarian concepts to recognise the effects of socio-political constraints on individual autonomy and appreciate how moral and legal norms interact in pluralistic societies; Norrie (1996a) 383, 392.

66 See Findlay (2010b).

about the appropriateness of punishment, the forms this might take, and the legitimacy attached to penal justice, as well as accounting for the nature of those interests that underpin them. The latter is crucial for understanding the governance implications of values that draw their attachment from both global and local constituencies.

A criminal justice perspective that reflects the moral significance of penal law suggests a pluralistic engagement with concepts such as harm, duty, liability and responsibility, and examining their construction and function in diverse social settings at the global and local level. However, as discussed, deconstructing constructs of 'justice' or 'legitimacy' invariably forces us to engage with the eternal conundrum of how to explain the relationship between the empirical and the moral world.

For criminological theorists, bridging this epistemological divide has been fraught with difficulty. As with phenomenology, it involves elaborating the dialectic between objective and subjective accounts of social reality. Hence, in the present context, objectivism is likely to consist of a functionalist, or conflict-theory approach to explaining what penal law signifies and how it impacts on relevant audiences. Subjective approaches, on the other hand, are more likely to focus on how moral perceptions of penal law and their subjective impact influence attitudes and behaviour. In other words, the tendency is for theory to polarise thinking about how sentencing might be implicated in transforming penal ideology into morally significant outcomes.

Theorising penal law as moral and social

The concept of attachment

In his analysis of the relationship between law and community, Cotterrell[67] reminds us that a sense of attachment is an essential subjective component for understanding the concept of 'community' as a social phenomenon. The notion of a sustained and mutual attachment which provides the sense of continuity necessary for communities to exist is crucial to this understanding. Consequently, attachment to 'community' may be conceptualised in terms of its 'objective' quality as a manifestation of social reality, or as something which is essentially 'subjective', consisting of a complex interrelated set of individual background variables, such as attitudes and beliefs, the development of which is crucially dependent upon social context.

Whilst attitudes and beliefs may reflect unique individual qualities of feeling and emotion, values derived from membership of a particular 'community' with its distinctive characteristics may also be identified and described in terms of their social significance. From this perspective, it is not difficult to argue that the criteria by which we measure 'objective' attachment to 'community'

---

67 Cotterrell (2006) 70–71.

should also be capable of engaging with its 'subjectivity', especially relationships between human agency and social structure within that 'community'.

There are important parallels here with debates about the nature and role of attachment in criminology, especially the idea that that self-control may be conceived as internal to the individual, whilst social control is external and relevant to explaining criminal behaviour only to the extent that it influences self-control. The proposition that external controls are internalised through the process of 'socialisation' is a significant focus for deconstructing notions of 'community', particularly its role in shaping moral values and influencing behaviour. In the international context, for example, Mark Drumbl[68] employs Hirschi's control theory[69] to illustrate the paradox of the frequently strong bonds of attachment that unite perpetrators of mass atrocity to both state and society,[70] although he largely ignores Hirschi's later work with Gottfredson, which emphasises the importance of the relationship between contingent and psychological variables.[71]

Responding to social change

Such an appreciation of the relationship between the moral and the social is crucial for conceptualising the recursive and developmental nature of penality and its ability to respond to fundamental shifts in the cohesiveness of social organisations and their moral values. This observation is especially pertinent in conceptualising penal law's engagement with the value-pluralism of post-modernity. Cotterrell describes[72] law's linkage to social change in the following terms:

> Law may define the social as it regulates it, but it does so under conditions that the social itself provides. Law presupposes a conception of the social that defines not only its technical jurisdiction, but also the arena in which its interventions require rational integration, and the general source of its legitimation and cultural meanings. It follows that, as the identity, coherence and shape of the social are questioned, assumptions about the nature and efficacy of law are also put in issue.

The implications of this argument are profound when we begin to consider the rationales for punishment and, more particularly, the increasingly divergent moral foundations underpinning the legitimacy of trial justice described in this book; whether at the global or local level. Furthermore, as we begin to move away from the rationale of risk/security to that of environmental

---

68 Drumbl (2007a).
69 Hirschi (1969) 16–33.
70 Drumbl (2007a) 35.
71 Gottfredson and Hirschi (1990) 65.
72 Cotterrell (2006) 20.

degradation and climate change, the role of the social comes under greater scrutiny. Although the 'community' from whom legitimacy is sought remains universal because of the global and ongoing nature of the threat, penal law and practice will need to draw its legitimacy from localised areas of catastrophe where social relations of community may have been obliterated or fragmented. Consequently, communitarian foundations for rationalising punishment or signifying its moral value may change radically. Hence, in terms of 'community', the legitimacy of punishing environmental crimes that impact on the social relations of the human species must be conceived in global *and* local terms. Each context must be subjected to penetrating analysis.

However, what of environmental degradation which leads to the systematic depletion and obliteration of animal and plant species, rather than impacting directly on human forms of 'community'? In exploring this question, it is worth pausing for a moment to reflect upon whether or not the basic assumptions underlying the above argument are correct. To put it another way, are we justified in arguing that morality is largely shaped by social relations, so that we need to take note of this when considering the moral legitimacy attached to punishment in different kinds of 'community', or is it indeed more accurate to suggest that social relations are largely shaped by morality?

The answer to this question has profound consequences if we consider why the norms and structures that regulate social life take a particular form, and in accounting for changes in their composition over time. Logically, such phenomena impact on social reality and therefore social relations and 'communities'. Indeed, it may be appropriate to accord legally enforceable rights to non-human species, not just because species conservation is intrinsically good, but because humanity has a shared moral interest in preserving the integrity of species and habitats. In that sense, morality is best described as social morality. The relationship between social life and social morality is best viewed as in a constant state of flux. This is reflected in the changing legitimacy accorded to penal law and practice over time and space.

It may be argued that a systems approach to answering these questions tends to decouple the idea of social morality from a consideration of system. For example, economic systems may be justified purely in terms of what benefits the maximisation of profit. Such an approach appears to support the notion that morality influences social relations more than the reverse proposition. The reason for this is simply that a successful economy will impact on social relationships and give rise to a shared social morality. Yet system theory ignores the fact that discrete systems do not operate in a moral vacuum. Despite value-pluralism, I would argue that social harmony reflects the balance between social structure and social morality.

Theorising the social function of morality

Emile Durkheim's notion of moral individualism, referred to earlier, has some utility in clarifying these issues. It is important to note that Durkheim himself was not engaging in a discussion about the nature of moral values.[73] On the contrary, his principal objective was to describe and explain the function of morality in society. Whilst for Durkheim there was some identifiable moral consensus based upon a shared attachment to religious values, the secular-isation of post-modern societies has rendered the idea of a unitary shared moral consensus about the nature and function of penal law untenable.

Instead, moral constituencies are now fragmented and may owe no particular allegiance to a specific religious or other moral code. However, the very existence of value-pluralism poses a fundamental challenge to the future legitimacy of punishment and suggests a need for the sociology of punishment to engage with this issue. The first stage is to speculate about the kinds of moral constituency from which punishment seeks to draw its legitimacy. Such an account might include an analysis of the function of shared value judgements about the appro-priateness of certain forms of behaviour and how they should be punished.

Taking international criminal justice, for example; on this view, we might conclude that the basis for a shared moral culture is derived from humanity's shared interest in preserving fundamental human rights, such as the right to life and liberty. Such a sharing reflects a universal moral bond between human beings based on a common need to preserve essential qualities of humanity. However, there is an underlying difficulty in conceptualising penality in terms that link the universal nature of this shared morality to its partisan realisation in different social contexts. This dialectic between the universal and the relative presents a significant obstacle to theorising the relationship between penal values, norms and outcomes within the trial context. However, particular insights may be derived by accounting for the recursive relationship that exists between the moral and the social.[74]

Social theory suggests certain ways of describing and explaining social life. The actions of human agents can be measured in objective terms, but there are limits to the extent that we can generalise about the subjective meanings attached to these observable facts. Moral values and the principles for action derived from them fall into this category. Although these principles may be set out as normative frameworks and objectified in legal form, the moral values they enshrine can only be realised through human action. Human agency reflects the subjective influence of moral values through action. Therefore, humans are moral as well as social agents. In this sense, the reciprocity of social action reinforces moral values.

Consequently, from the perspective of structure, it might be argued that the normative framework of penal law facilitates outcomes that impact on moral

---

73 See Cotterrell (1999) ch. 4.

74 The recursive relationship that exists between structure and agency is important in developing sentencing models. For example, Giddens's structuration theory allows us to conceptualise how the criminal trial process is created recursively over time and space and suggests different levels or layers of meaning for understanding sentencing contexts comparatively which can modelled at different levels of abstraction. These issues are explored in more detail in chapter 4.

values and influence attitudes and behaviour. This is a fundamental tenet of deterrent and communicative theories of punishment. Correspondingly, from the perspective of human agency, we may argue that judicial discretionary power directs how the morality of penal ideology is transformed through sentencing (see Figure 2.1 above). Sentencing principles may be regarded as a combination of legal and moral norms that reflect a conception of 'justice' (a morality of sanctioned punishment) supportive of judicial and/or executive ideology. In this sense, therefore, sentencing jurisprudence is suggestive of how sentencing law ought to be applied in a social context through the medium of a sentencing decision. Although this normative framework is a component of structure, it is constantly changing through the recursive practice of sentencing. Therefore, the ability of social theory to deconstruct the recursive relationship between structure and agency over time can provide important insights into the extent to which sentencing reflects shared moral values about penal purposes and practice.

These issues are significant for conceptualising how the moral and the social are reflected in the context of conflict resolution. Therefore, if we think of conflict as intrinsic to the human condition, we might argue that the resolution of conflict is intrinsically beneficial to humanity and consequently a universal moral good. The converse is to argue that, although conflict fulfils an important social function, its resolution may not necessarily be intrinsically good. This view suggests that conflict resolution may sometimes be perceived as good by certain sections of humanity. Another position might be to argue that since conflict is an integral aspect of human behaviour, humanity cannot exist without conflict, even though this could precipitate the eventual destruction of the human race.

Societies therefore provide structures to regulate the 'appropriate' balance between peace and conflict which citizens (in democratic states) agree as necessary precursors to perpetuate social life. Hence, the extent to which structures for conflict resolution such as trials are deemed to be intrinsically 'good' depends upon how a particular society or community comes to define what is 'good'. This is essentially a moral question. Where conflicting interests weaken the legitimacy attached to penal ideology, it weakens the legitimacy of trial outcomes and undermines the regulatory governance of the state.

Consequently, the nature of the dialectic between conflict and its resolution is a constantly changing aspect of social life. This realisation forces us to confront the problem of hegemony and its potential for suppressing human rights, since the forces of hegemony are partisan in identifying conflict and supporting structures devised to resolve it.

I have argued that the essence of trial justice must be respect for the universal primacy of human rights over hegemonic power and the discriminatory impact it achieves through punishment. For this reason the trial's function in resolving conflict should be viewed as intrinsically 'good'. Therefore, although it may be a moral choice to view trial outcomes as either 'just' or not, the criminal process itself should not be seen in purely instrumental terms. To conceive of the trial as intrinsically 'good' because it has the capacity to resolve conflict is to recognise that trials have a moral capacity. That morality and its practical delivery through the mechanism of the trial is an essential thread in supporting human rights and therefore sustaining humanity itself. However, to reflect this moral value, the penal ideology that underpins the trial should represent the legitimate interests and expectations of those constituencies seeking 'justice' within a relevant social context.[75]

As argued in chapter 3, imbuing those structures charged with delivering justice with qualities of 'goodness' does not imply any moral attachment by the 'relevant audience' to the outcomes they produce. Rather, the legitimacy attaching to different forms of conflict resolution depends upon the nature of social relations within particular contexts and the extent to which shared values exist regarding the appropriateness of certain acts or omissions. This does not mean that social relations shape morality; rather, they provide a shared social context against which the rightness or wrongness of particular behaviours is judged. Therefore, one would expect moral consensus about the appropriateness of criminalising particular behaviours to be reflected in the perceived legitimacy that a moral constituency attaches to the punishment of those behaviours. Such legitimacy extends to the rationales or purposes for punishment and by implication to particular forms of distributive justice.

Accounting for hegemony

The significance of this observation is evident if one considers the nature of trial justice from a hegemonic perspective. In an insightful paper James Cockayne[76] draws on Garfinkel's seminal contribution on the conditions of successful degradation ceremonies[77] to focus attention on the way in which international and domestic forms of international penality have the capacity to degrade the status of humanity at large, as well as the national and ethnic status of perpetrators, victims and communities in conflict zones. Cockayne suggests that hybridised forms of international justice – such as the tribunals for Kosovo and East Timor, the Special Court for Sierra Leone and, more recently, the Cambodian Extraordinary Chambers and The War Crimes Chamber of the State Court of Bosnia-Herzegovina – frequently engender moral confusion by 'defeating the process whereby war crimes trials transform local morality to align it with international norms', and have a tendency to reinforce local ethnic prejudices and solidarities.

Referring to the differences between the transformative significance of international and domestic criminal trials, Cockayne argues that:

---

75 See, further, Findlay and Henham (2010) ch. 1.
76 Cockayne (2005) 455, 456.
77 Garfinkel (1956).

The transformation of the individual perpetrator is used to maintain the community's moral *status quo*. But war crimes seek a different kind of transformation: the degradation of the perpetrator is not intended to affirm the community's moral *status quo* but to transform it, replacing the values present during a period of conflict with some other set of determinate values[78]

... Too often, we ignore the transformative project inherent in international criminal justice and assume that it is simply a supranational analogue of state criminality.[79]

The hegemonic aspect of the transformative potential of the trial is neces-sarily a function of penal ideology and the forces that privilege its dominion. Furthermore, the key point about legitimacy to be drawn from Cockayne's analysis is that it is a function of the trial itself to provide the moral capacity for that transformation and that the moral significance of both the trial and its outcome should be judged against the values held by those constituencies directly affected by them. Hence, the analysis acknowledges the need to account for the plural partisan influences that determine the trial's transformative potential.

Notwithstanding, it may be argued that there is more convergence in the transformative function between international and domestic forms of trial justice than Cockayne acknowledges. The idea of the trial as transforming the status of perpetrators to maintain the community's moral *status quo*, when juxtaposed against that of using the trial to supplant conflict values, is not necessarily so contradictory if we think of the issue in terms of the moral impact of post-modern penality. The main reason for this is that the increas-ing value-pluralism within states during the post-modern era has produced a situation where penal ideologies are no longer predicated on the idea that trial outcomes automatically engage with moral constituencies in terms of communicating or expressing a universally accepted moral message.

Consequently, conjecture exists about conceptualising the trial as capable of delivering universally accepted moral truths, either in terms of establishing the 'facts' of a particular case and what should amount to appropriate punish-ment, or how victims and communities view the criminalisation of certain behaviours and the nature of the state's response. If trial justice does not confront such conflicts, the state risks alienating significant minorities.[80]

Accordingly, trials of whatever complexion are being forced to confront the consequences of greater social conflict as characterised by varying degrees of division and violence. As Garland argues,[81] a focus on a criminology 'of the other' requires a closer engagement with moral themes; something that has

---

78 *Ibid.* 466.
79 *Ibid.* 469.
80 A classic example of this is the work of Lea and Young (1984).
81 Garland (2001) 184.

increasingly eluded criminal justice as it shifts more towards the positivist preoccupations of crime causation and prevention which have increasingly characterised post-modern penality.[82] Garland suggests that, far from seizing the opportunity to engage with the conflicting moral demands of value-pluralism, post-modern penality has instead resorted to a 'pre-modern, mechanical' notion of shared values[83] with which to tighten its grip on social control, thereby increasing intolerance and exacerbating social division.

Grounding the moral authority of penal law

The implications of this moral detachment for the authority and legitimacy of penal law remain a matter of debate. From a Weberian perspective, for example, the strengthening of law's political authority increases the legitimacy of the rule of law, irrespective of whether its rules and procedures have any moral purchase among citizens in the wider community.[84] According to Weber, the legal norms which regulate punishment are founded on principles of substantive rationality, in so far as they are informed by a mixture of moral and other beliefs *existing beyond the formalism of the legal rules* themselves. However, in reality such norms are highly formalised in structure, and there exists a complex balance between formal logical processes which facilitate the recursive reproduction of law as an autonomous system of rules and the extent to which ideology about the moral acceptability of social action informs decision-making.[85]

Therefore, in Weberian terms, legal rationality becomes bureaucratised to the extent that the criminal process recursively perpetuates the development of internally consistent principles which tend to reinforce dominant political ideologies. A system of formal rationality reproduced in contexts where political and moral ideologies are at odds (as may well be the case both within and between modern pluralistic states) means that legal formalism predominates and increasingly causes the alienation of the criminal process from the outcomes it produces. This process inevitably has the effect of strengthening the power of those who have dominion over law-making.

By way of contrast, Habermas reaches beyond law by grounding its authority and significance in the communicative rationality of the 'lifeworld'.[86] Habermas follows Durkheim to the extent of seeking to ground law's authority

---

82 In effect, reversing the oft-repeated political rhetoric of 'tough on crime and tough on the causes of crime'.

83 An example is the media-driven notion of penal populism characterised by the sentencing legislation of the late 1990s.

84 See Cotterrell (1983).

85 A similar effect noted by some social psychologists is that perceived legitimacy provides a kind of 'reservoir of support' for institutional practices which may override the interests of those whom such structures are meant to serve. See Tyler (2006) 281.

86 See Habermas (1987), Habermas (1996).

in principles of rationality drawn from forms of social solidarity and from that to describing ways in which social processes of consensus-formation and interpretation are constructed and transmitted through law.[87] However, he goes further than this in asserting the key function of law as effectively balancing the instrumental demands of society's institutions (so-called instrumental rationality) against those of the communicative rationality of groups within society having a shared moral agenda. Whilst maintaining that law and morality remain distinct, for Habermas the rationality of consensus formation and its true reflection in law is crucially dependant upon the political relationship between law and democracy, since this determines the extent to which communicative rationality can find true expression through law.

Hence, criminal processes such as the trial are conditioned to facilitate the rational expression of communitarian interests in so far as this is not repressed by partisan penal ideology. Unfortunately, the value-pluralism of post-modern society impedes the likelihood of moral consensus on questions of crime and punishment, and with it the realisation of a non-partisan penality. Whilst Durkheim's notions of law as reflecting social solidarity grounded in the universal moral consensus of the state are clearly outdated, as Cotterrell suggests,[88] it may well be that his notion of a value system deriving its moral authority from our collective concern for human equality is the only way to envisage a truly global community of values.

Linking theory and method

The ongoing theoretical debate concerning the relationship between law and morality has had a limited impact on approaches to comparative method in sentencing research. As discussed in chapter 4, models of sentence decision-making have largely developed along secular jurisdictional lines and often owe their basic assumptions to particular theoretical perspectives about the nature of law and legal process. Not only does the adoption of a particular theoretical approach potentially distort any subsequent empirical conclusions reached about the nature of the social reality investigated, it necessarily misrepresents or marginalises significant contextual information which may be crucial for understanding the normative significance of specific aspects of the analysis. Consequently, it may be argued that existing models of criminal justice have limited utility in the comparative analysis of trial justice at both the global and local levels, especially the extent to which they are capable of engaging with the normative aspects of sentencing.

In order to make sense of sentencing comparatively we need to understand what 'penality' signifies in different contexts and how international and

---

87 In this connection, see further commentary on Hutton's use of Bordieu's notion of the 'social field' or 'habitus' in chapter 4.
88 Cotterrell (1999) 168–69.

domestic penal systems interrelate. This section draws attention to some significant weaknesses in this respect in the recent development of the theory and method of comparative criminal justice. Accordingly, it suggests appropriate connections between theory and method, with a view to expanding our capacity to appreciate the relationship between the perception and the social reality of trial justice.

Comparative analysis and context

However, before turning to these questions, it is important to clarify what is meant by comparative analysis in this context. This task is best accomplished by first summarising some specific limitations of existing approaches. For instance, comparative analysis should *not* consist of what Nelken[89] describes as 'comparison by juxtaposition', nor should its purpose be perceived as a thinly 'disguised hegemonic project', or a search for 'globalised legal concepts'.[90]

Nor is it adequate to draw a simple dichotomy between what Pakes[91] describes as so-called 'relativist' and 'positivist' approaches. Anthropological research typifies the former in emphasising that everything in social reality is relative: it is a function of the environment. Pakes suggests that explaining how something works elsewhere can lead to looking at one's own society and social life in a different way. The equivalent to this approach in social science research is 'interpretivism', which involves examining crime and criminal justice in context and trying to understand why criminal justice processes have come into existence and work in the way they do.[92]

By contrast, 'positivist' approaches attempt to identify core sets of principles underpinning criminal justice and distinguish them from merely external features. Such approaches tend to assume that criminal justice and social control are universal phenomena, implying that arrangements existing elsewhere can be given meaning in the domestic context, whereas for relativists the most important issue is that the meaning of a phenomenon should be derived from its own context.

The most significant question to ask before embarking on any comparative analysis is therefore why the comparison is being made. In the present context, one might then question the relevance of comparative analysis to the study of trial justice. As has been suggested, one answer is to argue that we need to understand the relationship between global and local forms of trial justice in order to make sense of recent developments in the globalisation of criminal law and process, such as international courts and tribunals, or the myriad hybridised forms of post-conflict justice. Appreciating these effects involves a consideration of

---

89 Nelken (ed.) (1997).
90 See Zedner (1995).
91 Pakes (2010) 13.
92 For a recent appraisal, see Nelken (2010).

context. This suggests a profound analysis of several dimensions of understanding, ranging from penal ideology through to the operation of particular criminal justice processes – in other words, from macro to micro, from theory to practice.

This being the case, we now examine the utility of existing methodological approaches for understanding criminal justice comparatively. In prefacing his detailed analysis of French judicial culture, John Bell[93] argues that one has to engage in inference from conduct and statements, plus some questioning of participants. He considers the sort of evidence required of legal culture and concludes that it must combine description of activity and the operation of physical institutions with the analysis of attitudes. This can include the agenda of the institution. Analysis of attitudes will rely heavily on what parties say about themselves, or the stories they recount about the legal process. However, it will also make use of analysis of the fundamental structures of thinking (legal reasoning) and the assumptions that lie behind what is expressed and done. Bell points out that the linguistic dimension is not the only one; courtroom architecture, procedure and dress are all ways of communicating things about the law.

Arguably, however, Bell's focus on legal culture is too narrow. Pakes,[94] for instance, looks at the use of case studies, focused comparisons and statistical analysis.[95] The most obvious limitation regarding the latter is that quantitative data on measures of penal severity and judicial practice from different jurisdictions are not comparable. Several scholars, notably Albrecht[96] and Frase,[97] have pointed to the fact that the comparative analysis of quantitative data on the effect of penal processes in different jurisdictions is suspect because it ignores legal and cultural context. Consequently, statistical comparisons tell us little (if anything) about the socio-political forces that determine the interactions which statistics purport to represent, nor the nature of those interactions.[98]

Comparative sentencing statistics may be manipulated for ideological and/ or political purposes.[99] For example, they may purport to show a relationship between judicial practice and apparently low levels of sentence severity for particular types of offence or offender across jurisdictions. There is a danger that such information could be taken as an indication to policy-makers that

93 Bell (2001) 20.
94 Pakes (2004) 16.
95 However, Bohlander (2004) criticises this study on the basis that Pakes employs a very narrow database, the validity of his methodology is not made explicit, and his assumptions and conclusions overgeneralise what is a complex issue requiring a more penetrating analysis.
96 Albrecht (2001) 293, 294.
97 Frase argues the need to identify and control for factors which make sentencing fundamentally non-comparable in different jurisdictions, so that when policy-makers make choices involving the possible adoption of ideas from foreign jurisdictions they are able to minimise major sources of non-comparability between systems; Frase (1998) 109, 119.
98 This is consistent with earlier work by Cicourel and others in the 1960s; see Cicourel (1968). A classic example is the International Crime Victimisation Survey; see van Dijk, van Kesteren and Smit (2008).
99 See Hall *et al.* (1978).

more rigid legislative control of sentencing discretion through the construction of sentencing guidelines is imperative.[100]

In an insightful review of Nelken's[101] edited collection of essays on different comparative approaches, Paul Roberts[102] cautions against over-reliance on local expert commentary. He suggests that national experts speaking from within a particular cultural 'milieu' may be no less skewed or partial, and could be even more limiting than an outsider's perspective. Roberts agrees with Hodgson[103] that:

> The comparativist (whether or not conducting empirical work) is engaged in a form of legal anthropology and is a participant observer ... She is attempting to permeate another culture, at the very least to understand its institutional structures, laws and procedures, but hopefully also its languages, customs, ideologies, legal cultures and practices ... A contextual approach to the study of law and legal processes is vital to our understanding of legal culture: rules, procedures and judicial decisions are insufficient. Just as with the study of domestic law and legal problems, this approach creates only an illusion of understanding.

However, although agreeing that the 'comparativist must beware of constructing models and precoding information from the bias of her own legal culture', Roberts takes issue with Hodgson's view that 'all observation is subjective' and its implication that nothing can be taken as given, suggesting that this would render research impossible. Self-evidently, if everything is relative, there cannot be any kind of objectivity, and it becomes futile to discuss the normativity of law.

Similarly, being a participant observer provides opportunities to delve deeper into the multi-layered, nuanced, dynamic and conflicting meanings of social practices by immersing oneself in a foreign language and culture over an extended period of time. For example, understanding the role of the layman or the victim in criminal justice suggests a need to investigate the reasons why laymen or victims are treated as they are within any particular criminal process, and what law and policy symbolise in this respect. However, as Roberts argues, this approach may produce just as biased an account as one produced by an indigenous expert.

In terms of assessing the strengths and weaknesses of these methodologies for the comparative analysis of trial process, it is important to note the predominance of narrative analysis. However, to understand the rationale and operation of international or local trial processes involves the identification,

---

100   This conclusion might also be implemented at the regional level, such as within the EU.
101   Nelken (ed) (2000).
102   Roberts (2002).
103   *Ibid.* 545, Hodgson (2000).

description and analysis of communication structures and social interaction. Where necessary, therefore, narrative analysis needs to be supplemented by various ethnographic approaches, including direct observation (participant or otherwise), interviewing and expert contextual commentary.

Although narrative itself records dimensions of formal process, it does not permit us to understand how each player in the trial process subjectively interprets any aspect of that process. A narrative simply records the ways in which formal requirements are interpreted (acted upon) as external processes. However, as Twining[104] suggests, there is an absence of a definite and uniform legal vocabulary and also a 'fringe of vagueness' or 'open texture' within legal methodology that is compounded where the analysis of difference and synthesis is applied across different procedural traditions. As such different meaning may be given to the same text. This tendency is compounded in the case of sentencing, where the text conceals a greater level of subjectivity on the part of the decision-maker, and, where inquisitorial trials predominate, the narrative is more likely to be minimal and formulaic.

Another significant issue is the fact that physical gestures are not normally recorded despite their obvious impact upon an account. Similarly, translations may lose the symbolic nature of the original text, or may reflect the (or a) dominant cultural stance (without regard for other minority influences), once again relating back to the problem of cultural bias in interpretation. Furthermore, as Jackson[105] suggests, the order of procedural rules is not accidental within any given legal context. Consequently, trials may be conceived as the site of a set of discourses, each with its own set of codes and participants.

To counter these limitations the kind of comparative contextual analysis described in chapter 4 is designed to facilitate culturally sympathetic understanding where rules are applied to previously unforeseen contexts and situations. For instance, the elaboration of narrative through selective observation and expert commentary is advocated to counter the tendency towards methodological distortion. Additionally, comparative contextual analysis should be sensitive to phenomenological description in providing accounts of the subjective reality of process at the symbolic and ideological level.[106] It should also aim to counter the problem of cultural bias implicit in conventional comparative methodologies through ongoing critical evaluation by expert commentators and subsequent interpretations of their accounts. In short, it should be sensitive to the different levels of meaning and understanding attributed to action and process by trial participants in different legal cultures.

---

104 Twining (1999).
105 Jackson (1988).
106 See, for example, Sudnow (1965).

Comparative analysis and trial justice

Having outlined several weaknesses of comparative method, I now propose to identify some specific issues relating to the comparative analysis of trial justice where improvements could be made. To begin with, it is worth noting that conventional paradigms for evaluating punishment in both common and civil law jurisdictions attach great symbolic significance to the formal pronouncement of sentence and the elaboration of its rationale by the judiciary in individual cases. The rhetoric and symbolism of the moment not only marks the conclusion of the trial process by acknowledging the extent of criminal liability through appropriate punishment, it also signals an apparently[107] natural break between the determination of guilt through verdict delivery and the consequences of its pronouncement.

Furthermore, the conventional trial process recursively reinforces relationships of power and subjugation within the jurisdictional boundaries of states, and so selectively appropriates presumed mandates[108] for punishment. Such mandates are normally based on an identifiable ideology and rationality for punishment. In the case of international trial justice, these may be forged *ex post facto* following analysis of the causes and consequences of a particular war or social conflict, but they are nevertheless generally taken to represent coherent and legitimate rationales for depriving individual citizens of their liberty through formalised punishment. Nevertheless, as Garland[109] implies, for both international and domestic forms of trial, the ideology of freedom and liberty is increasingly being replaced by that of control, so that the social reality of the trial may bear little resemblance to its proclaimed rationale, or the social context in which it operates.

Such an interpretation forces us to confront the dichotomy that exists between objective representations of the trial and its relative reality for the lay and professional participants and wider social audience. In the present context, the crucial issue is whether the different phases of the trial actually represent key moments which have some moral or normative significance extending beyond its boundaries, so that they can be said to connect in some profound moral sense with what citizens regard as demonstrably necessary requirements for justice delivery. Correspondingly, from a comparative perspective, it is necessary to question whether such processual divisions have a substantive ideological significance, and, if so, the extent to which they mirror shared

---

107 Arguably, it is only 'natural' in the sense that the verdict marks the end of one stage in the criminal process. However, a Classical Liberal approach to punishment would dictate that the gap between verdict and sentence is as short as possible, and the scope for exercising sentencing discretion reduced.

108 The word 'mandate' is used to draw attention to the fact that the executive's power to legislate in penal matters derives from the democratically expressed will of the people.

109 Garland (2001).

perceptions of how penal ideology should be reflected in the structure and function of the trial.

As argued more fully in chapter 4, recognising that our experience of law and the power of normative judgements are relative and reflective of value-pluralism means that the answers to these questions can no longer be revealed by testing social reality against conventional paradigms of trial justice. Conversely, they are unlikely to be answered by an approach which fails to question the moral integrity of penal law and its ideological foundations. We are therefore left with the apparent paradox that any comparative understanding of criminal procedure must be approached from a perspective which is tolerant of context and its effect on the social reality of discretionary decision-making for trial participants and their relevant social audiences.[110]

These observations serve as an important reminder of the need to appreciate the influence of legal and social variables when formulating so-called 'objective' understandings of trial structure and human action within specific jurisdictional contexts. In particular, whilst the trial process is fluid, dynamic and recursive in terms of structure, its social reality is largely constituted through human agency and the instrumental exercise of judicial discretionary power. Consequently, human experience of what constitutes the normative and social reality of the trial is firmly grounded in context. This insight has particular relevance where, as with international courts and tribunals, the judges who exercise discretionary power are themselves drawn from diverse legal cultures and personal and social backgrounds. Thus, understanding how attitudes and perceptions towards punishment and motivations for judicial behaviour influence discretionary decision-making within criminal trials is a major challenge for policymakers who aim to establish trial cultures that are responsive to restorative justice ideology and practice.

Some alternative approaches

Richard Frase[111] has recently evaluated the work of Damaska and Cavadino and Dignan (amongst others) in the context of sentencing and comparative law theory. Cavadino and Dignan[112] offer a fresh perspective on theorising comparative penology based on a typology of 'late-modern' capitalist societies. This seeks to distinguish between countries included in their study[113] on the basis of political economy and then to relate these differences to variations in penality. Whilst acknowledging that differences in political economy and culture alone are unable to explain *all* variations in punishment and penality

---

110 See Vogler (2005). For comment, see Roberts (2008).
111 Frase (2008).
112 Cavadino and Dignan (2006).
113 Namely, the United States, England and Wales, Australia and New Zealand, South Africa, Germany, The Netherlands, France and Italy, Sweden and Finland and Japan.

among the countries examined, Cavadino and Dignan make the important point that:

> One cogent factor may well be the variable interrelationships that exist in different kinds of countries between ideological factors and attitudes on the one hand and the institutional contexts within which these attitudes may be shaped, influenced and expressed on the other.[114]

This insight reflects this book's emphasis on sentencing as a crucial space where penal ideology and human agency interrelate within the normative framework and social context of the trial

Frase suggests that comparative research into explaining sentencing variations over space and time would be enhanced if factors such as those identified by Cavadino and Dignan were added to the more system-based modelling approach of Damaška.[115] Frase rightly emphasises the organic nature of sentencing and the dangers of gross overgeneralisation on the basis of what appear to be comparable data.[116] However, it is equally important that separate consideration be given to questions of how each aspect of sentencing arises and functions within the context of this organic whole.

Concluding comment

The preceding discussion not only illustrates that there are conflicting theoretical approaches to conceptualising the relationship between morality, punishment and sentencing, it also reminds us that there is consequently no accepted or conventional wisdom regarding the appropriate linkages to be drawn between theory and method in this area of scholarship. In other words, this plethora of theoretical insights may merely serve to obfuscate the development of comparative scholarship in criminal justice.

So, despite the fact that law and legal processes may be regarded as vital for upholding fundamental human rights, theoretical assumptions about how such shared moral values come to be reflected in law, and their social significance, remain controversial. Whilst such conjecture is perfectly acceptable as a matter of theoretical debate, contextualised understandings of concepts such as duty and responsibility, and what these may signify as 'shared' meanings within a

---

114 Cavadino and Dignan (2006) 35.
115 Frase (2008) 368. Generally, Frase concludes that Damaška's comparative procedure models are rather rigid and one-dimensional and incapable of explaining contextually influenced phenomena such as the approach to victims of many European justice systems. This is consistent with the findings of Henham and Mannozzi (2003). Nor are Damaška's models considered effective in accounting for the different meanings attached to the purposes of sentencing across jurisdictions, because the postulated ideals and examples of his models tend not to correspond with observed differences of sentencing purposes; Frase (2008) 359.
116 A similar cautionary note may be directed towards international surveys such as the International Crime Victimisation Survey; see note 98 above.

particular social context, have crucial practical consequences for the effectiveness of criminal justice as a form of governance. Such understandings may not necessarily be derived through any particular theoretical lens.

It is for this reason that chapter 4 argues in favour of comparative contextual modelling to explain the relationship between shared values about punishment and the perception of trial outcomes in particular social settings. As explained, such modelling is based on a merging of theoretical insights through the synthesis of inductive and deductive approaches to methodology.

3   Punishment Rationales in a Comparative Context

This chapter analyses a critical issue in the relationship between sentencing and the legitimacy of trial justice. Understanding why it is that particular cultures, communities, social groups or individuals hold certain attitudes and beliefs about the justifications for punishment and, more significantly, how this affects their perceptions of legitimacy is crucial to establishing the normative significance of sentencing in any context.[1] As argued in the preceding chapter, it is only by integrating a more normative perspective into sociological explanations that relevant and meaningful interpretations of sentencing can be achieved for each context.[2] Therefore, I would argue that increasing our understanding of how social and normative factors interrelate in any context holds the key to providing more informed comparative analyses and enhances the debate about the role of punishment and sentencing as an aspect of criminal justice governance.

Introduction

The aim of this chapter is to identify and analyse some of the pervasive themes and features that impact on the justifications for punishment and their realisation through sentencing in both global and local contexts. In particular, it explores the relationship between the philosophy of punishment and the sociology of sentencing. The object of this analysis is to consider how moral questions about the legitimacy of sentencing can be better accommodated within sociological accounts.

As suggested in chapter 2, Garland's[3] point about the signifying nature of penality has special resonance in the present context by implying that

---

1 The expression 'Punishment' is often used generically to refer to those justifications and practices concerned with the implementation of penal law. As stated in chapter 1, this book distinguishes between the notion of 'Punishment' as being concerned with debates about values, justifications and norms, and 'Sentencing' as referring to the social reality of discretionary decision-making, including penalty selection.
2 See also Duff and Garland (1994).
3 Garland (1990) 254.

sociological accounts should be reflective of generally understood cultural meanings about crime and punishment and, consequently, the boundaries of morally acceptable behaviour. In other words, these accounts should provide accurate insights into the different contexts of legitimacy. Accordingly, the chapter's emphasis is on analysing the rationales for punishment in terms of their relationship with the legitimacy of sentencing, and exploring some of the issues and reasons which influence particular manifestations of penality in different contextual settings. The final section, therefore, includes a number of case studies that examine the legitimacy of trial justice and its significance, focusing especially on the extent to which sentencing outcomes reflect a 'shared morality' about the appropriateness of punishment and its impact.

Symbolism and power

The ideology of retributive justice is a criminal justice dynamic which plays a dominant role in shaping penal policy and sentencing practice in most complex industrialised societies, irrespective of whether their models of criminal procedure are adversarial, inquisitorial or 'mixed'. Paradoxically, it is also a major element in many indigenous forms of justice delivery which are often thought of as essentially restorative.

Naturally, one may theorise about the reasons for this, either in the abstract or by evaluating the empirical findings of studies conducted from a variety of theoretical perspectives; anthropological, historical, legal, sociological or political. However, the relativism and narrow disciplinary focus of such studies are the very features which tend to inhibit our capacity to generalise about the contextual significance of particular penal ideologies and practices, or indeed what they might signify for more globalised forms of criminal justice governance. This raises the question of how we should conceptualise the moral significance of phenomena such as punishment in sociological terms, especially how we might give due consideration to subjectivism within the context of abstract macro-sociological explanations of criminal justice. The argument developed in this book is that attributions of responsibility and accountability made through punishment are only meaningful if understood as essential aspects of shared moral experience. It is therefore seen as essential when theorising transformative processes such as criminal justice to establish conceptual links between values and actions that will help us to understand what sentencing outcomes actually signify.

This poses a fundamental problem when deconstructing different penal contexts because sentencing praxis essentialises and distorts penal ideology and obscures its moral foundations. Not only is there the difficulty of identifying the ideology itself, but the problem of describing social reality is exacerbated because the processual activity of sentencing both interprets that ideology and contextualises it through the decision-making process.[4] Thus, identifying the role of morality in what transpires is problematic. The question might be answered from a functional perspective, arguing that the expressive value of the outcome is all that matters, but this would be to ignore the role of the underlying philosophical foundations of punishment and the impact of differing moralities in each jurisdictional context.

A classic example of this difficulty at the global level is revealed in the sentencing justifications invoked by the United Nations International Criminal Tribunals for the Former Yugoslavia and Rwanda (ICTY and ICTR respectively). The following extract from the ICTY's judgement in *Furundžija*[5] is typical:

> It is the *infallibility* of punishment, rather than the severity of the sanction, which is the tool for retribution, stigmatisation and deterrence. This is particularly the case for the International Tribunal; penalties are made more onerous by its international stature, moral authority and impact upon world public opinion, and this punitive effect must be borne in mind when assessing the suitable length of sentence [emphasis added].

Such obfuscation of purpose is compounded by the rhetoric of moral justification expressed by the tribunal, and the implication that the ICTY (or any similar international forum) has the capacity to turn these sentiments into a fully articulated penalty of proportionate retribution. The relativity of concepts such as justice and penality is ignored, it being assumed that these are synonymous for both the ICTY and international trial justice. This kind of rhetoric therefore undermines any notion that international criminal justice might be regarded as a representative form of governance based on a global moral consensus. However, the important point is that it appears to do so *only* if one accepts the argument that the legitimacy of international trial justice depends on something beyond symbolism.

The idea that trial justice may need to be something more than symbolic[6] in order to gain moral legitimacy raises some complex philosophical issues. Superficially, the tribunals themselves raise the possibility that the legitimacy of trial justice may depend on something more than retributive symbolism by invoking consequentialist justifications for punishment; especially in suggesting that their legitimacy and contribution to post-conflict justice satisfy particular demands such as reconciliation.[7] Arguably, these claims are not only obscure but largely unsubstantiated, and therefore remain conjectural.

Nevertheless, the fundamental point at issue is much more difficult to answer because it ultimately depends upon the philosophical persuasion of

---

4 The complex connections between the philosophy of punishment and penal policy are explored in Duff and Garland (1994) 16–20.

5 *Prosecutor v Furundžija* (Case No. IT-95-17/1-T), Judgement, 10 December 1998, para. 290.

6 Of course, symbolic impact may be regarded as a perfectly acceptable outcome for sentencing.

7 See, further, Henham (2005b) ch. 1.

the observer. For example, retributivists in the Kantian tradition might argue that punishment is an affirmation of right, and justifiable as a categorical imperative, so long as it is inflicted as an end in itself rather than as the means to an end. On this basis, the affirmation of right through punishment and 'justice' are seen as morally equivalent in validating the use of retributive punishment to support the universal law of freedom. It may indeed be argued that the symbolism of punishment so justified lies in the fact that it expresses the sanctity of human freedom, since it clearly defines the morally justifiable parameters for penal intervention in the liberty of the individual.

Thus, it may be argued that the normative compass of the criminal process should be circumscribed by retributive ideology because it limits the extent to which individuals may be used as means. However, questions about the moral status of the criminal process remain, especially whether it has intrinsic moral worth, in the sense of not being simply means. Paul Roberts,[8] for example, has recently questioned whether criminal process, global or local, can be regarded as intrinsically valuable, in the sense that say, friendship or marriage may be, by asking the question, what is it good *for*? Roberts goes on to suggest that criminal process has no intrinsic moral worth beyond its instrumental capacity to secure good ends. What constitutes acceptable moral ends for morally significant social mechanisms such as criminal process is (and always has been) highly contested terrain.

Roberts rejects most forms of consequentialism as morally acceptable ends for criminal process on the basis that consequentialism undermines the dignity principle,[9] whilst arguing that retributive justice is an inherently valuable and morally acceptable response to crime. Nevertheless, he acknowledges that a full account of retributive justice would need to specify the conditions under which the criminal courts might exercise legitimate authority to pass judgement and impose penal censure and punishment.

Such observations raise several issues which concern the transformative potential of the trial, the most significant of which touches on the instrumentality of criminal process. It may be argued in response to Robert's assertion that the 'criminal process appears to be devoid of intrinsic moral worth' that criminal process is intrinsically good as a regulator of purposeful social intercourse. The intrinsically good moral end served by criminal process is that it prevents social anarchy in providing a means for regulating human behaviour. Certainly, such an assertion elevates criminal process beyond the level of object and instrumentality – a view endorsed by Nicola Lacey,[10] who

---

8 Roberts (2006).

9 Although retributive justice may be abused to offend the dignity principle, Roberts argues that this is merely contingent and pragmatic, rather than by design as is always the case with consequentialism. It may be countered that the impact on access to justice and rights is nevertheless the same, and that the moral acceptability of consequentialist measures depends on the utilitarian calculation that effective harm-prevention is as important as individual accountability for criminalised behaviour.

10 Lacey (1988) 173.

invokes the communitarian argument that the moral boundaries of criminal process should extend beyond the 'individuals never being used as means to social ends' argument because of the essential and intrinsic goodness for humans of a peaceful and just society.

Furthermore, whilst Roberts agrees that social relationships such as *friendship* are intrinsically good, others also remind us of the broader social dimensions of friendship in the sense of what Oderberg[11] has called 'social living'. This might include 'living in a self-governing community, or perhaps state, whose sole purpose is to promote the peaceful and harmonious coexistence of its members.' One might therefore identify as intrinsically good those structures of social life (such as criminal process) which generally 'exist *for* man, in order to enable him to flourish, and so is [are] good *for* man', as Oderberg suggests.[12]Although this line of reasoning is compatible with the view that the human capacity for self-determination and autonomy is shaped by society's capacity to reduce social conflict, it should not, as Kymlicka argues,[13] be taken as a complete negation of individual autonomy, especially the capacity of individuals to pursue those ends which they perceive as morally virtuous.

Although these arguments take us beyond the scope of this chapter, they are extremely pertinent to the present discussion. If one takes the utilitarian view that the resolution of social conflict is intrinsically good, it follows that those structures and processes which promote the maintenance of social cohesion are elemental for social life. Consequently, reducing damage to social relationships by developing social structures that promote values of reconciliation and peace becomes an underlying ideological imperative for achieving justice. Such an ideology has reciprocally beneficial individual and social functions. This is because notions of individual responsibility and accountability are developed with holistic relational conceptualisations of social life.[14] Ultimately, of course, it is a matter of moral judgement as to

---

11 Oderberg (2000).
12 *Ibid.* 43. In similar vein, Sandel criticises Rawls for ignoring the social origins of our conceptions of the good, thereby drawing attention to how the political objectives of power and hegemony threaten the perceived neutrality of individual autonomy, a theme central to Rawls's philosophy; see Rawls (1973) 433, Sandel (1982). Sandel's communitarian theory differs from the Rawlsian view of the self as logically prior to social roles and relationships, preferring instead to conceptualise self-determination as something that is intrinsically bound up with 'the politics of the common good'; see, further, Mulhall and Swift (1966) 56.
13 Kymlicka (2002) 220, 222.
14 The Zulu concept of *ubuntu* provides a useful illustration of such a context. As Louw suggests, *ubuntu* provides a spiritual foundation for African societies based on a deep understanding of humanity and its potential. It is exemplified in the maxim *umuntu ngumuntu ngabantu* ('a person is a person through other persons'), suggesting the nature of the moral balance between individual and group. Louw argues that *ubuntu* provides a distinctly African rationale for values such as compassion, warmth, understanding, caring, sharing and humanness. More broadly, it may be argued that *ubuntu*, along with other similar indigenous foundations for social morality, is rooted in the notion that it is only through others that one becomes a whole person; Louw (1988), Wilson (2001) 9.

whether or not criminal process has any intrinsic value, and a fine distinction exists between something being intrinsically constitutive of the good, and something (merely) being an instrument to good ends.

However, the need to reconcile differing perspectives and interpretations complicates the task of developing cogent links between the moral and the social when theorising the relationship between sentencing and the legitimacy of trial justice. For example, scholars such as Moore[15] and Dolinko[16] have argued for the beneficial consequences of retributive punishment, whilst Anthony Duff's[17] communicative theory of punishment argues that society's disapproval is communicated to the offender through the pronouncement of the sentence and received by serving the sentence. Punishment is therefore seen as a penance endured as a demonstration of the offender's acceptance that the crime is indeed blameworthy. Suffering allows the offender to rejoin society's moral consensus by acknowledging the state's judgement that the crime is wrong. Seen in this light, the purpose of punishment is to reconnect the offender with society's values.

Duff maintains that his theory is retributive rather than consequentialist because it relies on the notion that individuals are autonomous rational moral agents whose rehabilitation is achieved through internal reasoning and moral choice, rather than through coercion and the instrumentality of the state. However, the important issue in the present context is not whether Duff's ideas should be labelled as retributivist or consequentialist; it has much more to do with the communicative aspect of his theory, particularly the nature and origins of the moral message that is conveyed when punishment is applied through the process of sentencing, and its social significance.[18] In other words,

---

15 Moore (1993).
16 Dolinko (1997).
17 Duff believes that this reconciliation is brought about through the process of punishment itself, which induces repentance and aims to alter the moral sentiments of the offender. Thus, the idea of punishment as non-coercive and aimed to communicate to the offender the condemnation of his conduct moves beyond von Hirsch's emphasis on the censuring aspects of punishment. See Duff (1998), Duff (2001), Duff (2003). However, von Hirsch counters that, although censure provides the offender with the opportunity to make a rational moral choice to desist from crime, it cannot do so on the basis of the kind of moral repentance envisaged by Duff; von Hirsch (1999).
18 Sue Rex sought to develop Duff's communicative theory of punishment in the context of community penalties. On the basis of empirical research, she argues the case for giving community-based sanctions a central place in a sentencing framework based on a strategy that develops the communicative dimension of community penalties. This would be achieved by persuading offenders that their offences are morally unacceptable and so encourage a greater degree of social responsibility. However, in her review, Worrall expresses methodological doubts about Rex's ability to establish a closer relationship between 'high-level normative thinking and ground-level practical decision-making', and points to her failure to address the problem of implementing a communicative system of punishment that takes proper account of issues of social exclusion and legitimacy. Worrall also makes the important point that a communicative approach to sentencing based on rational moral choice and 'legitimate' expectations is lacking through its failure to account for the role of sentiment and emotion. Consequently, the

Duff focuses on something which has a great deal of relevance to our discussion about the legitimacy of trial justice: how are the processes and outcomes of sentencing perceived and interpreted by others, particularly offenders, victims and the 'community' where the 'criminality' occurred.[19]

There are clearly conceptual difficulties in accommodating philosophical insights about the morally educative function of punishment into sociological accounts of the social reality of sentencing. Nevertheless, appreciating the communicative role of punishment, whether achieved through censure, penance or more restorative forms of justice, is crucial for understanding the legitimacy attached to sentencing in different contexts. Therefore, introducing a more normative perspective such as Duff's into sociological accounts helps us to speculate more effectively about the ways in which moral questions about punishment impact upon social life.

In particular, such insights can help us comprehend the relationship between perceptions of justice and its social reality. As has been argued, this link is vital for appreciating the role of legitimacy, and especially the idea that 'legitimate' trial justice depends upon a sharing of moral values about the justifications for punishment, and its implementation. The argument may be extended to suggest that such a sharing of values is necessary for penal legitimacy to exist as feature of civil society.[20] By accepting the beneficial consequences of penal legitimacy as sustaining social cohesion, one should be able to argue for an ideology that promotes it. The achievement of this aspiration of course depends on social reality.

The nature of the relationship between morality and justice is by no means a straightforward issue. Different philosophical approaches become important from an empirical perspective if we begin to think about describing the relationship between moral and social factors in the everyday practice of sentencing. Although there are clear links between moral philosophy and the adoption of certain sociological methods, such as phenomenology, philosophical discourse does not describe social reality. As Hudson points out,[21] justice in Kantian terms is chiefly concerned with giving expression to rationality and will, whilst Rawls's principles of social justice envisage a notionally egalitarian society, ignoring social inequality and similar constraints on the exercise of free will.

However, where scholars have considered the role of emotion and sentiment in shaping morality, such debates are directly relevant to the idea of developing more normative approaches to understanding penal legitimacy. Hume's argument that moral distinctions are founded on sentiment, and

---

relationship between penal communication and its perception as fulfilling 'legitimate' expectations will never be certain, but always contingent upon moral influences that are fluid and subjectively contingent; see Rex (2004), Rex (2005), Worrall (2006).

19 As Duff and Garland (1994) 15 suggest, the nature of moral communication or education is essentially a political issue.

20 That is, beyond the idea of legitimacy remaining a purely subjective attribution.

21 Hudson (2003a) ch. 1.

Mackie's[22] moral subjectivist view that reason and sentiment cannot be conceived as objective reality, despite the fact that social considerations may play a part in shaping them,[23] provide pertinent examples.

To get beyond the notion that there are no objectively verifiable moral truths is a perquisite for generalising about the social reality of sentencing and its effects. Recognising that moral objectivity may simply be a matter of intuitiveness about right or wrong at least raises the possibility of some form of generalisation. However, the idea that 'truth' is somehow recognisable externally, or that we can generalise in any meaningful way about its existence as intuition is problematic. This is particularly so when thinking about the notion that morality might be shared in contexts of social relations.

Russell[24] suggests that individual emotions and senses reflect sensory information which has an external 'objective' existence. Nevertheless, this is not the same thing as being able to explain and generalise about subjectively held feelings and emotions. Such arguments highlight the contentiousness of the proposition that there is an identifiable 'shared morality', or that shared moral principles can somehow be identified. However, their relevance to the present discussion cannot be overstressed, not merely from a philosophical perspective,[25] but because they draw attention to some crucial yet unresolved questions of social science epistemology and methodology concerning our ability to identify and explain the social significance of sensory information.

It is beyond the scope of this book to evaluate the implications for sentencing of competing philosophical arguments. Rather, the present purpose is to highlight the significance of these debates for understanding penal legitimacy and its relationship to sentencing as a form of social reality. As suggested, the ability to verify actions and reactions and to speculate about their normative[26] significance as reflective of particular values depends upon one's position on a number of complex, and possibly irreconcilable, philosophical issues.

It may be argued that to move forward requires acceptance of the possibility of moral objectivism and the adoption of an ethical stance that is tolerant of instrumentalism; that is to say, that actions informed by values have consequences which are to some degree foreseeable, and observable, as a matter of empirical fact.[27] For present purposes, the latter proposition implies that it may be possible to make objectively verifiable generalisations about the

22 Mackie (1982).
23 For Mackie, the moral relativity of different cultures is evidence supporting subjectivism.
24 Russell (1914) Lecture III, 70.
25 For further discussion, see Harman (1999). For an instrumental reading of value judgments readers are referred to the moral pragmatism of John Dewey; see, Hickman and Alexander (eds) (1998).
26 Again, it is important to emphasise that the expression 'normative' is being used here in a sociological sense as something that influences or guides action.
27 See Duff and Garland (1994) 21. Argument may, of course, persist as to the appropriate methodology.

impact of social experience on value judgments, such as the perceived legitimacy of trial outcomes, and, most importantly, the extent to which sentiments
and emotions interact with such external stimuli.[28]

As suggested earlier, a number of deficiencies in social theory become
apparent as a result of accepting this proposition. More specifically, sociological
approaches are deficient in providing convincing accounts of the relationship
between subjective experience and objectively verifiable facts. Interpretative
theories such as phenomenology,[29] and more recent deconstructionist approaches like semiotics,[30] are notoriously difficult to operationalise, producing
descriptively rich but frequently ungeneralisable conclusions. For example, the
study by Rogers and Erez of cultural interpretations of 'objectivity' in sentencing
among legal professionals in South Australia is particularly instructive in this
respect. The authors found it necessary to deconstruct this concept because
legal practitioners appeared to have differing perceptions about whether certain
actions associated with the operation of a victim impact statement scheme
were 'objective' or 'subjective'. The study therefore aimed to 'decode' symbolic
references ascribed to these linguistic, social and relational constructs of
'objectivity' by analysing the subjective experiences of legal professionals and
their relationship to this construct. Hence, the study appears to suggest ways
in which the objectivity of process is constructed subjectively.

Similarly, Casanovas[31] further narrowed the interpretative vision by suggesting
that reconstructing the 'reality' of the courtroom is only possible at the micro-
situational level, since this avoids distorting the relationship between cognition
and action. Consequently, we are left with the conclusion that existing interpretative approaches produce 'descriptions' of social life that are not only
context-specific but extremely limited in their capacity to explain the normative
significance of processes such as sentencing and relating them convincingly to
sociological accounts. Therefore, it seems reasonable to conclude that the
extent to which it is possible to generalise sociologically about the significance
of values and ethics in sentencing will always be hindered by our incapacity to
describe and explain human feelings and emotions and relate them to so-called
observable 'facts'.

The failure of social theory to adequately reflect the impact of morality in
explanations of sentencing is a matter of some conjecture. Whilst Durkheim's
concept of moral individualism,[32] discussed in the previous chapter, suggests

---

28 This epistemological assumption underpins much social psychological research into the fear of
    crime; see, for example, Jackson (2004), Jackson (2005).
29 Hogarth's study of Canadian magistrates remains the best example in sentencing research;
    Hogarth (1971).
30 Rogers and Erez (1999).
31 Casanovas (1999).
32 See Cotterrell (1999) ch. 7. These ideas were developed from Durkheim's earlier work in *The
    Division of Labour*, which provided a functionalist analysis of the relationship between morality
    and the conditions necessary for social life. Such theorising retains limited empirical credibility

a possible way forward, the problem remains of how to identify the value system of individualism in terms of a shared moral culture existing at either the global or local level, and which manifests itself in regulatory structures such as those associated with punishment and sentencing.[33] Despite these conceptual difficulties, the notion of a moral imperative linked instrumentally to the conditions necessary for social life is an attractive one, suggesting the possibility of a meaningful sociological explanation of the impact of shared moral values.

The weaknesses in Durkheim's sociological theorising are well-documented.[34] Although he theorises the role of social morality in shaping penal ideology, his conclusions do not resonate with the value-pluralism of post-modern societies. Furthermore, Durkheim avoids engaging with philosophical arguments, such as those concerning deontological objections to consequentialism.[35] Significantly, in developing his notion of moral individualism, Durkheim adopts a pragmatic view of the instrumental capacity of moral values; one that envisages a reciprocal relationship between social solidarity and morality. Arguably, Durkheim's most important contribution to this debate is the notion that sociological inquiry can and should be utilised to explain the nature of shared morality in any particular society, presuming such conditions exist empirically.[36] Cotterrell summarises this idea as follows:

> It is for sociology to observe morals as social facts and to interpret moral experience to show how it relates to social development. Sociology, for Durkheim, is the key to a positive science of morality. It threatens to displace philosophy in so far as the latter fails to conduct and interpret the empirical social inquiries without which the meaning of moral prescriptions cannot be understood.[37]

This book adopts a similar approach, embracing the notion that social theory and methods are capable of observing morality from a social perspective and thereby generalising successfully about the impact of morality on social life. However, it also argues for an interdisciplinary approach whose epistemological principles admit the possibility of moral objectivism and the validity of sociological descriptions of moral experience. Notwithstanding that such generalisations may be limited by sociology's incapacity to proceed beyond its own 'objective' accounts of subjectivity, it is nevertheless possible to speculate from these about the impact of morality on social life,

---

in the pluralistic and largely secular societies of the early twenty-first century and their rapid globalisation. The notion of social solidarity being based on a unified morality has long since evaporated. However, the argument that social relations and the conditions necessary to sustain social life affect the sharing of moral views in pluralistic contexts remains persuasive.

33 Durkheim's account does not address the consequences for social theory of moral subjectivism.
34 Most notable are Durkheim's failure to theorise power and hegemonic causes of social inequality.
35 Such arguments are simply not addressed by Durkheim.
36 Cotterrell (1999) 57.
37 *Ibid.*

particularly the relationship between the social fact of sentencing and its perceived legitimacy as moral experience.

In that sense, therefore, an approach that merely equates penal legitimacy with the symbolism of punishment is misplaced. Sociological inquiry into the attitudes and perceptions that validate penal measures is clearly possible. However, more significant is the fact that social inquiry can extend beyond mere description of punishment's symbolic effects to produce theorised and methodologically valid accounts of how they impact on social life as shared moral experiences.

A functionalist account of legitimacy such as Durkheim's might therefore suggest that social cohesion is largely the function of a shared morality, and that a reciprocal relationship persists between these two variables. However, this still omits a more sophisticated conceptualisation of the relationship between human agency and structure, including particularly the impact of hegemonic variables, to satisfy the requirements of a more holistic explanatory theory.

As an exercise in comparative sociology such theorising needs to be capable of engaging with different levels of social context and conceptual abstraction in order to facilitate the development of appropriate paradigms for comparative contextual analysis.[38] It should therefore be possible to speculate more convincingly about the relationship between morality and the perceived legitimacy of punishment and sentencing from such a theoretical perspective. This in turn may lead to new insights about the significance of trial justice as a form of symbolism and an expression of power.

Values, norms and legitimacy

The problem of exceeding the rhetoric and symbolism of punishment may be due to some structural or procedural deficiency.[39] More fundamentally, however, it often conceals a more deep-seated and intractable difficulty which goes to the core of criminal justice governance; namely, a lack of connection between the ideology which informs punishment and the perceived legitimacy of its normative expression in the form of sentencing outcomes.[40] This problem is exacerbated in more complex, pluralistic societies where the ideological and physical resources of criminal justice are monopolised by power elites as part of the apparatus of control through the exclusion and stigmatisation of individuals or groups which threaten their hegemony. As Garland implies,[41] these shifts in governance over time makes the task of understanding different punishment rationales and studying the relationship between values,

---

38 As discussed in the preceding chapter.
39 Such as weak sentencing guidance or poor judicial education.
40 This is certainly arguable in the case of the ICTY and ICTR; see, further, Henham (2007a). The era of the collapse of the rehabilitative ideal in the United States provides a local example of such disjunction.
41 Garland (1990).

norms and the legitimacy of trial justice in different contexts extremely complex.

This complexity is further magnified where hegemonic ideologies deliberately obfuscate conventional understandings of criminality and punishment within state or regional contexts, as occurred in the Balkans and Rwanda.[42] Such effects often mirror a profound divergence in the morality which informs penal ideology and criminalises particular actions, and may precipitate a realignment of forms of political and criminal justice governance. This shift may then be projected onto existing paradigms of criminal justice at the global and local level, distorting and magnifying orthodox conceptualisations of governance. Findlay describes this effect in the context of the so-called 'war on terror':

> The dominant hegemony in this climate of international terrorism ... has significantly transferred militaristic intervention at least in part to the jurisdiction of international criminal justice.[43]

Consequently, concepts of risk and security, predominant concerns of post-modern penal ideology, are transformed by the deliberate merging of the political imperatives of the 'war on terror' with those of conventional criminal justice concerns. Thus, the hegemony of western political ideology may justify significant incursions into the civil liberties of citizens in areas of criminal justice which have little, if anything, to do with the perceived threat to security of global terrorism.[44] In this way political hegemony may categorise those exposed to diminished forms of due process in the name of criminal justice,[45] and aim to stigmatise and exclude those whom it perceives as a threat.

The tendency for political ideologies to deliberately encourage citizens to 'misrecognise their enemy' is not new,[46] nor is it unusual for criminal justice to be used duplicitously in order to exclude or oppress certain minorities for reasons of hegemony. Mathiesen's[47] seminal conceptualisation of the 'power-draining' function of prison in advanced capitalist societies may be utilised more generally to illustrate this particular tendency. For example, at the global level, political hegemony might be directed against state leaders, or outsiders, who threaten political or economic objectives. Arguments may be deployed to justify military intervention or provide aid for reasons which

---

42 This failure to engage with local morality is accentuated by internationalised forms of justice; see Cockayne (2005).
43 Findlay (2008).
44 Typically, these take the form of increased surveillance, militarised forms of policing, random identity checks and detention without trial.
45 See, further, Zedner (2005).
46 See Hall *et al.* (1978) in the English context.
47 Mathiesen (1990).

support democracy,[48] when the pretext is that of gaining control of economic resources. Equally, at the local level, utilising imprisonment to 'divert' attention from greater social harms perpetrated by those in control is not uncommon; for example, those perceived as socially 'dangerous', or a 'threat' to the prevailing social order, may be subjected to selective forms of incapacitation. In terms of criminal justice governance, such practices may be rhetorically justified for reasons of risk or security,[49] and therefore portrayed as morally just,[50] because they help to sustain democratic principles and preserve the freedom of the individual under the law.

Such strategies distort the moral foundations of criminal justice governance, stigmatise the morality of those whose actions or tendencies are condemned, and assert particularised forms of moral dominion as governance. As Armstrong and McAra point out,[51] the distorted logic of risk assessment is translated into disproportionate precautionary action against powerless minorities without adequate predictive evidence. A similar effect in the case of international criminal justice is described by Ewald,[52] where the 'approval' of risk as posing a 'relevant threat' may depend on it qualifying as a perceived threat to hegemonic interests. Seen in this light, it may be argued that the structures of criminal justice are manipulated to selectively appropriate particular moralities in order to accommodate perceived threats to political hegemony. In this way, for example, the morality of the 'victim' has been appropriated to broaden the reach of criminal justice as a response to politically defined threats, such as terrorism. As Simon puts it:

> ... crime victims emerged as idealized citizens whom lawmakers could invoke to expand governmental powers freely without serious political risk, as long as they responded to the twin calls for safety and vengeance that victims are idealised as making.[53]

The blurring of the dimensions of risk and security, and their moral appropriation by political elites is effected through their ability to continually redefine those individuals and contexts requiring precautionary legislation. The introduction of Control Orders in England and Wales under the Prevention of Terrorism Act 2005 is a case in point.[54] Such erosions of civil liberty

---

48 The concept of 'democracy' itself may be perceived as potentially hegemonic by some moral codes because it subverts religious orthodoxy.
49 For useful illustration of approaches to dangerousness and issues of risk and governance, see Brown and Pratt (2000).
50 See Morris (1994).
51 Armstrong and McAra (2006) 27.
52 Ewald (2006) 171, citing Hardt and Negri (2000).
53 Simon (2007) 268.
54 As suggested earlier, Control Orders subject terror suspects to tight restrictions on their activities. Individuals considered to pose the most serious risk to national security can

effected by extending the reach of criminal justice governance confuse the morality of social conflict and war with that of 'ordinary' crime. For those minority groups who are disproportionately subject to such laws, they may precipitate further alienation without renewed attempts to rationalise and redefine the contexts for sharing morality within the pluralistic state. As Lea and Young[55] argue, these effects may spiral towards militaristic policing and increased social exclusion as those who are oppressed gradually withdraw moral legitimacy from the organs of state and the structures of governance.

Another issue frequently overlooked in current theorising about the effects of globalisation on criminal justice governance is the fact that changes in the morality of punishment and the perceived legitimacy of sentencing have occurred throughout history, and the global significance of such changes has paralleled the spread of economic and political hegemony.[56] Since morality and its relationship to punishment is in a constant state of flux, purely descriptive, empirical accounts of apparent paradoxes in criminal justice governance provide inadequate understandings of the forces that actually drive these changes. A useful example is the ongoing paradox of the 'colonisation' of local and global forms of criminal justice by the ideology and praxis of restorative justice, which originates from indigenous societies.[57] As noted, the analysis of such trends requires a deep understanding of the morality of indigenous forms of justice and its social origins.

Similarly, the fluid and reflexive nature of criminal justice as representing changing values for governance over time is evident in the English transition from the Bloody Code of the late eighteenth and early nineteenth centuries to the penal liberalism of the Gladstone Committee in 1895.[58] The reasons for this are complex,[59] but essentially reflect changing hegemonies and views about the purposes of punishment and the causes of crime[60] in an era of rapid industrialisation and increasing social mobility. Consequently, the history of incarceration in England reflects a broad spectrum of values and justifications for dealing with the infringement of socially approved norms over time.[61] Clearly, the reasons why certain behaviours are criminalised, and how this occurs, vary according to context and interpretative perspective, but for all of them the role of hegemony is a fundamental determining factor.

---

be ordered to observe a curfew, and a residential requirement may be imposed. Suspects can be electronically tagged, face visiting restrictions, be banned from accessing the internet, and face restrictions on their place of religious worship. They can also be ordered to surrender their passports and report daily to a monitoring company or to the police.

55 Lea and Young (1984).
56 See Garland (1990).
57 For further detail, see Johnstone (2002).
58 As Emsley points out, unlike much of Europe, such liberalism did not extend to the abolition of the death penalty, or the use of corporal punishment; Emsley (1996).
59 See, further, Garland (1985) ch. 1.
60 Ewald (2008).
61 See, generally, Radzinowicz and Hood (1990).

Therefore, the criminalisation of certain behaviours may or may not be regarded as morally appropriate at certain times in history, depending on whether the behaviours in question threaten particular hegemonic paradigms for governance.[62]

The relationship between the organs of state and the role of morality in criminal justice are crucially important for governance. Loader[63] has recently considered the significance of shifts in this relationship in England during the twentieth century. He describes how the era of 'moral paternalism' in criminal justice, when it was generally accepted that the establishment was invested with the capacity to 'do the right thing', was gradually replaced by a more inclusive, political approach.[64] This in turn became increasingly driven by a form of punitive and reactive penal populism during the 1990s. An important reason for the eventual demise of 'moral paternalism' was the inability of the establishment to control public feeling and emotion about crime and punishment once, as Loader puts it,[65] 'the genie ... ha(d) been let out of the bottle'. This had a corrosive effect on the perception that the courts and the judiciary, in particular, had the capacity to reflect public sentiment.[66] The paradox of increased public expectation, and a corresponding failure on the part of the institutions of liberal democracy to respond effectively to these demands, suggests to Loader[67] a crisis of legitimacy in criminal justice, and the need for a political ideology capable of enhancing social solidarity.

More generally, Loader's analysis points to the increasingly tenuous moral foundations of the post-modern or neo-liberal state, and the inability of its ideology and structures to fully grasp and respond to the pluralistic demands for justice of its citizens. The state's response has prompted such phenomena as the rise of the 'crime victim', the focus on 'territorialising' communities, and the move towards more 'collective forms of responsibility'. However, some commentators, Loader included,[68] have taken issue with the thesis that the schism between liberalism and (post) modernism is catastrophic for criminal justice and penality, suggesting instead that there are signs of continuity and positive adaptation,[69] as well as transformation.[70]

Nonetheless, a significant gap remains between the social reality of criminal justice and its public perception, and it is this lack of credibility which goes to the root of governance. A recent and continuing example of this at the local

---

62 Loader (2006).
63 *Ibid*, 568.
64 *Ibid.* 575.
65 *Ibid.* 582.
66 See Roberts and Hough (2005) 72.
67 Loader (2006) 582.
68 Loader and Sparks (2004).
69 An example is the widespread use of risk assessment to create more inclusive and relevant correctional programmes.
70 For a review of the arguments, see Hutchinson (2006).

level concerns the issue of overcrowding in English prisons.[71] This crisis, which has been ongoing since the late 1970s,[72] has mirrored major shifts in the perceived legitimacy of criminal justice, caused by such factors as the demise of 'moral paternalism', the increased politicisation of criminal justice, and the increasing gap between citizens' expectations and the state's response, resulting in the progressive alienation of citizens from the institutions and moral ideology they perceive criminal justice to represent. As argued in chapter 1, the role of the judiciary as an organ of the state has more recently come under intense scrutiny, and perhaps more significantly, its legitimacy as a fundamental element of criminal justice governance has been seriously questioned. In particular, the foundations of judicial discretionary power have been gradually eroded by the executive through increased legislative control of the sentencing function.

A more emotive and difficult question is whether, in matters of punishment and sentencing, the judiciary is perceived as the last bastion of the liberal state or as a mere blinkered defender of the rule of law. Such pointed observations highlight current concerns about the nature of state responsibility to citizens for criminal justice and the sentencing role of the judiciary within that framework. Arguably, the issue of prison overcrowding is evidence of a more general failure on the part of the state in fulfilling its moral responsibility to protect its citizens. Arguments supporting the bifurcation of penal policy, and the need to strengthen the public perception of community penalties as providing suitable alternatives to imprisonment, have been virtually continuous since the White Paper that preceded the Criminal Justice Act of 1991, yet it seems that all such initiatives have failed to convince the public.[73] Conversely, although public attitudes appear to support the principle of just deserts and the concept of protective sentencing for dangerous offenders,[74] there appears to be a lack of information generally about the circumstances in which such sentences may be imposed and the exact nature of the available penalties. When examining the gap between judicial practice and public sentencing preferences,[75] it is significant that this narrows when information

---

71 For detailed analysis, see Cavadino and Dignan (2002) ch. 6. For coverage of recent exchanges between the judiciary and the executive on this issue, see BBC News (2007); Judiciary of England and Wales 'Statement from the Lord Chief Justice: Sentencing and Prisons' 27 January 2007 at http://www.judiciary.gov.uk/publications_media/general/sentencing_prison.htm (accessed 2007); *The Times* 'Prison more Punitive with Overcrowding' 16 February 2007; *Rv Seed and Stark* [2007] EWCA Crim 254; BBC News (2007b); and see http://www.judiciary.gov. uk/docs/speeches/lcj08032007.pdf (accessed 2007) for the full text of the Lord Chief Justice's speech at the University of Birmingham on 7 March 2007.

72 The late Merlyn Rees, then Home Secretary, instigated the first major inquiry into the crisis in 1979.

73 See Roberts and Hough (2005) 82. Significantly, sentences such as community service are perceived as the most popular because of their emphasis on compensation and reparation, with probation the least popular; the use of community sentences generally being seen as less appropriate for more serious offenders and those with previous convictions; *ibid*, 83.

74 Roberts and Hough (2005) 78.

75 *Ibid.*

increases, as do public perceptions about the suitability of community sentences.[76] These findings are consistent with those reporting limited public knowledge about the courts and the functions of the court system.[77] Given that public perceptions of appropriate punishment and court sentencing practice generally coincide, but differences increase as crime seriousness decreases, it appears that increased information may be significant in raising public confidence about community sentences.

Nevertheless, despite the enormous increase of the last ten to fifteen years in the levels of information available about sentencing and its justifications, the public's perception of the judiciary is that they are 'out of touch' with the views ordinary people hold about crime and punishment,[78] whilst popular 'trust' in politicians has correspondingly declined dramatically during the same period.[79] As Garland explains,[80] the politically expedient short-term reactive 'solutions' that have characterised the penal populism of late post-modernity have done little to address the social causes of crime; the politics of social democracy of the mid-twentieth century has been replaced by a politics of security and economics that is disconnected from issues of social justice and reconstruction.

As the organ of state charged with the implementation of penal policy, the judiciary is caught in the middle of a widening credibility gap. Although the public appear to believe in the impartiality and integrity of the judiciary, there has been a general, but gradually diminishing, belief that sentencing levels are too low,[81] which, added to the perception that judges do not represent the views of the communities they serve, exacerbates the apparent detachment of the judiciary from the everyday experience of crime and the morality of punishment. Public ignorance about established sentencing policy which, until recently, took no account of matters such as overcrowding and early release when fixing the appropriate penalty, has compounded this sense of moral detachment. If this is added to the judiciary's often palpable resentment at the gradual erosion of its discretionary power in sentencing and the increasing bureaucratisation of the judicial role, its apparently over-defensive posturing over the prison overcrowding issue is perhaps understandable. Arguably, this situation has arisen because the judiciary finds itself unsure of its governance role. It has not lost sight of the principle that judicial independence is a matter of constitutional balance. However, the exact nature of the judiciary's role in maintaining that balance has too frequently been obscured by the exigencies of political pragmatism.

These events also demonstrate how the recent demise of criminal justice governance tends to reflect back on the organs of state, exposing rifts and

---

76 *Ibid.* 83.
77 *Ibid.* 70.
78 *Ibid.* 73.
79 See, for example, BBC News (2005), Ipsos MORI (2003).
80 Garland (2001) 199.
81 Roberts and Hough (2005) 77.

forging allegiances – the impression being given that ideological and strategic rifts in penal policy are exploited purely for reasons of power. All this contributes to negative public perception and a breakdown of trust.

This downward spiral also suggests (as argued in chapter 1) that the judiciary (like other state organs) is increasingly less able to assert a convincing connection between its perceived role as defender of the rule of law and the legitimacy of that law for citizens. In terms of punishment and sentencing, this weakness undermines the judiciary's capacity to punish in ways which may be perceived as morally relevant for different constituencies seeking justice.

Legitimacy and moral consensus

The final section of this chapter explores the relationship between values, norms and the legitimacy of trial justice in comparative contexts through some specific case studies, both global and local. Emphasis is placed on analysing this issue from a 'relational' or 'communitarian' perspective. Accordingly, the purpose of each case study is to examine the extent to which justifications for punishment and sentencing practice can be said to correspond to an identifiable shared morality and to speculate about the origins and significance of this for the perceived legitimacy of trial justice. The analysis is approached from the perspective of the paradigm for conceptualising the legitimacy of trial justice elaborated in Figure 2.1. Consequently, it seeks to explain how far sentencing outcomes tend to reinforce trial ideology rather than engage with communitarian moralities of justice.

Deconstructing penal justifications

An examination of some of the philosophical justifications for sentence provided by the ICTY illustrates why it is necessary to develop such rationalisations with a firm commitment to ground rationality in context.[82] It also suggests the need for punishment rationales to be developed within a more holistic paradigm which connects global and local aspirations for justice in the aftermath of war and social conflict. The need for such an inclusive sentencing paradigm is evidenced by the fact that consequentialist rationales in the ICTY have remained largely undeveloped and disconnected from the contexts in which they are meant to have effect.

An illustration is provided by the tribunal's curious interpretation of the concept of rehabilitation. Part of this persisting obfuscation is caused by a failure to engage with notions of individual and collective rehabilitation as fundamentally interrelated concepts. Orthodox post-modern conceptions of rehabilitation have developed in such a way that the underlying rationales for rehabilitation are associated more with crime reduction and preventative strategies than with the liberal-modernist agenda of providing 'curative', or

---

82 See Henham (2005b).

'healing' disposals. This tendency reflects a reconfiguration of the welfare principle within the post-modern context, and does not necessarily indicate, as Hutchinson suggests,[83] the abandonment of welfare ideology.

It is difficult to deduce any such underlying morality for the use of rehabilitation as a penal justification in the sentencing judgments of the ICTY, or, indeed, evidence of any reasoning which might lead to it. For example, the ICTY Trial Chamber in *Delalić*[84] described the objective of rehabilitation in the following terms:

> The factor of rehabilitation considers *the circumstances of reintegrating* the guilty accused into society ... so that they can become useful members of it and enable them to lead normal and productive lives upon their release from imprisonment [emphasis added].

In the Appeals Chamber,[85] the Tribunal, whilst acknowledging its significance, reaffirmed its belief that rehabilitation could not 'play a *predominant* role' in the decision-making process,[86] and was clearly subordinate to deterrence and retribution as the main purposes of sentencing in the *ad hoc* tribunals. In their deliberations, the Appeals Chamber went on to refer to the primacy accorded to rehabilitation in many national jurisdictions and certain international and human rights instruments, such as the International Covenant on Civil and Political Rights.[87] Unfortunately, the ICTY has failed to develop the notion of rehabilitation in the wider transitional justice context in terms of its potential for changing perspectives of individual and collective responsibility and accountability, especially through the notion of community reintegration, or to suggest how this might transform the guilty into 'useful' members of society.[88]

Mathiesen[89] makes an important point regarding the relative moral influence of rehabilitative ideology within prisons, which has some relevance in this context – especially his suggestion that the rationality of such ideology is maintained to fulfil the demands of system interests. Similar observations seem equally pertinent to describe how the concept of rehabilitation is characterised as an aspect of international penality, particularly since those few references which have been made to it appear to be more rhetorical than substantive. This gives a

---

83 Hutchinson (2006).
84 *Prosecutor v Delalić et al.* (Case No. IT-96-21-T), Judgement, 16 November 1998, para. 1233, (the '*Čelebić i*' case).
85 *Prosecutor v Delalić* (Case No. IT-96-21), Appeals Judgement, 20 February 2001, para. 806.
86 *Ibid.* (emphasis in original); ' ... although rehabilitation (in accordance with international human rights standards) should be considered as a relevant factor, it is not one which should be given undue weight.'
87 Article 10 (3) of the ICCPR states: 'The penitentiary system shall comprise treatment of prisoners the essential aim of which shall be their reformation and social rehabilitation.'
88 See comments by Drumbl (2007a) 149. Some support for rehabilitation, especially for younger offenders, is also provided in *Prosecutor v Furundžija* (see note 5 above), para 291.
89 Mathiesen (1990) 29.

misleading impression that the rationality of rehabilitation is self-evident and that rehabilitative justice is intended to be merely symbolic.

Certainly, such an interpretation is supported by the ICTY Trial Chamber's comments in the *Furundžija* case,[90] where the ideology and scope of rehabilitation was considered only within the context of notions of retributive and deterrent justice. This is particularly ironic in that Beccaria, whose philosophical approach to punishment was invoked by the Trial Chamber,[91] failed to explore the relationship between the consequences of punishment and the social causes of crime; something that is crucial to contemporary notions of rehabilitation, and any coherent argument for relational justice. This failure to exploit the nexus between notions of individual and social rehabilitation within a more far-reaching and inclusive paradigm for punishment which recognises the crucial link between process and outcome is significant. More broadly, it illustrates perfectly why the political realities that determine the relationship between rationalisations supporting rehabilitation and those supporting the institutions of hegemonic power cannot be ignored.[92]

The current limited conceptualisations afforded by international criminal tribunals for rehabilitative and restorative justice are undoubtedly circumscribed by their adherence to a traditional retributive model.[93] To progress beyond this penal limitation would require a philosophical reorientation which favours the moral utility of rehabilitative goals aimed at achieving greater social reintegration, and the adoption of a more relational model for justice delivery that empowers victims and communities.[94] The latter, however, would be largely dependant upon ideological as well as structural change,[95] since the criminal process[96] is seen by some scholars as an inappropriate locus for re-integrative ceremonies and popular forms of justice.[97]

---

90 *Furundžija* (see note 5 above), para 290, 'The Trial Chamber is further guided in its determination of sentence by the principle proclaimed as early as in 1764 by Cesare Beccaria: "punishment should not be harsh, but must be inevitable … "' (para. 291); 'Finally, none of the above should be taken to detract from the Trial Chamber's support for rehabilitative programmes in which the accused may participate while serving his sentence; the Trial Chamber is especially mindful of the age of the accused in this case' (footnote 285). As Beccaria put it, 'one of the greatest brakes on crime is not the cruelty of the punishment but its infallibility, and, consequently, the vigilance of judges' (Beccaria C *Dei delitti e delle pene* (1766 ed., para. XXVII, Venturi (ed.), 1965, 59)).

91 See, further, Radzinowicz (1966).

92 As exemplified by Article 33 of the SFRY Criminal Code, which includes the following as two of its three reasons for the imposition of sentence:
   (1) preventing the offender from committing criminal acts *and his rehabilitation*; …
   (3) strengthening the moral fibre of a socialist self-managing society and influence *on the development of the citizens' social responsibility and discipline*' [emphasis added].

93 Dignan and Cavadino (1996).

94 *Ibid.* 156.

95 See Findlay and Henham (2005).

96 Whether adversarial, inquisitorial or hybridised.

97 Zedner, for example, suggests that prevailing notions of reparative justice and retribution tend to 'ignore the structural imperatives of deprivation and disadvantage under which many offenders

Evidently, this kind of fundamental change depends on what is feasible as a matter of political reality. It must be recognised that for any new penal ideology to inform criminal justice in a socially diverse and morally pluralistic society will always demand the exercise of hegemonic power. From the perspective of developing notions of relational justice, the important issue is how power is shared; especially through recognising those values and interests deemed necessary for any pluralistic community to exist. The extent to which hegemony fosters social conflict rather social cohesion will always reflect the extent to which the democratic process accurately represents the 'real' interests of communities and social groups.

The morality of procedural justice

As the work of Tyler and others illustrates,[98] procedural justice may be more important than distributive justice in determining individual perceptions of the overall fairness of regulatory regimes. More specifically, trust and the ability to exercise some control over process emerge as particularly significant variables in perceptions of the legitimacy of international trial process and its sentencing outcomes. For example, the practice of plea bargaining has spawned a vast, often critical, literature in common law jurisdictions, and the almost universal approval which has greeted its adoption by the ICTY has provoked some trenchant criticism.[99] As the following discussion illustrates, the way in which procedural justice serves broader ideological goals, and the nature of those goals, is crucial to its legitimacy, especially in terms of whether it is perceived as reflecting hegemonic morality, or, alternatively, a more socially inclusive mandate that effectively links the outcomes of trials to communitarian needs.

The case of *Prosecutor v Plavšić*, heard before the ICTY Trial Chamber in September 2003,[100] provides an excellent illustration of the moral ambiguity associated with procedural mechanisms such as plea bargaining within the retributive justice context of international criminal trials. Mrs Plavšić, who was 72 years old at the date of her trial, had at one time been a distinguished academic. She entered politics in 1990, becoming acting co-President of the Serbian Republic of Bosnia and Herzegovina and, ultimately a member of the Presidencies of Republika Srpska. It was established that the Bosnian Serb leadership, including Mrs Plavšić, had 'disregarded reports of widespread

---

act', whilst more developed conceptualisations of reparative justice might be capable of addressing communitarian ideals of social justice. Zedner advocates a vision of reparative justice predicated on the utility of all criminal justice practices sharing responsibility for social inclusion and control and the equal distribution and enforcement of rights; Zedner (1994) 226, 250.

98 See, for example, Lind and Tyler (1988), Makkai and Braithwaite (1996).
99 Henham and Drumbl (2005), Henham (2005).
100 *Prosecutor v Plavšić* (Case No. IT-00-30&40/1-S), Trial Chamber, Judgement, 27 February 2003. The implications of the Plavšić case for plea bargaining in international criminal trials are considered further in Scharf (2004).

ethnic cleansing and publicly rationalised and justified it'.[101] The original indictment contained counts alleging genocide, complicity in genocide and the following crimes against humanity: persecutions, extermination and killing, deportation and inhumane acts. Although she had initially pleaded not guilty to all counts at her first appearance before the Trial Chamber in January 2001, she subsequently entered a guilty plea to count 3 (persecutions, a crime against humanity) in October 2002. This plea was contained in a plea agreement made in September 2002,[102] whereby the Prosecutor agreed to move to dismiss the remaining counts on the indictment following the accused's guilty plea. Accordingly, such counts were dismissed in December 2002.

Mrs Plavšić filed a statement in support of her motion for a change of plea at the same time as a written factual basis describing the crime to which she pleaded guilty and her involvement in it. In the former, she accepted responsibility and expressed remorse, inviting others to 'examine themselves and their own conduct.'[103] Significantly, she accepted responsibility as a leader for the grave crimes committed by others, whatever might have been their allegiance during the conflict:

> To achieve any reconciliation or lasting peace in BH, serious violations of humanitarian law during the war must be acknowledged by those who bear responsibility – regardless of their ethnic group. This acknowledgement is an essential first step.[104]

The Trial Chamber was particularly impressed by the testimony of Dr Alex Boraine[105] who suggested that, given Mrs Plavšić's prominence and symbolism as a Serb nationalist and political leader, her apology and apparently full, genuine and voluntary expressions of remorse were highly significant indicators

---

101 *Ibid.* para. 18.
102 The plea agreement was made pursuant to Rule 62 *bis* of the ICTY Rules of Procedure and Evidence which provides:

> If an accused pleads guilty in accordance with Rule 62 (vi), or requests to change his or her plea to guilty and the Trial Chamber is satisfied that:

> (i)   the guilty plea has been made voluntarily;
> (ii) the guilty plea is informed;
> (iii) the guilty plea is not equivocal; and
> (iv) there is a sufficient factual basis for the crime and the accused's participation in it, either on the basis of independent indicia or on lack of any material disagreement between the parties about the facts of the case,

> the Trial Chamber may enter a finding of guilt and instruct the Registrar to set a date for the sentencing hearing.

103 *Prosecutor v Aleksovski* (Case No. IT-95-14/1), Judgement, 24 March 2000, para. 182.
104 *Ibid.*
105 Former Deputy Chairperson of the South African Truth and Reconciliation Commission and founding President of the International Centre for Transnational Justice.

for reconciliation. Recognition of the pain and suffering experienced was particularly significant in providing a degree of closure for victims and their families.

The ICTY Trial Chamber in *Plavšić*[106] concluded that the accused's guilty plea and acknowledgement of responsibility should carry significant weight in mitigation as having a 'positive impact on the reconciliatory process'. It therefore accepted that her guilty plea and other expressions of remorse contributed towards establishing the 'truth' of what took place.

However, this raises the important issue of whether such a procedural mechanism operating in the context of a (predominantly) adversarial trial paradigm is best placed to determine 'truth',[107] and indeed, raises questions about the context in which this particular version of 'truth' is being produced, and for whom. This observation highlights a significant paradox for sentencing in international criminal trials; how to produce sentencing outcomes that engage with victims and victim communities whilst concurrently satisfying retributive demands for punishment. It might be argued that it is impossible to envisage an international trial paradigm that could reconcile both sets of aspirations without some recourse to non-judicial means. A more radical alternative is to call for a complete reconceptualisation of the trial paradigm as necessary for the engagement of restorative themes.[108]

These difficulties were illustrated by the outcome in *Plavšić* itself. Despite acknowledging that it would give significant weight to the accused's plea of guilty, expressions of remorse and the positive impact on reconciliation, the Trial Chamber was eventually swayed by the heinous nature of what had taken place and its effects. The Prosecution was criticised for giving insufficient weight to (*inter alia*) the accused's guilty plea and her post-conflict conduct, yet there was a distinct lack of clarity in the Trial Chamber's determination of exactly what the effect of the mitigation (described as 'very significant') should be on the sentence. Such an outcome tends to support Zappala's suggestion,[109] based on the Appeal Chamber's unwillingness to entertain a sentence discount in the ICTR case of *Kambanda*,[110] that it may not be appropriate to allow plea-bargaining and plea agreements for crimes of extreme gravity.

The apparent absence of any willingness on the part of the international tribunals to preclude such practices, or lay down guidelines for sentencing practice, indicates their tacit acceptance as institutional procedural mechanisms. However, their moral significance has broader implications for the legitimacy

---

106 *Supra,* note 100, para. 81.
107 Zappala (2003) 89 makes the important point that the determination of 'truth' where a guilty plea is entered is neither judicial nor pedagogical, and, therefore, appears to contradict the mission of international criminal courts to take account of victims' interests. However, it may be argued, for example, that Article 65, para. 4, of the ICC Statute counters this effect.
108 See Findlay and Henham (2005).
109 Zappala (2003) 89.
110 *Prosecutor v Kambanda* (Case No. ICTR 97–23-S) Trial Chamber, Judgement and Sentence, 4 September 1998.

of international trial justice. Although the parameters of crime seriousness and its balance with expediency have yet to be drawn at the international level,[111] Zappala's reasons for supporting the practice are not totally convincing, since he advocates the pragmatic use of guilty plea discounts and plea agreements on the basis of their prosecutorial advantages in shortening investigations, and of cost, as being in the public interest to shorten the trials of minor participants. Yet in many jurisdictions sentence discounts for guilty pleas, or indeed any form of plea bargaining, is forbidden for the most serious crimes, such as first-degree murder, where mandatory minimum sentences are often provided.[112] A similar paradox in the appropriate penal response applies to the ICTR and the Special Court for Sierra Leone, where the death penalty is available for those less serious offenders who are tried locally, whilst the most serious perpetrators may be punished less severely if tried and convicted at the international level.[113]

These disconnections between local and global perceptions of justice are crucial because they reflect differences in the morality of punishment and the limitations this imposes on the extent to which we are able to generalise about the rationales which justify it. This disjunction is further magnified by the hegemony of punishment, whether global or local, which reinforces social and cultural divisions through partisan choices about whose opinions and actions are labelled as deviant and criminalised within each context. It is not surprising, therefore, that it is hard to find any evidence of a 'shared morality' between the global and the local which manifests itself in the sentencing outcomes of international criminal trials, or in hybridised processes which have been infiltrated by trial ideologies and practices alien to indigenous contexts of war and conflict.

Participation and legitimacy

The roles which offenders, victims and other participants, lay or professional, are *actually* permitted to play in the manufacture of trial justice are equally crucial for its moral credibility. For example, although commentators have hailed the Rome Statute of the ICC as providing significantly advanced levels of participation for victims, this is arguably more myth than reality.[114] An illustrative precursor to the way in which the ICC might handle the issue of participative rights more generally, including those concerned with sentencing, was recently provided in the area of pre-trial

---

111 Frulli (2001), Carcano (2002).
112 See, further, Seiber (2003) vol. 1, 83.
113 See Drumbl (2007a) 158.
114 Henham (2004c). More generally, as Findlay suggests, access to justice at the international level fails to reflect that accorded to victims in several common and civil law jurisdictions, where direct access is given to the sentencing process. Certainly, in the case of the ICC it does not extend much beyond protection for victim witnesses and victim compensation; see ICC Statute, Articles 43(6), 68(2), (3) and (4), 75, 79; Findlay (2002).

investigation.[115] This concerned objections raised by the ICC Prosecutor regarding the effects of victim participation in the investigations following the referral of the situation in the Democratic Republic of Congo to the ICC.[116] In fact, despite the fact that the ICC Statute makes far more significant attempts than the *ad hoc* tribunals to provide for the recognition and participation of victims at all stages of the criminal process, these proceedings illustrate how the modalities of adversarial trial as enshrined in the ICC criminal process effectively circumscribe the context for victim participation.

The ICC Prosecutor's application for leave to appeal against an earlier ruling of the Pre-Trial Chamber[117] relating to the participation of certain victims in the investigation stage is salutary for a number of reasons beyond the merely legalistic. The application itself was based on Article 82(1) of the ICC Statute, which provides:

1. Either party may appeal any of the following decisions in accordance with the Rules of Procedure and Evidence [...]

---

115 It should be noted that various pre-trial rights are provided for victims in the case of the ICC. Article 15(3) of the ICC Statute permits victims to make representations to the Pre-Trial Chamber with respect to any request made by the Prosecutor to proceed with an investigation. Article 19(3) provides that victims may submit observations to the Court with regard to proceedings relating to jurisdiction and admissibility. Further, by virtue of Article 53(1)(c), the Prosecutor may conclude, despite having taken the gravity of the crime and the interests of victims into account, that an investigation would not serve the interests of justice. In such circumstances the Prosecutor must inform the Pre-Trial Chamber and the State making a referral or the Security Council (as appropriate) of his or her conclusion and the reasons for it; Article 54(2). See, generally, Section III, Victims and witnesses, ICC Rules of Procedure and Evidence.

116 Observations of the Legal Representative of VPRS 1 to VPRS 6 following the Prosecution's Application for Leave to Appeal Pre-Trial Chamber I's Decision on the Applications for Participation in the Proceedings of VPRS 1 to VPRS 6, Situation in the Democratic Republic of Congo, Case No ICC 01/04, Pre-Trial Chamber I, 27 January 2006. The Prosecutor's objections were:

    (1) that 'external participation' adversely affected the integrity of the investigation and the safety of victims and witnesses;
    (2) that it might precipitate a serious imbalance between victims' rights and those of the Defence;
    (3) that the Pre-Trial Chamber was giving rulings about the existence of crimes when only the Court itself had jurisdiction (para. 9).

117 Decision on the Applications for Participation in the Proceedings of VPRS 1, VPRS 2, VPRS 3, VPRS 4, VPRS 5 and VPRS 6, Situation in the Democratic Republic of Congo, Case No ICC 01/04, Pre-Trial Chamber I, 17 January 2006. In reaching its decision that victims may participate in all stages of the proceeding, including the investigation stage, the Pre-Trial Chamber applied Article 68(3) of the ICC Statute, which provides 'Where the personal interests of the victims are affected, the Court shall permit their views and concerns to be presented and considered at stages of the proceedings determined to be appropriate by the Court and in a manner which is not prejudicial to or inconsistent with the rights of the accused and a fair and impartial trial. Such views and concerns may be presented by the legal representatives of the victims where the Court considers it appropriate, in accordance with the Rules of Procedure and Evidence.' See further ICC RPE, Section III, subsection 3.

(a) A decision that involves an issue that would significantly affect the fair and expeditious conduct of the proceedings or the outcome of the trial, and for which, in the opinion of the Pre-Trial Chamber or Trial Chamber, an immediate resolution by the Appeals Chamber may materially advance the proceedings

The Pre-Trial Chamber refused the application, ruling that the Prosecutor was effectively attempting to pre-empt decisions which might be made by the Court at some future time relating to the exercise by victims of their procedural rights under the Statute by denying to victims the possibility of participating in the investigation stage. As such the rationale for the application itself was not a relevant issue.

The point of the Statute is to guarantee victims' rights of access and carries with it a positive obligation for the Court to facilitate their effective use.[118] As the Pre-Trial Chamber put it:

It would therefore be quite illogical to authorise an appeal against a decision which does no more than implement certain aspects of the proceedings in full accordance with the basic documents.[119]

The Pre-Trial Chamber acknowledged that the various legal requirements dealing with victims' rights to participation contained in the Statute and the Rules and Regulations of the ICC were designed to ensure a 'fair and impartial trial', being closely linked to the concept of 'equality of arms', or balance between the parties during the proceedings:

The balance of criminal trials is not affected by the participation of the victims; on the contrary, taking their interests into account constitutes one of the factors contributing to the balance ... [120]

The difficulty with this assertion is that it needs to be evaluated in the context of the adversarial nature of the existing form of international criminal trial. As argued, these rights are not really participatory in the fullest sense. Certainly, they permit victims the right to be represented and to participate procedurally at various stages in the ICC trial process. But, they are not participative in the sense of giving victims a voice in actual decision-making.[121] Therefore, it is also questionable

---

118 *Ibid.* para 6.
119 *Ibid.* para 7.
120 *Ibid.* para 18.
121 The rights provided are what Ashworth might describe as 'service rights' rather than 'participatory rights'. 'Service rights' are best described as *non-participatory* victim rights, including such things as the right to receive relevant information at various stages of the court process, and the right to compensation for victims. 'Participatory rights', on the other hand, refer to more fundamental rights to consultation and participation in the criminal process – participatory rights in a tangible sense that mandate some form of procedural participation for victims. These might include rights to consultation regarding prosecution, acceptance of plea, sentence and release decisions. It is

how far they go towards satisfying the emotional and cathartic needs of victims.[122]

Additionally, the Trial Chamber's recognition that 'victims have their own interests to defend, which are different from those of both the Prosecution and the Defence',[123] is not merely a self-evident truth; the words capture the fundamental paradox of juxtaposing notions of 'participation' and 'rights' against the modalities of adversarial trial. In so doing, what might constitute an 'interest' is defined in essentially confrontational and polarised terms. By way of contrast, the idea of a trial ideology liberated from such constraints invests the concept of an 'interest' with a broader dimension – one which recognises that retribution and healing are not necessarily incompatible objectives. Conceptualised in this way, access to justice is interpreted to mean access to decision-making possibilities that maximise the likelihood of achieving outcomes which address the real concerns of victims and communities seeking justice.

Ideological conflict

The punishment practices of indigenous peoples are another context where notions of morality and legitimacy are brought into sharp relief. Within particular states and regions, the hegemony of dominant structures of criminal justice governance may dilute, distort or destroy traditional indigenous forms of conflict resolution. The nature of these contradictions is evident from the following example:

> In the Navajo Justice and Harmony Ceremony, the Peacemaker does not ask if the existing relationship is bad or good. Such value judgments are neither respectful, helpful or truthful. The Navajo peacemaker will ask, 'Hashhkeeji' – is this relationship moving towards disharmony? – or 'Hazhooji' – is this relationship moving towards harmony? It is important to emphasise the movement aspect of these words. The Aboriginal belief is that all living things are in a constant state of flux, moving towards or away from harmony ... The reasons for the wrongdoing are said to be the result of the person's relationship with the community moving towards disharmony ... The valuation of good and bad is not present. There exists only the constant flux of the movement of relationships within the community towards disharmony or harmony.[124]

The focus of such explanations is necessarily subjective and contextual. Distinctive notions of humanity and its essential characteristics are proposed with

---

necessary to draw a distinction in the characterisation of so-called 'participatory rights' between those rights that *allow for the possibility* of some form of participation by victims, and those rights that are tangible as a matter of social reality; Ashworth (1993).

122 For further discussion, see Wexler and Winick (1996), Sherman (2003).

123 *Supra*, note 117, para 18.

124 Guest (1999). See, further, Yazzie and Zion (1996).

which it is impossible for 'outsiders' to comprehend or empathise. Similarly, hegemonic morality is rejected and replaced by a notion of morality as serving a social function; namely, the interests of humanity as inclusively defined. Accordingly, the predominant rationale for intervention is to restore a sense of harmony in social relations. In one sense, it can be argued that the morality of the process is defined by the cultural origins of social relations.[125] However, this functional approach to explaining the significance of a shared morality, whilst undoubtedly valid for a specific social context, also acknowledges a universal moral truth; namely, that human discord and conflict are destructive of social life, howsoever conceived.

As argued in the previous chapter, conflict resolution through structures aimed at restoring social harmony is intrinsic to social life. The extent to which different interests need to be balanced in order to maintain social harmony varies according to context, as does the level of social harmony deemed acceptable for social life to continue. Hence, the morality attached to conflict resolution is a shared reality unique to a particular social context. It symbolises something that is necessary for social life to exist in that social context because it effectively regulates social relationships within the confines of that context. However, it is not a shared morality that outsiders can experience, because they do not share the heritage of emotional and social bonds of indigenous cultures.

Where socially inclusive communities such as those of indigenous peoples are concerned, the ties that bind their moral experiences are likely to be much closer than those of more socially complex, morally pluralistic societies. This shared moral bond may be likened to a stream of moral consciousness which constantly reinforces indigenous forms of conflict resolution with a shared vision of humanity.[126]

Concluding comments

Beyond the indigenous world of customary norms and practices, it would be naive to suggest that there exists a shared morality of punishment, in the sense that there is any kind of moral consensus about its rationales and how justice should be administered. This proposition remains true whether one examines global or local forms of criminal justice, or in terms of their horizontal and vertical relationships.

This chapter has not been arguing for, or seeking to identify a shared moral consciousness or sentiment about trial justice, however formal or informal that may be. Rather it has sought to establish why we need to find a basis for recognising and explaining the social significance of morally divergent views about punishment by developing better understandings of their contextual

---

125 This view corresponds to Durkheim's functional analysis of morality.
126 Comparable in it effects to Durkheim's notion of moral individualism.

significance. More specifically, this means understanding how the morality of punishment and the social reality of trial justice relate to one another, within and between different social contexts. The importance of this debate cannot be overstated. Nor should it be overshadowed by internecine debates between law, sociology or moral philosophy about the place of morals in explanations of social life; or the extent to which moral objectivism is possible, or indeed desirable.

4 Discretionary power and sentencing

Introduction

In general terms, the aim of this chapter is to describe and evaluate different sociological approaches to modelling judicial sentencing behaviour with a view to assessing the balance between universal factors in decision-making and particular contextual influences on sentencing practice. This implies that it is indeed possible to detect all the variables which might impact on the sentence decision-making process and that, in examining any given jurisdiction, it is also possible to pinpoint discrete variables peculiar to that specific context which influence sentencing. This is, of course, an objective that is extremely difficult to achieve

The best that can be hoped for is that we can make informed generalisations about the sorts of variables which inform sentencing as a type of discretionary decision-making, and their relative influence, taking social context into account. This would include factors that influence judicial culture,[1] such as judicial education and social background, as well as the wider cultural milieu of politics, morality and social life which are critical in shaping the perceptions and attitudes of all citizens towards matters of punishment and the role of criminal justice.

My reason for adopting such a cautious view of our capacity to explain sentence decision-making from a sociological perspective[2] lies in the inadequacy of the conceptual and methodological tools at our disposal. It will be argued that present conceptualisations of discretionary decision-making and sentencing in particular offer only partial insights into this complex world. More specifically, we seem unable to produce accounts of sentencing which deal adequately with the role of morality or social context. Part of the problem is caused by the complex nature of sentencing itself, especially the interrelationship of social and psychological factors. Clarity in this area is vital if one considers the

---

1 Bell (2001).
2 Our understanding of the psychological aspects of sentencing and the modelling of sentence decision-making has been increased significantly by the work of Mandeep Dhami; see, for example, Dhami (2007), Dhami and Souza (2009), Mueller-Johnson and Dhami (2010).

degree to which the morality of sentencers influences their perception of offenders, victims, and community interests, or their approach to justifying penal measures.

These shortcomings in understanding punishment and sentencing are fundamental. Put simply, if our knowledge about the role of sentencing in interpreting penal ideology is imperfect, we cannot begin to make informed analyses of its impact in different social contexts. Crucially, this requires a fundamental appreciation of the transformative capacity of the discretionary element in sentence decision-making, as discussed in chapter 2. The social and moral impact of penal law can only really be understood by developing our knowledge of how sentencing decisions are reached, and, equally importantly, what influences them.

Better evaluation of the governance role of punishment therefore rests on improving our knowledge of how sentencing decisions respond to social morality. As has been argued, descriptions and explanations of the social reality of sentencing must not only accommodate a normative perspective, they must also consider the interdependence of moral and social judgements in the psychological processes of decision-making. This includes the assertion that the relationship in sentencing between moral and social factors is reflexive and recursive. Hence, sentencing is mutually re-interpretative and reinforcing of penal ideology and its social milieu. This analysis holds provided one accepts that moral sentiments have some kind of objective existence, as argued in the previous chapter.

To attribute responsibility is a moral act, since it is judgemental as to the appropriateness of action. However, as discussed in chapter 2, there is a difference of view as to whether law is instrumental, declaratory or interpretative of morality, or a categorically distinct and therefore closed system of norms. Even if one takes the view that penal law is so distinct, sentencing itself is a moral and social experience which has social consequences.

Furthermore, as Hutton suggests,[3] due to the wide discretion generally given to sentencers in common law jurisdictions, there is a considerable area for decision-making which lies well beyond the conventional rationales and certainties of law and the substantive and procedural rules that govern its interpretation and application. Although governed by normative constraints, the exercise of discretionary power is infused by the need to take into account moral and social considerations which, while appearing to have an objective existence, are at the same time subjectively perceived and interpreted in different ways by the participants in the trial process.[4] This blending of moral and social perceptions is extremely difficult to disentangle, since to do so would require the development of a theory and method which can distinguish how social experience is constructed subjectively, and experienced objectively. For

---

3 Hutton (2006) 155; see also Hutton (1995).
4 Rogers and Erez (1999).

this reason discrete studies, such as that conducted by Rogers and Erez, are valuable in shedding light on this conundrum because they attempt to deconstruct how a particular version of social reality is created and what it means subjectively for certain participants in the sentencing process. This does not imply any claim that we can experience their 'reality', but it does go some way towards helping us understand what it means to articulate certain descriptions of that reality, in a moral as well as a social sense. Of course, the partiality of the theoretician, or that of the observer, cannot be overcome, so 'reality', contextualised or not, is always projected through a distorted conceptual or methodological lens.

I have argued elsewhere[5] for the transformative capacity of sentencing to be recognised, meaning that some account should be taken of the way in which the process of sentence decision-making in effect actualises the moral significance of the offender's conduct. So conceived, sentencing can be seen as a decision that gives individual practical effect to punishment following a process of reasoning which draws on interpretations of law and facts that are determined by penality and ultimately by context, as discussed in chapter 2.

This chapter considers the implications of such a conceptualisation of sentence decision-making for penal governance. It focuses specifically on developing the modelling framework, so that we are in a better position to examine how the relationship between moral and social factors evident in the exercise of discretionary power manifests itself through individualisation of the sentencing decision.

Tamanaha[6] argues that the processual activity of trial decision-making is where value is attributed to fact and that our capacity to comprehend this is relative to context. The ability to appreciate the contextual significance of moral values is therefore crucial,[7] especially how moral meanings come to be attributed to actions. This includes understanding how values are implicated in sentencing decisions and what those decisions represent in moral terms.

Our understandings of what may be taken to represent the 'truth' of what takes place in the trial – whether relating to discretionary decisions about the admissibility of evidence, determinations about the relevance of evidence to sentence, or the significance of sentencing decisions themselves – depend upon whether we possess the conceptual and methodological tools needed to facilitate such a multi-dimensional interrogation of different processual contexts. We begin this quest with a brief evaluation of the capacity of existing sentencing models to answer this question.

---

5 Henham (2001).
6 Tamanaha (1997).
7 Whether this is observable and capable of description objectively, or as a matter of subjective experience.

The nature of sentencing norms

An important but neglected aspect of the debate, and one which has important implications for how we conceptualise the norms of penal law and sentencing, is the extent to which they share similar moral foundations with those of substantive criminal law. This discussion draws particular attention to the capacity of the sentencing process to transform moral values into normative guides to conduct. Distinctions between substantive and procedural norms in this respect are significant for modelling the sentencing process.

Legislation about punishment – sentencing law

Sentencing law may state the purposes and options for punishment and the criteria which must be fulfilled in order for it to be imposed, but it differs from the criminal law in the sense that the latter sets out the criteria for establishing responsibility rather than accountability. The framing of both is influenced by the morality of time and place, which is itself a reflection of social context. In post-modernity, societies are likely to be characterised by a plurality of normative structures designed to regulate behaviour. Some of this behaviour is criminalised, and may be dealt with by the apparatus of state law and punishment.[8]

However, it could be argued that sentencing law has distinctive moral characteristics because the practice of punishment communicates a moral message[9] about how society sees fit to respond to the guilt of the accused. It gives decision-makers morally significant options, depending on the amount of sentencing discretion at their disposal. These options may have a moral significance in their own right, in the sense that they represent particular ideological views about punishment. Penal options may be morally ambiguous (as with community service) because they suggest different moral justifications and possibilities for punishment generally, these being individualised depending upon the circumstances of each case. Here a distinction is normally drawn between the general justifying aims of punishment and the principles existing for their distribution.[10]

When punishment is imposed through sentencing the moral ideology which informs sentencing law is made concrete. This does not mean to say that moral values are simply transformed through sentencing, rather that morality is crystallised in some way through the transformative process of decision-making. The moral ideology which informs sentencing law is not necessarily representative; there will invariably be a plurality of moral values in post-modern societies. Similarly, the extent to which competing interests are able to assert their morality through law will vary. So by saying that sentencing is

---

8 See, further, Tamanaha (2007).
9 Duff (2001).
10 Hart (1968).

morally transformative, I mean that it somehow transforms the moral character of sentencing law. It does this by particularising the chosen punishment; the sentencer ascribes to the offender a punishment relevant for that offence. This is a moral act, because the sentencer is justifying the punishment in terms of the seriousness of the offence and the culpability of the offender. It is also moral, because it is a reality that stands to be judged by 'significant others'.

Assessing seriousness and culpability involve moral judgements that are guided to a greater or lesser extent by legal norms, depending on the extent of discretionary power available to the sentencer. The culpability of the offender is ascribed a moral value which is balanced against other relevant factors. Therefore, determining seriousness in sentencing is a moral decision as well as a legal one, because it represents a judgement about how society (depending on the degree to which law is the product of a 'democratic' process) wants criminalised behaviour[11] to be dealt with by the legal system. In a sense, therefore, the sentencer is interpreting and operationalising social morality; judging criminalised behaviour as a moral wrong in the way that citizens might, were they to find themselves in the sentencer's position.[12] What citizens cannot do, of course, is to judge the moral culpability of the offender. This is entrusted to the sentencer who is the only person privy to the information and structures to facilitate that decision.

This crucial moral nexus between the justification for punishment and the decision to impose a particular penalty relates directly to our discussion of governance in criminal justice, because it is linked to the issue of state responsibility. Specifically, this refers to the state's responsibility to ensure that the sentencing system commands public confidence. As I have argued, this should mean that sentencing outcomes are perceived as legitimate by citizens and that this legitimacy can only be measured by understanding the extent to which sentencing outcomes reflect shared values about punishment and sentencing. This issue has become increasingly critical for governance due to the fragmented and diverse nature of value systems in liberal western democracies.

Hence, in addition to complying with penal norms, sentencing responsibility lies in making decisions about punishment in individual cases that accord in a moral sense with the perceptions held by citizens of what amounts to justice. However, the extent to which sentencers can, or should, be required to identify and refer to the penal morality of relevant interests remain a significant problem. I have argued that this can only be achieved by gradually moving away from the constraints imposed by retributive penal ideology and adversarial

---

11 A question that arises here concerns the criteria by which behaviours are criminalised.
12 Whether that judgement reflects social reality is another matter. This highlights the problematic connections between the philosophical justifications for punishment and the social reality of sentencing and why it is so important to understand more about the role of sentencing in bringing them together; see, for example, Hudson's criticisms of Rawls's 'original position' and the 'veil of ignorance'; Hudson (2003a) ch. 1.

justice and embracing a more communitarian approach to conceptualising penal ideology. Furthermore, this should be accompanied by a rethinking of the role of judicial discretionary power in sentencing in terms of its capacity to transform the values underpinning punishment, so that judges can feel more confident that sentences engage more directly with social reality and the moral concerns of citizens.

Notwithstanding, although the idea of justice is crystallised through sentencing, the exact nature of justice as a form of 'moral balancing' – as fairness and equity; in other words, the social significance of the 'truth' or moral message it conveys – is outside the immediate control of citizens. Although punishment is particularised, through the recursive process of sentencing, the latter also promulgates the generality of what is perceived as justice. This is especially critical to the maintenance of criminal justice governance because the cumulative effect of this recursive process contributes to the existing ideology of justice (hegemonic and pluralistic) and reaffirms it, or may produce change from within.[13]

Sentencing principles and guidance – sentencing control

In the English context, there has been some debate as to whether sentencing principles and the guidance developed by the Court of Appeal on the advice of the Sentencing Advisory Panel and Sentencing Guidelines Council[14] are legal norms in the strict sense. In principle, sentencing decisions *per se* do not have the status of conventional legal norms in that they do not (strictly speaking) create binding precedents. However, failure to follow relevant sentencing guidance can prompt an appeal. This kind of guidance can vary in terms of how much it restricts the capacity of sentencers in exercising their discretionary power, and can produce incoherence and inconsistency in sentencing.[15]

Nevertheless, the important point in the present context is that such guidance has more than simply normative effect. It directly influences the operational context of sentencing, so has a moral impact, both in terms of its immediate effect on the decision-making process and, consequentially, on how sentencing outcomes are perceived. Structurally, guidance (of whatever form) can be utilised as an effective mechanism for injecting moral messages directly into sentencing. These messages may originate for all kinds of reasons, often socio-political and hegemonic,[16] and from different sources, the degree of interference permissible being the most significant factor. On the other hand, interference may be perceived, and is often portrayed as such by the state, as

---

13 As evidenced by judicial resistance to the ideology of just deserts introduced by the 1991 Criminal Justice Act in England and Wales.

14 Now replaced by the Sentencing Council; see Part 4 of the Coroners and Justice Act (2009).

15 See Henham (1992).

16 Such as the desire of the executive to have greater control over the resource implications of sentencing.

a legitimate means for reacting directly and effectively to the 'expressed' concerns of citizens about crime and punishment and channelling them directly into the sentencing process. On this reading, state intervention is portrayed as democratic and representative; part of the apparatus of responsible criminal justice governance. However, as suggested, where the moral gap between judicial sentencing and public confidence is exacerbated by continued tension between the executive and the judiciary, as in England and Wales, the prospect of increased state control of this kind is a cause for concern.[17]

Modelling sentencing discretion

The limitations of models reflect those of the theories that inform them. These, in turn, may offer partial representations of social reality, either because of particular political predilections of the author, or more simply because their epistemological roots are grounded in a particular era. Neither limitation, of course, invalidates the integrity of the model, nor the reality it purports to project. This is an important point to grasp when attempting to model the social reality of sentencing. The issue is important in thinking about whether models can be effectively refined and developed to reflect changes in social life. Arguably, the answer should be affirmative, since modelling, like theorising in the tradition of causal determinism, can serve a distinctly heuristic function.

However, the experience of modelling sentence decision-making casts doubt upon this kind of approach.[18] Thomas,[19] for example, provides a purely positivist analysis of legal norms, which, whilst jurisprudentially invaluable, is largely devoid of any analysis of social context. It is an exercise in doctrinal legal method, seeking to give shape and substance to a continually developing and otherwise diverse set of decisions made by the English Appeal Court about the appropriateness of particular sentences handed down by Crown Court judges. Such an exercise does not equate with heuristic social modelling in the conventional sense, because its purpose is not to describe the social reality of sentence decision-making as a dynamic processual activity. As Hawkins states:

> The law in action is a system of meanings, a fluid normative system, not an abstract system of rules mechanically applied ... In the creation and re-creation of reality in formal legal processes fundamental models of human character and motive are central. The legal process is a morality play.[20]

Other models, such as the early work by Green on the role of legal factors,[21] or, more recently, Lovegrove's[22] numerical model, similarly lack any

---

17 As discussed in chapter 1.
18 See Henham (2001) for a detailed account of such models and their weaknesses.
19 Thomas (1970), Thomas (1979), Thomas (1982 as updated).
20 Hawkins (2002) 443, 444.
21 Green (1961).
22 Lovegrove (1989), Lovegrove (1997).

contextual analysis of social or psychological factors,[23] or speculation as to their role in sentencing; such variables being considered only sporadically by earlier studies; for example, Nagel,[24] Smith and Blumberg,[25] or Hood's[26] early work on magistrates' sentencing.

A significant criticism of all the above studies is their obsession with explaining the reasons for inconsistency rather than consistency in sentencing, regardless of whether these are due to legal or social factors. This tendency reflects a signal concern with one of the underlying principles of retributive justice – equality of impact – a principle that has grown to prominence with the post-modern emphasis on desert and proportionality. However, more recent interpretative approaches have focused on situational and contextual explanations of discretionary sentencing behaviour.

The precursor of such studies is Hogarth's[27] seminal work on Canadian magistrates. His phenomenological approach relied upon prior identification by the magistrates themselves of those areas and issues which they considered relevant to sentence decision-making, so informing the development of the hypotheses for the research and their operationalisation through a wide variety of methodological techniques. Hogarth found that the attitudes and beliefs of Canadian magistrates tended to reflect the communities in which they lived. His examination of the complexity of magistrates' thought processes in sentencing concluded that magistrates' identification of what they considered 'essential' information, and the importance they attached to the various categories of it, was consistent with their penal philosophies and attitudes. Therefore, the most important variables in explaining sentencing behaviour which emerge from Hogarth's study are the penal philosophies and attitudes of magistrates, the characteristics of the communities where the courts are situated, and the nature and extent of the information available to magistrates before sentence, factors which were largely ignored in previous sentencing research.

More recently Tata[28] and Hutton[29] have questioned the rationality of sentencing because the factors that are operative in decision-making cannot be identified. Firstly, Tata suggests that most contemporary attempts to explain sentencing 'misrepresent decision-making as a deductive, linear, analytical and mechanical activity', preferring instead a more transparent intuitive account of sentencing involving a 'schematic-holistic' or 'whole case' approach that conceptualises sentencing as an activity whereby decisions are constituted and reconstituted according to 'context' and 'audience'. Consequently, decisions are

---

23 See Dhami's work, *supra*, note 2.
24 Nagel (1962).
25 Smith and Blumberg (1967).
26 Hood (1962).
27 Hogarth (1971). A similar approach to modelling sentencing was adopted in Hood (1972).
28 Tata (1997).
29 Hutton (2006).

seen as unstructured, relative, pragmatic and situational; 'reasons' are regarded as suspect (*post hoc*) rationalisations of case stories 'largely constructed and typified by the criminal process even before they reach the judge'. In similar vein, Hutton argues that sentencing involves *post hoc* rationalisation and justification:

> Thus, an understanding of sentencing from this perspective is an understanding of the range of legitimate accounts which judges can construct to justify their sentence.[30] ... Sentencing decisions are not generated by the application of legal rules but through the routine, largely unreflective, day-to-day practices of judges working in a distinctive legal culture and in a local court environment.[31]

Hutton draws support from Roberton's[32] work on House of Lords judges, suggesting that the sort of 'pragmatic utilitarianism' which Robertson suggests characterises their approach to decision-making has considerable relevance to sentencing.[33] Whilst Hutton is no doubt correct in asserting that individualised sentencing militates against the development of rational principles for sentencing,[34] I would argue that he overemphasises the extent to which sentence decision-making is a predominantly *post hoc* activity. For example, he suggests that:

> There is virtually no reference to anything which might be described as 'technical' evidence, for example, about past sentencing practice, about the effectiveness of punishment, or about the costs and benefits of sentencing policy. Furthermore, there is little reliance on past practice.[35]

This generalisation fails to acknowledge the fact that these matters will invariably be referred to by Crown Court judges in their preparation of judgments, the extent of the evidential considerations depending on the complexity of the case, and considerations as to the appropriateness of particular punishments depending, not only on references to similar decided cases and sentencing guidance, but also broader considerations about the justifications for punishment, which may involve difficult questions about public protection and the perceived acceptability of the penalty.

Hutton's further suggestion[36] that the individualisation of sentences militates against the articulation of reasons for consistency has some merit, but it may be argued this is to some degree inevitable given the nature of the task.

---

30 *Ibid.* 168.
31 *Ibid.* 173.
32 Robertson (1998).
33 Hutton (2006) 171.
34 *Ibid.* 173.
35 *Ibid.* 171.
36 *Ibid.* 173.

Accordingly, the crucial point is for the balance between the need for consistency and the demands of individualised sentencing to be monitored and adjusted as necessary by the Appeal Court and the Sentencing Council.[37] In any event, such moves towards rationalisation and transparency in sentencing were anticipated by the provisions of S174 of the Criminal Justice Act (2003) which for the first time imposed obligations on courts to give reasons for and explain the effect of their sentencing decisions.

More specifically, S174(1) provided that any court passing sentence on an offender:

(a)   must state in open court, in ordinary language and in general terms its reasons for deciding on the sentence it has passed, and
(b)   must explain to the offender in ordinary language–

   (i)   the effect of the sentence
   (ii)   the effect of non-compliance with any order it has imposed
   (iii) powers of the offender or any other person to seek variation or review of any court order forming part of the sentence.
   (iv)   the consequences of failing to pay a fine where this is the sentence or part of it.

A number of other significant matters to be borne in mind by the court in complying with its obligations under S174(1) were set out in S174(2). These included the issue of sentencing guidelines:

- Where guidelines indicated a sentence of a particular kind, or within a particular range, the court was placed under a duty to state its reasons for departing from these if it decided to do so.
- Where the sentence was non-custodial, and there were no reasons for excluding a custodial sentence, the court had to explain why it was of the opinion that a non-custodial sentence was appropriate.
- Where the court passed a community sentence instead of a fine, and the decision did not seem to be in the interests of justice (as defined), the court had to explain why it considered such a course appropriate.
- Where the court discounted the sentence in return for a guilty plea under S144 it was mandated to state the fact.[38]

---

37 Hutton implicitly acknowledges this, suggesting that judicial resistance to controls on their discretion, whether through guideline or information systems, must be overcome; *ibid.*
38 See, further, Henham (1999b). However, the obligation to state reasons and issues surrounding the appropriate degree of discount were not clarified until definitive guidance was issued by the Sentencing Guidelines Council in 2007 following widespread consultation; see Sentencing Guidelines Council (2007).

- The court had to mention any aggravating or mitigating factors which it regarded as being of particular importance.[39]

Furthermore, these statutory obligations had to be considered in conjunction with the Practice Direction on custodial sentences originally issued to the courts by the Lord Chief Justice in 1998, the main object of which was to provide model forms of words to help sentencers explain the effect of their decisions in clear and accurate terms.[40]

Taking a much broader sociological perspective in a more recent paper, Tata[41] develops the notion of sentencing as craftwork:

> ... by paying more serious attention to sentencing processes at street level (as well as being aware of official and public discourses), it becomes possible to explore the conception of sentencing as a craft. A conception of

---

39 Arguably, this provision was superfluous since courts would normally do this anyway, particularly in view of the possibility of an appeal under S36 of the Criminal Justice Act 1988 on the basis that the sentence was 'unduly lenient'.

40 Practice Directions (Custodial Sentences: Explanations) [1998] 1 WLR 278; [1998] 1 All ER 733; [1998] 1 Cr App R 397; 22/1/98. This direction now appear in the Consolidated Criminal Practice Direction, which provides as follows:

1.7 EXPLANATIONS FOR THE IMPOSITION OF CUSTODIAL SENTENCES.

  1.7.1 The practical effect of custodial sentences imposed by the courts is almost entirely governed by statutory provisions. Those statutory provisions, changed by Parliament from time to time, are not widely understood by the general public. It is desirable that when sentence is passed the practical effect of the sentence should be understood by the defendant, any victim and any member of the public who is present in court or reads a full report of the proceedings.

  1.7.2 Whenever a custodial sentence is imposed on an offender the court should explain the practical effect of the sentence in addition to complying with existing statutory requirements. This will be no more than an explanation; the sentence will be that pronounced by the court.

  1.7.3 Sentencers should give the explanation in terms of their own choosing, taking care to ensure that the explanation is clear and accurate. No form of words is prescribed. Annexed to this Practice Direction are short statements which may, adapted as necessary, be of value as models (see Annex C). These statements are based on the statutory provisions in force on 1 January 1998 and will, of course, require modification if those provisions are materially amended.

  1.7.4 Sentencers will continue to give such explanation as they judge necessary of ancillary orders relating to matters such as disqualification, compensation, confiscation, costs and so on.

  1.7.5 The power of the Secretary of State to release a prisoner early under supervision is not part of the sentence. The judge is therefore not required in his sentencing remarks to provide an explanation of this power. However, in explaining the effect of custodial sentences the judge should not say anything which conflicts with the existence of this power.

41 Tata (2007).

sentencing as craftwork destabilises long assumed binaries in sentencing ...
By conceiving of sentencing as craftwork these binaries are revealed as
fluid, mutable, and protean. Sentencing as craftwork allows us to conceive
of the judicial process as about *both*: choice *and* order; implicit routine
and explicit normative principle; analysis *and* intuition; individualisation
and consistency; rationality *and* emotion; mind *and* body. These qualities
co-exist dynamically, are synergistic, and inhabit each other.[42]

In seeking to elaborate this thesis, Tata provides a somewhat limited portrayal
of judicial sentencing, albeit that this may be for heuristic purposes[43] For
example, he fails to provide a clear definition of discretion in the sentencing
context; particularly as to whether he is referring to its origins in legal,
procedural or social norms.[44]

More fundamentally, his initial premises appear to rest on a false dichotomy,
since he begins by oversimplifying existing paradigms of sentencing in terms
of either juridical/legal-rational, or as new-penology/risk-based.[45] As regards
the former, Tata makes reference to several adherents of this perspective
including the present author, ignoring more recent work on the development
of comparative contextual modelling.[46] However, before exploring the implications of this in greater depth, there are some additional points worthy of
comment.

Arguably, Tata exhibits a general tendency to overdramatise the significance of particular observations,[47] or to reformulate previous discourses in
ways that sustain his argument. Even the dichotomies he occasionally suggests appear somewhat contrived. For example, the distinction Tata draws
between tariff and individualised sentencing[48] may have been accurate for
England and Wales before the Criminal Justice Act of 1991,[49] but the inflex-
ibility of this paradigm is exaggerated. Instead, more recent effects, such as
the creative role played by the pragmatic use of judicial discretion in breaking
down the rigidity of the just deserts framework imposed by the 1991 Act
should have been noted.[50]

---

42 *Ibid.* 427 (emphasis in original).
43 For example, his characterisation of most sentencing work as mundane and boring (*ibid.* 428)
    and his emphasis on socially produced justifications (*ibid.* 440); developing Kritzer's conception
    of two levels of clientele audience, external and internal, (*ibid.* 444), both contrive to create
    rather than dispel false dichotomies in sentencing.
44 *Ibid.* 429. For example, what is meant by 'legal discretion'.
45 *Ibid.* 426. See Henham (2005b) ch. 2, in particular, for further discussion of the distinction
    made between ideological, normative, descriptive and contextual paradigms.
46 Henham (2001).
47 For example, as to the fluidity of rules and discretion, Tata (2007) 430.
48 *Ibid.* 437.
49 See Thomas (1979).
50 For further discussion; see Ashworth (2010) chs 1, 2.

Also important is the fact that individualised approaches to sentencing predominate where there is wide discretionary power.[51] Its importance is dictated by the ideology that drives the process and embodied in penal norms. These may be lacking or incoherent, as in the case of international criminal trial structures. Therefore, it may be argued that the important issue is why and how that ideology is driven through the processes of trial and sentencing, and the extent to which it engages with commonly accepted (or contested) notions of 'justice'. As argued, this is essentially a moral question. Fundamentally, it provides the rationale for my argument that sentencing must come to terms with, and provide, frameworks for understanding the role of morality in decision-making.

Tata's assertion that emotion[52] is regarded as an enemy of legal-rational scholarship because it is the enemy of objectivity is surely correct.[53] However, he does not engage with the theory and methodology of comparative contextual modelling and its implications for transforming sentencing mentioned above. Tata effectively ignores such broader contextual approaches to sentence modelling in describing discretion as fundamentally determined by penal principles.[54] Unlike contextual modelling, it may be argued that Tata's conceptualisation focuses too much on characterising the use of discretion in sentencing as an abstracted exercise; in the sense that he adopts a pragmatic interpretative approach that focuses disproportionately on case construction. Although, Tata does point out that sentencing is constructed from already processed information through discretionary decisions made earlier in the process, the sociological significance of this is hardly new.[55]

Fundamentally, Tata fails to distinguish between factors that influence discretionary decision-making and the significance *of the decision* itself.[56] Similarly, in his use of the word 'legitimating',[57] Tata's analysis appears to separate understandings of what goes on *as* sentencing from its effects. For example, in his discussion of the meaning of rhetoric and reality in sentencing,[58] Tata fails to explore the most important issue of whether the rhetoric of sentencing symbolises something more than retributive justice; the appropriate

---

51 In the international context, this is exemplified by the very wide discretion accorded to the judges of the ICTY, ICTR, and to a slightly lesser extent, the newly created ICC; see Henham (2003a).
52 Again, Tata's reading of the significance of emotion may be regarded as somewhat misplaced, and perhaps exaggerated in its support for the argument that emotion may be deployed rationally; Tata (2007) 432.
53 *Ibid.* 431.
54 *Ibid.* 433.
55 Cicourel (1968).
56 Tata (2007) 435. The importance of local context and how the perception by sentencers of their social responsibilities influences their decision-making practices is highlighted in Parker, Sumner and Jarvis (1989). It is the accuracy of these perceptions and their social impact through sentencing that requires further elaboration.
57 'These binaries constitute a currency of legitimating reference points'; *ibid.* 442.
58 *Ibid.* 440.

question being; what does sentencing represent externally, *not* just internally? The sentencing outcome may be symbolically (possibly morally) transformative, but the extent to which we can understand these effects as subjective experience, and draw meaningful conclusions from such observations, remains a matter for debate (as discussed in chapter 3).

Moving from local to global

Paradoxically, Hutton's interpretative approach may have important implications for thinking about how sentencing takes place at the international as well as the local level. His description of judges deploying justifications for sentence *post hoc*; of discretion not being determined by law but characterised by 'pragmatic utilitarianism', implies a need for some form of fundamental change in the ideology and operational context of the judicial function. Hutton's analysis may have more resonance at the level of sentencing in international criminal trials precisely because of the enormous, and currently largely unregulated, discretion afforded to the judiciary operating in this context.[59]

Ewald's recent analysis of truth construction in international criminal justice is particularly instructive.[60] His account of how 'material facts' come to achieve the status of 'judicial truth' as a result of discretionary decisions made about the admissibility of discrete pieces of evidence in international trials suggests how important it is for theories and models of sentencing to consider the wider socio-political contexts of criminal trials and, more particularly, the impact ideology has on the rationality of trial norms and the exercise of discretionary power.

Ewald argues that the links between rationality and hegemony and its evidential impact on the construction of what counts as 'truth' are likely to be established at different procedural stages, well before the trial proper begins. It is therefore important to bear this in mind when conceptualising the role of punishment through sentencing, particularly its evaluation as an exercise of normative power and its capacity to engage and seek legitimacy with relevant audiences such as victims and victim communities.

In common with Tata and Hutton, Ewald emphasises the notion that judicial reasoning of evidentiary decisions in international trials is essentially circumscribed by pre-existing and externally determined contexts of rationality. This recursive process of reasoning reinforces the relationship between the hegemony and rationality of criminal justice, especially the accuracy of the 'truth' narrative espoused by Western civilisation.

> The risk of a significant disjunction of 'material' and 'judicial truth' in international criminal justice, as described above, through the hegemonic discourse is usually disguised by a rationality (and formal legal

---

59 See, further, Henham (2005b).
60 Ewald (2008).

language) which – in its own perspective – presents facts and inferences in an 'objective' way and meets the formal requirements of a reasoned judgement ... Thus, the selection of sources and originators of evidentiary information and ultimately the judicial decision making on the presentation, admission and rational use of evidence provide the functional context in which the hegemony of normative models is reproduced as 'knowledge' and 'truth' and (selective) criminalisation strategies are conducted.[61]

Although such observations have important implications for the exercise of discretionary power in sentencing at both the global and local level, careful note should be taken of how existing normative structures are responsible for shaping the contexts of discretion. Therefore, how trial evidence comes to be treated for the purposes of sentence and the relative impact of distinct verdict and sentencing hearings on that evidence are matters of huge significance in shaping the contours of discretion, especially the extent to which rationalities of 'truth' are capable of being created and transformed into outcomes which have a moral significance beyond hegemony.[62] For trial justice to engage with the pluralism and relativity of 'truth', and for this to be conceptualised in sentence modelling, calls for a fundamental change in how we conceive of the purposes of sentencing in moral terms and its accommodation within existing norms and structures of decision-making.[63]

The changes for modelling sentencing discretion envisaged in this book are more fundamental than any which might be contemplated through the development of Hutton's or Ewald's analytical framework. As suggested elsewhere, they call for a complete reconceptualisation of sentence decision-making at the international level,[64] such changes being crucial for the theoretical development of sentencing more generally and the evaluation of its role as an element of criminal justice governance. Its primary objective is to make sentencing more instrumental than symbolic, more capable of engaging with the demands for justice of victims and victim communities through mediated and integrative outcomes. Such a change in the ideology, rationale and practice of sentencing requires a contextual approach to modelling which is capable not only of describing but also of explaining, the relationship between moral and social reality and its reflection in discretionary decision-making. Consequently, it argues that key concepts such as responsibility and accountability are better understood in terms which have objective and subjective resonance for their relevant audiences.

---

61 *Ibid.*
62 See Findlay and Henham (2010) ch. 4.
63 For a preliminary discussion of these ideas, see Henham (2001).
64 Henham (2005b) ch. 8.

Developing a contextual model

Before elaborating such a model of the sentence decision-making process, it is important to provide a brief summary of its theoretical foundations and situate it within the discourse of other contemporary work. For example, Hutton[65] and Hawkins[66] have each suggested different approaches for conceptualising the broader social context in which discretion is exercised and how this impacts on the actual process of sentence decision-making. Hutton and Hawkins have similar visions of how social structure impinges on the social practice of discretionary decision-making. Hutton develops Bordieu's conception of the social field, or 'habitus',[67] whilst Hawkins elaborates notions of 'surround' and 'decision field' – the former representing the broader social and political context that influences individuals and structures of decision-making, the latter representing the more defined and controlled structural setting where discretionary decisions are actually made.[68] Hutton goes on to elaborate the relevance of certain elements of the habitus of sentencing, such as 'populist punitiveness', broader criminal justice system goals and pressures, judicial and legal culture, and the significance of judicial power ('capital').[69] Ultimately, Hutton envisages judicial decisions on sentence as patterned, socially constructed, somehow 'emerging' from the largely fixed and inflexible habitus of sentencing.

Hawkins also suggests that decision fields in criminal justice are relatively stable, since they operate with well-established cultural and operational assumptions and norms; for example, in relation to the values and ethics of legal practitioners in the courts. However, the most interesting aspect of Hawkins's analysis is the development of his concept of 'framing' to account for the way in which external factors are interpreted in the immediate situation of discretionary decision-making in a legal context. Hawkins states:

> A frame is a structure of knowledge, experience, values and meanings that decision-makers employ in deciding ... A frame can be seen as a set of rules for steering the performance of a task, or for organising the ascription of meaning to events or for classifying as relevant other raw material in the field[70] ... frames are reflexive in the sense that they both constitute reality and they selectively identify the facts that sustain a social reality.[71]

---

65 Hutton (2006) 161.
66 Hawkins (2003).
67 Described by Bourdieu as: 'Interactions between institutions, rules and practices, rituals, designations, conventions, appointments and titles which produce and authorise certain discourses and activities'. Bourdieu (1977) 21–22, cited in Hutton (2006) 161.
68 Hawkins (2003) 189.
69 Hutton (2006) 165.
70 Hawkins (2003) 190.
71 *Ibid.* 191. See also Hawkins (2002) 433–35.

Hawkins describes how the interpretative act of framing in decision-making gives meaning and classifies acts and information, making the point that different frames will dominate particular aspects of process which may change.[72] An example in the English sentencing context concerns the way factual information admitted and acted upon during the trial phase is reconstructed and re-interpreted for the purposes of sentencing, material relevant to sentence often being excluded from the trial as potentially prejudicial, or simply as beyond the remit of what the defence requires in order to contest the charges effectively.

In developing the theory and method of contextual analysis, Mark Findlay and I propose an interpretative framework for trial analysis derived from Anthony Giddens's macro-theory of structuration.[73] We argue that structuration theory[74] provides a reflexive theoretical construct that recognises structure, organisation and interaction as interconnected aspects of the same social practice, offering three levels of understanding depending on context. It provides a set of organising or interpretative constructs that allow researchers to identify elements and processes concerned in the recursive nature of the application of rules and resources by social actors. The theory makes it possible to understand the way in which different structures of trial process exist and are recursively created and patterned over time, whilst also appreciating the ways in which they are created by human agency through institutional practice. For example, the patterning of sentencing principles and their existence as formal rules can be conceived as a structural context in which the situational reality of sentence decision-making takes place.

This sensitising and interpretative approach is designed to elucidate the major dimensions of decision-making. Accordingly, the processes of decision-making may be seen in context as a series of frames of action; the context of the trial process is envisaged in terms of a series of pathways of decision-making wherein each outcome depends upon understanding how and why relationships between trial participants are resolved at crucial sites for decision-making within the trial. Each such frame of action contributes to moulding the trial process since each pathway is dependent upon influences that shape, drive and emanate from these relationships. Socio-historic accounts of the manufacture and development of process are dependent on the constituents of previous frames of action in as much as instantiation recursively contributes to our understanding of contextualised social action.

Crucially, the relationship between structure and agency depends for its relative existence upon context, from which it is never separate or autonomous. The relativity of each frame of action is established through our ability to consider interaction within the context of the frame against past and

---

72 *Ibid.* 192.
73 See Findlay and Henham (2007).
74 See, especially, Giddens (1979), Giddens (1984).

present action outcomes. This analysis therefore envisages the various dimensions of decision-making, their contextualisation and comparison in terms of a series of frames which comprise a moving picture – contextualised social action.

Based on this theoretical approach, contextual modelling provides a conceptual tool which combines interpretative and quantitative approaches and has the potential for broader application in the analysis of the various dimensions of trial decision-making.[75] In its application to sentencing, it conceptualises the psychological appropriation and assimilation of relevant information from interconnected objective and subjective perspectives used in decision-making as constituting a holistic explanation – objectively, in the sense of externally verifiable manifestations of sentence decision-making as a processual activity; and subjectively, in terms of the extent to which sentencers appear to share similar images of relevant case material and legal rules in the context of perceived audience expectation.

The methodology implicit in contextual modelling therefore involves the identification, description and analysis of communication structures and interactive processes in sentencing through contextual analysis. The model accommodates methodologies which facilitate the deconstruction of the social reality of sentencing by developing an approach which combines inductive and deductive strategies. These signify objective and subjective dimensions of social action by facilitating the conflation of those theoretical and empirical imperatives that are dictated by different epistemological positions. In so doing, the social context of the sentencing process, in terms of its objectivity (both conceptual and concrete), and subjective accounts of that objectivity (in terms of its phenomenological content) may be revealed.

The contextual analysis of sentencing and its associated methodological capability allows us to appreciate the reality of the sentencing process as manufactured at different levels of abstraction as an objective or subjective phenomenon. The distinction between action and value is readily conceptualised in terms of the model, since it is capable of elucidating the context of sentence decision-making in a criminal trial (with its specific audiences, players, processes, institutions, power relations and symbolic structures), and lends itself to reconstruction at various analytical levels, including the analysis of decision-making in socio-historic context.

The model conceptualises the nature and direction of the relationship between action and value in sentence decision-making in terms of a recursive and reflexive process. Thus, the context of action proceeds through the analysis of interaction (process) as objectivity, and interpretation (value) as subjectivity. In other words, both interaction (as process) and interpretation (as value) have an external and internal dynamic which is revealed through analysis of the sentence decision-making process. Therefore, any methodology

---

75 For a full account, see Findlay and Henham (2005).

compatible with contextual modelling must be capable of reflecting both the objective and subjective dimensions of interpretation and be sensitive to different levels of meaning and understanding attributed to action and process in sentencing by trial participants.

Conceptualising the moral and the social

As suggested in chapter 3, our capacity to comprehend how subjectivity and objectivity interrelate; whether there can be any 'shared' understandings in any moral sense; and how these might find expression in sentencing are all questions which depend on adopting a compromise position about the possibility of objectively describing certain aspects of subjective experience. Accordingly, subjective understandings can only be revealed for different levels of analysis in sentencing research to the extent that we are able to adopt interpretative methodologies capable of identifying points where 'shared meanings' exist.

As indicated, this means developing constructs and methods that assist in comprehending the relationship between moral and social experience in sentencing. This entails a focus on how we conceptualise the relationship between objectivity and subjectivity and consequent further refinement of contextual modelling.

Figure 4.1 postulates how relational justice, or convergence between the individual and collective morality, is perceived in terms of objectivity and subjectivity. At the level of objectivity, a relational context means that individual and collectively held values about behaviour coincide, to the extent that this is externally verifiable; similar emotions and sentiments are expressed by everyone about the morality of behaviour and how it should be dealt with.

At the level of subjectivity, individual and collective consciousness, the subjective meaning that everyone attaches to what they are experiencing is shared. In other words, there is accommodation and convergence between the subjective and objective. A shared vision of the individual and the community based on deeply rooted cultural values – as often characterised by indigenous tribal communities – means that objectivity and subjectivity are more likely to coincide. Therefore, concepts of responsibility and accountability are evaluated against a holistic or relational vision of justice.

Such a holistic sharing of moral consciousness is frequently reinforced through the symbolism of external events in situations of war and social conflict. A typical example is the destruction in 1993 of the sixteenth-century 'Stari Most' bridge over the Neretva river in Mostar, Bosnia-Herzegovina, and its re-opening ten years later after the end of the Balkan War. For the indigenous Croat and Muslim communities, the bridge's destruction at first symbolised mutual hatred, division, destruction and death; then came some degree of healing, closure, sense of community and hope when the bridge was rebuilt.

The Mostar Bridge analogy raises a particularly salient point in the punishment context; the extent to which sentiment and emotion can be externalised through their attachment to structure and outcome. Conceptually, this concerns

PERCEPTION   **INDIVIDUAL**   **COLLECTIVE**

Objectivity   **Relational context**

Subjectivity   **Shared consciousness**

Figure 4.1 A model of relational justice

the crucial balance between what is 'real', as a matter of objectivity, and what is taken to be 'real' only because it can be generalised from subjective accounts. This is often a matter of speculation, since we can never really have epistemologically objective knowledge about what is metaphysically a subjective issue.

Consequently, sociological accounts must seek epistemologically acceptable methods of describing the moral foundations and normative power of relational justice. However, this must be preceded by conceptual modeling, such as Figure 4.1, that suggests a framework for relating the relevant norms and values of relational justice to social experience.

Relating concepts to governance

In this context, Hutton usefully invokes Weber's concept of charismatic authority[76] in relation to judicial sentencing and the problem of reconciling this with public perceptions of the judiciary as 'out of touch'. Utilising this concept of authority is particularly insightful when discussing the normative significance of punishment and sentencing[77] and its relationship to governance in criminal justice. The gradual ebbing away of authoritarianism, definitive forms of 'truth' and notions of universal morality has been a pervasive feature of post-modernity.[78] This phenomenon has undermined the notion that those who have power also have authority, in the sense that their decisions automatically imply moral allegiance on the part of the relevant audience. Individualism, moral pluralism, cultural diversity and social exclusion have all contributed to the fragmentation of those moral principles which had previously sustained a rational notion of 'civil society' in the modern state.

One reason why the moral authority of the police and other agents of criminal justice have diminished more readily than that of the judiciary is the latter's deeply entrenched power base, and the significant influence it is able to exercise constitutionally over the executive and the legislature in matters of sentencing policy.[79] It is also true to say that the conceptual framework which

---

76 Citing Cotterrell (1992).
77 See also the discussion of Loader (2006) in chapter 3 above.
78 See Smart (1999).
79 An example is the fact that, until recently, the judiciary was not permitted to have regard when sentencing to issues such as the cost of sentences, prison overcrowding or the effectiveness of sentences.

legitimises the moral authority of other criminal justice agencies is more exposed to public scrutiny than that of the judiciary. So, for example, the role of the police in the neo-liberal consensus that followed the Second World War, although conceived very much in the tradition of Beccaria's social contractarianism,[80] has been radically altered by the ever-pressing need for increased measures of crime control and crime prevention,[81] especially in the wake of the 'terrorist threat' precipitated by the events of 9/11. By contrast, the relentless expansion of penal law, the continuation and consolidation of judicial discretionary power through the development of sentencing principles, and the erosion of individual liberties through sentencing, continued largely unchecked until the demise of the rehabilitative ideal in the early 1970s and the gradual encroachment of human rights principles into matters of sentencing after 1998.

With the advent of the managerialism,[82] political pragmatism and penal populism of the 1980s and 1990s,[83] the judiciary has increasingly felt the corrosive power of media-led campaigns and suffered a degree of public vilification, often ill-informed, at the hands of political pundits and others with more sinister motives.[84] Paradoxically, this weakening of judicial authority and the rule of law has been accompanied by a re-affirmation of neo-liberal ideals of participatory democracy for the administration of criminal justice, as personified by the jury and the lay magistracy. Of course, the irony of this situation is that, at the same time as successive governments have been engaged in narrowing the scope of penal governance and control, they have also been encouraging more communitarian forms of sentencing, such as restorative justice. In terms of penal governance, such relinquishing of responsibility and accountability can be described as a form of abdication on the part of the democratic institutions of state for significant aspects of crime and its causes. Despite this reality, the notion of community involvement in matters of trial and punishment has come to represent a validation of penal policy, particularly in terms of public confidence as expressed through opinion polls and focus groups.[85] Its personification in the form of lay justice looks set to continue.

The ongoing debate in English criminal justice concerning the desirability of having lay or professional decision-makers in the magistrates' courts provides a perfect example of the disconnect that exists between public perceptions of sentencing and its social reality, and the consequent need for adequate

---

80 See Beccaria (1995) Introduction, xvii, for discussion of Beccaria's approach to contractarianism and utilitarianism.
81 These have paralleled the social fragmentation of British society since the Second World War.
82 Lacey (1994), Raine (2005) 291.
83 Bottoms (1994).
84 It is only recently that members of the judiciary were permitted to comment on sentencing decisions in the public arena.
85 See Roberts and Hough (2005).

conceptual and methodological techniques for analysis.[86] Arguments in support of lay decision-making in the magistrates' courts have tended to be based on the virtues of participatory democracy, localised justice, its symbolic legitimacy and on grounds of cost.[87] If the lay magistracy is truly a paragon of communitarian justice, then one would expect this to be reflected in measures of public confidence – also that there would be some way of evaluating whether or not the lay magistracy was (in reality) representative, and, if so, to what extent this reflected a sharing of moral values about crime and punishment more generally, or for specific contexts.

However, these issues are never fully explored. Research studies[88] have long highlighted the problem of making the lay magistracy more representative of the communities they serve, but, beyond demographic analysis, such studies invariably consist of comparisons of opinion and attitude between magistrates and a representative sample of the local community, or more generally. A recent example of this approach is provided by Morgan and Russell.[89] They were given a specific brief,[90] the main purpose of the research being to consider the appropriate 'balance' between lay and professional magistrates in the light of their findings.[91] However, they did not interview magistrates and ask them questions designed to find out more about how sentencing decisions are reached, and what influences them.[92] Instead, arguments about costs and efficiency savings seem to predominate. For example, despite the fact that the significant indirect costs[93] of the lay magistracy probably outweigh their advantage over professional magistrates in terms of direct costs, this was balanced against the additional costs incurred as a consequence of the latter sentencing more severely. This raises the question of whether issues of cost are relevant to justice,[94] and therefore, to the further question of how justice itself is defined and evaluated.

---

86 The debate has spawned a vast literature. Notable recent contributions to the debate include: Auld (2001), Darbyshire (1997), Davies (2005), Diamond (1990), McBarnet (1981b), Morgan (2002), Morgan and Russell (2000), Raine (2000), Raine (2002), Robson (2002), Sanders (2002a).

87 Morgan and Russell (2000) 6–10.

88 Hood (1962).

89 Morgan and Russell (2000).

90 The research remit is stated, *ibid.* 5.

91 *Ibid.* vii.

92 For example, specific case studies and other techniques could be developed and a questionnaire administered to a representative sample of magistrates designed to elicit information about their attitudes and beliefs about punishment and how these might manifest themselves in sentencing particular kinds of offender or offence. Interviews with legal advisors and clerks would also be useful, particularly as to how they view their advisory role in sentencing and the significance of their relationship with magistrates. Furthermore, such research should consider issues relating to the distribution of work between the magistrates and the Crown Court, such as mode-of-trial decisions, or effect of plea, since these have an important impact on sentence.

93 For example, the provision of legally qualified legal advisors, infrastructure and expenses.

94 This is not to mention the fact that more serious cases are heard by the professional judiciary.

Arguably, Morgan and Russell's research ought to have explored how local differences of ethnicity, gender and social class impact on sentence decision-making in the magistrates' courts, and whether there were any significant differences between the lay and professional magistracy in the influence of these factors on sentencing. Furthermore, respondents in any public opinion survey should be asked for their views on the role of punishment in dealing with crime generally, as well as their particular community, and how they see the role of lay sentencers in achieving communitarian objectives. The relationship between crime causation and punishment is particularly important, not only in considering regional variations, but also when assessing effectiveness and the kind of justice model against which the lay/ professional issue should be evaluated. Given the importance attached to recent initiatives in restorative justice, it is also unfortunate that Morgan and Russell were not able to adequately address the interests of victims and local communities.

The above criticisms reflect the fact that Morgan and Russell did not develop a model of justice, lay or otherwise, and use it to inform their research methodology and validate their subsequent findings against its criteria.[95] For this reason, their concepts of 'quality' and 'validity' are devoid of any notion of how the ideology of summary justice is constructed,[96] and the relative differences in justice delivery between lay and professional magistrates. Evidently, what kind of justice model might be thought appropriate depends on many factors, not least of which are the ideological and epistemological persuasions of the observer. For example, Sanders[97] identifies the core criminal justice values of fairness, democracy and efficiency against which to evaluate magistrates' justice, but such an approach may be criticised as lacking any critical engagement with the fundamental issue of governance. In other words, we should be looking at the question of values within the broader context of what ought to be the legitimate expectations of criminal justice and its ability to deliver them.

As argued throughout this book, although legitimacy is essentially a moral question, we need to understand how this relates to punishment and sentencing from a sociological perspective, particularly the extent to which sentencing can be seen as morally transformative.

---

95 See also Sanders (2002a) 333, noting Morgan and Russell's comment that: 'We were not in a position to assess the rectitude, appropriateness or justice of the decisions made by lay and stipendiary magistrates.' Morgan and Russell (2000).
96 See McBarnet (1981b), Carlen (1976).
97 Sanders (2002a) 325 *et seq.*

5 Procedural Justice and Due Process

The idea that procedural justice is important in determining individual perceptions about the legitimacy of the whole justice system is not new. Indeed, it might be suggested cynically that many so-called reforms in Western criminal justice are procedurally symbolic, but substantively insignificant. Nevertheless, the fact that procedural justice may affect perceptions and attitudes about punishment, as well as behaviour, confirms its central role in determining the legitimacy of punishment.

This chapter, however, has broader concerns than this, because it seeks to explain why we should improve our understanding of how procedural justice impacts on the relationship between social context and punishment. This is directly related to the governance issue discussed in chapter 2, especially the crucial role procedural justice plays in linking penal norms and their supporting ideologies to the attitudes and behaviours that ultimately define the parameters for criminal justice governance. Crucial to this understanding is the way in which procedural justice has the capacity to distort or misrepresent the relationship between penal ideology and the social reality of punishment. How such phenomena are conceptualised in criminal justice theory remains conjectural. However, the focus of this chapter is to consider why it is necessary to enhance the conceptual framework for understanding the relationship between such procedural constraints and the social impact of trial outcomes, and how this might be achieved.

Introduction

There are no prescriptions for identifying which normative aspects of sentencing may be regarded as concerned with procedural justice. As Tyler points out,[1] the idea of procedural justice has moved away from Thibaut and Walker's original conception of it as being concerned with instrumental or facilitative decision-making. Rather, it is now widely recognised that procedural justice is

---

1 Tyler (2006) 175.

equally concerned with non-instrumental matters,[2] in the sense that it has much more to do with the quality of decision-making[3] and its effects than with a perceived need for direct involvement in decision-making itself.[4] Significantly, therefore, Tyler identifies 'inferences about the motives of the decision-maker' and the nature of interpersonal contacts with the relevant authorities as crucially important variables.[5]

However, the most pertinent link Tyler draws[6] is between ethical judgements about the fairness of procedures and the perceived legitimacy of decision-making by state institutions and authorities. Noting that legitimacy is largely concerned with thoughts, feelings and behaviour, Tyler emphasises[7] the need to develop social theory in order to take greater account of these normative aspects of legitimacy. He further acknowledges the hugely important practical implications of this for developing relevant and sustainable forms of governance.[8]

Nevertheless, this chapter is not concerned with discussing the relevance of so-called therapeutic jurisprudence in this context; in other words, the extent to which the sentencing process benefits those persons affected by it. Rather, it is confined to exploring how to conceptualise the link between value judgements about the procedural aspects of sentencing and the perceived legitimacy of trial justice, and its implications for criminal justice governance. Nevertheless, the fact that research suggests[9] an important link between the therapeutic impact of procedures perceived as fair and the effectiveness of criminal justice governance is crucial for the future development of criminal justice policy.

Deconstructing procedural justice

The evaluation of whether particular procedures are fair is not merely a question of subjective judgement. It also depends on how the penal norms of each jurisdiction are configured; their social context and historical origins, and how such norms are made concrete through the process of sentence decision-making. As Rogers and Erez argue,[10] it is vital for researchers to question the meanings that participants in the process, both lay and professional, attach to what appear to be objectively uniform and value-neutral descriptions of events or processes, as well as their understanding of penal norms and their impact.

---

2 So-called 'relational criteria'.

3 Here Tyler includes such matters as representation, neutrality, bias, honesty and consistency; Tyler (2006) 175.

4 It should be noted that the instrumental perspective has important implications for conceptualising social control.

5 As Tyler suggests, the most important aspect of these interpersonal contacts appears to be linked to their impact on personal self-worth and self-esteem; Tyler (2006) 277.

6 *Ibid.* 278.

7 *Ibid.* 282.

8 *Ibid.* 287.

9 Waldman (1998).

10 Rogers and Erez (1999).

Sentencing practitioners will hold common understandings regarding the objective significance of particular procedural elements in the decision-making process. These procedures might involve such matters as the role of mitigation, the function of the prosecutor, the impact of plea, or the framework for determining the seriousness of offences. Nevertheless, their subjective appreciation of what these procedures mean, how they operate, and their overall significance for sentencing, will vary considerably. However, the penal ideology that underpins sentencing practice is a common defining characteristic for both subjective and objective interpretations of the trial's procedural norms and their implementation.

To focus the discussion this chapter takes the vexed question of plea bargaining and analyses it from a procedural justice perspective.[11] The purpose is not only to illustrate the significance of social context to procedural justice, but also to identify some core themes in an attempt to advance socio-legal analysis of the relationship between plea bargaining practices and sentencing within such contexts. The analysis focuses specifically on the impact of this relationship on the capacity of sentencing to promote the rights of victims and communities at both the international and national level, and more broadly on criminal justice governance.

Plea bargaining as theory and context

Where offences are broadly defined (as in international criminal law) the tendency for evidential matters relating to sentence to be ignored or treated superficially is accentuated. The problem is exacerbated where a plea of guilty has been entered to some or all of the offences charged. The implications are considerable, since the absence of substantive uncontested material relating to sentence may encourage inconsistency in sentencing and injustice in particular cases.[12] Where a guilty plea exists, a dispute regarding the nature of the factual evidence contended as relevant by the defence for mitigation of sentence may need to be challenged by the Trial Chamber, either in terms that require the

---

11 Plea bargaining poses a direct challenge to some fundamental rights associated with due process such as the presumption of innocence, equality of arms, the privilege against self-incrimination, the right to be treated fairly without discrimination, and the right to a fair and public hearing. However, the rationale for selecting plea bargaining as a focus for examining procedural justice in this chapter extends beyond these rights considerations, since it has broader social significance. For example, it may be argued that plea bargaining is fundamental to sustaining the ideology of crime control and undermines alternative justifications for sentencing. It is also questionable whether procedures based on expediency can engage with issues of social justice, especially where cultural misunderstandings exist as to the effects of such procedures. Finally, there are important issues regarding the extent to which victims should participate in plea bargaining.

12 This may constitute a breach of Art. 14.1 of the International Covenant on Civil and Political Rights (1976). For further discussion in the context of the ICTY and ICTR, see Kittichaisaree (2001) 291.

defence to adduce further evidence to substantiate its version of events, or through the instigation of some kind of procedural device,[13] whereby various approaches may be adopted in order to elicit an agreed version of the facts before proceeding to sentence.[14]

Profound criticism has been levelled at plea agreements in the international context, especially their capacity to distort the 'truth' of previous events to suit processual goals. This tendency produced a powerful dissenting judgement from the then Presiding Judge Wolfgang Schomburg[15] in the ICTY case of *Deronjić*,[16] in which he criticised the compromising effect of plea agreements and their adverse impact on maintaining proportionality in sentencing. Schomburg's primary objection to the sentence of ten years imprisonment imposed on the offender for a single conviction for persecutions (a crime against humanity) was that the factual basis for the conviction was enshrined in a plea agreement that provided an arbitrary and selective account of what took place, and in no way reflected the offender's undoubted participation in a much larger premeditated criminal plan of ethnic cleansing as a relatively high-ranking perpetrator. Whilst accepting, in principle, arguments advocating the utility of plea agreements for reasons of judicial economy and limited resources, Schomburg's chief objection lay with their possibly detrimental effect on the quality of justice subsequently administered by the court:

> The test should be, whether individual separable parts of an offence or several violations of law committed as a result of the same offence are not particularly significant for the penalty to be imposed. In those cases the prosecution may be limited to the other parts of the offence or violations of law[17]

Schomburg was also uncompromising in attributing to the Prosecutor a clear duty to safeguard justice by ensuring that 'there is no arbitrary selection of persons to be indicted and no arbitrary selection of charges or facts in case of an indictment.'[18] Regarding the significance of the guilty plea *per se*; after taking into account the comparative evidence,[19] Schomburg was unequivocal in his rejection of the notion that a guilty party should be capable of derogating from the gravity of a crime[20] and showed particular concern for the fact

---

13 Such as the English so-called 'Newton hearings'; see, further, Ashworth (2010) 375.
14 Rule 69, ICC RPE provides that any prior agreement between the Prosecutor and the defence not to contest an alleged fact is subject to the overriding discretion of the Trial Chamber to order a more complete presentation thereof in the interests of justice (particularly those of victims).
15 *Prosecutor v Deronjić* (Case No IT-02-61-S), Dissenting Opinion of Judge Wolfgang Schomburg, 30 March 2004.
16 *Prosecutor v Deronjić* (Case No IT-02-61-S), Sentencing Judgement, 30 March 2004.
17 *Supra*, note 15, para 8.
18 *Supra*, note 15, para 19.
19 Seiber (2003).
20 *Supra*, note 15, para 14(a)(b).

that 'no victim or person has been given the opportunity to address the Trial Chamber in person ... '.[21] Hence, the clear message conveyed by Schomburg was his insistence that the ICTY would be failing to fulfil its mandate if it did not adhere to the fundamental principle that a perpetrator deserved a sentence proportionate to the gravity of the crime, and that the mitigating effect of post-crime conduct should be strictly limited.[22]

The above observations about plea agreements and their increasing use in international criminal trials reflect the way in which procedural norms and processes in conventional adversarial, and to an increasing extent inquisitorial, trial paradigms may distort the 'real' facts to produce a version of the 'truth' which conforms to the exigencies of the trial context, with all its political ramifications, rather than the real experiences of the offenders and victims, and the communities in which they live. This conclusion suggests that, since plea bargaining[23] is a function of the criminal process, it is necessary to consider

---

21 *Supra*, note 15, para 20.
22 It is also important to note the deleterious effect that disproportionate sentences for such grave and aggravated crimes as genocide might have on sentences for murder cases in national jurisdictions such as those of the UK; van Zyl Smit (2002).
23 In England and Wales a clear distinction is drawn between charge, fact and plea bargaining, although all three are generally described as forms of 'plea bargaining'. Charge bargains occur when the prosecution agrees to drop a 'more serious' charge in return for a guilty plea to a lesser included offence, or in circumstances where the defendant faces two more charges and intends pleading not guilty to all of them, the prosecution agrees to drop one or two charges provided the defendant pleads guilty to one of the charges. Fact bargains occur where the prosecution agrees to present a particular (usually less serious) version of the facts in return for a guilty plea. Technically, a plea bargain, only occurs where there is a change of plea from not guilty to guilty, but no charge or fact bargain is involved. In such circumstances, the 'bargain' relates to the defendant exchanging his right to trial (and possible acquittal) for the certainty of a lower sentence than he would have otherwise received upon conviction. There is no 'bargain' in the sense of negotiation and agreement on sentence with the judge. This corresponds to the practice where a sentence discount is given in return for a guilty plea.
In the US the expression 'plea bargain' is also used generically. In many states judges encourage the prosecutor and defence attorney to agree a plea rather go to trial. This is more in the nature of a 'charge bargain'. If the offender does not accept this 'plea bargain' and elects to go to trial and is subsequently convicted, some judges may impose a 'trial tax', meaning a more severe sentence than might otherwise be imposed for the same offence. This is specifically designed to encourage defendants to 'plea bargain' rather than go to trial. All this is done informally, and is not part of the official case record, thus making it very difficult to study, more particularly so since most trials are for very serious offenders who pressures are greater, while practice may vary considerably from county to county.
In some jurisdictions prosecutors do not bargain, while in other, they might overcharge at the outset, knowing that they will 'bargain away' some of the charges. There are variations on a theme, whereby prosecutors will 'charge bargain', meaning an agreement with a criminal suspect before formal charges are laid, or 'sentence bargain', where the prosecutor will agree with the defendant on a lenient sentence recommendation to the judge in exchange for a plea of guilty to the original charge. In England and Wales, the expression 'sentence bargain' is normally taken to refer to an agreement between judge and counsel whereby the former indicates the likely reduction in sentence if the defendant pleads guilty.

its contribution to procedural justice within the social context that informs the framework and operation of that process. Needless to say, the observer's particular theoretical predisposition will necessarily dictate how the relationship between plea bargaining and social context is conceptualised. The most significant aspect of this is the impact theory has on the conceptualisation of procedural justice. If it is argued that procedural justice is to do with understanding the relational context of punishment, then one would expect this to be reflected in the theoretical perspective adopted to explain the impact of plea bargaining on sentence and its perception. Consequently, the kind of theoretical approach adopted to conceptualise procedural justice is likely to have a significant impact on how the *function* of plea bargaining is explained.

To begin with, the social reality of plea bargaining may be theorised as instrumental and reciprocal, in the sense that it generally follows a set of predetermined routines or processes which are designed to produce a particular result, consistently over time. The process itself may be conceptualised in a number of ways.

As an aspect of control ideology

From this perspective, plea bargaining may be viewed as a minor component in the armoury of social control. In other words, it is conceived as part of the apparatus employed by the state to label and stigmatise those whose actions have been criminalised.[24] However, a problematic moral issue concerns the role of the bargain in delineating the scope of the criminalised action, and in qualifying the extent of the individual responsibility that is attributed to it. Thus, whilst the bargain contributes to the smooth functioning of the control machinery, it also makes a normative contribution to society through its moral symbolism, since the bargain itself is a moral act with moral and normative[25] consequences beyond the courtroom. As such, it promotes a culture of moral compromise – of negotiated justice – that can seriously undermine the legitimacy attached to the criminal process, and the purposes of punishment in particular.[26]

A recursive validation of law

This approach is more consistent with a Weberian perspective on the relationship between law and social context.[27] Weber took the view that legal

---

24 This is consistent with Becker's view of moral entrepreneurship; Becker (1973).
25 The expressions 'moral' and 'normative' are used here in the conventional sociological sense. Therefore, 'moral' refers to penal values, whilst 'normative' refers to the impact of such values. Plea bargaining is morally symbolic in the sense of representing certain values about how the criminal process operates. It is also normative in the sense that the values symbolised by plea bargaining impact on the values of others and influence their conduct.
26 This is evidenced by the outrage that greeted Baldwin and McConville's original study; Baldwin and McConville (1977).
27 Cotterrell (1992) 153.

rationality becomes bureaucratised to the extent that the criminal process recursively perpetuates the development of internally consistent principles which tend to reinforce dominant political ideologies. A system of formal rationality reproduced in contexts where political and moral ideologies are at odds (as may well be the case both within and between modern pluralistic states) means that legal formalism predominates and increasingly causes the alienation of the criminal process from the outcomes it produces.

On this view, the fact that plea bargaining may be morally contentious cannot prevent it from becoming an integral part of the criminal process, or undermine any penal rationale which justifies this. On the contrary, the absence of any moral consensus tends to reinforce the moral authority plea bargains derive from being embedded within the law's normative framework, and so validates the penal ideology that sustains it.

Another form of legal closure may be achieved through the lens of autopoiesis or systems theory. Seen from this perspective, the task of theory is to identify ways in which criminal justice processes such as plea bargaining are reconstituted within systems other than law, and to consider how greater congruency might be achieved between the expectations which other systems have of law, and the ability of law to meet those expectations.[28] King argues[29] that autopoiesis theory focuses on three specific areas; the internal operations of different systems; the interfaces between these systems; and, the different social worlds of meaning that each constructs. He suggests that autopoiesis theory may operate as a 'liberating force' from conventional social science explanations which evaluate the operation of the law from external criteria derived from such explanations.

However, as argued in chapter 2, knowledge about the construction of discourses within and between systems is valuable to the extent that it may allow us to widen our understanding of how criminal processes are perceived, but the significance that systems theory attributes to law's instrumentality suggests that law, rather than human agency, creates the conditions for securing its own legitimacy by controlling the way in which the legal system prioritises communication inputs. Accordingly, the role of human agency is minimised by the normative requirements of the criminal process, which regulates social expectations and the influence of social context.

The idea that law creates the conditions that sustain its own validity is superficially attractive, but it may be argued that this autonomous view of law's instrumental capacity for legitimating its own activities and processes, beyond those related to the doctrine of law, is counter-intuitive. It gives too much emphasis to the power of law. Instead, it may be argued that the motives which determine action cannot be controlled by law. Rather, the value attributed to law and legal processes and the normative impact of law

---

28 Nobles and Schiff (1995) 299, 301.
29 King (1993) 218, 230.

all depend upon human agency. It is this that validates law and its consequences as an aspect of social life. In this sense, the social reality of plea bargaining and its normative consequences are regulated by law, but law does not control how the process is interpreted and what it signifies. This is achieved through human agency and its interpretation of penal ideology.

A recursive and structured process facilitated by human agency

This perspective differs from the last in that it sees control of the relevant communication channels, or pathways of influence, as being firmly in the hands of the legal professionals who facilitate the smooth functioning of the legal system and its processes. From a functionalist perspective, human agency, not law, is viewed as largely responsible for validating the actions and processes of the system.[30] Hence, system goals are seen as self-serving.

Clearly, this perspective attaches a greater importance to action than structure, and is consistent with the premises of structuration theory discussed in chapter 4.[31] As suggested, a crucial factor in Giddens's formulation is that the consequences of human action are recursively implicated in their social reproduction, subject to their rationalisation by social actors. Hence, social practices, such as plea bargaining, become integral to the recursive reproduction of the criminal process. According to this view, the role of legal structure, which includes the norms that regulate plea bargaining, is to enable and constrain the production of social practices such as plea bargaining. The system itself determines the framework of the communication structures that facilitate the process, but human agency shapes them as reproducible social practices. Therefore, plea bargaining may be conceived as a self-validating processual necessity to the extent that human agency controls the conditions for its social existence.

A technology of power

The work of Michel Foucault[32] and others[33] drew attention to the use of penal policy as a thinly disguised tool of social hegemony through oppression and discrimination. This type of analysis emphasises the following themes to a greater or lesser degree:

- Structural mechanisms such as plea bargaining are designed to facilitate the hegemony of penal ideology.[34] They are part of a deliberate smokescreen

---

30 Cicourel (1968).
31 Giddens (1979), Giddens (1984).
32 Foucault (1977).
33 Pratt (1995).
34 See Vogel's discussion of the instrumental use of plea bargaining by the power elite in the United States; Vogel (1999).

created by state or international forms of hegemony to give an illusion of 'justice, legitimacy or due process' to a phenomenon which, in reality, diminishes the right of parties to equal treatment by the criminal process.[35] As Mathiesen argues,[36] such activities are deliberately designed to divert attention away from other oppressive consequences of hegemonic power.

- Plea bargains 'negotiate' the reality of what has taken place; they distort facts for hegemonic advantage. For example, the epithet 'victor's justice' is frequently applied to international trial justice, and to the structural imperatives of the processes that produce it. Such a view makes it difficult to claim that the 'truths' international trials produce could contribute to transitional objectives such as reconciliation and peace.[37] In this sense, hegemonic theory finds it impossible to conceptualise the outcomes of criminal justice as benign or morally neutral.

Ultimately, the circularity of this perspective leads one to suggest that social context can be the only criterion against which to judge the 'legitimacy' or otherwise of hegemony and its structures of criminal justice governance.

Developing the argument

The fact that a number of constituencies may be implicated in ruling on legitimacy does not offer a satisfactory solution to these difficulties. Whether human agency, or structure, or both, are theoretically privileged as validating procedural decisions such as plea bargains is irrelevant in understanding their social significance, since procedural 'legitimacy' reflects different purposes for different constituencies. What is important is that we recognise and understand what these purposes are and their significance within different contextual settings.

The ICTR case of *Kambanda*[38] provides a good example of the problems that can result from such tensions between theory and context. The decision

---

35 See references to the effects of race and gender on sentencing in chapter 7.
36 Mathiesen (1990).
37 Such as the claims made by Dr Alex Boraine in the Plavšić case before the ICTY. Mrs Plavšić filed a statement in support of her motion for a change of plea at the same time as a written factual basis describing the crime to which she pleaded guilty and her involvement in it. In the former, she accepted responsibility and expressed remorse and invited others to 'examine themselves and their own conduct.' Significantly, she accepted responsibility as a leader for the grave crimes committed by others, whatever might have been their allegiance during the conflict: 'To achieve any reconciliation or lasting peace in BH, serious violations of humanitarian law during the war must be acknowledged by those who bear responsibility – regardless of their ethnic group. This acknowledgement is an essential first step.' The Trial Chamber was particularly impressed by the testimony of Dr Boraine who suggested that, given Mrs Plavšić's prominence and symbolism as a Serb nationalist and political leader, her apology and apparently full, genuine and voluntary expressions of remorse were highly significant indicators for reconciliation. Recognition of the pain and suffering experienced was particularly significant in providing a degree of closure for victims and their families; see Scharf (2004).
38 *Prosecutor v Kambanda* (Case No. ICTR-97-23-S), Judgement and Sentence, 4 September 1998.

illustrates the adverse consequences that have arisen as a result of a lack of clarity in the ICTR mandate. For some commentators, this mandate extends no further than retribution and deterrence, whilst others recognise a greater role for the ICTR in national reconciliation, as mandated by the Rwandan Organic Law. However, it may be argued that the ICTR has failed to place sufficient emphasis on its statutory 'reconciliation' mandate, particularly by failing to engage directly with the Rwandese people. Although the former Prime Minister pleaded guilty to genocide, little effort was made to capitalise on his confessions and admissions of guilt in the process of reconciliation at the local level.

Arguably, such a narrow approach to penal ideology undermines the educative and reconciliatory purposes of the trial process and its legitimacy. In terms of penal policy, it provides a further example of the consequences of failure to clarify the purposes for punishment and the principles of distributive justice. This lack of engagement between objectives and outcomes is not simply concerned with vertical relationships between international and local forms of trial justice. The analysis is equally applicable to comparisons of plea bargaining practices between different national jurisdictions,[39] and the limitations of the conclusions that may be drawn from them. This in turn mirrors the weak relationship within many national jurisdictions between penal ideology and sentencing outcomes and its adverse impact on the perceived legitimacy of procedural justice.

A consequence of this is a lack of engagement in some jurisdictions between victims and 'plea bargaining' practices, as in England and Wales. Although there are important considerations regarding the extent to which victims should participate in the decision to accept a guilty plea in return for a sentence discount, victims (actual and potential) clearly have an interest in seeing a true offender convicted, and many victims may be prepared to face the ordeal of a court appearance rather than seeing the offender receive a significant sentence reduction in return for a guilty plea.[40] Research by the Sentencing Advisory Panel,[41] for instance, confirmed this in the case of rape, where some victims reported that they would have been prepared to give evidence, if given the choice, in order to ensure that substantial mitigation was not based on a guilty plea. This frustration is often compounded by what are perceived as unwarranted charge reductions, where the victim or the victim's family has not been consulted.

Such exclusivity in plea bargaining is a consequence of the adversarial and retributive nature of trial justice. In the United States, for example, a guilty plea discount (or sentencing or confession reward) is frequently referred to as a 'trial penalty' to emphasise its coercive aspects. This may be justified by the egregious nature of the crime, as revealed in evidence given at the trial, which

---

39 See Jung (1997), Yue (2002), Langer (2004).
40 See Fenwick (1997), Henham (1999a).
41 See Sentencing Advisory Panel (2002); Clarke, Moran-Ellis and Sleney (2002).

would otherwise be concealed by a sterile guilty plea.[42] Indeed, some may argue that certain defendants do not deserve discounts under any circumstances, even if they are pleading guilty.

Alternatively, the guilty plea discount may be justified on the basis of its remorse rationale.[43] It may be argued that a truly remorseful offender would be prepared to accept any just punishment and, therefore, should plead guilty without expecting any sentencing concession. However, remorse may conceal the true nature of the transaction being undertaken; namely, bargaining away or buying-off the accused's due process rights in return for the economic benefits of a low trial rate, and (or) absolving victims and witnesses from the ordeal of oral testimony.

As McCoy convincingly argues,[44] it is undeniable that some offenders do indeed accept responsibility for their crimes, and many actually feel deep remorse. But the inherent subjectivity in knowing whether this is truly so, and how much credit, if any, an offender should receive for being remorseful, are thorny questions, not answered by the knowledge that remorse is sometimes real. This gives rise to difficult issues. The American federal system explicitly states that defendants who plead guilty may receive credit for 'acceptance of responsibility', but not necessarily. It may be questioned therefore whether an accused accepts responsibility because he or she is remorseful, or in acceptance of the prosecution's ability to prove the crime. 'Acceptance' is not necessarily the product of remorse.

The link between remorse and rehabilitation may also be obscure. Arguably, a remorseful offender has taken the first step towards rehabilitation and possible reform, and, having in a sense already served some portion of the sentence, should receive a lesser term. However, remorse does not necessarily lead to rehabilitation. In short, the remorse rationale is less satisfying than thoughtful judges, upon reflection, might be willing to acknowledge.[45]

In the light of these shortcomings it may be argued that procedural mechanisms such as plea bargaining should provide a more inclusive context for accountability that reflects the interests of the wider constituency of victims

---

42 McCoy (1994).

43 Bagaric and Amarasekara argue that the doctrinal basis for the recognition of remorse as significant in sentencing is untenable. Certainly, remorse does not fit easily into philosophical categories; Bagaric and Amarasekara (2001). For example, just deserts theorists, such as von Hirsch, argue that punishment must be assessed objectively on the basis of the degree of harm and offender blameworthiness, with remorse becoming relevant (if at all) at the post-sentencing stage; von Hirsch (1993) 72. On the other hand, the notion of a sentencing or confession reward corresponds closely with utilitarian considerations designed to prevent future crime by adopting a humane approach to the offender. Remorse may even be seen as punishment in itself and, therefore, justifying mitigation of sentence on the basis that the net cost in suffering would equal that of the non-repentant offender serving a longer sentence; McCoy and Henham (2004).

44 McCoy (1994).

45 McCoy and Henham (2004).

and communities, and that these aspirations should be capable of being realised through a modified normative framework.[46] Consequently, normative frameworks should be flexible enough to contribute as far as possible to the satisfaction of such 'interests' within any particular context. However, reflecting the 'interests' of victims and communities in the social reality of procedural decision-making will demand answers to the following questions:

- How are victims and their 'interests' to be defined?
- How are the rights of offenders, victims and those of the state to be balanced?
- What level of participation should be accorded to victims?
- How are victims to be represented in the trial?
- What is to be the role of the victim as witness?
- How is the trial to be structured in terms of verdict and sentence, and how will this impact on the evidence?
- How will the pre-trial, trial and post-trial phases of the trial impact on the victim's role?

In theory, the moral basis for what the state considers to be an appropriate balancing of interests is a matter of rational debate and political will. For example, the moral principles by which the state balances such interests may reflect the values and norms of particular human rights standards, and be embodied in legal instruments having universal validity. Yet, those standards are not sensitive to the reasons for the differing social and cultural complexities of particular contexts, such as social inequality or other forms of discrimination. They are moral principles whose normative effect is relative to context.

Therefore, such universalised values and the norms for their enforcement need to be grounded and validated by the values that underpin the social morality of differing social contexts. To achieve that kind of context-driven accountability requires the construction of a socially inclusive framework for justice delivery that is based on a clear social agenda. Accordingly, as Findlay and I argue,[47] a more inclusive kind of accountability for the trial should be underpinned by the following values:

- **DEMOCRACY** – Ensuring relevant interests are identified, understood and given their voice;
- **HONESTY** – Establishing trust and credibility;
- **TRANSPARENCY** – Promoting 'truth-telling' through process;
- **MEDIATION** – Facilitating reconciliation of conflicting interests;

---

46 Therefore, plea bargaining should enhance the trial's inclusive capacity.
47 Findlay and Henham (2010) ch. 6. Such values apply equally to domestic and international criminal justice.

- **PEACE-MAKING** – Supporting outcomes which engage with the promotion of peace and reconciliation;
- **RECONSTRUCTION** – Identifying ways of operationalising outcomes.

The extent to which these values are able to underpin procedural justice is currently limited by the hegemony of retributive ideology and adversarial trial. There is a distinct lack of harmony between victim interests and the crime-control agenda of encouraging and rewarding guilty pleas, suggesting the need for entrenched rights of consultation and participation by victims in plea agreements and sentence discount decisions. From a social perspective, sentence discounts for guilty pleas are particularly unsatisfactory, since neither the sentence nor the offence reflects the degree of harm actually suffered by the victim, or the community. More significantly, the capacity for achieving social accountability through the greater involvement of communities is severely restricted. These include the ability to pursue restorative objectives, such as rehabilitation, reparation and reconciliation, that are responsive to the needs of each social context and support its moral foundations.

Redefining ideology and context

The conventional starting point for any discussion of theoretical modelling of the criminal process in common-law jurisdictions has been Herbert Packer's[48] seminal distinction between crime control and due process. Whilst a paradigm of due process (such as Packer's) is not normatively prescriptive, it can be used to judge whether a particular process measures up to its taxonomy of idealised due-process characteristics. Despite the many qualifications and critiques of Packer's modelling,[49] it remains important in highlighting fundamental distinctions affecting the balance between individual and system interests in criminal processes.[50] These distinctions might be portrayed in terms of the following basic paradigms of trial justice:

- **THE PRAGMATIC MODEL** – in this conceptualisation judges equate trial justice as consistent with the achievement of system objectives. Hence, the ideology of trial justice is conveyed through symbolism and rhetoric. In this model guilty pleas/plea agreements are valued as contributing to the achievement of bureaucratic goals of speed, efficiency and the maximisation of resources.[51]

---

48 Packer (1969).
49 The most significant being his failure to account for context and power variables. For a useful summary, see Zedner (2004) 116–20.
50 Hudson suggests that tensions between liberty and security are replicated for criminal justice in the due process/crime control dichotomy; Hudson (2003a).
51 This model appears largely consistent with Packer's notion of crime control, except that the paradox between crime control and due process lies in what controls the significant discretionary power that resides in sentencing judges. The impetus against due process may therefore derive from judicial power exercised pragmatically, or the political hegemony of penal policy.

- **THE LEGITIMACY MODEL** – here trial justice is conceived in terms of a synergy between ideology and outcomes. Consequently, criminal trials are seen as transformative structures whose primary function is to provide the means of reconciling the ideology and the morality of punishment for citizens. This model conceives of guilty pleas/plea agreements as lacking moral legitimacy if they are not set against rationalisations for punishment that are supported by identifiable and relevant interests within society. Although it may be argued that enhancing the speed of punishment, saving court time and expense, absolving the need for victim/witness testimony, encouraging co-operation with the authorities and the further identification of suspects, are all beneficial consequences of plea bargains, these are administrative and bureaucratic rationalisations. It cannot be assumed that they support a penal ideology which has moral legitimacy in the eyes of all the significant players in the process.[52]

As suggested, the adversarial contest and retributive justice currently filter and distort the nature and impact of the 'truths' which form the historical record of alleged events. To enhance legitimacy in a restorative sense suggests a reconceptualisation of plea bargaining as an element of trial justice aimed at producing 'truths' that heal the community, rather than alienating and stigmatising individuals and social groups. This would give greater penal autonomy to damaged communities, including victims. Accordingly, moral engagement with trial justice within each context should be seen as a bottom-up process, rather than the 'top-down' approach currently prevalent.[53]

As Combs[54] suggests in the context of international trial justice:

> … proceedings now bear a much closer resemblance to the official inquiries of Continental jurisdictions, which are predominantly directed from above, by the court, rather than propelled from below, by the parties.[55]

The potential for greater victim engagement in aspects of procedural justice such as plea bargaining has been advanced considerably through the normative structures of international criminal justice institutions, such as the ICC. The work of the ICC's Outreach Programme has been significant in defining the justice needs of victims and communities in transitional states, but, as Clark argues,[56] there is considerable scope for development:

> … if war crimes tribunals are going to use plea agreements, and if these agreements are to stand any chance of having a positive impact, one of the priorities for these courts' outreach units should be to inform and to

---

52 The legitimacy model goes beyond Packer's notions of due process because it focuses on the perceived morality and social impact of trial decisions.
53 See McEvoy and McGregor (eds) (2008).
54 Combs (2002) 1, 103.
55 The issue here is the extent to which the 'top-down' approach ignores social context.
56 Clark (2009).

educate local communities – and in particular victims – about these agreements. This lesson is perhaps particularly pertinent to the ICC, as a permanent court. Learning from the ICTY's experience, it has recognised the importance of outreach work and it is to be hoped that it will also come to appreciate the crucial relationship between outreach work and plea bargains.

Arguably, there is a need to go further in identifying and realising the transitional needs of victims and communities by reconceptualising penal ideology and effecting victim engagement through a modified normative framework for the trial.[57] Such a reconceptualisation is equally valid for national as for international forms of criminal justice. However, to develop such a context for 'legitimacy' within any particular jurisdiction will require a theoretical approach and dependant methodology involving comprehensive comparative contextual analysis. The objective would be to deconstruct the social context of plea bargaining with a view to exploring the potential for reconceptualising it within a penal ideology more focused on restorative justice.[58]

Plea bargaining – illustrating the contextual approach

This section explores how this objective might be achieved. More specifically, it examines how the conceptual paradigm described in chapter 2 could be utilised as a framework against which to deconstruct those aspects of trial justice considered relevant for understanding sentencing in different contextual settings. As suggested, plea bargaining provides a useful setting through which to pursue this objective, since it is a generic expression that describes a broad array of criminal justice practices. These practices are culturally distinct and informed by penal ideologies having different contextual origins and significance. Plea bargaining is also a phenomenon that takes place at all levels of criminal justice; global[59] to local.[60]

The purpose of the paradigm is to provide a framework for linking issues conceived as relevant for understanding the relationship between sentencing and the legitimacy of trial justice in different contexts (see Figure 2.1). The issues identified in Figure 2.1[61] are envisaged as interrelated aspects linking the morality of punishment and its perceived effects. A number

---

57 Findlay and Henham (2010).
58 See generally in the international context: Combs (2007).
59 For detailed analysis of the practice of plea bargaining in the ICTY, see Henham and Drumbl (2005). See, generally, Henham (2005b) ch. 4.
60 For example, in the context of England and Wales, see, generally, Darbyshire (2000). For a European overview, see Tulkens (2002).
61 Namely: ideology, ethics, practice, perceptions, reaction and impact.

of theoretically informed themes are suggested to facilitate each analysis.[62] The choice of these themes is arbitrary in the sense that each is chosen to address specific issues considered relevant to understanding the social reality of plea bargaining and its impact on sentencing. It has been argued elsewhere that, by developing such a paradigm, the theoretical orientation and methodology for any contextual study may be fixed, and the empirical findings analysed against the chosen criteria.[63]

A description of how this paradigm might be developed in the case of plea bargaining is provided in Figure 5.1.

Theory

SELECTED THEORETICAL ISSUES

The relationship between law[64] and morality – This reflects the ongoing debate as to whether law is a closed system of rules, or whether law and morality are irrevocably interconnected. If the latter, it then becomes possible to argue that particular value positions should, or could, provide the moral basis for that relationship.

The social function of law – Here the purpose is to identify and evaluate theoretical insights about the nature and function of law from a social perspective. In this respect, Durkheim's theorising about the cohesive function of morality and his notion of moral individualism may prove fruitful in explaining how the perception of punishment and its social impact are linked.

Conceptualising process and punishment as symbolism – The theoretical insights of labelling theory can help to explain the interactive aspects of processes such as plea bargaining, as well as providing a perspective that favours a more holistic appreciation of its relationship to sentencing.

The significance of hegemonic power – Foucault's notion of technologies of power and its associated theorising provide a means for conceptualising the power dimensions of plea bargaining, especially its strategic controlling function of facilitating process ideologies that serve to alienate and stigmatise individuals and social groups.

---

62 For example: the notion of process as symbolism, the relationship between law and morality, sentencing as social interaction, the relationship between hegemony and punishment.

63 Consistent with the notion of contextual modelling, the paradigm may be refined following the use of inductive or deductive methodologies; see Henham (2001).

64 'Law' is used here to denote sentencing law in the broader sense of including substantive and procedural norms.

Modelling

SPECIFIC QUESTIONS ARISING FROM THE THEORETICAL DEBATE

Law and morality – whether plea bargaining is compatible with victims' perceptions of trial justice.

The social function of law – whether Durkheim's ideas help us to understand how victims and communities relate to processes such as plea bargaining in a moral sense, and the social repercussions of this in terms of the perceived legitimacy of the criminal process.

Symbolism – whether labelling theory is able to clarify the practical social reality which lies behind the rhetoric used to justify plea bargaining.

Hegemony and control – whether plea bargaining is a strategically significant aspect of social control which helps sustain the dominion of powerful elites through criminal justice.

Methods

Issues of law and morality – theoretical evaluation; questionnaires and surveys (victims/participants)

The social function of law – theoretical evaluation; victim surveys

Punishment as symbolism – theoretical analysis; covert and participant forms of observation; structured and open-ended interviews; narrative analysis; expert commentary

Control – theory and policy evaluation; interviews; observation; narrative analysis; expert commentary

Figure 5.1 A paradigm for deconstructing the social contexts of plea bargaining

METHODOLOGICAL IMPLICATIONS[65]

To summarise; this paradigm is intended to facilitate the analysis of the previously identified themes of morality, ideology, ethics, practice, perception, reaction and impact in terms of their social significance for plea bargaining. The analysis is focused[66] on issues of law and morality, punishment as symbolism, sentencing as social interaction and the relationship between hegemony and punishment. Themes are explored through a variety of theoretical lenses, chosen because they are thought likely to enhance knowledge about a particular aspect of plea bargaining. This in turn furthers our understanding of the connections between criminal process and its perceived legitimacy.

---

65 The main focus here is on combining inductive and deductive methodologies. For further discussion, see Henham and Findlay (2002).

66 These categories are not exhaustive, nor are the theoretical approaches suggested. They have been chosen because they are thought to be the most useful route to understanding how punishment and sentencing relate to legitimacy in any given context.

It is suggested that there is some underlying relationship between law and morality which is fundamental to grasping its true nature and significance for the sentencing process. More importantly, the paradigm takes full account of the fact that knowledge about the moral foundations of penal law is pivotal to appreciating its authoritative social function. Hence, the degree of moral attachment between citizen and penal law is a measure of the state's authority to punish. These observations apply equally to globalised forms of legal authority, such as international penal law and its underlying ideology.

Tensions between procedural justice and community protection

The final section explores one aspect of this paradigm in more depth. It analyses the social context of sentencing as an instrument of hegemony and social control and the relevance of this for understanding penal legitimacy, drawing on Foucault's theorising about the role of punishment and sentencing as technologies of power.

What constitutes the appropriate balance between community protection and the rights of those offenders judged to be 'dangerous' provides an archetypal example of the tension between procedural justice and social context. Recent legislation[67] in England and Wales, for instance, has removed the presumption[68] that an offender with a previous conviction for a specified offence (as defined) is to be presumed 'dangerous', unless the court, on the basis of the evidence before it, finds this to be unreasonable. Notwithstanding that this eliminated judicial discretion, its wider significance concerns the reverse burden placed upon the offender in such circumstances to adduce evidence that would lead a court to find the presumption of 'dangerousness' was rebutted. The consequences were profound for the offender, especially given the widely recognised difficulties of reliability inherent in the methodologies available for reaching a finding of 'dangerousness' sufficient to trigger the relevant provisions.

Given these problems, it has long been debated whether the adversarial trial provides an appropriate context for making such decisions.[69] It may be argued, for example, that the legitimacy of these findings is not enhanced by the fact that they are essentially non-legal judgements made by judges about an individual's propensity to commit serious offences, notwithstanding that they are based on the 'best possible' evidence available. To structure the relevance and weight of such evidence according to legal criteria not only introduces a further normative layer, with its own ethics and procedure, it tends to obscure the already weak foundations for decision-making. Therefore, to force the offender to rebut a presumption of dangerousness unjustifiably privileges legal procedural norms over the rights of the accused. This diminishes prospects for adopting

---

67 Criminal Justice and Immigration Act (2008).
68 Originally contained in S229(3) of the Criminal Justice Act (2003).
69 See, generally, Ashworth (2010) ch. 6.

more socially reflexive approaches for determining dangerousness. On the contrary, it suggests an excessive use of law as a means of social control.

These arguments should also be scrutinised in the light of the long-running ethical disputes that surround the aims of punishment and their relevance for sentencing 'dangerous' offenders.[70] The debate between utilitarian and retributive approaches for dealing with the problem of punishing 'dangerousness' is generally conducted at a level that considers its role in balancing the rights of the offender against those of the community's right to protection against the possible commission of further serious acts by the offender. In this sense, each member of the community is seen as a potential victim. Wood has argued that legal distinctions such as guilt or innocence, intention or lack of intent, do not justify the differential treatment of so-called 'dangerous' offenders from 'dangerous' non-offenders in terms of the risk of future harm. Consequently, subjecting 'dangerous' offenders to harsh treatment beyond civil detention is not justified. These arguments tend to reinforce the suggestion that determinations of 'dangerousness'[71] should be made for all alleged offenders before they are considered for further processing by the criminal justice system, and that the latter should not be automatic.[72]

To explore the social context of these developments from a hegemonic perspective, it may be argued that ideologies of 'dangerousness' comprise one or more of the following elements:

- **BIFURCATION**: This refers to the strategy of diverting scarce penal resources to what are portrayed as more constructive and cheaper alternatives to short prison sentences; the remainder being targeted at so-called 'dangerous' offenders. Whilst it hints at rehabilitative and economic justifications, penal bifurcation primarily fulfils what Mathiesen[73] has termed the 'action function' of penal policy, in suggesting that something is being done about what the ruling elite has designated 'a significant social problem' against which it is taking immediate and decisive action.
- **SOCIAL CONTROL**: This is achieved where politicians dictate the moral parameters for law and order by mandating custodial sentencing for 'dangerous' offenders while increasing the use of community punishment for

---

70 See, for example, Wood (1998).

71 Not only by 'experts' but also including community representatives, so that a more socially integrated response to offending behaviour can be developed and incorporated in representations put before a trial process, should that be the preferred option.

72 The dangerous offender legislation of the Netherlands represents an improvement on the clinical approach of some nations. In the Netherlands, mental health assessments do not focus solely on predicting dangerousness or base their assessment only on a mental disorder. Rather, the assessments examine mental state, offender history and circumstances, and behaviour at the time of the present offence, which provides a more rounded picture of the offender and the offence, potentially improving behaviour predictions. For recent evaluation of the Dutch model, see de Boer and Gernts (2007).

73 Mathiesen (1990).

designated others. It raises difficult questions about the reasons for including particular social groups and individuals within these designated categories.[74]

- **RETRIBUTIVE JUSTICE:** The penal strategy of 'bifurcation' increases the problems of reconciling consequentialist measures aimed at reform or rehabilitation with the predominantly retributive framework for sentencing prevalent in western industrialised societies. The political goal of hegemony favours the latter and leads to a distorted emphasis being placed on retributive sentencing practice.

- **COMMUNITARIANISM:** Community punishments tend to conform to restorative values of bringing offenders, victims and communities together. Although they are operationalised through multi-agency, socially supportive and integrative approaches, this is not the case for those offenders who are unfortunate enough to be labelled and processed as 'dangerous'. For this group, the scope for the individualised use of judicial discretion in sentencing and the adoption of alternative approaches is minimised through the state's hegemonic penal ideology of stigmatisation, repression and exclusion.

Hence, in the case of so-called 'dangerous' offenders, the social reality of hegemonic power and control is achieved by criminalising the future behaviour of a group of individuals who have been singled out for harsh treatment because they have offended in the past. Conventional approaches for dealing with 'dangerousness', as in England and Wales, cannot be justified satisfactorily through conventional retributive rationalizations, such as restoring unfair advantage, communicating censure, or otherwise enforcing the rule of law. Current explanations fail to take into account the social reality of hegemony in this area of penal law and its adverse consequences for those individuals unfortunate enough to be subjected to it.

Summary and conclusion

Despite the apparently self-validating nature of law's authority, and hence procedural justice, a reconceptualisation of that authority based on the social utility of restorative objectives is nevertheless destined to remain context-specific and self-validating. Nowhere is the fragmentation of legal authority more apparent than where forms of local justice are reconstituted for transitional purposes. As Clark explains,[75] not only are communities and local forms of justice delivery essentialised by outside commentators, the complexities of local forms of transitional justice are difficult to characterise because their procedures have been modified and are no longer representative of the original. There may also be variations of what purport to be the same form within a transitional state. Additionally, where cultures are broken, authority figures

---

74 See, further, Brown and Pratt (eds) (2000).
75 Clark (2008).

change, so there may no longer be a well-established form of local justice, and no undisputed authority. Consequently, previously identified and documented indigenous processes cannot be held out as being authentic.

This is not simply a question of the effects of temporal change on forms of local transitional justice in post-conflict states, it also raises important questions for understanding how the legitimacy of procedural justice is constructed in both global and local contexts. The assertion of local justice, as against international jurisdictions such as the ICC, is made primarily on the basis of its perceived greater legitimacy for resolving the conflicting interests of post-conflict societies. Arguably, this phenomenon mirrors similar tensions that increasingly afflict the so-called civil society of nation states, where social fragmentation reflects inequalities of gender, race, religion, ethnicity or social circumstances, and where the control apparatus of state criminal justice is no longer founded on shared moral values about what should constitute 'crime', or how it should be dealt with.

The challenge for theory and method is to develop ways of identifying and explaining the social significance of these changing relationships for procedural justice. In achieving this it is increasingly important to distinguish the different agendas that may be set for the trial process and those expectations that are aimed at achieving social change. It is at this juncture that the relationship between criminal justice and governance becomes critical.

6   Deconstructing Evidence for Sentencing

The emphasis in this chapter is on exploring the broader context in which information is attributed the status of fact and 'truth' for the purposes of sentence. It describes and evaluates the procedural contexts which determine the factual basis for sentence in global and local forms of trial justice, and considers the likely impact on this process of adopting alternative punishment rationales and trial models. The chapter also examines the significance of sentencing norms and practice within different jurisdictional contexts and trial traditions. For example, the chapter focuses on problems associated with conventional approaches to establishing the factual basis for sentence, considering differences between adversarial, inquisitorial and hybridised forms of trial justice; the relevance of substantive law issues and their impact on sentence determination; the significance of the verdict; the relevance of previous convictions; and the adequacy of mechanisms for resolving disputes about evidential status.

The chapter's focus on these procedural questions seeks to establish their wider significance for trial justice. More particularly, this specific aspect of sentencing procedure – how testimony is attributed the status of fact, and therefore 'truth', for the purpose of decision-making – represents a critical nexus between the normative and the social in trial justice. This is because it is through the processual activity of sentence decision-making that value is attributed to those 'facts' available[1] for sentence. This merging of the normative and the social is facilitated through the human agency of discretionary decision-making, yet current criminal justice theory fails to consider adequately the significance of these processes, or how they function. The most important aspect of this concerns our limited understanding of how sentencing norms and principles are implicated in the merging and transformation of fact and value, especially how legal and social factors actually impact on decision-making, and the broader significance of this for understanding the legitimacy of justice.

---

1 Not legally excluded, or unavailable for tactical reasons.

Conceptualising evidence

Conceptualising fact and truth from the perspective of legitimacy

The objective of this section is to illustrate how present conceptualisations of the relationship between evidence and sentencing fail to deal adequately with the issue of legitimacy and to suggest how criminal justice might better theorise this relationship and its significance for trial justice from a communitarian perspective. For present purposes, the notion of 'communitarianism' implies that the nature, presentation and admissibility of evidence relevant to sentence should be firmly linked to establishing a version of events, or 'truth', that has moral significance beyond the trial in terms of its relevance to and impact on those 'communities' and citizens primarily affected by the criminalised behaviour.

Consequently, as suggested in chapter 1, it is important to consider how notions of 'fact' and 'truth' are constructed in sentencing and their interrelationship in terms of:

- the aims of punishment;
- the relationship between penal ideology and penal norms;
- the transformative capacity of sentencing;
- perceptions of trial justice;
- the social impact of trial justice.

The aims of punishment

We may begin by asking why the aims of punishment take their present form and how they are represented in penal ideology. I would suggest that there is a recursive link between sentencing outcomes and penal rationales that has a significant impact on the truth-finding capacity of the trial. This notion is not novel, in that, for example, one may assert that a trial informed by a purely retributive ideology is likely to produce much less 'contextual' evidence than one which gives equal prominence, or a significant role, to rehabilitation or more restorative forms of justice delivery. Whether the penal rationales in question operate within a normative environment that is adversarial, inquisitorial or hybridised will also clearly impact on the nature and quality of the evidence, in addition to its presentation and admissibility. It might also be argued that the recursive nature of the trial and the outcomes it produces has the effect of re-affirming perceptions of legitimacy attaching to the penal ideology which informed it.[2]

---

2 Such reasoning is consistent with Weber's view of legal-rational authority as sustaining the legitimacy of normative rules.

The relationship between penal ideology and penal norms

How does penal ideology find expression in the legal framework for sentencing?[3] This question raises the possibility that there is a significant link between penal ideology, the normative framework for sentencing, and the nature and quality of the evidence available for sentence. More specifically, it draws our attention to the structure of the criminal process, especially the configuration of the different phases of the trial and sentencing processes, and their evidential impact.

The transformative capacity of sentencing

How does sentencing facilitate the transformation of penal ideology into concrete outcomes? In general terms, this involves the notion of sentence decision-making as a transformative mechanism, the explanatory capacity of sentencing and the transformative potential of judicial discretionary power, all of which are considered in detail in chapter 4. However, in the evidential context, the important point to make is that the potential of trial evidence to contribute to any transformative project through its impact on sentencing will largely depend on the realisation that judicial discretionary power, within appropriate ideological and normative boundaries, can be deployed to serve more communitarian interests, rather than being increasingly constrained by ever more prescriptive guidelines, or used as an instrument of political repression.

Perceptions of trial justice

This concerns the extent to which sentences are perceived as legitimate by 'relevant audiences'. There is clearly a crucial link between the source and quality of the evidential base for sentencing decisions and the likelihood of those decisions being perceived as legitimate. However, the fundamental issue here is the need for that evidence to fairly reflect broader communitarian interests in the crime and its effects. This means that evidence beyond that which is purely crime-based must be drawn from the affected 'community' in order to establish the collective impact of the alleged criminality and to identify those 'interests' having a 'legitimate' claim to some form of criminal redress. In this sense, the objective is also to establish the relevant constituency for collective liability, if there is one, but mainly to ensure that the accountability of the individual charged with the offence is situated within a proper evaluation of collective accountability, and that the penal response to the harm caused reflects clearly identified and appropriate communitarian concerns.

---

3 Both substantive and procedural.

The social impact of trial justice

This is concerned with the relationship between perceptions of legitimacy and subsequent behaviour. More specifically, we focus here on the moral and social status of sentencing decisions in terms of their impact beyond the trial proper. However, in order to appreciate this, it becomes necessary to conceive of the criminal trial as a transitional process, thereby extending our understanding of its communitarian purchase. This means thinking more creatively about what trial outcomes can actually contribute and achieve as social phenomena occurring within a particular local or global context. In so doing, the trial needs to be situated within its appropriate socio-political context

These observations may be elaborated further in terms of the legitimacy model described in chapter 1.

Evidence and the legitimacy model

Beyond thinking about how to conceptualise the role of evidence and its relationship to the sentence decision-making process in sociological terms, we also need to consider how this perspective is connected to moral judgements made about such events by 'relevant audiences', and its significance. In terms of the model elaborated in chapter 1, this involves extending our conceptualisation of the recursive nature of sentencing as a transformative enterprise by injecting a moral dimension into the analysis. The purpose of this is to enable us to model more accurately the relationship between the social construction of criminal trial justice and its moral evaluation at various phases of the trial.

The exercise is complicated by the fact that the theoretical dimensions requiring analysis range from the elaboration of higher-order concepts, such as penal ideology, down to the description and explanation of interactions involving procedural norms, such as the impact of evidential norms on the quality of the information available for sentence. In relation to the latter, for example, conceptualising process for the purpose of modelling sentencing would need to take account of its qualities as:

- **RECURSIVE** – particularly the role of human agency in the reproduction of sentencing structure;
- **PROCESSUAL** – in that the nature and impact of sentencing is influenced by the outcome of discretionary decisions made at specific decision points both before, during and after the trial; and
- **INTERACTIVE** – the fact that the social context of judicial, professional and lay interaction is fundamental to decision-making.

As suggested, the model's capacity to explain the relationship between evidential issues and the perceived legitimacy of trial outcomes can be extended by elaborating each dimension of the model from a moral perspective. This can best be thought of in terms of two distinct areas. The first is concerned with the moral ideology that informs the normative structure of the trial; here we would include issues of morality, ideology and ethics. The second is concerned with the praxis of sentencing in the broadest sense; here we include sentence decision-making, perceptions and reactions to it, and its wider significance for the legitimacy of criminal justice as a fundamental component of governance.

In terms of the relationship between evidence and sentencing, the most important theoretical issue to consider is the extent to which the evidential process may be seen as mirroring shared values about punishment and sentencing. Different theoretical approaches to understanding criminal justice produce conflicting views about the role of evidence in sentencing and its significance; for example, the extent to which the criminal process is hegemonic, discriminatory and oppressive. Such a perspective would necessarily see penal ideology and its normative framework, including the purpose and form of its evidential norms, as instrumental in achieving these objectives. Therefore, perceptions of the aims of punishment and their reflection through sentencing as principles of distributive justice, or conceptions of trial justice as predominantly adversarial or inquisitorial, are all distorted if viewed through a particular theoretical lens. To change this penal mind set and arrive at a point where a more communitarian approach is taken as to the purpose and quality of the evidence deemed acceptable for trial purposes is likely to involve fundamental changes to penal ideology and the ethical framework for justice delivery.[4]

Developing a more inclusive and integrated approach for explaining the nature and function of evidence as regards sentencing requires both a detailed understanding of the social context of penal law and of the role played by morality in the specific social environment of the trial. This requires us to think more effectively about the contingent nature of penal morality within any social context, and its reflection in the trial process. The contested nature of 'fact' and its assertion as a form of 'truth' having social consequences within each trial reflects this contingency. To appreciate this insight further, we also need to develop the capacity to construct meaningful accounts of human experience within each trial. Such subjective accounts should probe understandings of the way evidence for sentencing is perceived and utilised by participants and the trial's 'relevant audience' in specific social contexts. They should also address the wider point that the relationship between evidence and sentencing forms part of a recursive process of trial justice; in other words, it is an accepted feature of a particular penal realm, be that a specific society, or the international stage.

Therefore, as Rogers and Erez argue,[5] our understandings of what actually counts as 'fact' depends on the extent to which we can generalise from subjective accounts of what a 'fact' is and means. In this sense, deconstructing the meanings which relevant participants attribute to aspects of the trial in terms of their subjective experience should add considerably to so-called

---

4 See, further, Findlay and Henham (2010) ch. 4.
5 Rogers and Erez (1999).

'objective' accounts of these events. Such an approach should therefore help researchers get closer to appreciating the normative significance of what is taking place because it provides an insight into why and how individuals attach value to what they perceive within the context of the trial.

However, as Tamanaha suggests,[6] decision-making within the criminal process effectively merges the relative realities of 'fact' and 'value'. Arguably, appreciating this insight is an essential prerequisite for any meaningful examination of the praxis of punishment, since it enhances any conceptualisation of the relationship between the norms and practice of sentencing. In particular, it suggests that the capacity of the trial to produce 'truth' is limited by the following factors:

- the exigencies of the adversarial contest which pre-selects relevant material;
- the penal ideology which informs the normative structure of the criminal process;
- the social morality attaching to the punishment of certain forms of behaviour and types of offender.

The case of Julius Streicher, the Nazi propagandist, who was tried and executed at the Nuremberg trials after the end of the Second World War[7] provides a interesting illustration of the influence of context on the nature and quality of the evidence adduced at trial and its impact on sentencing. Eastwood considers how the legal case against Julius Streicher was constructed and developed from the interrogation stage through to final judgement. From the perspective of international criminal justice, the work is significant for a number of reasons. First, it confirms through detailed documentary analysis how the Nuremberg prosecutors operated within a rigid and uncompromising retributive framework designed to deliver 'victors' justice. Secondly, Eastwood documents how the adversarial context of Streicher's trial facilitated the development of the evidence necessary to sustain the indictments alleged against him. This was achieved within an atmosphere heavily charged with prejudice, and loathing of those whom the Allies judged as culpable for presiding over one of the darkest periods in human history.

Despite a pretext of due process and equality of arms, Eastwood demonstrates how the account of the 'truth' of Streicher's inciting behaviour which was carefully constructed during the trial amounted to a 'self-fulfilling prophecy'. Although a 'truth' derived from the evidence, it seemed predestined to correspond with what the Allies already 'knew' to be the case; that beyond any (reasonable) doubt, Streicher was an instrumental figure in the incitement of acts so heinous as to be beyond 'normal' human comprehension. Significantly,

---

6 Tamanaha (1997).
7 See Eastwood (2006), Eastwood (forthcoming).

Eastwood also draws attention to the relationship between these issues and the apparently disproportionate nature of Streicher's punishment.[8]

Eastwood deals adequately with issues of comparability and context in drawing attention to the legal analysis of the trial evidence and its relationship to the development of 'incitement to genocide' as an international criminal offence. Nevertheless, the analysis might have been enriched by a broader consideration of how the legal manufacture of 'justice' and the nature of the 'truth' it delivers are essentially matters of temporal and contextual significance.

Thus, as has been argued, it is a matter of conjecture as to whether a purely 'legal' doctrinal approach, or even analysis of the 'law in context', are capable of providing lessons for the development of law which can be generalised, beyond its essentially technical advancement. Regarding this, it may be asked whether Eastwood's work, in common with others that draw links through history and time, can really tell us much about 'justice'. Rather they confirm the view that context validates law's authority to deliver 'justice'. However, this does beg the question of whether international trial justice has much to do with the development of international criminal law, or, indeed, whether it should. The question achieves added complexity where trial processes are hybridised, or where international trial justice is examined merely as a component of what might be considered necessary to promote reconciliation and peace in the aftermath of war and social conflict.

On this point, it is worth noting that Eastwood is careful not to go beyond an essentially legal remit. In so doing, she establishes parameters for comparison and context which need to be acknowledged. Nevertheless, her assertion that 'selective interpretation and reinterpretation operate at the core of the legal process' raises a fundamental point. Since this depends on the exercise of discretion by trial professionals, it may be argued that it is not possible to get a comprehensive picture of the decision-making processes involved in the trial without taking a broader contextualised approach. Clearly, it is impossible to avoid the law and morality debate if one is attempting to explain the 'law in action', because the social reality of the legal process has normative significance. As argued, an appreciation of this is essential if it is desired to engage with the notion of legitimacy. In the case of Streicher, for example, a narrow legalistic perspective may lead us to question the extent to which his trial was an appropriate context for understanding the 'truth' about the cultural impact of hate speech in pre-war Germany.

As explained in chapter 2, a number of broad analytical themes are engaged in order to simplify the analysis and enhance our understanding of the legitimacy of trial justice. These themes are concerned with the symbolism of trial justice; the relationship between law and morality; how the social interaction of sentencing is theorized; and the relationship between hegemony and sentencing. This chapter explores issues of symbolism and hegemony

---

8 Streicher was hanged in October 1946.

and their implications in the context of establishing the factual basis for sentence.[9]

Symbolism

The symbolic significance of the punishment process for individual defendants may lie in its conceptualisation as a ritual of denunciation and degradation, in that certain offenders might internalise sentiments of moral condemnation and denunciation expressed by the court to the extent that their own moral sentiments are altered irrevocably.[10] In this sense, the symbolism of punishment rests in its perception as a personification, conduit or transmitter of moral sentiment about punishment; a message intended equally for the condemners and the condemned. However, because punishment is relative in its symbolic and real effects, and these do not necessarily coincide, it is suggested that conceptualisations of symbolism in this context need to be developed against notions of 'community' which take full account of the demands for 'justice' of the 'relevant audience' at both the local and global level.

The symbolism of punishment is conveyed through the declaratory or expressive nature of sentencing. However, the intended communication of any moral message through the delivery of the sentence may itself be compromised as a result of normative imperatives such as plea agreements (see chapter 5). A specific criticism is the distorting effect of plea agreements and their capacity for downgrading the 'truth', in terms of how the trial marks the seriousness of what has taken place through punishment. The result can be major concern about the factual basis underlying the conduct charged.

A typical example of the evidential impact of plea agreements is the ICTY decision in *Momir Nikolić*,[11] where the accused was originally charged with numerous crimes, including genocide. Following an amended plea agreement the accused eventually pleaded guilty to the lesser charge of persecutions (a crime against humanity), and all remaining counts on the indictment against him were dropped. In considering Rule 62 *bis* of the ICTY's Rules of Evidence and Procedure,[12] the Trial Chamber observed that it was satisfied that the

---

9 The relationship between law and morality and the analysis of sentencing as social interaction are discussed in chapters 2 and 4 respectively.

10 Lemert (1972).

11 *Prosecutor v Momir Nikolić* (Case No. IT-02-60/1-S), Trial Chamber, Sentencing Judgement, 2 December 2003. The Appeals Chamber subsequently confirmed the Trial Chamber's earlier interpretation of this (and other) principles, particularly relating to the timing and credit for a guilty plea; *Prosecutor v Momir Nikolić* (Case No. IT-02-60/1-A), Judgement on Sentencing Appeal, 8 March 2006.

12 This provides: 'If an accused pleads guilty in accordance with Rule 62 (vi), or requests to change his or her plea to guilty and the Trial Chamber is satisfied that:

(i) the guilty plea has been made voluntarily;
(ii) the guilty plea is informed;

factual basis upon which the charge of persecutions was based reflected the totality of the defendant's criminal conduct.[13]

Whilst the sufficiency of the factual basis for the crime eventually charged, and the accused's participation in it, is not in doubt, the application of this rule ignores the fundamental capacity of plea and other forms of negotiation for manipulating evidential 'truth' to suit normative goals. Not only does the plea deny the possibility of testing the evidence in open court, its acceptance of a charge as reflecting the totality of the accused's criminal conduct effectively denies the court the opportunity to give full expression to the totality of that criminality through the imposition of a penal sanction which adequately reflects the seriousness of the crime(s) and the culpability of the offender. In effect, the moral symbolism of the specific sentence, and international penality's wider expressive impact in terms of publicly denouncing serious breaches of international criminal law, may be seriously compromised if the totality of the punishment is not seen to be proportionate to the totality of the defendant's criminal conduct.

Conditions of successful degradation ceremonies

James Cockayne's[14] insightful analysis of the symbolic transformative effects of international trial justice, discussed in chapter 2, not only illustrates the utility of labelling theory for modelling the social reality of trial process, whether local or global, but also suggests the efficacy of this approach for deconstructing the social reality of specific trials. Therefore, in this sense, it carries with it a strong methodological imperative.

In addition, as Sudnow[15] and Cicourel[16] showed in their seminal analyses of trial processes, labelling theory is especially useful for drawing attention to stereotyping and the ways in which procedural rules are systematically redefined in order to satisfy systemic pressures for conformity. Similarly, Skolnick's[17] insight that legal rules provided 'a context for the behaviour of legal men', envisages studies of the 'law in action' (such as the social reality of discretionary decision-making within the trial) as essentially concerned with deconstructing

---

(iii) the guilty plea is not equivocal; and
(iv) there is a sufficient factual basis for the crime and the accused's participation in it, either on the basis of independent indicia or on lack of any material disagreement between the parties about the facts of the case,

the Trial Chamber may enter a finding of guilt and instruct the Registrar to set a date for the sentencing hearing.'

13 *Supra,* note 11, para. 51.
14 See Cockayne (2005) 455, 456, Garfinkel (1956).
15 Sudnow (1965).
16 Cicourel (1968).
17 Skolnick (1966) 27.

the meanings attributed to action by social actors, and the interrelationship and transformation of legal principles and rules within legal institutions.

Three specific characteristics of labelling theory make it especially useful for theorising the recursive nature of the trial process over time, and in different social contexts:

1. It rejects the static model of causal determinism, emphasising the process of interaction and its symbolic elements.
2. It views the individual self and human experience as constantly changing, so it becomes important to interpret that experience and its significance.
3. It recognises value-pluralism, focusing attention on the fact that notions of criminality and the perceived legitimacy of punishment are contingent upon context.

As Cohen and Young suggest,[18] 'facts' are frequently represented as 'truth' based on an implied moral consensus, whereas in reality this consensus is a myth, since it comprises what are presented as attitudes that are widely held. Hence, it may be argued that excessive stress on particular aspects of information, particularly through the way in which evidence is identified and presented at the trial, when taken together with the enormous symbolic impact of the verdict and sentence, tends to reinforce existing prejudices and stereotypes. This can lead to social breakdown and the incapacity of 'community'; the stigmatisation of 'community' and individuals through reinforcing negative imagery; increased penal severity through the distorted emphasis on particular forms of behaviour and accountability; and, as Mathiesen argues,[19] it may provide a smokescreen for wider, more political objectives.

The most positive aspect of labelling theory in terms of its heuristic potential is its capacity for deconstructing the transformative context of sentencing and its perception as individual and collective forms of shared experience on a micro or macro scale. At the micro level, as King points out,[20] for individuals this suggests a focus on those variables that influence the behaviour of participants within the court process; for example, contextual reasons for delay, inconvenience and disruption to the accused's case. Significantly, these influences may also be instrumental in their impact on the identification and presentation of 'relevant' evidence and its subsequent contribution to the factual basis for sentence.

The above suggests that the significance of the evidence employed for the purposes of sentencing is frequently obfuscated by the symbolism of the sentencing decision, especially its declaratory nature.[21] This tends to confirm

---

18 Cohen and Young (1981).
19 Mathiesen (1990).
20 King (1978) 167, 218.
21 For example, it was stated by the ICTY in *Aleksovski* that 'A sentence of the Tribunal should make plain the condemnation of the international community was not ready to tolerate serious

the view that the discretionary power of sentencing is instrumental in constructing symbolic images of relevant case material, legal rules and punishment justifications for participants and the 'relevant audience' in criminal trials, and that the normative structure of the trial is implicated in this process. The proposition also suggests that failure to engage with the relative realities of symbolism and context (local and global) are significant obstacles to any constructive dialogue with alternative perceptions of trial justice.

Social control

This section examines the proposition that the construction of what becomes trial evidence and therefore accepted as 'fact' is crucially affected by the way in which penal justice operates as a form of social control. This suggests that there a direct relationship between the development of penal ideology as an instrument of hegemonic power and the instrumental use of criminal sentencing to implement divisive and discriminatory penal policies.

Stan Cohen's[22] early critique of the 'justice model' of sentencing that replaced the 'rehabilitation model' following its demise in the early 1970s highlights significant aspects of the debate. Cohen[23] makes the point that the justice model produced a refocusing of judicial discretion in sentencing, in the sense that substantive justice became increasingly obscured by the rhetoric of formal justice. This resulted in a substantial increase in penal severity and in the overall length of prison terms. However, the most significant change was the refocusing of penal policy on individual responsibility and the gradual abdication of the state's responsibility for addressing the social causes of individual criminality. Cohen saw this as a distortion of the neo-classical project, in the sense that the state was gradually moving away from its essential role in protecting citizens and leaving them to face the consequences of the exercise of their free will without the state accepting reciprocal accountability for the social causes and consequences of crime. Hence, those qualities of fairness, compassion and individuation that were the hallmark of judicial discretionary power under the rehabilitation model were fatally compromised.[24] Cohen concluded that the attack on discretionary decision-making was therefore misplaced. He suggested that the impact on sentencing was directly correlated to socio-political changes, pointing to the need for greater moral congruence between citizen and state in matters of penal policy:[25]

---

violations of international humanitarian law and human rights'. As Frulli points out, one of the most important functions of the sentencing judge in the international tribunals should be to give effect to the degree of wrongdoing expressed in international criminal law; Frulli (2001).
22 Cohen (1985).
23 *Ibid.* 113, 114.
24 *Ibid.* 246, 247.
25 *Ibid.* 249–51.

... justice has to be 'reaffirmed' as an honourable moral value in itself
and not something which the law mechanically requires ... personal
responsibility and the moral purpose of law ... If people lose their sense that
'things are working' and that they are living in a 'fair and just' society ...

More recently, Pratt[26] has described how, utilising Foucault's notion of 'technologies of power', the relationship between state moral authority and law
is reciprocally created and maintained through the state's control of that
body of knowledge which both defines the criminal law and determines the
characteristics of those who are labelled as criminal.

A further insight in the present context concerns the relationship between
social control and accountability, especially its role in manufacturing 'truth' –
'the notion that it is necessary to discover the truth about the past in order to
achieve justice in the present'. Cohen[27] posits the possibility that structures
of international punishment, for example, provide a form of social control
which is instrumental in negotiating and defining what becomes known as
truth and counts as justice. He suggests that any discussion involving
redefinition – whether resulting from trial justice, truth and reconciliation,
lustration, or any other means – inevitably has significant implications for
social control and governance during and beyond the transitional justice
phase. This is because, as Cohen so aptly describes,[28] any determination
about the facts of what has happened in the past inevitably creates an artificial barrier – a breaking of the relationship between past and future – so that
policing the past becomes more a question of making sure that the past
remains closed. Social control becomes a process involving the selective
control and manipulation of memory.

In the post-modern era the certainty of this discourse has been replaced by
what Cohen calls the 'centrifugal' falling away of information and memory.[29]
The relativity of values and their controlling ideologies become increasingly
difficult to identify, let alone predict, making it harder to prevent the absolution
of the human rights abuses carried out by totalitarian regimes, such as that
of Argentina in the 1970s. In other words, to a greater or lesser extent, we
gradually come to accept degrees of denial without necessarily being aware
of the insidious effects of this acceptance on our perceptions and actions
towards present and future human rights abuses, especially those amounting
to international crimes, such as genocide and crimes against humanity.

There is a sense, of course, in which all trial evidence is concerned with
the control and manipulation of memory, depending on the objectives of
those who are in a position to exercise such control in a practical way.

---

26 Pratt (1995).
27 Cohen (1995) 7, 15. Cohen goes on to develop a paradigm of regimes of continuity; *ibid.* 48.
28 Citing Spitzer; *Ibid.*
29 *Ibid.* 48.

However, the extent to which individual participants, lay or professional, can manipulate the system depends as much on its bureaucratic and administrative goals as it does on the ideology that informs its normative framework. The need to identify both the system and sub-system goals of the trial is as important as an appreciation of the holistic nature of the criminal process and the points of tension and synthesis existing between its component parts.[30]

Evidence of prior criminality and sentencing

Issues of principle

One of the most enduring debates in sentencing concerns the extent to which an offender's prior criminal record should be taken into account in arriving at the correct sentencing decision.[31] As Roberts suggests, it is a relationship that features heavily in how the general public perceive the legitimacy of sentencing:

> Sentencing ... involves the expression of community censure, and a legal system which ignored community sentiment would ultimately lose the power to condemn – hence the need to ensure that expressions of censure bear a close connection to public ascriptions of blameworthiness. If legal censure ignores a variable considered by the public to be highly relevant to blameworthiness, the legitimacy of the sentencing process will be undermined.[32]

The conventional terrain for this debate lies between those who adhere to some form of retributive justification for punishment and those who favour more consequentialist aims. Although this is not the place to rehearse these arguments in full, a brief résumé of the main positions is necessary in order to make sense of the argument that follows.

Roberts[33] draws a clear distinction between cumulative sentencing, 'flat-rate' sentencing and the progressive loss of mitigation approaches. The rationale of cumulative sentencing, which grew to prominence in the second half of the nineteenth century, is based on the notion that repeat offending should be dealt with by successively more severe punishment, irrespective of the offender's circumstances, although it may be modified to take account of mitigation. Its main justification is that of individual deterrence, but it may also be justified in terms of general deterrence, incapacitation, denunciation or 'just deserts'. The 'flat rate' approach is purely retributive and argues that previous convictions should never be taken into account in sentencing. Such convictions

---

30 See Henham (2004a).
31 For a detailed analysis, see Roberts (2008b).
32 Roberts (2008a).
33 Roberts (2008b) 8. See also Ashworth (2010) ch. 6.

have no relevance in determining what should be the appropriate penalty because retributive punishment can only be justified in the instant case, not on the basis of what the offender is judged to have done in the past. A middle position is provided by the progressive loss of mitigation test which focuses more on the issue of culpability. This approach basically allows first offenders to receive a discounted sentence for their hitherto blemish-free record, but the discount is gradually reduced to correspond with any repeat offending. As von Hirsch has argued,[34] repeat offenders are more deserving of punishment by virtue of their repeat offending, although this approach depends for its success on maintaining the difficult balance between notions of offence seriousness (ordinal proportionality) and the possible impact of individual culpability on sentence lengths. Consequently, there have to be clear limits on the extent to which the discounting of sentences can go.

The moral justification for limiting the effects of retributive punishment implicit in the progressive loss of mitigation approach is that of recognising human frailty where an individual has lapsed into repeat offending. The first offender, having been censured, is deemed, as a rational human being, to be capable of drawing the appropriate moral conclusions about what they have done in the past, and it is therefore assumed that this knowledge will influence their future intentions. However, this kind of approach remains value-neutral in terms of those influences that might cause a particular offender to draw, or not, the 'appropriate' moral conclusion from the censure of punishment.

As von Hirsch describes,[35] the basic tenets of commensurable sentencing can be traced back to the Enlightenment principles of fairness, which were founded on very definite views regarding the moral function of penal law and therefore its moral boundaries. As a crucial component of the social contract between citizen and state, the function of liberal penal law was to preserve Man's natural right to liberty. Paradoxically, both as regards punishment and crime prevention, classical principles deliberately failed to eschew notions of moral welfare and how they might be realised through penal law. It was simply assumed that the 'appropriate' moral decisions would be reached by both the individual offender and the criminal justice system that processed them. As argued earlier, the neo-liberalism of the mid- to late nineteenth century did nothing to broaden the concept of criminal responsibility, or to widen the notion of moral blameworthiness beyond that of the individual offender. Similarly, moral justifications are largely absent from the discourse of modern deserts theorists, such as von Hirsch, who rely on so-called objectively verifiable notions of 'justice' and 'fairness', known to 'most' members of society.

However, this kind of intuitive approach does little to engage with the pluralistic values of post-modern society to explain how this moral diversity is reflected in different views about the legitimacy of punishment. As suggested,

---

34 See von Hirsch (1976).
35 *Ibid*. 195.

Roberts has clearly argued the case for a more nuanced reflection of public opinion in the approach of the courts to sentencing offenders with previous convictions, and cautioned against the consequences of failing to do so:

> A wide discrepancy between the practice of the justice system and the views of the community with respect to basic principles will lead to public disaffection with the sentencing process. This, in turn, may well *undermine attempts to ensure compliance with the law.* A departure from community views on an important issue like proportionality or the appropriate use of previous convictions will drain away much of this legitimacy – hence the need to *pay some heed to community reaction* [emphasis added].[36]

Whilst Roberts recognises the continuing need for sentencing to reflect community values in order to retain its legitimacy, he does so by arguing that failure to do so will tend to undermine the rule of law. At one level, this is, of course, perfectly accurate, but there is another sense in which the relationship between legitimacy and the rule of law needs to be tested in the penal context. This is based on the notion that there is a point where the dialectic between community values and the rule of law becomes so acute that the latter is no longer able to respond to changing community values, or the ruling elite prevents this for hegemonic reasons. The former is exactly the scenario described in chapter 1, where it was emphasised that the proper exercise of judicial discretionary power in sentencing is the first thing to be scrutinised where the moral nexus between legitimacy and the rule of law begins to break down.

This book contends that the value-pluralism of post-modern societies forces us to go beyond conventional paradigms of trial justice in order to close the gap between the rule of law and legitimacy. It has been argued that penal norms should be democratised in the sense that the moral values that underpin them should reflect more accurately those interests of the diverse moral audiences over which it holds dominion. Clearly, a complete reconceptualisation of trial ideology that favours the merging of retributive and restorative notions of justice would provide a reconstituted basis for identifying and evaluating the prior criminal history of the offender.[37] However desirable that may be, there may be other ways in which a more communitarian approach could be adopted in our consideration of previous convictions within a 'just deserts' framework for sentencing.

This would entail a move away from the conventional focus of previous convictions evidence on individual culpability towards a broadening of that concept to allow the admissibility of more community-based evidence. However, the intention would not be to extend the relevance of culpability-based evidence, but rather to allow such community-based evidence where it can be

36 Roberts (2008a) 478.
37 See, further, Findlay and Henham (2005).

demonstrated that culpability effectively extends beyond the individual offender to the community itself,[38] so that the parameters of culpability become both individual and collective.

Accordingly, the primary focus would be on the harm[39] that has been caused through previous criminality and on extending the notion of deserts to encompass that of social deserts. The latter means that not only should deserts be viewed as including harm which goes beyond victim impact in the sense that it also impacts on the community, but also that the impacted community may have a reciprocal responsibility to account for what has taken place. In terms of victim and community impact, fresh individual convictions should be treated as adding to the sum total of behaviour that the community judges harmful. However, viewed from the perspective of shared individual and collective accountability, the retributive justification for the increased penalty holds because it is the cumulative impact of that behaviour on both the individual *and the community* that is being punished. Therefore, from a retributive perspective, deserts punishment is based on a more communitarian assessment of harm and culpability. Notwithstanding, although the offender is not being punished for consequentialist and/or utilitarian reasons, these may be side-effects of the primary rationale.

If behavioural impact is judged against such a broader notion of deserts, one that is related to social justice (howsoever conceived), this does not weaken the categorical imperative towards retributive punishment provided there is *prior* agreement about what counts as harm. In other words, this is not punishment *for* recidivism in the narrow sense, but punishment *because* recidivism damages the community.

As suggested, offender culpability would need to be judged against a broader notion of community accountability, one that accepts the possibility that the community itself may bear a significant responsibility for the individual's past and present criminality. The concept of 'seriousness' for sentencing purposes would reflect the degree of harm caused to community interests and not be based solely on an individually focused assessment of harm and culpability. For example, the extent of community harm would feature more directly in assessing the relevance for sentencing of factors such as offender premeditation and remorse.

The ceiling for crime seriousness would thus be judged against a broader communitarian conception of harm and culpability. Presuming it would be possible to identify community perceptions about the harm caused by certain forms of repeat offending, through public opinion surveys and local representation, this information could be factored into determining the parameters of ordinal proportionality. Therefore, what would be achieved in terms of

---

38 Such as repeated institutional or systemic failure.
39 Immediate and consequential, although relevant criteria would need to be developed to delimit the latter.

deserts is to take the issue of previous convictions as possible aggravating circumstances out of the penal equation when sentencing.

These suggestions can be compared with those of other scholars. Zedner,[40] for example, identifies the need for a theoretical reorientation to achieve a greater integration of retributive and reparative forms of justice[41] based on the abandonment of culpability as the central focus for sentencing and paying much closer attention to the issue of harm and its social distribution. Her argument for a move away from culpability to a broader based conception of social harm is founded in part on an appreciation that crime infringes rights held in common socially and that the conception of harm should be widened because citizens have rights to a presumption of security.[42]

Such arguments resonate with the notion of some movement towards merging retributive and restorative forms of justice, but there are differences in emphasis. The most important of these is that the rationale for extending notions of harm and culpability so that they are more grounded in plural community values recognises that 'legitimacy' is a contextually relative concept. Thus, the legitimacy of trial justice is conceived in terms of how sentencing engages with competing moral values and the extent to which it is successful in doing so. Therefore, changes should be rights-protected rather than simply rights-based as Zedner argues, since this ensures that rights of access are given 'real' practical effect.[43]

The re-orientation of international trial ideology proposed by Mark Findlay and myself suggests a fundamental recasting of the moral foundations for international trial justice.[44] What I have argued for here is a more limited re-appraisal of the role of previous convictions within the existing adversarial trial and retributive sentencing paradigm. I have not explored this rationale further by advocating changes to the normative framework of the criminal trial[45] based on a greater synergy between notions of individual criminal responsibility and those of individual culpability for sentencing purposes, since this would be beyond the remit of this book. However, suffice it to say that any reconceptualisation of the notion of culpability for sentencing of the kind discussed above carries with it the implication that there should be a corresponding adjustment in the formalised notions of fault embodied in the norms of substantive criminal law.

To summarise, my greater focus on the harm caused to the victim and the community is not gained at the expense of individual culpability. Rather, it

---

40 Zedner (1994).
41 Zedner suggests that arguments for incorporating reparative elements into the criminal justice process are mainly pragmatic and economic.
42 Environmental and corporate crimes become relevant within this broader formulation.
43 Henham (2004a).
44 See Findlay and Henham (2010) ch. 1.
45 This would have implications in terms of the relationship between the verdict and sentencing phases of the trial.

recognises that culpability as a concept needs to reflect its broader communitarian context – namely, some greater reflection of how the morality of the behaviour in question is judged by those who are directly affected by it. Similarly, concerning the assessment of harm, this should not be seen in purely objective terms, but needs to be related more effectively to victim and community perceptions of harm and reflected in the judgements made by those charged with delivering justice in the courts. As always, the difficulty remains that of devising principled criteria for decision-making. In this, human rights principles and their influence on the norms of access and decision-making are crucial.

Previous convictions and international trial justice

The Rome Statute of the International Criminal Court (ICC) is largely silent about the role of previous convictions in sentencing.[46] Article 76(1) of the ICC Statute simply provides:

> In the event of a conviction, the Trial Chamber shall consider the appropriate sentence to be imposed and shall take into account the evidence presented and submissions made *during the trial*[47] that are relevant to the sentence [emphasis added].

However, some minimal elaboration is provided by Article 78 of the ICC Statute which contains a general direction regarding those factors to be taken into account in the determination of sentence according to the ICC Rules of Evidence and Procedure (RPE), as follows:

> 1. In determining the sentence, the Court shall, in accordance with the Rules of Procedure and Evidence, take into account such factors as the gravity of the crime and the individual circumstances of the convicted person

Rule 145(1)(b) of the ICC RPE refers to the Court's duty to balance any mitigating and aggravating factors when sentencing. The type of factors that might be regarded as appropriate aggravating factors are stated in Rule 145(2)(b)(i) of the ICC RPE as including 'Any relevant prior criminal convictions

---

46 The ICTY and ICTR provisions are extremely vague, with judicial discretion being the primary determinant of the weight to be attached to any evidence deemed relevant to sentencing. Rule 101(B) of the ICTY RPE provides that 'in determining the sentence, the Trial Chamber shall take into account the factors mentioned in Article 24, paragraph 2, of the Statute, as well as such factors as are (i) aggravating circumstances'. This is mirrored by the ICTR provisions. There appears to be no other reference to previous convictions in the sentencing regime of either tribunal.

47 Note the implication in favour of one hearing to include both verdict and sentencing phases.

for crimes under the jurisdiction of the Court or of a similar nature'. However, Rule 145(2)(b)(vi) of the ICC RPE also requires the Court to take into account 'other circumstances which, although not enumerated above, by virtue of their nature *are similar* to those mentioned' (emphasis added). A point arising in this context is the extent of the ICC Prosecutor's obligation to bring previous offending behaviour on the part of the accused to the attention of the Court where the offences concerned do not appear to fall directly within the ambit of Rule 145(2)(b)(i).

Rule 145 only serves to obfuscate the possibility of achieving a coherent sentencing approach. It refers to the determination of sentence pursuant to Article 78, paragraph 1, which is clearly directed towards fixing the level of sentence appropriate to the offender and the offence; namely the individualisation of the sentence, once the question of seriousness has been settled in principle.[48] In other words, Article 78 is concerned with what Hart might describe as distributive justice, or Tonry and Morris as the purpose *at* sentencing. Rule 145(1)(c), in particular, includes factors relating to harm and culpability – such as the harm caused to the victims and their families, the nature of the unlawful behaviour and the means employed to execute the crime, and the degree of intent and participation of the offender – which are normally considered as primary determinants of seriousness based on just deserts considerations of harm and culpability, that forms the basic rationale for the retributive element of sentencing in the ICC.

There are a number of other more specific difficulties with these provisions concerning the issue of previous criminality. To begin with, it is not clear whether the 'other circumstances' referred to in Rule 145(2)(b)(vi) relate to the broader social context of the instant case, to offences for which the offender has previously been convicted, or evidence which was previously utilised in judging the offender's future propensity to commit crime. All three possibilities may conceivably apply.

Correspondingly, the reference to 'other circumstances' which are by their nature 'similar' to the instant case is equally unclear. If, for example, the similarity lies in the fact that violence was present in previous offending behaviour, then the issue becomes one of deciding how to reflect different degrees of previous violence as an aggravating factor when individualising the penalty for the instant offence.

---

48 Very little (if any) guidance on this matter is provided by the ICC Statute. Article 76(1) of the ICC Statute provides:

> In the event of a conviction, the Trial Chamber shall consider the appropriate sentence to be imposed and shall take into account the evidence presented and submissions made during the trial that are relevant to the sentence.
>
> Patently, this provision neither provides nor refers to any rationale or statement of purposes for sentencing. Neither does it indicate (even in outline form) the nature and form that any sentencing guidance might take.

To take the third possibility above, it may be asked whether previous offending behaviour that attracts a longer than 'normal' or 'commensurate' sentence on the basis of the offender's perceived 'dangerousness' should be treated as an aggravating factor. The issue here concerns the extent to which a finding of 'dangerousness' can constitute 'other circumstances', so making the previous offending behaviour 'similar' and hence relevant to that in the instant case. This is a difficult question because a determination of 'dangerousness' includes findings which relate both to the nature of the harm that has been caused by the offender in the past and an assessment of the likelihood that the offender will commit similar offences in the future. Any determination of 'dangerousness' is highly equivocal because it is partially based on a qualitative evaluation of the characteristics of the offender 'which are susceptible of change with the passage of time.'[49] The role of the court in making the determination is equally equivocal.[50] This is not simply a matter of technical distinction. It illustrates a fundamental difficulty in deciding the extent to which 'other circumstances' that relate to the commission of previous offences are relevant to the instant offence if they reveal aggravating features which tend to establish a pattern of offending or characteristic traits of the offender.

Similar difficulties of interpretation arose in connection with the ill-fated Section 29(1) of the English Criminal Justice Act of 1991, which Roberts describes as representing:

> ... the most ambitious attempt by any legislature to distance the sentencing process from a cumulative sentencing model[51]

Section 1 of the 1991 Act stated that the courts were only allowed to take account of the present offence and one other associated offence in considering whether an offence was serious enough to impose a custodial or a community sentence on the offender. Section 29(1) itself provided:

> An offence shall not be regarded as more serious for the purposes of any provision in this part by reason of any previous convictions of the offender or any failure of his to respond to previous sentences

Although the Government's intention was to give statutory effect to the progressive loss of mitigation principle, the section caused a considerable amount of confusion because it was so poorly drafted. One interpretation was that it allowed the court to take into account the circumstances of any offence of

---

49 These words were used in the ECHR case of *Thynne, Wilson and Gunnell v United Kingdom* (1991) 13 EHRR 666, para. 70.
50 For detailed analysis, see Henham (1997).
51 Roberts (2008b) 100.

which the offender had been previously convicted, or of any other current offence, if considered relevant to assessing the seriousness of the present offence.[52] As Ashworth pointed out,[53] one of the difficulties of this formulation was that it relied on a vague notion of what 'circumstances' relating to the previous offending behaviour might be sufficient to increase the seriousness of the present offence and so push the penalty beyond that normally considered appropriate.

Such obfuscation is compounded in the context of international trial justice, and its significance increases still further if the previous criminality in question is taken as evidence of 'dangerousness' requiring some kind of preventative response on the part of the court. The concept of protective sentencing and its justification has long been a matter of intense debate among criminal justice scholars.[54] With regard to selective incapacitation, views range from the utilitarian to the purely retributive. The former holds that it is justifiable for sentencers to order precautions to be taken against those offenders who seem likely to commit harmful offences in the future – even when these precautions, added to the penalty, exceed what is regarded as commensurate to the offence. Such an approach is both reductivist and utilitarian, since it holds that the perceived social utility of protective sentencing in terms of crime prevention outweighs the humanitarian cost to a small minority of offenders and their families.[55]

For the committed retributivist, precautionary sentences are always unjustifiable since they consist of punishment for crimes as yet uncommitted.[56] This view holds good against both selective and collective forms of incapacitation. In relation to the latter, Crocker[57] has argued that the only basis for its justification relies on the notion that the offender, having failed to serve previous sentences in full, has not suffered full retribution, so that his moral culpability merits more severe punishment. Owens[58] goes so far as to suggest that collective incapacitation is more ethically acceptable than selective incapacitation because the former does at least reflect previous serious misconduct rather than a presumed tendency towards it.

These contrasting views regarding the morality of protective sentencing form the moral basis for justifying the ascription or derogation of individual offenders' rights[59] in a situation where they are adjudged dangerous. Bottoms

---

52 See Ashworth (1991) 151 *et seq.*
53 *Ibid.* 152.
54 Floud and Young argue that protective sentencing is morally *un*objectionable, since dangerous offenders, having forfeited their right to be presumed harmless, must inevitably carry the burden of accepting the principle of just distribution of risks; Floud and Young (1981).
55 Tonry (1992).
56 For an attempt at reconciliation of the two extremes, see Wood (1998).
57 Crocker (1995).
58 Owens (1995).
59 The significance of rights for international sentencing is addressed in chapter 6.

and Brownsword[60] argue that preventative detention is always a wrongful violation of detainees' rights, but justified in the case of a 'vivid danger' (where serious harm is likely to be perpetrated in the near future).[61] However, two important questions remain unanswered; firstly, Who is to determine the distinction between a 'vivid' and 'something less than an imminent danger' in predicting whether individuals may commit serious breaches of international humanitarian law in future social conflicts? and, secondly, are these taxonomies in any event adequate or relevant frameworks for analysing such contexts? Surely, the unconditional nature of any potential aggressor's actions is more difficult (if not impossible) to predict where societal breakdown and armed conflict persist. It is also legitimate to question whether the conventional bases upon which the relationship between predicted harm, commensurability and culpability are determined in western domestic sentencing systems are appropriate foundations for punishment in the context of international criminal trials.

It is instructive to examine the reasoning of the international judges in this respect. For example, some obfuscation is apparent in the deliberations of the ICTY Trial Chamber in *Kunarac*.[62] This appears unconvincing in suggesting that the 'propensity to commit violations of international humanitarian law, or, possibly crimes relevant to such violations' can be discerned only on the basis that an offender might have a record of previous criminal conduct '*relevant to those committed during the armed conflict*',[63] since, 'in practically all cases ... the convicted persons would be first time offenders *in relation to international crimes*.'[64] The Trial Chamber concluded:

> Violations of international humanitarian law, by their very nature, can be committed only in certain contexts which may not arise again in the society where the convicted person, once, released, may eventually settle.

However, it might equally be asserted that the reasons for conflicts of the kind which arose in the former Yugoslavia and Rwanda are deeply rooted in the historical and cultural fabric of those societies. Consequently, returning offenders who discover upon release that the moral justifications for their previous involvement in armed conflict remain will surely have a propensity to commit further violations of international humanitarian law, more particularly so in their desire to seek revenge against those seen as responsible for committing acts in furtherance of a policy of ethnic cleansing. The approach of the ICTY in *Kunarac* is one which relates propensity solely to the immediate

---

60 Bottoms and Brownsword (1982). For an analysis of this approach in the light of proportionality theory, see von Hirsch and Ashworth (2005) ch. 4.
61 The concept of 'vividness' includes seriousness, temporality, immediacy and certainty.
62 *Prosecutor v Kunarac et al* (Case No IT-96-23-T & IT-96-23/1-T) 22 February 2001, para. 843.
63 Emphasis in original.
64 Emphasis in original.

circumstances surrounding an offender's participation in the instant conflict, whilst ignoring the past and future context of conflict situations.

The moral basis for any predictive detention is further weakened where the legitimacy of the decision-making body may be impugned, or charged with an institutional bias towards retributive punishment, as has been the case with the *ad hoc* tribunals. The suggestion that international sentencers may be encouraged to use preventative detention in response to perceived public reaction against inadequate or unduly lenient sentences may prove a dangerous threat to individual rights and a guise for the further abuse of retributive punishment exacted against citizens of 'punished' states. It is also worth noting that, since sentence lengths for international crimes are necessarily high, the scope for additional preventative margins is correspondingly reduced, albeit that the concept of a 'preventative margin' is in itself highly conjectural.

Given the dubious ethical foundations for protective sentencing, there should be serious misgivings regarding the extent to which evidence relating to an offender which formed the basis of a previous finding of 'dangerousness' should be admissible as an aggravating factor for the purposes of sentencing in international criminal trials.

Establishing the factual basis for sentence: conventional approaches

This section focuses on some of the salient features of existing approaches to establishing the factual basis for sentence in both national and international contexts. It provides a foundation for adopting possible modifications to the structures and relationships which influence the exercise of judicial discretionary power over the determination of factual evidence for sentencing in criminal trials.[65]

Adversarial systems are driven by the overwhelming need to make a formal determination of guilt, whether or not this results from plea or verdict. Unfortunately, neither outcome necessarily establishes a sufficiently precise factual basis for the sentencer to assess the culpability of the offender. In addition, according to Ashworth,[66] the problem is likely to be exacerbated (particularly following a guilty plea) where the system of criminal law is based on broadly defined offences.[67] As Thomas suggests,[68] the facts on which the sentence is based must be consistent with the formal determination of guilt. Consequently, if the offender is acquitted of a graver charge or pleads guilty to a lesser offence, the sentencer must accept this as forming the factual basis for the determination of the sentence. However, sentencers normally have a

---

65 For further elaboration in the international context, see Henham (2009b).
66 Ashworth (2010) 374–75.
67 The issue is significant because it may impact directly on the choice between a custodial or non-custodial sentence, or determine the length of any prison sentence.
68 Thomas (1979) 367.

discretion regarding whose version of events to believe where there are conflicting accounts as to whether the offender was engaged in a continuous course of conduct, as long as they do not assume the existence of facts clearly negated by the formal finding of guilt.

A crucial question that arises in this context is the extent to which general principles relating to the burden and quantum of proof apply in reaching a decision as to whether a fact is relevant to sentence. This issue gains in significance where the sentencing phase of the trial process is separated from that which determines guilt or innocence, and its form is determined by conventions, principles, relationships and interactions which differ from the main body of the trial. In England and Wales, for example, not only has the sentencing phase of the trial traditionally been one where the principle of judicial independence has found its fullest expression, it has also developed its own philosophical rationales, procedural rules, sentencing principles and policy.

The separation of the verdict and sentence phases of the trial, whether within a unified or a two-stage process, also poses significant structural questions. One of these concerns the most appropriate processual context for realising the potential of judicial discretion to influence praxis and advance the integration of restorative themes in trial decision-making.[69]

Arguably, the most significant practical consequences resulting from the separation of the verdict and sentence phases of the trial concern the need for evidence to be reconstructed to serve the purposes of the sentencing phase. For example, evidence relevant to sentence (such as provocation) may not be sufficiently explored, even during a full trial. Where the offender pleads guilty these shortcomings are exacerbated, since the prosecution and defence accounts of the facts may differ considerably. Yet this phenomenon may also occur within an integrated criminal process model. In Italy, for example, specific criteria establish the boundaries for the exercise of discretionary power relevant to sentence, but it is witness testimony elicited during the trial phase that is evaluated against these legal constraints. Judicial deliberations follow immediately after the close of the trial and, after considering any unresolved preliminary matters and/or procedural issues, judges must consider each issue of fact or law, as well as the proper sentence. Needless to say, such abbreviated proceedings and procedures may facilitate sentence bargaining and distort the extent to which the facts upon which sentence is based actually correspond with those that occurred. Similarly, rights accorded to victims[70] are directed towards the trial (verdict and sentence) rather than to sentence alone.

Whether there should be a distinction between the verdict and sentence phase, or provision made for a separate sentencing phase, is one of the most important issues to impact on the way sentencing decisions are reached within

---

69 For an example that considers the potential of pre-trial decision-making in international trials, see Jackson, J. (2009) (discussed later).

70 Under Article 90 of the Italian Code of Criminal Procedure (1988).

domestic criminal justice systems and has fundamental evidential repercussions for sentencing outcomes in the case of international criminal trials.

As far as the international context is concerned, both the *ad hoc* tribunals for the Former Yugoslavia and Rwanda and the ICC have a predominantly unified structure. In other words, the verdict and sentence phases are conducted as one continuous process. In the case of the *ad hoc* tribunals, both the Defence and the Prosecution have the right to present evidence relating to sentence and argue for an appropriate sentence at the end of the trial phase once formal pleadings have closed:

Rule 85: Presentation of Evidence

(A)   Each party is entitled to call witnesses and present evidence. Unless otherwise directed by the Trial Chamber in the interests of justice, evidence at the trial shall be presented in the following sequence … (vi) any relevant information that may assist the Trial Chamber in determining an appropriate sentence if the accused is found guilty on one or more of the charges in the indictment.

However, this was not initially the case with the *ad hoc* tribunals where the respective Rules of Procedure and Evidence for the ICTY and ICTR (Part Six, Section 4) implicitly provided for a system whereby evidence relating to sentence could only be heard once the decision as to guilt or innocence had been made:

Rule 100: Pre-sentencing Procedure

If a Trial Chamber finds the accused guilty of a crime, the Prosecutor and the defence may submit any relevant information that may assist the Trial Chamber in determining an appropriate sentence.

Early *ad hoc* tribunal cases such as *Tadić* (ICTY)[71] and *Akayesu* (ICTR)[72] even went so far as to hold separate sentence hearings, but their respective rules were later amended to remove this possibility. The rationale for this was essentially the bureaucratic and administrative one of greater speed and efficiency. The new procedure ensured that the presentation of evidence and pleadings on sentencing matters occurred *before* the verdict was determined with the result that both phases of the trial are now reflected in a single judgement based on the merits of the case.

Rule 86 (C) of the ICTY/ICTR Rules of Evidence and Procedure effectively provides that after the presentation of all the evidence pertinent to the trial of

---

71 *Prosecutor v Tadić* (Case No. IT-94-1-S), Sentencing Judgement, 14 July 1997.
72 *Prosecutor v Akayesu* (Case No ICTR-96-4-T) 2 September 1998.

the issues the closing arguments of the Prosecutor and the Defence must 'address matters of sentencing'.

Rule 86: Closing Arguments

(A)   After the presentation of all the evidence, the Prosecutor may present a closing argument; whether or not the Prosecutor does so, the defence may make a closing argument. The Prosecutor may present a rebuttal argument to which the defence may present a rejoinder.

(B)   Not later than five days prior to presenting a closing argument, a party shall file a final trial brief.

(C)   The parties shall also address matters of sentencing in closing arguments

The ICC Statute adopts a similar model. Article 76(1) provides that following a conviction the Trial Chamber should move on to the sentencing issue, taking into account evidence presented and submissions *made during the trial* that are relevant to sentence. Significantly, in Article 76(2)[73] it goes on to provide that (in contested cases only and before completion of the trial) the Trial Chamber may direct (or must, if requested by the Prosecutor or the accused) *a further hearing* to hear any additional evidence or submissions relevant to sentence.[74]

Schabas[75] suggests that this procedure creates a strong presumption in favour of a distinct sentencing hearing following conviction but this has not been the experience of the *ad hoc* tribunals. Nonetheless, Zappala[76] argues that the position regarding the ICC remains unclear as to whether there should be one decision containing both verdict and sentence, or two distinct decisions. More constructively, Van Zyl Smit[77] suggests that the provision for separate hearings and pronouncement of sentences under Article 76(2) may prove a fruitful avenue for the development of sentencing jurisprudence on the appropriateness of life imprisonment.[78]

Clearly, within a unified process, evidence relating to mitigating and aggravating factors will be constrained by the fact that it follows on from the trial proper, where the evidence is confined to that which is necessary to prove the commission of the crime. As stated, in the case of the *ad hoc* tribunals,

---

73 See Rule 143, ICTY RPE.

74 Art. 76(4) confirms that (wherever possible) the sentence must be pronounced in public in the accused's presence.

75 Schabas (2007) 305.

76 Zappala (2003) 198.

77 van Zyl Smit (2002) 14.

78 This being currently hampered by the failure of the *ad hoc* tribunals to develop principles of cardinal and ordinal proportionality, which in turn reflects the absence of a hierarchy of offence seriousness for sentencing purposes. This would allow different degrees of culpability to be reflected in the adoption of different penalties. See, generally, Henham (2003a) 93 and 98.

Rule 85(A)(vi) of the respective Rules of Evidence and Procedure provides for the presentation of 'any relevant information that may assist the Trial Chamber in determining an appropriate sentence' after all other evidence led by the Prosecution and the Defence (or otherwise ordered by the Trial Chamber) has been presented, unless otherwise directed by the Trial Chamber in the *interests of justice*.

Significantly, since the removal of Rule 101(B) there is no implication that the Defence should present evidence pertinent to mitigation of sentence on the basis of the accused's guilt, but rather that its emergence should be as part of the normal course of the trial and, therefore, directed towards assisting the tribunal to determine the relative merits of the case against the accused.[79] Since the Rules refer to the submission of 'all relevant information', there is some doubt regarding the exact nature of the evidential material permitted and whether it may be treated as equivalent to evidence submitted in accordance with the Rules.[80] Similarly, whether trial rules on the submission and admissibility of evidence also apply to the Trial Chamber's deliberations during the sentencing phase is a matter for conjecture.

Arguments in favour of holding a separate sentencing hearing after conviction are considerable. For instance, in a mono-phase hearing the necessary omission of mitigation evidence during the trial stage may prove prejudicial to the defence when it comes to sentencing, because it restricts information concerning the offender's personal role in the commission of the crime and its immediate aftermath.[81]

According to Wald[82] this probably contributed to the defence's failure to make any submission on sentence in the ICTY case of *Krstić*:[83]

> ... the Tribunal Rules call for the verdict and sentence to be issued simultaneously, thus putting the defence counsel in the unenviable position of having to make any pleas for leniency at the same time as he is maintaining that his client should be acquitted.[84]

---

79 As would be consistent with an inquisitorial truth-finding purpose for the trial.
80 ICTR decisions have attempted to clarify what information relating to aggravation and mitigation is relevant to sentencing and the appropriate burden of proof. For example, in *Prosecutor v Niyitegeka* (ICTR-96-14-T), Judgement and Sentence, 16 May 2003: 'It has to be borne in mind that the principle according to which only matters proved beyond a reasonable doubt are to be considered at the sentencing stage extends to the assessment of any aggravating factors, while mitigating factors are to be taken into consideration if established on a balance of probabilities. This Chamber reiterates that a particular circumstance shall not be retained as aggravating if it is included as an element of the crime in consideration' (para. 488). This approach is consistent with domestic adversarial trial practice.
81 Keller (2001) 68.
82 Wald (2003) 467 at note 63.
83 *Prosecutor v Krstic* (Case No IT-98-33-T) Judgement, 2 August 2001.
84 Keller (2001) 69 uses *Krstić* to illustrate 'the negative impact that the presentation of sentencing evidence during the trial can have on the perception and possibly the reality of the fairness of the proceedings'. *Ibid*, 71, further suggests how remarks made by Judge Wald regarding the

The introduction of such evidence may also impact adversely on the accused's rights of silence and protection against self-incrimination. In particular, the defence may be induced to introduce more witnesses during the trial process in order to establish the accused's good character and personal circumstances.[85] Alternatively, from the prosecutor's point of view, a second hearing is likely to permit the introduction of aggravating factors (such as the accused's criminal record) that might be considered inadmissible for reasons of irrelevance during the trial proper.[86] In any event, the range of admissible material for sentencing purposes is potentially considerable where there is a second hearing.[87]

Clearly, *Krstić* does raise some difficult questions, and although at first sight these appear to concern purely procedural matters, it is evident upon closer examination that they highlight some fundamental concerns about the future credibility of international criminal justice more generally, not just international sentencing. The relevant points may be summarised as follows:

(1)   Judge Wald questions the basis upon which the Defence were able to make a plea for leniency at the same time as maintaining that the accused should be acquitted. However, as Keller suggests,[88] it is surely illogical for the Defence to present evidence about what might be the appropriate sentence for crimes to which the accused has pleaded not guilty and not yet been convicted.

(2)   The accused's right of silence and the right against self-incrimination were compromised. It is surely correct to argue that, if an accused chooses not to give evidence, or having been sworn, without good cause refuses to answer any question, the court may not draw adverse inferences about individual criminal responsibility from this failure to give evidence or refusal, without good cause, to answer any question.[89]

---

impact of certain testimony relevant to sentencing could have easily been interpreted as influencing her decision on the verdict.

85 As Zappala (2003) suggests, this is hardly likely to prove expeditious.

86 Schabas (2007) 306. This does not permit the prosecution to call evidence for the purposes of establishing the commission of offences other than those which have been proved, regardless of their nature and gravity.

87 This includes the detailed consideration of expert medical, psychiatric and personal circumstances reports and witness testimony that are admitted and evaluated purely for sentencing purposes.

88 Keller (2001) 68.

89 In *Funke v France* (Case A/256-A) European Court of Human Rights [1993] 1 CMLR 897, 25 February 1993, the ECHR decided that the right to silence was implicit in the general right to a fair trial under Article 6(1) of the Convention. However, the ECHR does not expressly guarantee the precise constituents of the rights actually comprised within Article 6 of the Convention. The substantive content of the law of evidence has been left largely to domestic law, with the ECHR concerning itself more with questions of procedural justice. Accordingly, in the UK it

Commentators agree[90] that eliminating the possibility of a separate sentence hearing, as has been the experience of the ICTY and ICTR, undoubtedly diminishes the accused's right to silence, and causes problems for the Defence where it wishes to introduce evidence in mitigation, such as that relating to the accused's role as a possible accomplice rather than principal, or efforts that the accused might have made in trying to reduce the suffering of victims, either during or following the commission of the crime. It is difficult to envisage the introduction of such evidence without at least risking the possibility of self-incrimination. It is also arguable that evidence relevant to sentence introduced during the trial phase, such as that relating to victim impact, may adversely affect a judge's perception as to the guilt or innocence of the accused, and therefore be unfairly prejudicial because it has the potential to compromise the accused's right to a fair trial.

I would argue that such restrictions and their effects should be exposed for what they really are; namely, procedural devices which exist to facilitate the adversarial context of justice delivery. They are crucial for establishing the nature and credibility of a particularised form of evidence (or 'truth') which is conventionally validated by the test of whether or not it is of *probative value*. Consequently, it is evidence conceived and manufactured to serve the ends of adversarial justice or, more specifically to establish the guilt or innocence of the accused within such a normative framework. As such, these norms not only represent procedural obstacles to achieving greater inclusion for victims through integration within the trial process, they also tend to perpetuate the narrow focus on retributive and deterrent punishment so characteristic of international criminal trials.

In essence, those exclusory rules of evidence which arguably protect the accused from otherwise prejudicial testimony are designed to safeguard the presumption of innocence – the cornerstone of adversarial trial. The merging of the verdict and sentence stages of the trial further threatens the protection of these basic rights. Paradoxically, however, the mere separation of these two stages would not change this negative assessment of the rationale and value of the evidentiary rules as they currently exist, because it would not deal with the fundamental failure of the present system of trial justice to deliver a more inclusive communitarian resolution to the problem of achieving justice following mass atrocity.[91]

---

remains the case that the silence of an accused at trial cannot be commented upon by the prosecution, although the reverse is true for a co-accused. But the Human Rights Act 1998 does include the right to remain silent, not to testify during the proceedings and not to be compelled to give self-incriminating evidence as specific rights to be included within the general right to a fair trial. It is also worth noting that Article 14.3(g) of the International Convention on Civil and Political Rights provides that 'In the determination of any criminal charge against him, everyone shall be entitled ... not to be compelled to testify against himself or to confess guilt'.

90 See Keller (2001) 69.
91 For an informed analysis of the kinds of resolution necessary in the case of Rwanda, see Drumbl (2002).

Accordingly, it may be argued that those specific evidential protections and artificial structural impediments to justice discussed above should be replaced by new ethical rules for conduct which are developed from broader, more inclusive moral foundations. Clearly, nothing can prevent judges from drawing adverse inferences about the conduct of any participants (whether lay or professional, offender or victim) within the context of any trial process. However, the crucial issue is whether the rationale and structure of the process in question serves to achieve something more than merely facilitating retributive forms of justice within a predominantly adversarial trial framework.

As Mark Findlay and I elaborate,[92] whilst such a transformation would include a determination about whether or not the legal requirements of an offence have been established, the purpose of such changes would extend far beyond this aspiration. In particular, the trial process would be designed to encourage the maximum participation of all those 'legitimately' claiming justice, especially through the possibility of mediated settlements which seek to promote a more inclusive and restorative resolution. Consequently, a broader framework of participative rights would be balanced by an equally robust set of norms designed to protect those who come forward with evidence which could lead to progress in achieving outcomes that promote peace and reconciliation.

Findlay and I argue that the need for change is evident from cases such as *Krstić*. More specifically, we refer to the fears voiced by Keller[93] concerning Judge Wald's remark following the conclusion of Witness DD's testimony, that it 'will help us in making our decision'.[94] Such remarks might imply that victim impact testimony could be potentially prejudicial to the accused because of its possible impact on a judge's perception of the evidence. However, the dangers of such unfair prejudice are relevant primarily to the determination of guilt or innocence within the context of an adversarial trial, and are driven by the need to deliver retributive justice. Hence, Keller's[95] assertion that the presentation of such evidence on sentencing during the trial phase could 'endanger the integrity of the judicial process' needs to be evaluated within that narrow context.

At first sight, the foundation instruments of the international institutions, particularly the ICC, go much further than many domestic legal systems in providing procedural safeguards to ensure the fair trial of the accused and for the participation and protection of victims and witnesses at all stages of the criminal process. For example, Article 67(1)(a) of the ICC Statute is unequivocal in stating that the accused must be informed promptly and in detail of the nature, cause and content of the charge in a language which he or she

---

92 Findlay and Henham (2010) ch. 4.
93 Keller (2001).
94 Keller (2001) suggests that Judge Wald's remarks were almost certainly made out of politeness to the witness: 'I have no questions for the witness except to thank you for coming and sharing your very sad story with the Tribunal. I think it will help us in making our decision. Thank you'; *Krstić* Trial Transcript, Wednesday, 26 July 2000, Page 5768.
95 Keller (2001) 69.

fully understands and speaks. Yet, these kinds of safeguards are largely absent when it comes to the deliberation and pronouncement of sentence. As described, the conventional practice, now adopted by both the *ad hoc* tribunals and prescribed for the ICC, is that all evidence relating to trial of the issues and sentence is heard before the verdict and sentence are delivered.[96] Furthermore, although sentence is pronounced publicly, and wherever possible in the presence of the accused (Article 76(4) of the ICC Statute; Rule 144 (1) of the Rules of Procedure and Evidence), deliberations are *in camera*, and there is no obligation for the reasons and an account of the process whereby the decision was reached to be made public.

This contrasts sharply with the ICC's provisions on verdict delivery, since Article 74 of the ICC Statute provides specifically that the decision must be in writing and contain a full and reasoned statement of the Trial Chamber's findings on the evidence and the conclusions reached. However, only a summary of the decision need be delivered in open court. Consequently, so far as sentencing is concerned, whilst the matters the court is required to consider are set out in some detail in Rule 145 of the ICC Rules of Procedure and Evidence, the legislative instruments do not go further than requiring that they should be taken into account during the private deliberations of the Trial Chamber.

Although, of course, the international courts have (in many instances) delivered consistent and lengthy accounts of their reasoning in sentencing offenders, the absence of any obligation in this respect is, nevertheless, a significant procedural limitation given the normal absence of a separate sentencing hearing. The existence of such hearings promotes the creation and development of a sentencing jurisprudence – one that encourages a culture of judicial transparency through the public reception and rational evaluation of evidence that is specifically relevant to the sentencing decision.

In addition, as the International Law Commission made clear in its comments on the work of its forty-sixth session,[97] the procedural guarantees inherent in the concept of a fair trial should be extended to a separate sentencing hearing (as was then proposed), since its purpose is to determine an appropriate punishment for the *individual* as well as the crime. In the absence of any obligation to hold such a hearing, an even stronger argument for transparency in sentence decision-making surely exists. Arguably, the absence of any mandatory procedure for transparency in sentence decision-making also stems from the major systemic weakness of the entire international criminal trial process; namely, that the procedural safeguards are more apparent than real, because there is no need for them to be otherwise. In effect, the justifications for punishment in international trials do not have to extend beyond the limitations imposed by the philosophies of retributive justice and deterrence.

---

96 Notwithstanding the ICC Trial Chamber's power to hold a further hearing on matters related to sentence under Rule 143, ICC RPE.

97 Comment to Art. 46 'Sentencing' Yearbook of the International Law Commission (1994).

There are, however, broader issues raised. First, there is an argument for supporting separate sentence hearings for symbolic reasons. This holds that marking out the public deliberation and pronouncement of sentence as something distinct from the verdict has an enormously powerful symbolic effect in drawing attention to and dramatising the punishment, as well as promoting psychological and emotional feelings relating to atonement and closure.[98] Arguably, a unified verdict and sentencing process encourages obfuscation in the justification of sentences.[99] Since it does not promote an alternative context for sentencing, a unified process is likely to negate and stultify those arguments which might explore issues leading to the constructive development of sentence decision-making and greater legitimacy for sentencing outcomes in favour of those that sustain the status quo.

Secondly, an argument can be made out for suggesting that a two-stage verdict and sentencing process serves to emphasise the qualitative distinction between the pre- and post-conviction phases of the trial by signifying that different substantive and procedural norms apply. It is significant that in the English context, where similar wide judicial discretionary powers in sentencing exist within a two-stage process,[100] the sentencing phase of the trial is often used by judges to make what Ashworth[101] refers to as 'moralistic homilies', and that the systematic analysis of relevant aggravating and mitigating factors is associated and developed within this process culture. Arguably, such a tendency is suppressed with a unified trial process, particularly where, as with the international criminal trial institutions, the process is dominated by a predominantly retributive ideology which does not encourage transparency, or the more extended and constructive analysis of evidence for sentencing purposes.

Moreover, failure to clarify the relationship between substantive offence requirements and sentencing principles exacerbates these difficulties. The conventional common law approach for dealing with the conceptual problems of culpability and harm has followed the basic notion that the substantive law exists to fix the minimum conditions for criminal liability, whilst sentencing principles should help determine the degree to which any offender can be held responsible for the consequences that follow from his or her actions.[102] The moral distinctions between offences in terms of gravity and intent are drawn

---

98 This is consistent with the sociological insights of labelling theory discussed earlier; see, further, Sudnow (1965), King (1978). On therapeutic jurisprudence, see Wexler and Winick (1996), Sherman (2003), Petrucci (2002), Rottman and Casey (2000) 12–19, Kirchengast (2008), Erez (2004), Kenney (2003), Harber and Pennebaker (1992), Roberts and Erez (2004).

99 As the Italian experience tends to suggest, where the burden of formality and transparency is minimal.

100 Note that the sentencing phase of the trial is often heard separately – for example, because of the need for reports to be prepared concerning the offender's medical or social background. However, the basic principle is that the sentence should follow the verdict wherever possible.

101 Ashworth (2000c) 306.

102 Ashworth (2006) ch. 1.

through the framing of substantive offences, with specific factors having a bearing on the determination of an individual's responsibility for consequential harm and culpability being reserved for the sentencing stage. These distinctions have considerable significance in the context of international trials.

In *Aleksovski*[103] the ICTY endorsed the approach adopted in the *Čelebići* and *Kupreškić* judgements to the effect that the inherent gravity of the accused's criminal conduct must be reflected in the sentence, and that the determination of gravity requires a consideration of the particular circumstances of the case, as well as the form and degree of the accused's participation in the crime. However, this approach collapses what Carcano[104] identifies as an important distinction; namely, the determination of gravity *in abstracto* and *in concreto*:

> The gravity *in abstracto* is based on an analysis, in terms of the criminal law of the objective and subjective elements of the crime. The gravity *in concreto* depends on the harm done and the degree of culpability of the offender. ICTY and ICTR case law reveals divergences in the application of these concepts. The former focuses mainly on the concrete gravity of the crime inferred from the circumstances of the case. The latter assessment has been broader in that both the gravity *in abstracto* of the crime and its gravity *in concreto* were taken into account.[105]

Arguably, the ICTY and ICTR have failed to differentiate clearly or consistently between notions of gravity and seriousness for the purposes of the trial and sentence. The 'gravity'[106] of an offence in substantive terms depends on satisfying different criteria from those applicable to sentencing. For 'just deserts' sentencing, 'gravity' is regarded as a major element in determining the 'seriousness' of the offence. It is fundamental to the nature of the penalty and the appropriate sentence. In terms of the verdict, the concept of 'gravity' is integral to satisfying the requirements of particular substantive offence definitions. Although the sources of evidence may be the same within a unified process, its disclosure, presentation, testing, admissibility and prioritisation satisfy very distinct purposes.

In the same way that moral and political ideology influences the framing of the criminal law, so it correspondingly determines how offences are perceived for the purposes of punishment. This involves crucial decisions about the relative severity of penalties (cardinal proportionality) and how offences should be ranked according to their seriousness (ordinal proportionality). Obfuscation results where this is a failure to distinguish the consequences of

---

103 *Prosecutor v Aleksovski* (Case No. IT-95-14/1), Judgement, 24 March 2000, para. 182.
104 Carcano (2002).
105 *Ibid.* 609.
106 The concepts of 'offence gravity' and 'offence seriousness' and 'crime' and 'offence' appear to be used interchangeably in the jurisprudence of the ICTY and ICTR.

assessing offence 'gravity' for the purposes of determining the substantive issue of criminal responsibility from that of determining the appropriate sentence.

Despite the fact that the notion of the individualisation of sentences is apparently enshrined in Article 24(1) of the ICTY Statute (Article 23(1) ICTR Statute) through the reference to 'individual circumstances', the exact parameters of this concept are not elaborated. As a result confusion also persists in the sentencing decisions of the *ad hoc* tribunals regarding the interpretation of 'individualisation' as a sentencing concept. Zappala,[107] in particular, seems to elevate 'individualisation' for crimes under international law to the level of a due process right, on the basis that it is instrumental in defining the limits of individual criminal responsibility[108] for acts committed during the course of armed conflicts, although falling short of recognising an allied right to rehabilitation on the part of the convicted person. In any event, the precise ambit of the 'individualisation' concept and its relationship to rehabilitation as a possible sentencing objective for the *ad hoc* tribunals remains conjectural.

It is difficult to see how individualisaton as a philosophical approach to the resolution of the conflicting demands of sentencing can be conceived in terms of a legally enforceable right in international sentence decision-making. This would only be possible should the rationale(s) for sentencing international crimes accommodate such an approach. As things stand, the predominant ideological framework for international sentencing based on retributive and deterrent purposes suggests a particularly narrow interpretation of individualization, certainly not one that engages constructively with the wider social context of sentencing outcomes.[109]

---

107 Zappala (2003) 204.

108 Damaška suggests that it does so by emphasising the avoidance of collective responsibility; Damaška (2008) 332. Arguably, Damaška deals inadequately with the relationship between the 'justice' of the trial and its perceived legitimacy. Damaška's didactic approach has two dimensions; firstly, the realistic and practical one of what is deliverable within the existing adversarial context, and, secondly, the pedagogical one of whether the trial can deliver something more than symbolism, be it in the form of retribution, deterrence, restorative justice, or whatever. The mission of trial justice is not readily conceived by this dichotomy, since, in order to be effective, there must be some moral underpinning. However, it is probably unreasonable to expect trials to provide a context for delivering the kind of 'truth' that does not 'blur over moral distinctions shared by ordinary people'; *ibid.* 353. It is also probable that complete moral accountability is unlikely to be reflected through satisfying those evidential requirements that are tied to the substantive definitions of crimes, international or otherwise, or degrees of culpability taken as indicia of seriousness for sentencing purposes. Nonetheless, a move is advocated away from individual legal accountability towards a more inclusive and collective context for the trial as a forum for establishing 'truths' which reflect the pluralistic moralities of contemporary society and respect their social and historical roots.

109 An earlier study by Schabas also considers the general applicability of the provisions of the Universal Declaration of Human Rights (1948) and the International Covenant on Civil and Political Rights (1976), especially Articles 7, 10 and 15. Schabas suggests that Article 7 'encompasses the notion of proportionality in criminal punishment', whilst Articles 7 and 10

Finding the appropriate epistemic context for evidence

In a recent paper John Jackson[110] raises some important issues about the source and nature of admissible evidence in the international criminal tribunals which have significant repercussions when thinking about how the evidential process relates to the perceived legitimacy of trial outcomes in any particular context. Jackson begins by reiterating the view that there is a marked fluidity in the extent to which adversarial and inquisitorial approaches have influenced international criminal trial procedure, especially the fact there is no clear dichotomy between those contextual factors that have produced reactive and active trial styles in the domestic context,[111] nor any conclusive evidence to support the suggestion that an inquisitorial approach might significantly increase the truth-finding capacity of the criminal process.[112]

Jackson concludes that obfuscation surrounding the possible goals of international criminal justice has tended to hinder a principled debate about the most effective sources and uses of evidence in international criminal trials, and he takes the view that the possibilities for merging retributive and restorative approaches within the trial context[113] would only 'serve to exclude the interests of victims and others in the community who need to be included.'[114] Consequently, Jackson sees the way forward as one where the purposes of international criminal justice focus on the core aim of ascertaining the guilt of those indicted of breaches of international criminal law (and so preventing impunity) and to ensure that this objective is achieved in a non-partisan fashion by adhering strictly to international fair trial norms such as those established by the ICCP and the ECHR. Therefore, Jackson argues that enhancing the fairness of criminal procedure in the international context will correspondingly enhance the accuracy, transparency and probity of the evidence-gathering and admissibility processes.

As an example, Jackson suggests that the consistent application of the principle of equality of arms 'provides an opportunity for *equal* participation by the parties'.[115] One might counter this assertion by suggesting that the notion of 'equality' is, of course, itself a relative concept, so that to assert rights protection through adherence to fair trial norms should be considered in terms of their contextual significance. In other words, I would argue that the issue of establishing the purposes of the trial *in any context* is a critical

---

effectively insist on the importance of rehabilitation. Again, the normative significance of these aspirations is ignored, as is the possibility of their realisation within the existing philosophical context of international penality. See Schabas (1997).

110 Jackson (2009) 22.
111 Damaška (1986).
112 *Contra* Pakes (2004) 162.
113 As suggested by Findlay and Henham (2005).
114 Jackson (2009).
115 *Ibid.* 23 (emphasis added).

precursor to rights protection and cannot be overcome or sidestepped by advocating increased adherence to norms which are designed to ensure 'fair' trial if the ideological framework which establishes the process is itself flawed, unclear or inherently partisan.

Therefore, the issue of establishing a coherent ideology for the trial, local or global, must be seen as the first critical step towards greater acceptance of the legitimacy of its outcomes.[116] Rules for minimising inaccurate testimony and effective risk allocation in the probity of evidence as between prosecution and defence are certainly vital matters in bringing coherence and a principled approach to the gathering and admissibility of evidence, but I would argue that they should sustain an ideology for the trial which seeks a more communitarian and relational approach to justice – one, therefore, which seeks to enhance the legitimacy of trial outcomes from the perspective of context.

At the domestic level, I would argue that the comparison drawn by Damaska[117] – between the laissez-faire adversarialism of the common law world and the inquisitorial notion of the state as protector of citizens' liberty, reflecting the social contract and 'moral pact' of liberal ideology – remains an important conceptual starting point for considering what the legitimacy of trial justice means, how it should be conceived, and what the consequences should be. It is necessary to understand why and how the blurring of this neat dichotomy has mirrored changes in the relationship between the state and the administration of justice since the late eighteenth century. In this sense, therefore, one must reflect upon the proposition that both the structures which sustain penal ideology and the ideology itself are a function of context. Correspondingly, the relationship between the state and citizens and its consequences for penality vary according to social context, as do the ideological foundations which sustain it.

As argued in chapter 2, unlike Jackson, I do not believe that international criminal justice should be conceived as something entirely different in this respect, in the sense that its goals are essentially *not* to serve the needs of 'civil society', but some more nebulous and broader objective concerned with ending impunity for international crimes and upholding the principles of international humanitarian law. To be sure, superficially, local and global forms of criminal justice have apparently differing aims, but I would argue that there is an important connecting thread between all forms of penality which is far more important, and should not be ignored. This concerns the fact that structures of penality exist only to serve ends which are perceived as legitimate, so that there must be a moral consensus in order for such structures to serve social ends effectively. The nature of such a moral consensus may well be fluid, fragmented and pluralistic, as in post-modern states, but it is

---

116 As argued by Findlay and Henham (2010) ch. 1.
117 Damaška (1986) ch. 3.

equally tenuous and lacking in communitarian foundations where international trial structures are concerned.

Consideration of these arguments is important when thinking through the impact of a normative framework, such as the evidential procedures of the international tribunals and the ICC. The limitations of existing evidential norms in the international tribunals are effectively highlighted by Jackson in a close interrogation of the practice of adversarial fact-gathering and its evaluation against the principle of equality of arms.[118] For example, he focuses on the practical problems of evidence-gathering in international trials, particularly for the defence, caused by the inability to force states to co-operate and the disproportionate availability of resources for the prosecution and the defence, which can severely hinder pre-trial preparation for the latter.

Jackson also considers the advantages and disadvantages of adopting a free-admissibility regime in the context of adversarial procedure,[119] drawing particular attention to the apparently broad remit of Rules 88(C) of the ICTY and ICTR RPE to admit any relevant evidence deemed to have probative value, and special provisions extending admissibility, such as that relating to a consistent pattern of conduct. However, he also notes the significance of the move away from the principle of orality in Rule 90(A) effected by the new Rule 89(F), which allowed written testimony to be accepted where allowed *in the interests of justice*, the position being further complicated by the introduction of Rule 92 *bis* which sub-categorised written statements prepared for legal proceedings into evidence relating to the acts and conduct of the accused (retaining a preference for oral testimony), and that relating to so-called peripheral or background evidence, where written testimony was preferred and which has resulted in large amounts of evidence being admitted without it having been examined or led in chief.

Hence, the complexities of evidence-gathering in the international tribunals have been exacerbated by the distinction drawn by the tribunal between crime-based evidence and that relevant to the acts and conduct of the accused, and, as Jackson argues,[120] the difficulties of drawing distinctions between the two has proved disadvantageous to the defence, especially in so-called command cases, where the more contextual information about the circumstances relating to the criminality and that going directly to establishing the individual responsibility of the accused has been effectively ignored. As Jackson puts it:

> … 'linkage' evidence consisting of 'insider' witnesses who establish the workings of the government, army, police and paramilitary units can also be crucial in tying the 'crime-base' evidence to the accused.

---

118 Jackson (2009) 25.
119 *Ibid.* 29.
120 *Ibid.* 31.

Jackson quite rightly goes on to point out that the international tribunals should perhaps become more sensitive to the dangers of convictions which rely disproportionately on unsubstantiated testimony, and the consequent implications of this in terms of the reliability of verdicts and the 'truth-finding' capacity of such trials.

These observations have significant implications for establishing the factual basis for sentence, especially the relative merits of the unified trial process, as against the two-stage verdict and sentencing procedure. At the normative level, the possible exclusion of testimony that may have a bearing on the sentence is potentially disadvantageous to the defence where verdict and sentence immediately follow one another, as is the case in most inquisitorially-based systems of criminal process. Notwithstanding the dangers of over-reliance on unsubstantiated testimony, the lesser standard of proof required of mitigating factors in adversarial systems should in any event facilitate the admission of material going beyond that which is essentially crime-based for the purpose of sentencing. However, the essential issue remains that of providing an appropriate normative context (based upon firm ideological foundations) wherein material accorded the status of evidence for sentencing purposes can be utilised in such a way (with appropriate rights protection) to accommodate a more communitarian approach to sentencing, and therefore one which address more effectively the justice concerns of 'communities' and victims.

Having examined the considerably wider powers of 'free admissibility' of the ICC's Pre-Trial Chamber, Jackson concludes that the investigative opportunities afforded by the Court's hybridised pre-trial model, evidenced by the proactive prosecutorial approach to fact-gathering taken in the *Lubanga* case, suggests that such a pre-trial type of confirmatory hearing is likely to provide a more effective context than the trial itself for receiving evidence which goes beyond the crime, provided full access to the prosecution file is allowed. Such a move would also be particularly helpful in cases where delay may seriously impair the reliability of the evidence. Overall, Jackson's primary concern is to suggest a more balanced epistemic context within the international criminal process as it currently exists. This is reflected in his cautionary observations about the need for both exculpatory and inculpatory material to receive equal exposure and the potential dangers of enhancing the pre-trial prosecutorial function without adequate disclosure requirements.

However, there is another level at which change should be contemplated. Mark Findlay and I[121] argue that the criminal process itself, including pre-trial, trial and sentencing stages, should be conceived as an appropriate epistemic context for evidence which goes beyond that needed to establish individual responsibility for the crime, if informed by a penal rationale that enhances its capacity to receive more broadly-based evidence relating to collective liability. Although difficult to achieve, it may be argued convincingly that the *status quo*

---

121 Findlay and Henham (2010).

does not provide a constructive or acceptable way forward for international criminal justice. Its penality remains primarily retributive and deterrent, its procedures a fluid and unpredictable cocktail of adversarial and inquisitorial approaches, and its outcomes often bearing a loose connection with the expectations for justice of those who have been directly implicated or affected by the criminalised behaviour in question.

Hence, the social and moral relevance of international trial justice should be regarded as having a major influence on the quality of the evidence, as a direct consequence of the purposes which inform the criminal process. As I have argued, this is essentially a contextual issue that presupposes our ability to deconstruct the linkages between shared moral values about punishment and trial outcomes. I would suggest that important parallels can be drawn between international and domestic forms of penality in this respect. Although domestic criminal procedures are generally less fluid and unpredictable, hybridisation and cross-fertilisation of adversarial and inquisitorial approaches has increasingly become the norm in recent years. Notwithstanding, retributive justice remains the talisman of penal rationality for the majority of criminal trial systems, with the result that trial outcomes frequently fail to meet the legitimate expectations for justice of those implicated or affected by criminality.

Evidential issues and transforming trial justice

The broader debate concerning the desirability and effect of victim impact statements in sentencing is fundamental to any discussion about trial transformation within the adversarial context of the common law world. More recently, Ashworth[122] has repeated his reservations, also suggesting that the use of victim impact statements in the context of adversarial criminal justice tends to increase sentencing severity – that they are a cynical political ploy used to appease victims' concerns whilst, in reality, such statements tend to corrupt substantive and procedural justice goals. Erez,[123] on the other hand, has consistently championed the use of victim impact statements, stressing particularly their cathartic and therapeutic aspects,[124] and suggesting that they empower victims, helping them cope with victimisation and the criminal justice experience.[125] Erez also suggests that the incorporation of victim statements tends to enhance proportionality rather than increase penal severity, as Ashworth maintains.[126]

---

122 Ashworth (2010) 385. See also, Ashworth (2000d) ch. 9; Ashworth (2002b).
123 Erez (1994).
124 For further discussion of this issue, see Doak, Henham and Mitchell (2009).
125 See particularly, Erez and Tontodonato (1990), Erez *et al.* (1994), Erez and Roeger (1995); Rogers and Erez (1999), Erez and Rogers (1999), Erez (1999).
126 Erez (1999) 551. Erez concludes, 'Comparitivists encourage us to increase appropriate legal transplants and decrease inappropriate ones. There is sufficient evidence at this point to suggest that VIS (among other victim-oriented reforms) is an appropriate transplant' (at 555).

The evidential tensions produced by the juxtaposition of different rationales for victim's participatory rights in sentencing have recently been examined by Edwards[127] in the English context. Edwards draws a threefold distinction in the possible rationales for VIS; the most significant for our purposes being the *improving sentencing outcomes* rationales and the *victim-benefits* rationales. The chief source of evidential tension identified by Edwards concerns the degree of proof which should be required of evidence, depending upon whether or not the rationale for admissibility is a belief that such evidence will 'improve' sentencing or, alternatively, that it 'benefits' victims in some way. The words 'improve' and 'benefits' are emphasised deliberately here because they raise a number of difficult issues. One of these is the appropriate balance between objective and subjective approaches to determining the admissibility of evidence for sentence within a predominant adversarial and retributive justice framework. In terms of sentencing outcomes, for example, it remains a moot point whether VIS pose a threat to proportionality and 'just deserts', as Ashworth and others have consistently argued.[128]

Nonetheless, even within a predominantly retributive framework for punishment that favours some priority being accorded to particular consequentialist or utilitarian objectives, such as rehabilitation or restorative justice, there is a limit to how far the admission of VIS evidence should be able to threaten principles of procedural and natural justice, especially where it may unjustifiably impinge on the rights of the accused. Correspondingly, such principles may be equally threatened should VIS evidence be allowed on behalf of victims on therapeutic grounds.

I would argue that these tensions cannot be resolved satisfactorily within the existing predominantly adversarial and retributive rationales and norms which shape the criminal trial and sentencing. The underlying problem is clearly illustrated by Edwards's discussion of how these issues impact on the current approach to establishing the factual basis for sentence in English law. Evidently, if matters are raised in the VIS (because it is felt that they are pertinent to the achievement of a more 'beneficial' outcome for the victim or the community in which he or she lives, or for therapeutic reasons) alleging facts that are not relevant to the crime(s) of which the offender stands convicted, then the question arises as to whether and how the 'truth' of such material may be established. If such 'facts' are to be admitted within the existing ideological and normative framework, then this may involve cross-examination of victims and require proof of the alleged 'facts' according to the usual standard of 'beyond all reasonable doubt', or on the balance of probabilities.

As Edwards illustrates through his insightful analysis of the South Australian experience,[129] lack of clarity regarding the rationale for admissibility is likely to frustrate the achievement of any of the stated objectives for VIS. If, for

---

127 Edwards (2009).
128 See Ashworth (1986), Garland (1990) 252, Buruma (2004).
129 Edwards (2009) 302.

example, a therapeutic justification for admissibility is advanced as the sole criterion, then logically the evidence should only be accepted on this basis and not taken as having any potential impact on sentencing. If, on the other hand, the evidence is meant to have some impact on sentence, then clearly it should be susceptible to cross-examination. Where both justifications are alleged, as was the case in South Australia, then there is an irreconcilable tension between the victim as *information-provider* and as *expressor*, since the victim's participatory role as the latter may compromise procedural fairness for offenders.

The debate as to whether VIS information about the 'harm' suffered by the victim should be allowed to impact on any assessment of the seriousness of the offence is ongoing.[130] However, as Edwards points out, the fact that such evidence may be taken into account suggests that it should be subject to proof beyond all reasonable doubt and, where a 'substantial conflict' exists about the facts themselves, a *Newton* hearing should be held. Where the sentencer judges the information regarding victim 'harm' as having an evidential impact relevant to assessing offence seriousness for the purpose of sentence, this should be made clear.[131] In such a case, victims should be subject to cross-examination and the facts established beyond all reasonable doubt. If no such impact is anticipated, then the 'facts' in the VIS need not be put to proof.

As suggested, the source of the tensions Edwards describes come from the need for victim harm and the interests of victims and communities to be defined in terms that satisfy the exigencies of adversarial/retributive trial ideology and the normative framework it imposes. Consequently, norms of procedural justice and other existing rights frameworks are only considered within the parameters this demands. That is not to say that VIS material should be admitted without restriction and regardless of accuracy, but rather, as Findlay and I argue in the case of international trials, it should be informed by a trial programme that has been developed against a reconstituted ideological and normative framework for the delivery of trial justice; one which merges retributive and restorative objectives against a rights framework firmly anchored to notions of individual and collective accountability for the alleged crimes. The successful achievement of such an objective will depend fundamentally on the informed development of judicial discretionary power within the changed penal environment.

However, as Grazia Mannozzi and I[132] suggest in our comparative contextual analysis of victim participation in sentencing in Italy and England and Wales, the manipulation and redistribution of judicial discretion within adversarial criminal trial processes, and the apparent empowerment of lay

---

130 *Ibid.* 296.
131 Edwards suggests that this tendency may increase following the introduction of the VFS type of family impact statement in 2007. See discussion in chapter 1
132 Henham and Mannozzi (2003).

actors, is merely a functional response, rather than one that is indicative of any meaningful increased democratisation. This analysis is also consistent with a general willingness on the part of both civil and common law systems to institutionalise criminal processes that are unconstitutional or otherwise in breach of human rights norms on the grounds of managerial or bureaucratic efficiency. Such manifestations have little to do with notions of integration as models for penological change.

These observations are consistent with two important conclusions emerging from our research;

- That the normative content of any criminal justice model is not the main influence on the extent to which judicial discretionary power impacts on the level of victim participation
- That changes in the structure and form of criminal process, without a corresponding re-evaluation of the overall purpose of prosecution, trial and sentence, beyond the perceived need to remedy procedural deficiencies, produce penal structures whose philosophical justifications are not easily reconciled with the existing stated aims of punishment and the normative model which embodies them.

Changing the paradigm

By way of contrast, within the more inclusive context of the kind of transformed trial process suggested by Mark Findlay and I, victim impact testimony is seen as an essential constituent for delivering a more representative and consensual version of the 'truth'. The kind of deep contextual knowledge that is necessary to achieve this cannot be obtained by simply remodelling the current adversarial paradigm for international criminal trials. For instance, the proposal of commentators such as Keller and Zappala for re-establishing a clear two-stage distinction between verdict and sentence has significant practical implications for victim integration, more especially because the separation of verdict and sentence does not necessarily obviate the need for evidence to be reconstructed to serve the purposes of the sentencing phase. In England, for example, the difficulties caused by the need to establish the factual basis for sentencing are a direct result of dividing the trial into two distinct phases. In particular, evidence relevant to sentence (such as provocation, duress or mental capacity) may not be sufficiently explored, even during a full trial.[133] Where the offender pleads guilty, these difficulties are exacerbated, since the prosecution and defence accounts of the facts may differ considerably.

---

133 The nature and extent of the admissible evidence will be constrained by the constituent elements of the substantive offence(s) which need to be proved by the Prosecutor. Emphasis, context and relevance will necessarily be different for sentencing.

The transformed trial paradigm proposed by Findlay and I imposes a different rationale for seeking facts which consequently renders meaningless the introduction of artificial procedural dichotomies such as separate verdict and sentencing phases that simply replicate those of the adversarial paradigm, since this would detract from the primary objective of producing a more conciliated, integrated and potentially reconstructive outcome to the trial.

As explained, it is difficult to differentiate between evidential material relating to the accused's attitude and behaviour admitted during the trial on the basis of its possible relevance as aggravating and mitigating circumstances, and the wider significance such evidence would assume should the process be transformed and detached from the normative constraints normally associated with the admissibility of evidence in adversarial trials. As noted earlier, within the adversarial context, no obligation rests on the Defence to present mitigating evidence based exclusively on the assumption that the accused is guilty. Excluding the introduction of potentially mitigating evidence on these grounds serves to promote the adversarial goal of establishing the guilt or innocence of the accused.

Instead, Findlay and I argue that the emergence of such evidence during the course of the trial should be facilitated by a more flexible normative structure which is directed towards assisting the court or tribunal to determine the relative merits of the case against the accused. Whilst this broader kind of approach does not realise the potential of such evidence for deconstructing relationships of individual and collective responsibility, or those between alleged perpetrators and the harm done to victims and communities, it does provide a normative framework which facilitates their further investigation within a context sympathetic to the transitional needs of victims and communities seeking justice.

In the context of such a transformed trial, there is no reason why the responses and observable characteristics of the accused in terms of behaviour and general demeanour during the trial cannot be exploited for their relevance to outcome. Furthermore, there is no reason why the contents of expert medical, psychiatric and personal circumstances reports should not be requested at any stage of the process if pertinent to the pursuit of a constructive outcome. Not only would the focused inclusion of such evidence promote a deeper understanding of the causal relationships which impact on individual and collective action, it would also signal opportunities for exploiting conciliation and mediation and their healing potential as part of the ongoing function of the trial process.

So, for example, General Krstić's apparent lack of remorse during the trial regarding the role he played in the genocide at Srebrenica[134] could, within the context of a more restorative focus for the trial, be further explored through some form of mediated process, if directed as appropriate by the Trial

---

134 Referred to by Wald (2003) 467 at note 66.

Chamber. The process would then be transformed in order to interrogate this finding of fact by eliciting further detailed victim testimony. The dynamics of the process, and that of all the participants, could, in such a case, be directed towards investigating the possibility of obtaining the forgiveness of the families involved and exploring what contribution this might make towards building the kind of justice necessary for peace and reconciliation.

Pursuing the contextual reasons for individual criminalised behaviour is an important step towards establishing the boundaries of responsibility, and, by preventing the false collectivisation of guilt, it discourages further social division and alienation.[135] In short, a significant characteristic of the kind of trans-formed trial advocated by Mark Findlay and myself is its capacity to explore and exploit feelings of contrition and penitence in the service of achieving a more inclusive form of justice. These sentiments demand equal satisfaction by trial justice regardless of whether the jurisdiction in question is global or local.

---

135 Galabru (2006) 151, 152.

7 Access to Justice, Rights and Accountability

Introduction

The aim of this chapter is to examine the relationship between accountability and rights from the perspective of punishment and its perceived legitimacy. Consistent with the theme of the book, the notion of accountability is taken to be inclusive in the sense that it recognises the need to accommodate both individual and collective notions of accountability for the consequences of criminalised behaviour. However, it does not favour widening inclusion at the expense of compromising the fair trial rights of the offender, but seeks to establish a coherent and egalitarian framework for participation. This should facilitate the widest possible form of redress for victims. Correspondingly, it should also extend the trial's capacity to achieve a wider measure of collective accountability in sentencing. To expand the notion of redress without compromising the integrity of existing trial structures demands a close examination of the relationship between victimisation and punishment and consideration of the extent to which trial justice is capable of satisfying identifiable victim interests through a rights paradigm.

Accordingly, the chapter sets out to establish why present conceptualisations of the relationship between victimisation and punishment fail to convey the true nature of victimisation and its impact on perceptions of justice. This question concerns both the perceived justice of trial outcomes and the broader, but related, issue of how individuals and communities are connected in a moral sense to the ideologies and practices of criminal justice. In this latter sense, the context of victimisation may be conceived as actual or potential. It should therefore be emphasised that the purpose of this analysis is not to argue for a particular morality as justice, or indeed, to suggest a new approach for conceptualising the nature of justice. Its purpose remains the more modest aspiration of suggesting why contemporary criminal justice theory fails to provide an adequate account of:

- the nature of victimisation and its impact on the perceived morality of punishment; and

- the links between citizens generally and those criminal process structures and outcomes that purport to reflect the interests of different moralities and perceptions of justice within communities.

The chapter then focuses on the adequacy of current theory for analysing trial outcomes as paradigms of accountability, concentrating particularly on the influence of substantive and procedural norms and the extent to which notions of access to justice and the rights of offenders and victims correspond to the reality of trial practice.

The chapter extends this analysis by examining the impact of broader social factors on such processes and how they influence the normative imperatives of sentence decision-making. It is particularly concerned with exploring the proposition that trial outcomes contribute to victimisation and social exclusion and the significance of this for governance in criminal justice. The chapter goes on to suggest ways in which sociological perspectives on questions of trial access and reciprocal notions of rights and accountability could more readily acknowledge their normative significance and importance for determining the legitimacy of sentencing.

Victimisation and legitimacy: the theoretical context

Linking the notion of legitimacy to trial justice requires a focus on the relationship between victims' perceptions of the morality of punishment and sentencing and the extent to which these values are *actually* reflected in trial outcomes.[1] However, developing the theory and methodology necessary to realise this aspiration in different contexts is by no means a straightforward matter.

Providing contextual understandings of socio-legal phenomena like victimisation within different cultures and jurisdictional boundaries is problematic. These difficulties are multiplied when we seek to develop understandings both within and across jurisdictional boundaries. The balance between phenomenology and social reality (i.e. what counts as an epistemologically valid explanation) lies in the extent to which there is agreement as to what constitutes 'objective fact' or 'objectivity'. Although the reality of victimisation is epistemologically conjectural, we can nevertheless postulate (depending on our theoretical persuasion) some *a priori* principles by which to measure/evaluate whether such a phenomenon 'objectively' exists. The subjectivity of the phenomenon, on the other hand, is concerned with such issues as the perceived legitimacy of the causes and consequences of 'crime'; what it subjectively 'feels' like to *be* a victim, rather than simply having been ascribed that status;

---

1 In concrete terms, this can be explored by exploring the extent to which such outcomes reflect the interests and aspirations for justice of victims.

and how these intimate influences have shaped the individual attitudes of those claiming victimisation.

Any social theory which seeks to address the nature and significance of victimisation must necessarily address its legal, socio-historical, economic and political dimensions. For comparative analysis this involves appreciating the multi-layered nature of the relationships between the values and actions which produce victimisation within particular cultures and being able to make epistemologically acceptable generalisations about them. These theoretical dimensions have been comprehensively discussed by Mark Findlay and I[2] in elaborating theory and methodology for the comparative contextual analysis of trial process. We[3] argue that utilising a reflexive theoretical framework facilitates the construction of models which can be tested and refined against specific contexts to produce meaningful comparative generalisations. This work suggests that the solution to comparative understanding rests in the development of theoretical models capable of conceptualising the significance of the relationship between social structure, process and action and its normative effects in ways that are sensitive to cultural diversity and moral pluralism.

Thus, such models derive from the deconstruction of specific contexts against an application of insights from theories which are thought likely to have the potential to infuse the analysis with meaningful comparative conclusions. Although the selection of theoretical postulates for modelling is initially and necessarily predetermined, their verification and modification, and the ultimate content of the model, is derived from contextual analysis.

Since contextual models facilitate the integration of different theoretical and methodological approaches, they may be utilised to deconstruct the meanings attached to specific social constructs such as victimisation within a particular culture (with its specific audiences, players, processes, institutions, power relations and symbolic structures). Such models also lend themselves to reconstruction at various analytical levels which are relevant from culture to culture; vertically or horizontally.

Furthering our understanding of victimisation and its effects therefore depends upon our capacity to analyse its lateral and vertical dimensions. The latter may be made more explicit by adopting different theoretical perspectives. Thus, for example, issues relating to the ideology, procedure and outcomes of the trial and their relationship to victimisation may be perceived laterally, as global and local dimensions which impact reflexively and vertically, in terms of the different degrees of theoretical abstraction (higher to lower) implicit in understanding each analytical level. For example, the procedural level may be conceived conceptually in both global and local terms which reflect degrees of similarity and/or difference (for example, as to correspondence with particular process styles), thereby emphasising the developmental relationship between these two dimensions.

---

2 Findlay and Henham (2005). See chapter 2 for further discussion.
3 *Ibid.* ch. 2.

Correspondingly, a higher level of theoretical abstraction may be necessary to appreciate the cultural significance of procedural norms and their symbolic and hegemonic implications, whereas our understanding of processual activity itself, such as the nature of victim participation in the sentencing process, will demand lower-order micro-explanation. Understanding the meaning and significance of victimisation from a comparative perspective therefore entails the adoption of a multi-layered theoretical approach which is capable of locating and relating hypotheses conceived at different degrees of relevance and abstraction to a given phenomenon in a coherent way.

The notion of victimisation as a social phenomenon has both objective and subjective dimensions. In the international context, for example, research by Kiza and Rohne focuses on both dimensions, because it examines the relationship between the attitudes and perceptions of victims and a range of post-conflict justice issues. Consequently, the study deals with what 'ought' to be and what 'is' through analysing the subjective accounts which describe the experiences and feelings of victims. It is not a conventional empirical study in the sense that that it seeks to hypothesise about observed and quantifiable 'facts' such as sentencing patterns. Rather, it applies quantitative techniques to the analysis of what is essentially an account of the subjective perception of 'facts', describing what it is like to be a victim in a particular post-conflict society and how this impacts on the perception of what constitutes justice for war crimes. Consequently, the 'objectivity' of these accounts can be evaluated only to the extent that we are able to understand their meaning within particular contexts.

The repercussions of this are considerable because, both theoretically and methodologically, there are clear distinctions to be drawn between exploring the subjective and objective dimensions of social experience. The objectivity of any social phenomenon mirrors its subjectivity (and vice versa) – the relationship is reciprocal. One can attempt to 'explain' how definitions of 'objectivity' are produced through the analysis of subjective experience,[4] which is a recursive and constantly changing process. Hence, this approach tries to fix the meaning or contextualise social life by deconstructing the subjectivity of individual experience and making generalisations about the extent to which such experiences and understandings are held collectively. Self-evidently, such methodologies will be culturally contextual in suggesting ways in which the objectivity of process is constructed subjectively.

Victimisation is therefore best conceived as a social construct that involves the interplay between the causes and effects of crime and the perceived appropriateness of particular forms of legal and institutional response. The reciprocal relationship between the aspirational and the empirical dimensions[5]

---

4 For a relevant example; see, Rogers and Erez (1999).
5 'In the sentencing context, the 'aspirational' dimension is concerned with the justice values held by individuals and how these relate to trial outcomes. Correspondingly, the 'empirical' dimension is concerned with the objective measurement of shared values.

JURISDICTIONAL

INSTITUTIONAL   **IDEOLOGICAL**

INTERACTIVE

Figure 7.1 Ideology and the dimensions of context

of this relationship are portrayed diagrammatically in Figure 7.1. This reflects the notion that ideology[6] impacts on each dimension of context and that the reciprocal relationship between ideology and context is crucial to under-standing how the interplay between social structure and human agency becomes characterised as victimisation.

Such a conceptualisation envisages that the relationship between trial justice and victimisation should be theorised in terms of the following con-textual dimensions. However, they are equally applicable in developing our understanding of domestic trial outcomes and their perceived legitimacy.

IDEOLOGICAL DIMENSION: This refers to the ideology which informs social structure. It is determined by political and pragmatic values and driven by the desire among rival social groups for hegemony and self-preservation. The legitimacy of trial justice depends on the extent to which victims are recognised as essential voices in the processes and outcomes of criminal justice. This context includes victims' views on the appropriate means of providing justice and the general purpose and benefits of addressing the needs of victims.

JURISDICTIONAL DIMENSION: This includes the nature, function and discretionary choices presented by the legal rules and principles which exist in a particular jurisdictional context. Thus, substantive legal rights accorded to trial participants, legal procedure and relationships between legal form, policy and social control variables are regarded as important structural properties to be analysed. This context determines the structural conditions for victim inclusion which are operationalised through the sub-stantive norms and procedures of international and domestic trial structures, their teleological interpretation, and the development of appropriate profes-sional conduct norms and rights instruments. Questions concerning the desirability and legal foundations of prosecution; the responsibility for prose-cution in terms of *locus* and formality of the proceedings, and the degree of victim participation in the prosecution may all be addressed within this context.

---

6 'Ideology' is used here to denote a set of beliefs or principles which may (or may not) draw allegiance as morally appropriate or politically desirable.

INSTITUTIONAL DIMENSION: This examines strategic rationales for the operation and function of processual activity, particularly institutional communication structures which influence outcomes. Analysis of this context reveals the extent to which structural impediments to victim inclusion exist and suggests how the structured framework may need to change in order to facilitate more restorative outcomes at both the international and local level.

INTERACTIVE DIMENSION: This crucial context is concerned with the social reality of decision-making, and reflects the fact that the conditions which influence the exercise of discretionary power are patterned through the activities of trial participants who recursively create the meaning and social reality of discretionary decision-making as both action and structure. Consequently, this context is directed towards understanding how processual variables which govern the operation of pathways of selectivity[7] within particular jurisdictions influence the exercise of discretionary decision-making power. The context therefore analyses the relationship between victims' attitudes and perceptions of trial justice and what *actually* takes place.

Therefore, as described in chapter 5, a contextual model may be developed for a specific context by refining and synthesising some specific theoretical propositions relating to victimisation and trial justice. The modelling emphasis would be on *procedure, outcome* and *purpose*; in other words, how the concept of victimisation is constructed culturally against the contextual dimensions identified above, and how it relates to the wider issue of criminal justice governance. The theoretical challenge is how best to envision these complexities by developing models with theoretical evaluators designed to deconstruct these aspects of social reality.

Initially, the choice of contextual evaluators for inclusion in any model will depend on a preliminary identification of the relevant dynamics of victimisation. As discussed earlier, conceptualisations of victimisation must acknowledge the need for paradigms which are capable of operating at different levels of abstraction and have the capacity to accommodate varying empirical, temporal and spatial dimensions. The evaluators included in any contextual model will always remain contingent, since they are predicated on identifying 'theoretically relevant facts' about the nature of victimisation in a particular jurisdictional setting. However, such modelling of victimisation should address issues of power, symbolism, due process and rights protection for each context analysed.

Conceptualising redress and establishing rights

Extending the notion of inclusion for the purpose of trial and sentence is not simply concerned with understanding the nature of victimisation and

---

7 This refers to influences on the way in which information used in decision-making is selected that are repeated and recursive.

reflecting the aspirations of victims through increased participatory rights. It also requires a fundamental re-evaluation of the trial process as a context for delivering more communitarian and socially responsive forms of redress than currently obtain. This entails broadening the scope of accountability to recognise collective as well as individual forms of accountability for harm and its consequences, and a corresponding acknowledgment of collective 'interests' in the kinds of redress available through the mechanisms of trial justice. The achievement of this goal is frequently hindered by the false dichotomies resulting from the need to distinguish penal objectives where purposes conflict with those of retributive justice.[8]

The kind of conceptual confusion that can result may be illustrated by examining the relationship between reparative and retributive forms of justice within the adversarial context, and its implications for the perceived legitimacy of sentencing. As Zedner suggests,[9] much of the difficulty is caused by obfuscation about the exact scope of reparative justice, especially its civil law associations, and the perception that it lacks penal characteristics. These difficulties are not insurmountable, as discussed later, provided their resolution is contemplated against a broadened focus for trial accountability. The relevant issues are well illustrated by analysing recent developments in international trial justice.

In a recent paper McCarthy[10] focuses on the reparations regime of the ICC which he seeks to evaluate against the concerns raised by reparative justice theory. In so doing, he makes some significant observations about the capacity of the ICC provisions to fulfil the expectations of victims and communities in post-conflict states.

McCarthy begins by alerting us to the moral significance of the behaviour criminalised by international criminal law in terms of the harm caused to victims[11] before evaluating the extent to which the ICC reparations regime provides a means to effectively redress this harm. McCarthy rightly identifies the problem of defining the purpose of reparations under the Rome Statute as the core issue. In particular, he notes that the reparations provisions are contained in Part 6 of the ICC Statute, which relates to 'The Trial', rather than Article 77 in Part 7, which deals with 'applicable penalties', and so concludes that reparations are concerned more with the role of the trial in redressing the harm done to victims than the punishment of its perpetrators.[12]

---

8 A classic example of this problem is the concept of 'community service'. Although it can be justified in either retributive or restorative terms, this does not of itself facilitate the integration of restorative and retributive ideologies for the trial, nor the rationale for imposing such sentences in particular cases.
9 Zedner (1994).
10 McCarthy (2009). See also Ferstman (2002), Keller (2007).
11 *Ibid.* 256.
12 *Ibid.* 257.

McCarthy argues that the ICC reparations regime can learn important lessons from the treatment of reparation in international human rights law. In particular, he suggests that the latter's more flexible approach to assessing non-pecuniary damages could provide a template for developing the rehabilitative aspects of reparation within the ICC framework.[13] This refers to redress which alleviates psychological, physical and social harm suffered by victims, and, alluding to the jurisprudence of the Inter-American Court of Human Rights, McCarthy suggests that this might include programmes of community social rehabilitation following egregious violations of human rights.

McCarthy goes on to suggest that the ICC Trust Fund could provide the means for addressing issues of individual and collective rehabilitation within the scope of Rule 98(4) of the ICC RPE.[14] This argument is developed by reference to the Court's independent power to support victims under Rule 98(5), which provides that 'other resources of the Trust Fund may be used for the benefit of victims subject to the provisions of Article 79.' Programmes dealing with physical, psychological and material support for victims have been authorised by the ICC Trial Chamber, and, as McCarthy suggests, the potential exists for all victims within the jurisdiction of the ICC to be included, not just those who appear before the Court or otherwise participate in the proceedings. However, McCarthy rightly cautions against interpreting Rule 98(5) as authorising a broader mandate to assist victims in general, pointing out that there is a potential overlap with the activities of charitable organisations. He bases this on the fact that those who have suffered harm must fall within the jurisdiction of the Court under Article 79(1), which clearly limits the outreach capacity of the ICC Trust Fund.[15] In addition, Regulation 48 of the Trust Fund effectively restricts the use of the Fund's 'other resources' to that of redressing the harm caused to victims.

Whilst this may be correct and, notwithstanding that one could not disagree with McCarthy's observation that the redress provided by the ICC Trust Fund addresses the moral status of the individual *qua* victim, it may be argued that the issues he raises regarding the scope of its reparations regime highlight a number of fundamental concerns. The first of these is alluded to by McCarthy himself, although in another context:

> Whereas reparative justice theory may make the point that it is necessary to address the full range of relationships harmed by the criminal conduct,

---

13 *Ibid.* 261.
14 *Ibid.* 262. Rule 98(4) states that 'Following consultations with interested states and the Trust Fund to an intergovernmental, international or national organisation approved by the Trust Fund.'
15 Article 79(1) states: 'A Trust Fund shall be established by decision of the Assembly of State Parties for the benefit of victims of crimes within the jurisdiction of the Court, and of the families of such victims.'

the ability of the ICC to achieve this is necessarily limited to the responsibility of individuals for criminal conduct.[16]

To be sure, the focus of McCarthy's argument is the existing ICC regime, so that he attempts to test the potential scope of its reparations regime against a normative framework for the trial process which remains largely adversarial, and one for punishment that is predominantly retributive and deterrent in purpose.[17]

I would argue that the fact the reparations regime in Part 6 is distinguished from those provisions of the ICC Statute which deal with the determination of sentence in Part 7 serves to further confuse the objectives of the Court. To begin with, it may be argued that the purposes of punishment *are* relevant to Part 6 by virtue of the fact that Article 76 (headed 'Sentencing') is contained in Part 6 and, more particularly, since Article 76(1) specifically states that the Trial Chamber must consider the 'appropriate' sentence following a conviction, taking into account evidence and submissions made during the *trial* that are relevant to sentence. Therefore, although the substantive provisions relating to the determination of sentence are contained in Part 7, the inclusion of Article 76(1) in Part 6 brings the question of punishment and sentencing firmly within the remit of the objectives set for the trial, taken as a whole, including reparations. Consequently, the fact that Articles 75 and 76 are so included suggests the need for there to be a clear understanding of the relationship between the purposes of the reparations regime and the sentencing regime *within the context of the trial as a whole.*

Therefore, I would suggest that the ICC's reparations regime cannot be detached from the penality of the trial proper, either conceptually or practically. Indeed, one might argue that a rationale for the international criminal trial which envisages its function as a mechanism for providing redress mandates a broad range of possible strategies and structures to achieve them, including those concerned with reparation and punishment. In fact, it is arguable that, because reparative justice is elemental to restorative justice,[18] any attempt to detach the reparations regime conceptually from the penal ideology of the trial proper is inappropriate and counterproductive. This is because the extent to which reparative justice can be expected to redress the concerns of victims is severely constrained by the legitimacy attached to the purposes and practices of the trial proper, including the punishment of perpetrators.

More fundamentally, the above discussion raises the complex and wider issue of defining the role of victims and communities within the ICC process. In other words, it questions the extent to which reparations for victims can be

---

16 McCarthy (2009) 270.
17 Henham (2003a).
18 On the difficulties of distinguishing between symbolic and material reparation, see Retzinger and Scheff (1996).

effectively separated from the broader demands for 'justice' raised in the aftermath of mass atrocity. Arguably, the only way to ensure that the 'interests' of these groups are satisfied is to modify the rationale for the ICC trial to include a broader notion of redress that extends to both reparative and retributive justice. As it stands, the interrelated purposes of reparations and retributive punishment have not been fully addressed within the normative framework of the ICC trial.

An important illustration of this failure is that no thought appears to have been given to the relationship between the approach to rehabilitation taken in the trial and its potential use as part of the reparations regime by the ICC. As mentioned, McCarthy draws upon the more flexible and constructive approaches of international human rights law to illustrate the therapeutic potential of rehabilitative measures, especially the notion that such measures have a significant role to play in repairing broken communities. However, I would argue that any conceptualisation of reparative justice in terms of 'social rehabilitation' should be related more directly to broader notions of rehabilitation in developing coherent and inclusive rationales for international punishment and sentencing practice within the context of the trial as a whole.

Failure to think this issue through is evident in the deliberations of the ICTY. Part of the obfuscation that has persisted in defining the tribunal's penal rationale[19] is its failure to engage with the notion that individual and collective rehabilitation are fundamentally interrelated concepts. This may in part be due to the fact that post-modern conceptualisations of rehabilitation have tended to stress its capacity for individual crime reduction – the ethos of the justification being the provision of some kind of 'curative', or 'healing' disposal. The relationship between this individualistic approach and broader notions of social rehabilitation remains unclear in the deliberations of the ICTY Trial Chamber. For example, it was stated in *Delalić*:[20]

> The factor of rehabilitation considers *the circumstances of reintegrating* the guilty accused into society ... so that they can become useful members of it and enable them to lead normal and productive lives upon their release from imprisonment [emphasis added].

In the Appeals Chamber,[21] the Tribunal, whilst acknowledging its significance, re-affirmed that rehabilitation could not 'play a *predominant* role', and was clearly subordinate to deterrence and retribution as the main purposes of sentencing. However, the Appeals Chamber also referred to the primacy accorded to rehabilitation in many national jurisdictions and certain international and

---

19 See Henham (2005b) ch. 1.
20 *Prosecutor v Delalić*, (Case No. IT-96-21-T), Judgement, 16 November 1998, para. 1233.
21 *Prosecutor v Delalić* (Case No. IT-96-21), Appeals Judgement, 20 February 2001, para. 806 (emphasis in original).

human rights instruments.[22] Regrettably, whilst the ICTY acknowledged the need for individuals to be re-integrated into society, it clearly failed to elaborate how this merging of individual and social responses might be achieved within the context of sentencing. An additional aspect of this process is the realisation that a close relationship exists between rationalisations which support rehabilitation and the exercise of hegemonic power.[23]

Undoubtedly, current conceptualisations of rehabilitative and restorative justice are circumscribed by the predominantly retributive and deterrent model. To progress beyond this would require both a philosophical re-orientation which favours the moral utility of reparative justice in achieving reconciliation and, further, the re-integration and empowerment of victims by adopting a more communitarian model for the trial and sentencing.

The latter, however, is largely envisaged as being dependent on institutional change, whereas the traditional court processes[24] of Western liberal democracies are seen as an inappropriate locus for re-integrative ceremonies and popular forms of justice. Further, as Zedner suggests,[25] prevailing notions of reparative justice and retribution tend to 'ignore the structural imperatives of deprivation and disadvantage under which many offenders act', while more developed conceptualisations of reparative justice might be capable of addressing communitarian ideals of social justice. Zedner advocates a vision of reparative justice predicated on sharing responsibility for social inclusion and control and the equal distribution and enforcement of rights.

Zedner further identifies the need for a theoretical reorientation in order to achieve a greater integration of retributive and reparative forms of justice,[26] based on the abandonment of culpability as the central focus for sentencing and paying much closer attention to the issue of harm and its social distribution. Her argument for a move away from culpability to a broader based conception of social harm is founded in part on an appreciation that crime infringes rights held in common socially and that the conception of harm should be widened, since citizens have rights to a presumption of security.[27] Correspondingly, the rights of individual citizens to a presumption

---

22 For example, Article 10(3), ICCPR states that: 'The penitentiary system shall comprise treatment of prisoners the essential aim of which shall be their reformation and *social* rehabilitation.' (emphasis added).

23 As exemplified by Article 33 of the SFRY Criminal Code which includes the following as two of its three reasons for the imposition of sentence: '(1) preventing the offender from committing criminal acts *and his rehabilitation*; … ;(3) strengthening the moral fibre of a socialist self-managing society and influence *on the development of the citizens' social responsibility and discipline*' (emphasis added). On the relationship between state authority and rehabilitation, see Garland (1996), Rex (1998).

24 Whether adversarial, inquisitorial or hybridised in nature.

25 Zedner (1994) 250.

26 She suggests that arguments for incorporating reparative elements into the criminal justice process are mainly pragmatic and economic.

27 Environmental and corporate crime become relevant within this broader formulation.

of security could be extended to actual and potential breaches of international humanitarian law.

Ultimately, Zedner sees some rapprochement between reparation and retributive forms of justice. She distinguishes both from rehabilitation and deterrence, suggesting their commonality on the grounds that each is predicated on notions of individual autonomy and the fact that they both derive their 'authority' from the offence itself and impose penalties on the basis of the seriousness of the crime. Ultimately, Zedner advocates that social inclusion should provide the rationale for fairness in reparative justice. The elaboration of this dimension for linking the rationale of reparative to restorative justice is lacking in McCarthy's analysis. As has been argued, such conceptual linkage is necessary in order to inform a more inclusive rationale for trial justice.

Procedural justice, rights and accountability

Conceptual linkage of a different kind is necessary if progress is to be made in delivering a more inclusive form of trial justice. The translation of ideological imperatives into concrete outcomes through sentencing is primarily dependant on the relationship between discretionary power and the instrumental capacity it derives from the normative framework of the trial. Conceptualising this symbiotic relationship is a vital function of social theory, but that alone is insufficient to penetrate the normative significance of what theory is only able to describe. In particular, comprehending the significance of procedural justice involves its deconstruction at several levels:

- objective description of procedural norms – why they take the form they do, and what this signifies;
- objective description of the processes by which procedural norms are invoked and applied – the social reality of norm application;
- objective and subjective accounts of the exercise of discretionary power by decision-makers;
- theoretical insights into the significance[28] of what takes place.

However, what links the application of sentencing norms to perceptions of justice is their significance as part of the mechanism for communicating the purposes of punishment to the 'relevant' audience. It is important to realise that norms are not simply facilitative, in the sense that they provide the mechanical tools for punishment. Sentencing norms are morally contingent norms, because their justified use in particular cases depends upon human agency. Yet the conditions whereby these norms are given concrete form are only

---

28 The way individuals, especially victims and witnesses, are treated by the process is important in determining their feelings about the 'fairness' of the trial and its outcome; see Tyler (2003). For relevant analysis in the context of pre-sentence reports, see Tata (2010).

capable of providing true accountability if they connect with the expectations individuals hold (and share) about punishment.

Accordingly, the relationship of rights to accountability is crucial in defining the legitimacy of procedural justice. Participatory rights should be seen as instrumental for delivering socially inclusive responses to criminalised behaviour, rather than ensuring 'fair' trial within the exclusory framework of adversarial trial and retributive justice. Thus, although the degree of participation may be a measure of procedural justice, this must be seen in the context of the trial's ideological and normative capacity to deliver 'justice' in the first place. In other words, expectations of an existing process may fall well short of those that citizens aspire to, and have a right to expect.[29]

Social context, legitimacy and rights

This final section examines the impact of social factors on rights and account-ability and how this is reflected in the process of sentencing. It is particularly concerned to explore the relationship between trial justice and victimisation and its implications for social exclusion and the governance role of criminal justice. The analysis suggests that conventional socio-legal approaches for evaluating accountability in terms of trial access and reciprocal rights could more readily acknowledge their normative significance and importance in determining the legitimacy of sentencing.

Conceptualising the victim

The work of Uwe Ewald[30] is significant for highlighting how victim identity is constructed in international criminal justice through 'societal technologies' that determine the relationship between hegemonic groups and those who are excluded from rights of access and justice. He suggests that such identities of victimisation are 'inevitably linked to interest-based political and global control strategies' and that international criminal justice is crucially implicated in constructing false accounts of victimisation as a consequence.

The manufacture of such large-scale victimisation amounts to crime control on a global platform. In particular, hegemonic states pursue strategies of selective violence against those states, regimes or 'others' they wish to dom-inate, justifying coercion through falsely representing such states as 'threats' to the universal social order. In this sense, the regulatory structures of inter-national criminal justice exist to give effect to the ideology and norms of domination. Hence, the processing of false victim identities is enabled through the normative framework of international trial justice. An example of this is

---

29 This is not simply a matter of equal access to justice, since these egalitarian aspirations are not reflected in the justice on offer.
30 Ewald (2006).

the focus in international trials on the construction of individual perpetrators and the failure of international criminal law to reflect the collective nature of victimisation through the accountability it provides. Ewald argues, further, that the distortion of value relationships by the large-scale victimisation of international criminal law is validated through the value-related dimension of sentencing, since this justifies the ideology of international criminal justice. The consistency of this false labelling amounts to social victimisation because it systematically approves the selective appropriation of false victim status and promotes distorted deviant identities.

More recently,[31] Ewald has suggested how the 'plausible rationality' that underpins international trial justice produces a form of 'judicial truth' that bears little resemblance to the 'material truth' of commonly shared values. The ideology that informs this rationality comes from the hegemony of the socio-political context of international criminal justice, which comprises 'an international political process of global structuring and organisation'. Consequently, the possibility of developing rights or standards aimed at achieving greater 'material truth' is compromised by the partisan westernised definitions of risk perception and threat that inform the ideologies and normative frameworks of international trial justice. These 'regimes of truth' are reproduced through the generation of evidence that sustains their hegemonic ideology, despite the fact that they are accepted only by a relative majority of relevant social actors, including the global 'community'.

Ewald's account of the social reality of the merging of 'fact' and 'value' as evidenced through the social interaction of the international trial is insightful, if not altogether surprising. His empirical finding that evidentiary information derived from government institutions appears to predominate in international criminal trials leads him to conclude that:

> … judicial reasoning and inference in international criminal justice beyond issues directly related to the execution of the crimes and large-scale victimisation, might be strongly influenced by legal, political and social concepts as part of 'Western civilisation'

The manufacture of 'judicial truth' is therefore implicated in fulfilling this hegemonic ideal.

Ewald's observations concur with those of other scholars. For example, Armstrong and McCara[32] and Simon[33] have each described the 'centring' of the victim and the false construction of victimhood as commonplace phenomena in post-modern criminal justice discourse. Such tendencies are the result of the reciprocal construction of the relevant 'audiences' and penal

---

31 Ewald (2008).
32 Armstrong and McAra (2006) 8.
33 Simon (2007) ch. 4.

ideologies that sustain hegemonic power.[34] As Sparks points out,[35] these insights owe much to Hall *et al.*'s[36] seminal analysis of state hegemony and the strategic deployment of its agents and structures to falsely identify, stigmatise and criminalise particular minority groups, albeit that the dialectics of power and exclusion have changed significantly since the 1970s.

Farmer[37] reminds us that there is a general failure to account for 'the significance of rights, not only in terms of their function in relation to the development of particular penal strategies, but also in terms of their importance in legitimising state action or justifying the use of power'. In other words, there is a need to account for the role of law and rights in the exercise and justification of penal power. In terms of the dialectics of power, the increased attention given to victims' rights may be seen as a significant paradox, since the rights ceded to victims by the state have been accompanied by a relinquishing of state responsibility towards citizens as victims of crime, actual and potential. In this sense, the incremental ascription of rights to victims may be viewed as an implicit validation of the use of state power against those individuals or groups which it wishes to exclude from the full benefits of citizenship.

Howard Becker[38] might describe the creation of such 'outsiders' as integral to the moral entrepreneurship of the state, Mathiesen,[39] on the other hand, as reflecting the diversionary function of punishment; whilst a Durkheimian[40] analysis might view such moral re-alignments as necessary to reinforce the collective sentiments of society. However, whilst all these insights have in common the notion of penal law as reflecting the moral power of the state, each fails to recognise how the paradox of relinquishing state power in one area may serve to validate the extension of state control in another. Arguably, this phenomenon is simply a consequence of the state's diminishing moral authority in late post-modernity. The further ascription of victims' rights is not only a reflection of the state empowering its citizens, it is also a function

---

34 Rose (2000).
35 Sparks (2006) note 31 at 39.
36 Hall *et al.* (1978).
37 Farmer (2006) note 49 at 66.
38 Becker (1973).
39 Mathiesen (1990). Individuals or groups perceived as socially dangerous or as a threat to the prevailing social order may be punished in order to divert attention from greater social harms being perpetrated by those in control. The latter are perceived as inappropriate targets because they are implicated in supporting ideals which are perceived as morally just (e.g. the political economy, democracy).
40 Durkheim (1982), Durkheim (1984) 101–32. What constitutes a morality of the common good is something which Durkheim fails to explore adequately, beyond asserting that societies themselves determine what is necessary for sustaining social cohesion and civil society. Unfortunately, since social morality in post-modern societies is fragmented rather than collective, there is an increasing moral distance between trial justice and the social experiences of citizens.

of the state empowering itself and, in so doing, reshaping the moral terrain over which it holds dominion.

This weakening of the social contract has correspondingly reflected a greater assumption of state responsibility for dealing with what are defined as threats or risks to civil society, such as so-called 'dangerous' offenders. The anomalous identification and criminal labelling of 'dangerous' offenders not only provides a useful example of the difficulties inherent in constructing legal definitions of complex social behaviours, it also illustrates the shallow moral foundations for such labelling by the state, as well as its potential discriminatory and exclusory effects.

The main difficulties are defining 'dangerousness' for the purposes of sentencing[41] and devising criteria for evaluating whether offenders are, or might become, 'dangerous'. For example, Walker[42] suggests that a dangerous situation is one which raises the probability of serious harm above a certain level. Therefore, although difficult, it should not be impossible to define that level of harm. Clearly, the dangerousness of the offender varies with the nature of the apprehended harm. Walker therefore proposes the formula, dangerousness = seriousness x probability of harm. The problem with this is that it ignores the fact that, if either the seriousness of the behaviour or the probability of its occurrence is below a certain level, we must think of the situation as *not* being dangerous. This unfortunate conclusion means that those who are faced with the onerous task of sentencing such offenders are forced to rely upon unsatisfactory actuarial and clinical predictive techniques.[43] Therefore, it may be argued that, whilst such sentencing is instrumental in defining the limits of

---

41 Floud and Young define dangerous offenders as those who have inflicted or attempted to inflict serious bodily harm on other human beings and who are found to be suffering from a severe mental or emotional disorder indicating a propensity towards continuing dangerous criminal activity; Floud and Young (1981).This does not, of course, address the question of when and how an individual should be judged as 'dangerous' in any particular case.

42 Walker (1985) ch. 22.

43 Actuarial methods have three main shortcomings:

   • They are ethically objectionable, since selection is made on the basis that a person is assigned to a particular class or risk group, so it weakens the presumption of innocence. It also minimises the impact of individual will.
   • They not explain behaviour and leave out circumstances and characteristics which may be relevant to a particular individual.
   • There are technical problems of too many false positives, short follow-up periods, and a low base level of violence.

   Similarly, clinical methods suffer from:

   • information overload;
   • too many false positives, and unacceptably high levels of false negatives;
   • the fact that assessment by professionals is no better than by non-professionals.

the law's coercive power, it lacks the moral authority to do so. Hence, the legitimacy of penal law in this area is weakened.

Sentencing is pivotal in delineating the parameters of accountability through its validation of penal law's authority. However, as Garland suggests,[44] there is a fundamental paradox in the increasing individualisation of penal law, particularly in terms of victim impact and its purported reflection through increased participatory rights in the criminal process, whereas the reality for sentencing is a dramatic reduction in the possibility of individuation through the increasingly strict regulation of discretionary power. The projected image of victim and offender is therefore a distortion of reality to the extent that it suggests a relationship where the interests of both, and those of the wider community, appear incapable of 'balance'.

According to Garland, the distortion of 'balance' towards favouring the rights of victims at the expense of offenders is a deliberate control strategy that is designed to maintain the social and cultural divide of contemporary Western states. As a matter of principle, Ashworth[45] argues that victims' interests should count for no more than those of other citizens when considering in whose interests the criminal justice process is being carried out. Again, it is this dialectic between the social reality of partisan control and the moral right of each citizen to equality before the law which is at issue. This is evidenced by the need for competing values to find equal expression through access to justice with corresponding rights protection.

The notion of balance

As to the 'correct' balance between the interests of victims and others in the criminal process, Ashworth's position has been convincingly challenged by Cavadino and Dignan,[46] who suggest that, although the premise for the 'public interest' argument is essentially valid, the conclusion Ashworth draws from it does not automatically follow. Accordingly, they argue that, as long as the behaviour is officially sanctioned, any reparative requirements of the victim should be accommodated by the sentencing judge.

In recognising that victim satisfaction and empowerment constitute an aspect of the 'public interest', Cavadino and Dignan concede that victim allocution should be limited to reparative rather than retributive considerations. However, they advocate[47] that restorative themes are more likely to be maximised through the adoption of an 'integrated restorative justice' model which allows for a principled compromise between

---

44 Garland (2001) 179.
45 Ashworth (2002a) 77.
46 Cavadino and Dignan (1997) 237.
47 Cavadino and Dignan (2002) 54.

retributive and reparative/restorative justice themes based on Dworkinian rights theory.[48]

It is instructive to examine the question of balance in the context of the ongoing debate about plea bargaining in international criminal justice.[49] In terms of procedural justice, Zappala[50] makes the important point that the determination of 'truth' where a guilty plea is entered is neither judicial nor pedagogical, and, therefore, appears to contradict the mission of international criminal courts to take account of victims' interests. Furthermore, he appears to advocate the pragmatic use of guilty plea discounts and plea agreements, on the basis of their advantages to the Prosecutor in shortening investigations and that it may be in the public interest to shorten the trials of minor participants on grounds of cost.

Several justifications have been advanced for the use of plea agreements in the ICTY. For example, in *Todorović*,[51] great emphasis was placed on remarks made earlier in *Erdemović* to the effect that an admission of guilt is important because it encourages individuals to come forward, and saves the tribunal the time, effort and expense of a lengthy investigation and trial, especially the laborious task of protecting victims and witnesses. In addition, by pleading guilty, an accused relieves victims and witnesses of the necessity of giving evidence with the attendant stress this may incur.[52] As Judge Cassese put it in *Erdemović*, 'Thus, by pleading guilty, the accused undoubtedly contributes to public advantage'.

However, the expression 'public advantage' as applied to plea agreements can be interpreted in many different ways. It may be to the 'public advantage' for victims and witnesses to be relieved of the stress of travelling or giving evidence, or that plea agreements contribute to 'truth-finding', or that they secure managerial and bureaucratic advantages. However, if Zappala is correct in arguing that plea agreements have no judicial or pedagogic value, the argument is reduced to one of defining the 'public advantage' in purely economic terms. Certainly, while the ideology and goals of international criminal justice remain partial or repressive, this will determine which rights are secured and upheld in international criminal trials.

Changing the penal ideology which informs the trial, as Findlay and I suggest, would provide a moral justification for giving victims greater

---

48 Emmerson and Ashworth appear to suggest that if any participatory rights were to emerge in the future, these are likely to be limited to the making of a statement outlining the effects of the crime, rather than allowing victims to actually make representations as to the length or type of sentence to be conferred. They also suggest that any such statement might infringe the accused's right to a fair and impartial hearing under Article 6 of the ECHR; see Emmerson and Ashworth (2001) 18–78.

49 See chapter 5 for fuller discussion.

50 Zappala (2003) 89.

51 *Prosecutor v Todorovic* (Case No. IT-95-9/1), Sentencing Judgement, 31 July 2001.

52 *Ibid.* para.80.

participatory rights in plea bargaining decisions. It would therefore enhance the pedagogic mission of the trial in terms of 'truth-finding' and its social context, since the interests of all parties who can establish a legitimate claim to participation would be promoted equally. However, there remains a need for a principled approach to developing the normative framework for rights to fulfil this changed ideology. This should not only draw a distinction between the foundations for rights and practice, but also promote methodologies that produce a deeper understanding of each social context and the relationship between rights and accountability.

Modelling rights

We now turn to consider the implications of this body of work for conceptualising notions of access and rights in relation to the legitimacy of sentencing. If we think about access and rights and their significance for governance from a hegemonic perspective, the social reality of participation may be reflected as a continuum of exclusion. Victims may be excluded as citizens for social and economic reasons (such as poverty). Thus, they are deliberately neglected by the state, or demand less intervention, because they have less power. Citizens falling within this category then disproportionately become victims of crimes defined by the powerful. The laws of the dominant elite are enforced by processes that give effect to its penal ideology. These processes allow diminished rights of access and participation to those citizens who are already victimised by the state's hegemony, so becoming doubly victimised. This paradigm applies equally to international criminal justice, except that it is the socio-political elites of Western states who constitute the hegemony, define the content of international criminal law, and identify those who should be subject to it.

However, Ashworth[53] asserts that the search for models is less relevant than the need to develop a number of fundamental principles and corresponding rights, including those mentioned below.

Rectitude

- The need to ensure the reliability of evidence;
- protection of the innocent from wrongful conviction;
- the right to consistent treatment within declared policies;
- the principle that individuals should only be subject to the minimum burdens necessary.

---

53 Ashworth (1994) 29.

Integrity

Criminal justice agents and the courts should consistently apply morally acceptable practices.

In his rejection of the notion of 'balance', Ashworth[54] suggests a chronology for the adoption of a rights-based approach to the criminal process which can be summarised as follows:

- identification of the aims of a given part of the criminal process;
- establishing what rights ought to be accorded to suspects, defendants and victims;
- establishing an adequate foundation for rights;
- determining the proper ambit of rights. This essentially involves ascertaining the relative weight of any right, circumstances in which rights may be sacrificed and the consequent examination of alternatives, as well as careful investigation of any empirical basis claimed to support the curtailment of rights in the interests of crime control.
- Where choices must be made the principle of maximum respect for rights should be observed.
- Focusing on rights must not lead to the neglect of wider issues such as public accountability and the exercise of power.

Of course, what amounts to 'morally acceptable' practices is an agent-relative issue that depends upon context, and it is social contingency which determines the configuration of a state's power relationships and its impact upon penal law. Correspondingly, the social reality of the power/law nexus validates the foundation for rights, but the moral authority of penal law *as it is reflected in social life* depends upon the extent to which it reflects shared social values about punishment. Therefore, the degree to which rights modelling is able to provide a more accurate conceptualisation of the relationship between hegemony and rights depends upon its capacity to explain the linkage between the normative and social dimensions of rights.

To develop this approach more fully, I propose to elaborate Findlay's[55] tripartite conceptualisation of access to justice from a rights perspective.

Rights of access to the trial

Rights of access in this sense refer to the ability of victims to participate in pre-trial decision-making, including diversionary mechanisms. These may be described as *purposeful rights*, in that the penal ideology that underpins rights

---

54 Ashworth (1996a) 229–30.
55 Findlay (2002).

advocates equal access to the trial process. Therefore, such rights are pre-dicated on the assumption that the ideology and process of the trial should be inclusive and integrated, and directed towards the identification and balan-cing of conflicting demands for justice. Rights of access to the trial should also promote consistency of approach within this context and rely upon an agreed formula for balancing public and private interests, with outcomes guaranteed as freely negotiated and unfettered.[56]

Rights of access by those within the trial

Such rights include the ability of significant parties to influence discretionary decisions through, for example, allocation and/or victim impact statements. They are therefore *participatory rights* in the practical sense of ensuring that the nature and norms of the process are *actually* inclusive. Such norms cover the conduct of professionals, experts and victims operating within the trial context, and are designed to ensure that participants are not coerced, or discourses constrained, by unduly restrictive conduct norms, such as those designed to support a framework for retributive justice delivery.

Therefore, these rights are distinguishable from rights that purport to be participatory, but are in reality merely symbolic or far more limited than the rhetoric of penal law suggests. This problem may be illustrated in the inter-national context by examining the ICC's participatory regime. There is nothing that *obliges* the ICC to admit relevant victim evidence. Read in con-junction with Rule 145 of the ICC RPE, which deals with the determination of sentence, the ICC provisions concerned with victims do not provide for their unconditional participation in any stage of the proceedings. For example, Article 68 of the ICC Statute, which includes provisions dealing with victim participation in the proceedings, is conditional in several aspects. The decision as to what constitutes 'the personal interests of the victims' is left to the Court's discretion, as is the decision whether to admit the victims' views and concerns at all. Article 68(3) simply mandates the Court to '*permit* their views to be presented and considered at stages of the proceedings *determined to be appropriate by the Court*' and then goes on to qualify that possibility further by adding that any such presentation and admission must be 'in a manner which is not prejudicial to or inconsistent with the rights of the accused and a fair and impartial trial'.[57] Rule 145(1)(C) of the ICC RPE merely obliges the Court to '*give consideration*' to (*inter alia*) the harm caused to victims and their families. There is *no right* for them to lodge a victim impact statement which *must* be taken into account in fixing the sentence.

---

56 Von Hirsch, Ashworth and Shearing (2003) 21.
57 This is a necessary discretion to maintain balance between the competing rights of the parties.

Rights of access to the community by the trial

These rights look beyond the trial process and are especially important for evaluating the extent to which sentences reflect shared values for punishment. They are *proactive rights* to the extent that they are instrumental in ensuring that punishment reflects the pluralistic justice demands of civil society. Such rights may also be viewed as *outcome rights*, in that they should ensure that trial outcomes correspond with the purposes which those communities would like to see achieved by the trial process. In this sense, rights are co-extensive with community aspirations for reintegration and the reconstruction of damaged relationships. In the context of international criminal justice, these rights are important in promoting the contribution of the trial to transitional justice in post-conflict states.

Again taking an example from the transitional justice context of international criminal justice, the outcomes of international trials currently play an ambivalent role.[58] To become more effective, such outcomes should be evaluated against transitional justice objectives and consider measures of satisfaction which go beyond the immediate impact of sentencing on victims and communities. However, the broader implications of such perceptions need to be evaluated within the context of transitional objectives. Satisfaction may ensue because the process was inclusive and participatory, or because of feelings held about its intrinsic value in resolving conflict and aiding transition. Similarly, differences between high and low-ranking perpetrators and forms of trial, for example, all affect perceptions of legitimacy. In terms of timing, the window of opportunity and impetus for reconciliatory motives to be exploited may quickly dissipate. Reconciliation may be triggered at different times in transitional states. Such triggers may range from the indictment and prosecution of particular perpetrators, to the release of political prisoners, whereas the reform of institutional structures to achieve economic justice may be seen as more pressing, or equally, significant to the goals of criminal justice. The inter-relationship of each element for achieving transitional justice depends on the relevant context and its transitional needs. All these considerations need to be weighed carefully in determining how rights for victims and communities can be associated with the integration of trial outcomes within the transitional framework.

Rights and governance

The difference between the social reality of victim participation and its symbolism was recently conceptualised by Cockayne in drawing comparisons between international and domestic forms of criminal justice:[59]

---

58 Henham (2010).
59 Cockayne (2001).

In one [model], represented through the rhetoric of the Prosecutor and the official spokespeople of the Tribunals,[60] victims and witnesses are central actors in the trial process. The Tribunal is, according to this model, there as a mouthpiece, a chance for their voices to be heard, for them to participate in the formation of the historical record and to ensure that these crimes are not forgotten. This model suggests a sociological role for the trial process which is not often ascribed to domestic criminal trials. The Tribunals are a tool for the *construction* of an international civil order ... In contrast, domestic criminal trials are rarely justified in these terms, as contributing to the construction of the domestic public order. Instead, they are conceived as enforcing that order. The second model for the Tribunals' trial process is more like that. It treats victims and witnesses as instruments in the Prosecutor's quest for a conviction. Protective and rehabilitative measures are not conceived as a integral part of the Tribunal's performance of their mandates, reconstructing civil order, but as instrumental measures designed to ensure victim participation and the ability of the Tribunal to function [emphasis in original].

The instructive aspect of Cockayne's distinction concerns the clear dichotomy he draws between domestic and international trials in terms of their function in the governance role of criminal justice. This centres on the notion that international trials have a particular sociological role in the construction of international civil order, while this role is less significant in domestic criminal justice systems. This book suggests otherwise in seeking to illustrate how the moral pluralism that characterises post-modern societies has forced domestic criminal justice systems to re-examine the parameters of 'rule-of-law' penal governance. This has occurred at the level of the legitimacy accorded to penal ideology and its relationship to the way trial outcomes are perceived by citizens. It has been suggested that the prevalence of retributive ideology and adversarial trial in both the international and domestic contexts has hindered the development of victims' participatory rights in sentencing.

However, such a conceptualisation is no longer a viable option for evaluating the role of victims in the governance function performed by criminal justice. Instead, it has been argued that a broader, more inclusive, reflection of moral interests should be represented at the pre-trial, trial and post-trial levels of the criminal process. These interests should equate with meaningful access and rights compatible with their fulfilment. Although constructing civil society remains the cornerstone of criminal justice governance in liberal democracies, it has been argued that the rule of law model needs to be relegitimised to reflect the plurality of moral interests that constitute 'civil' society.

---

60 See, for example, ICTY Press and Information Office (1996).

Having asserted the importance of rights and access in promoting a more constructive governance role for punishment, consistent and principled limits must be placed on identifying and enabling rights within such a revised framework, as Ashworth argues.[61] The scale of the task becomes apparent when one attempts to adumbrate likely relevant concerns, before deciding upon those which could feasibly receive some recognition through the tripartite divisions of the criminal process outlined above.

Those victims' concerns potentially relevant to promoting a more constructive form of governance rationale for the trial might include:

- how victims perceive the role of punishment and sentencing when thinking about the 'problem of crime';
- victims' attitudes and beliefs about different penal philosophies, and how this is related to their perception of sentencing;
- how victims conceive the relationship between sentencing and 'justice';
- factors influencing victims' perceptions about the moral value of punishment;
- whether victims think of punishment and sentencing as important in maintaining a sense of 'community' or shared moral values;
- whether sentencing should be morally pragmatic or aim to reflect a 'moral' view (and, if the latter, whose?);
- the 'appropriate' balance between individualised sentencing and consistency and proportionality;
- whether sentencing should reflect public opinion, and, if so, what form this might take;
- the extent to which punishment should be concerned to assert rights over responsibilities;
- the relevance of procedural justice to perceptions about the legitimacy of punishment;
- the appropriateness of guilt and individual criminal responsibility as foundations for sentencing;
- the appropriateness of merging criminal and civil responses to crime;
- the relative importance of individual and collective accountability in sentencing;
- the desirability of victim participation in sentencing;
- whether some form of community involvement in the sentencing process is desirable;
- whether systems of punishment should be designed and administered locally to reflect local crime and social conditions;
- the relationship between criminal justice and other elements of state governance, such as health, education, social welfare and the economy;
- whether multi-agency sentence decision-making is desirable;
- whether the judiciary are perceived as helping or hindering the 'war on crime';

---

61 Ashworth (1994).

- the relationship between the executive and the judiciary, and the role of politics in sentencing.

Clearly, the emphasis accorded to each of these factors will depend on the particular social contingencies of each context, whether local or global. Given the large number of potentially relevant variables, the clarity and utility of the analysis is likely to be enhanced by focusing on a particular theme and evaluating the extent to which it affords access and rights protection. For example, if a specific aspect of trial justice, such as plea bargaining, is examined, the following weaknesses might be identified:

- the relative weakness of the accused's negotiating position;
- the relative absence of clear guidelines;
- the appropriateness of plea negotiations in relation to the crimes in question;
- cultural misunderstandings regarding the negotiating procedure and its effects;
- denial to victims and communities of rights to access and participation in negotiations;
- the fact that the procedure is constrained by retributive ideology;
- whether procedures based on expediency can engage with issues of social justice;
- lack of transparency about the process and its impact on the sentence.

The next stage might be to consider how the weaknesses that have been identified might be rectified through greater participatory rights for victims and communities with a 'legitimate' interest in the process.

Human rights and sentencing

Sentencing appears powerless to counter the social injustices of hegemony; it simply reflects the moral boundaries of the social context that informs the ideology, structure and operation of the criminal process. The future legitimacy of governance structures including criminal justice will depend on developing ties of horizontal and vertical trust among citizens. Many commentators[62] believe that the emergence of such shared moral networks will be enhanced through strengthening the framework for achieving fundamental human rights. Building relationships of trust with excluded and alienated social groups is a necessary precursor to restoring legitimacy to criminal justice.

Nevertheless, as Engstrom admits,[63] the conditions for achieving greater internationalisation of human rights norms within domestic practices ultimately depend upon political will. Therefore, despite the fact that, for example, Article 14 of the ECHR sets forth the principle that the rights and freedoms

---

62 See, for example, Donnelly (2003).
63 Engstrom (2010).

in the Convention shall be secured without discrimination on any ground (such as sex, race, colour, language, religion, political or other opinion, national or social origin, association with a national minority, property, birth or other status), fundamental human rights norms are meaningless unless they can be secured through the political process. This may, of course, result from international pressure on state hegemony, but the successful practical implementation of human rights norms must ultimately depend on the necessary degree of legitimacy being accorded to the rule of law. Risse *et al.*,[64] for example, have suggested that state pressure from transnational and domestic 'civil' society is the key to achieving the reality of fundamental human rights norms, but it is difficult to see how such forces can be mobilised without the appropriate political transformation.

In addition, there is an absence of any meta-principle to guide rational choice and so provide for the principled development of human rights norms.[65] Nevertheless, as I have argued:[66]

> It is not sufficient to suggest that any attempt to reconcile the notion of the universality of human rights with the relative reality of rights recognition and practice is futile; whilst rights law and the ideology of rights are regulatory principles for human behaviour, their theorisation as a phenomenon which has social meaning – the linkage between values, norms and action – is driven by the need to understand the relationship between ideology and legitimacy ... Developing concepts of participation and integration reaching beyond symbolism in international sentencing ultimately depends on how the dynamics of ideology and power are played out through process as relative realities for victims and victim communities. Principal institutional features of this process dynamic include the domination of victims

That said, there is still a strong case to be made for strengthening the procedural framework for sentencing from a human rights perspective.[67] There is an increasing need for this in the light of the relentless pressure for economic stringency and the diminishing terrain of state accountability for crime and its consequences. By way of example, a vitally important legal issue is whether breaches of human rights norms associated with the operation of the guilty plea and plea agreements in international sentencing might provide grounds for appeal or review. The position is not encouraging. Although appeals relating to the operation of guilty pleas have been considered by the ICTR

---

64 Risse-Kappen, Ropp and Sikkink (1999).
65 Douzinas (1996) 128.
66 Henham (2005b) ch. 6.
67 For the development of such arguments in the context of England and Wales, see Van Zyl Smit and Ashworth (2004).

and ICTY,[68] there are no specific provisions contained in the foundation instruments of any international criminal trial institution which deal with the possibility of what is to happen when the sentence it imposes infringes human rights norms which fall outside the ambit of its rules as presently interpreted. As Zappala points out,[69] some protection is provided under Article 14, paragraph 5 of the ICCPR, which provides that everyone convicted of a crime shall have the right of review of his or her conviction and sentence by a higher tribunal.[70] However, disagreement persists over narrow doctrinal issues, such as whether the right to appeal is limited to matters of law or mixed law and fact.

Although Zappala concludes[71] that the ICC provisions dealing with rights of appeal and revision are 'far more balanced and in conformity with human rights standards than the provisions governing these proceedings before ad hoc tribunals', there seems to be no alternative avenue available where the operation of an institution's procedural norms breaches the human rights of the defendant.[72] One possibility, suggested by Cockayne,[73] might be for recourse to the UN Human Rights Committee. Under Article 2 of the ICCPR, an individual could (in theory at least) bring a claim against all those State Parties to the ICC Statute who are also Party to the ICCPR and its First Additional Protocol on the basis that the following provisions of Article 14(1) of the ICCPR are relevant to the operation of plea agreements and sentence discounts in international sentencing:[74]

> All persons shall be equal before the courts and tribunals. In the deter-
> mination of any criminal charge against him ... everyone shall be entitled

---

68 Henham and Drumbl (2005).
69 Zappala (2003) 171.
70 A similar right is provided in regional instruments such as the ECHR by Article 2, Optional Protocol 7.
71 Zappala (2003) 193.
72 *Ibid.* 194, suggests an important interpretative role for ICC provisions where *ad hoc* Tribunal provisions are silent or ambiguous on certain issues, including the interpretation of provisions against international human rights law standards.
73 Cockayne (2001) 20.
74 Ashworth and Redmayne identify the right to a 'fair and public' hearing (Article 6(1)) and the right to be treated fairly and without discrimination (Article 14, ECHR) as particularly relevant to the operation of the guilty plea discount in England and Wales; Ashworth and Redmayne (2005) 290. Note, however, that the procedure whereby an individual may plead guilty without trial or examination of the evidence has been held not to be in breach of Article 6 by the Commission, irrespective of the availability of the procedure under national jurisdictions; *X v United Kingdom* (1972) 40 CD 64, 67. In *Deweer v Belgium* (1979–80) 2 EHRR 439, the Court even went so far as to hold that the payment of a penalty in exchange for the right to a hearing is not necessarily inconsistent with Article 6, provided there was no duress. The extent to which the willingness of the prosecution to accept a plea of guilty to a significantly less serious charge exerts undue pressure on the accused remains a moot point. See, further, Emmerson and Ashworth (2001) 506.

to a fair and public hearing by a competent, independent and impartial tribunal established by law.

Although the Human Rights Committee might issue a non-binding recommendation should a claim prove successful, it is unclear what its effect might be, since the State Parties to the ICCPR do not, except through the Assembly of State Parties, have the capacity to revise sentences, and the ICC, although having international legal personality is not a party to the ICCPR. Alternatively, an appeal may be possible on the basis that a sentence was in violation of Article 21(3) of the ICC Statute:

> The application and interpretation of law pursuant to [Article 21 Applicable law] must be consistent with internationally recognised human rights, and be without any adverse distinction founded on grounds such as gender ... age, race, colour, language, religion or belief, political or other opinion, national, ethnic or social origin, wealth, birth or other status.[75]

Notwithstanding, the dangers posed to human rights (particularly defendant's rights) by supranational organisations such as the ICC are considerable, driven as they are by a punitive dynamic and developing outside any institutionalised mechanisms of accountability. Further, if human rights norms at the state level are more likely to reflect their development at the international level as the internationalisation of trial process increases, questions of governance and accountability become more acute – for example, the nature of the relationship between international mechanisms acting as the authoritative source of these norms (such as the ICC), and the extent of control which State and non-State Parties will have over the development of procedural norms in the ICC.[76]

Two case studies

As the examples discussed below illustrate, whilst increasing procedural justice through rights may appear to fulfil demands for equality of access to sentencing, the ideal of justice is unlikely to be achieved unless such rights are *socially responsive* and reflect the needs and interests of offenders, victims and

---

75 Regarding the principle of equal treatment generally, see Article 26, ICCPR. As Emmerson and Ashworth (2001) 110 point out, the anti-discrimination provision in Article 14, ECHR may only be invoked in conjunction with a substantial convention right.

76 An important distinction between the ICC and the *ad hoc* tribunals in this context is the fact that the ICC operates within a framework of complementarity rather than jurisdictional primacy. Thus, an ICC process which allowed local procedural norms to be factored into international trials might not only have increased chances of legitimacy in the affected communities, but could also play a highly significant role in developing comparative criminal procedural jurisprudence; Cockayne (2001) 27.

the wider community. To achieve such accountability requires recognition that 'justice' is not simply about the specific accountability of individuals or conformity of procedural norms to particular systems or paradigms of rights protection.

Race and sentencing

An example of the difficulties of redressing apparent 'injustice' in this area and of re-establishing a more egalitarian foundation for rights is Roger Hood's 1992 study of race and sentencing in England and Wales.[77] In 1992 Hood published the results of a systematic study of the relationship between race and sentencing decisions in the Crown Courts within the West Midlands area (Birmingham, Coventry, Warwick, Stafford and Dudley). These areas were served by a single police force and had a relatively high population of minority ethnic origin. Hood's objective was to determine how far and in what ways the factor of a defendant's racial or ethnic group influenced the sentencing patterns of the courts.

Hood's main findings were as follows:

- The research confirmed that 'to a very substantial degree, the over-representation of Afro-Caribbean males and females in the prison system is a result of their over-representation among those convicted of crime and sentenced in the Crown Courts'. Hood estimated that 80 per cent of black male over-representation arose from conviction rates and the characteristics of the offences involved. However, the remaining 20 per cent of the over-representation of black males 'appeared to be due to differential treatment and other factors which influence the nature and length of the sentences imposed'. Two-thirds of this 20 percent could be explained by the fact that more black than white defendants pleaded not guilty, and (due particularly to the practice of 'discounting' sentences for guilty pleas) the *consequent* greater length of custodial sentencing imposed. However, the other one-third (or 7 per cent) of the residue remained 'unexplained' by such procedural outcomes, and could only be accounted for by a higher proportion of black defendants being sentenced to custody than would have been expected once all the characteristics of the cases had been taken into account.
- Once all other factors had been taken into account, black male defendants in the West Midlands Courts had a 5 to 8 per cent greater probability of receiving a custodial sentence than their white male counterparts. The research also found significant variation between the court centres and between individual judges, so that in some contexts the probability of differential treatment was substantially higher. Female black defendants, on the other hand, did not appear, once other factors had been taken

77 Hood (1992).

into account, to have a greater probability of receiving a custodial sentence than female white defendants. Nor on the whole did Asian defendants, whose overall probability of being sentenced to custody tended to be lower once other factors had been eliminated.

Hood's general conclusion was that, while 'there was no evidence of a 'blanket' race or colour discrimination against all ethnic minority defendants', there was nonetheless a differential in the pattern of sentencing of black males in the Crown Courts that remained after all the characteristics of the case had been taken into account. In part, the differential could be explained as a consequence of the higher proportion of not-guilty pleas among black male defendants, and was not a product of discretionary sentencing decisions of individual judges. The other aspect of the differential, however, appeared to result directly from black defendants as a whole being treated less favourably in the aggregate decision-making practices of judges themselves.

Von Hirsch and Roberts[78] subsequently analyzed the results of Hood's study and made a number of suggestions, short of alleviating discrimination, for reducing the racial imbalance in prisons. However, they also argued that there was little advantage in seeking to introduce the concept of 'social adversity'[79] as a form of mitigation in sentencing, and that more advantage was to be gained by changing penal policies before the trial stage itself.

Not only does Hood's study illustrate the importance of social context in providing the opportunity for access to the trial, it also confirms that rights protection (even full participation) is of little value unless there is something of value requiring protection in the first place. In other words, the study shows the importance of social context in fixing the moral boundaries for the operation of penal norms; in this case, the causes of the differential in custody rates resulting from black male defendants plea decisions. Again, this is a function of ideology, and therefore of the political hegemony that determines state criminal justice.

Gender and sentencing

It is axiomatic that any discussion of sentencing that is detached from the social context in which it takes place can only provide a partial understanding of its social significance. This is particularly true when it comes to understanding the sentencing of particular groups or types of offender and the reasons for, and purposes of, sentencing them.[80] The relative influences

---

78 Von Hirsch and Roberts (2002).
79 See Hudson (1998) 221, 241.
80 The need to focus on the social construction of sentencing is evidenced by research on the differential sentencing practices applied to indigenous and non-indigenous women in Western Australia; see Bond and Jeffries (2010).

of social and biological factors in the social construction of race and gender stereotypes are clearly a case in point. For this reason, understanding the sentencing of women is socially and culturally contingent, as are the choices of theoretical framework to underpin any such inquiry.

As Ashworth points out,[81] in the wake of numerous reports, the Sentencing Advisory Panel for England and Wales in its final report on the Overarching Principles of Sentencing to the Sentencing Guidelines Council made some recommendations for courts to take more account of gendered characteristics in sentencing.[82] This, in itself, might be regarded as a controversial move by those who take the view that gender-specific policies are inappropriate as discriminatory.[83] It raises an interesting question, posed by the Home Office report in 1997;[84] what exactly does the concept of fairness mean in this context?[85] The answer given in that report was that 'fairness' should mean consistency of approach, rather than uniformity of outcome:

> In other words, it involves asking the same questions about factors such as employment status, family responsibilities and financial circumstances regardless of the offender's sex, rather than presuming that certain questions apply to males and females.

Not surprisingly, the report concluded that the sentencing of women was the outcome of the interactive effect of a number of factors.[86] The difficulty was seen as:

> Finding ways to challenge stereotypical pictures of men and women, without ignoring the fact that they often (but not always) do have different needs and responsibilities (and these are often precisely the needs and responsibilities which fuel the stereotypes).

---

81 Ashworth (2010) 248.
82 Sentencing Advisory Panel (2010).
83 See Piper and Easton (2005) 326.
84 Hedderman and Gelsthorpe (1997).
85 'Fairness' in terms of 'equality' tends to signify differential treatment in the sentencing of women. For example, the Gender Equality Act (2006) imposed a duty on public authorities to develop policies and services that take potentially different gender needs into account. However, there is little research evidence regarding public opinion and the sentencing of women and no clear understanding of the relationship between the underlying rationales of penal policy and their impact on the sentencing of women by the courts. This may well have contributed to the penal welfare complex persisting in the sentencing of women offenders; see Gelsthorpe (2005).
86 The most important was the nature of the offence, but the way the offence and offender were portrayed by other participants; appearance and behaviour in court, and interaction with magistrates were also important. These factors collectively shaped the court's perception of the offender and the nature of its response.

The argument for achieving 'fairness' through improving consistency and uniformity of approach is certainly important but, beyond this, the idea of extending rights and improving procedural justice fails to deal with the fundamental question of the 'legitimacy' of the reforms that are proposed.[87] The reason for this, as has been argued, is the strong attachment of 'legitimacy' to 'justice' in the sentencing context, suggesting that individuals and communities should empathise in a moral sense with the *actual* decisions taken by the courts, rather than simply matters of procedural justice. I have argued the need for penal ideology to reflect these different moral constituencies through the practice of sentencing and suggested that we can only really begin to understand the social significance of sentencing if we can explain this relationship more effectively.

Barbara Hudson[88] considers debates about the influence of liberal forms of justice and their relationship to penal justifications in the context of feminist writing. Although beyond this book's remit, these arguments raise some fundamental points regarding the legitimacy of the sentencing context for women. The most important of these is recognition by some feminist writers that the rights discourse for women is exhausted, and that philosophies of morality and justice are themselves gendered in favour of men. In addition, Hudson points out that Enlightenment values and principles adopt universalised value-neutral notions of the individual and responsibility, whereas the social reality of everyday life is built upon male values and constructs; which are the constructs of power and domination.[89] These observations suggest the need for a re-conceptualisation of such ideals and values.

Such debates inevitably feed into feminist discourse about punishment, particularly about whether universal guarantees of equality are possible within the existing penal frameworks of western liberal societies. In drawing attention to Pat Carlen's two basic requirements for female penality,[90] Hudson suggests that such objectives can only be achieved through the parsimonious use of punishment, and its justification and application in particular cases needs to be more convincingly argued when sentencing female offenders. For women, this implies a move away from the hegemony of male penal norms and recognition of the specific social contexts of female harm.[91] Recent initiatives[92] signal a move in this direction. The SAP advice to the SGC issued on the 11th March 2010 included recommendations about the sentencing of women, including the need to take the psychological impact of custodial

---

87 Such issues were beyond the remit of the 1997 Home Office report.
88 Hudson (2003a) 111.
89 *Ibid.* 121.
90 1. That the penal regulation of female law-breakers does not increase their oppression as women still further;
    2. That the penal regulation of law-breaking men does not brutalise them and make them even more violently or ideologically oppressive towards women in the future.
91 Hudson (2003a) 142.
92 See Ashworth (2010) 248.

sentences on women into account, as well as recommendations about the use of custody and community sentences.[93]

What they do not do, however, is to consider the possible reconceptualisation of penal ideology to better reflect the aspirations and needs of women. As has been argued[94] in the international context, reconceptualisation is necessary in order to provide the moral foundations for sentencing outcomes that resonate more with the 'relevant audience's' sense of 'justice', rather than striving to achieve 'fairness' under existing forms of liberal penal regime. Notwithstanding the *status quo* of retributive and deterrent justice, there are significant practical reforms that might be considered in order to better integrate restorative initiatives for offenders before, during and after the sentencing phase.[95] These do not depend upon the rationale of retributivism to establish credentials of fairness or consistency, but follow the rationale of producing 'truth' to satisfy identifiable demands for justice. Therefore, in the case of international trials, the retributive focus on individual responsibility becomes dissolved into a collective search for justice, so that the process is more open to evaluating the meaning and significance of collective forms of behaviour and its contribution to whatever atrocity took place.

Seen in this light, structures for conflict resolution are concerned with restoring the relationships of community essential for human life, or, at the very least, enabling that potential in humanity to be realised. As I have argued, despite obvious differences in jurisdiction, criminality and purposes for trial and sentence, the experience and subsequent analysis of international sentencing practice does have important implications for domestic systems of criminal justice, and the sentencing of offenders. For example, in the sentencing of female offenders, I would argue that a focus away from individual responsibility towards a more relational form of justice that addresses the social identity, interests and relationships of women more directly is feasible and a necessary part of constructing relationships of community, but it requires a concerted campaign to reposition penal ideology towards more restorative objectives.[96] Retaining the present unsatisfactory balance between the ideal of justice and the ethics of care[97] within the current penal framework is not acceptable, because greater controls over the individualised use of judicial discretion in sentencing and increased judicial accountability continue to

---

93 Sentencing Advisory Panel (2010).
94 Findlay and Henham (2010).
95 *Ibid.* ch. 2.
96 It may be argued that nothing in the recent SAP advice to the SGC fundamentally changes the rationale and policy for the sentencing of women. This is reflected in the continuing disproportionate focus on the use of custody for women and the corresponding neglect of other areas of women's condition, such as the impact of conditional cautions, and the funding of community programmes for women; see Gelsthorpe (2010).
97 See Gregory (2010).

drive the agenda towards procedural justice goals, rather than achieving substantive justice for women.

Developing the framework

Increasing victims' rights in sentencing within existing trial frameworks is likely to involve the examination of three key areas:

1. the degree of victim integration in sentence decision-making;
2. the extent to which procedural norms providing for victim participation in sentencing are supported by enforceable rights for victims;
3. the degree to which sentencing outcomes engage with victims and communities.

The purpose of this approach is to assess the extent to which access to justice for victims in sentencing is *actually* achieved by advocating contextual analysis of those discretionary decisions that impact on sentencing processes and outcomes, and the nature and operation of norms purporting to protect victims' rights. By approaching the issue on this basis it is possible to assess the relationship between the degree of normative support for victim participation and the rights protection available to victims in criminal trials in so far as it concerns sentencing.

The analysis of victims' rights and their evaluation against normative frameworks in a comparative context is far more complex than a simple juxtaposition against these themes. A number of stages are advocated:

- Any analysis must begin by addressing the problems of conceptualising rights law in theory and practice from a comparative perspective.[98] In particular, the values attaching to rights and their equivalent (ethical) principles as represented in legal and policy instruments should be examined.
- The next stage should examine the reality of rights in *practice* and the extent to which this really gives effect to those values which originally inspired the principles embodied in rights law.
- The final stage should be to consider the values and ethical practice of rights from a comparative perspective.

The most important consideration from a comparative perspective is the moral and ethical parameters within which rights norms operate. This is necessary within each social context in order to understand how ideology and power impact on the conceptualisation and operation of rights. Consequently, a reasoned assessment can be made of how the symbolism of rights (as values) contrasts with their relative reality (as norms and outcomes). In this

---

98 Henham (2004a).

sense, it is possible to describe how relationships between values, norms and facts are constructed as functionally distinct aspects of contextualised experience. Thus, the connections between the ideology and legitimacy attaching to rights can be described and evaluated at the abstract and concrete levels.

This resonates with the relational approach to rights taken in this book. Instead of partisan penal ideology delineating access and rights, they are conceived as grounded in context, so that the moral values attaching to them are mirrored in state and international structures for justice delivery. In this way, contextualised understandings of the relationship between participation and rights inform the capacity of sentencing to reconcile competing moral claims for justice.[99]

---

99 An illustration of the difficulties in reconciling differing contextual interpretations of rights at the regional and national level is provided by the ECHR. Whilst the ECHR is not morally relative, in the sense that the moral principles it espouses have universal moral validity, it is normatively relative in its effects, since relations between citizen and state are a function of jurisdictional context; see Henham (2010b).

8 Sentencing and Legitimacy in France and Italy

Introduction

The purpose of this chapter is to give the reader an overview of the socio-political and historical influences that have shaped the sentencing systems of France and Italy and to draw comparisons where appropriate regarding the impact of adversarial, inquisitorial and hybridised forms of trial justice on sentencing practice and its public perception. Consistent with the theme of the book, the analytical approach taken is to consider the relationship between social factors and the normative framework that underpins sentencing. Although one objective is to evaluate the extent to which existing theories and concepts in criminal justice theory can assist in exploring issues of legitimacy, the primary purpose of the analysis is to consider expert commentary and empirical evidence concerning the relationship between moral and social factors and how this influences the theory and practice of sentencing and, ultimately, its impact on the governance role of punishment and sentencing in criminal justice. Of particular significance is the extent to which perceptions about the role of victims have influenced the way in which they are treated for the purpose of sentencing and the impact of any structural reforms designed to increase victim participation in the sentencing process.

Sentencing and legitimacy in France

General overview

According to Pradel,[1] the French sentencing system is informed by a predominantly retributive and deterrent framework. Notwithstanding, Article 132–24, para. 2 of the 1994 French Criminal Code provides that, depending on the circumstances of the offence and the offender's personality, the nature, amount and type of the penalty should be determined by reconciling the objectives of public protection, the punishment of the perpetrator and the

---

1 Pradel (2001) 492.

interests of the victim with the need to facilitate the resocialisation of the offender and the prevention of future offences.

The maximum sentence available depends on whether the offences are classified as *crimes* (serious); *délits* (major); or *contraventions* (minor).[2] Penalties for crimes classified as *peines criminelles*[3] include life imprisonment[4] and there are four other maximum levels of imprisonment fixed at 30, 20 and 15 years, respectively. A minimum sentence of 10 years applies to *crimes* sentenced as *peines criminelles*, but there is judicial discretion to go below this where a *peine correctionnelle* is chosen.[5] A wide range of penalties is available in the case of *délits* including imprisonment for a maximum of 10 years, ordinary and day fines, community work, certain restrictions on liberty and other rights, as well as so-called complimentary punishments (*peines complémentaires*), depending on the level of seriousness.[6]

Sentencing decisions in the *cours d'assises* are pronounced immediately after conviction and are reached by a simple majority following a secret ballot. However, for the maximum penalty to apply there must be a majority of at least eight to four in favour. If this is not achieved, then the same process is repeated with respect to the next most severe penalty until one of these is accepted by simple majority.[7]

It is important to note that under the rule of non-cumulative punishments consecutive sentences are very rarely allowed, nor may charges be structured so as to evade this rule. Consequently, only one sentence for the most serious current offence may be pronounced, and this may not be enhanced on the basis of another current charge, except where the second offence is committed

---

2 See Articles 131–1 to 131–18 of the French Criminal Code. *Crimes* are tried in the *cour d'assises* and are punishable with imprisonment of five years or more; *délits* which carry prison sentences of between two and five years are normally tried in the *tribunal correctionel*; and *contraventions* which may attract prison sentences of up to two months are normally dealt with by a single judge sitting in the *tribunal de police*. Cases in the *cour d'assises* are tried by three professional judges (one president and two assessors), who constitute the court, and a jury consisting of nine members of the public. Cases in the *tribunal correctionel* are heard by a panel of three judges without a jury. Both judges and jurors deliberate together as to matters of guilt and sentence. A right of appeal on the merits to a *cour d'assises* in a different area was created in 2000 by a change in the law, with appeals on points of law remaining, as before to, the *Cour de cassation* (*Chambre criminelle*). See, further, Dervieux (2002) ch. 4.
  For an overview, see Elliot (2001).
3 Articles 131–1 to 131–34 of the French Criminal Code distinguish between *peines criminelles* and *peines correctionnelles* and imprisonment for *crimes* as *réclusion criminelle* as opposed to *emprisonnment* for *délits*.
4 The death penalty in France was abolished by Law n 81–908 of 9 October 1981.
5 Article 132–18 of the French Penal Code.
6 Additional penalties are available for serious crimes under Article 221–22 of the French Criminal Code, for example in the case of homicide, depending on whether there is a finding of voluntary or involuntary homicide, violence causing mutilation or permanent infirmity, torture and inhumane acts, as well as various categories of aggravated rape.
7 Dervieux (2002) 288.

after the offender has been convicted of the first offence. The rationale for this approach is based on the view that consecutive sentencing may exaggerate the offender's culpability and the feeling that the first conviction might serve as a preventative warning of a recidivist premium to follow any subsequent offending behaviour. Similarly, multiple-charge convictions have a limited impact on sentence severity, since the recidivist premium is based on the seriousness not the frequency of prior convictions.[8]

Challenges to existing paradigms

Foundations in The Enlightenment

Following the traumatic events of the French Revolution of 1789, the Code Pénal of 1791 introduced a rigid system of fixed penalties which were predetermined both as to type and degree for each category of crime.[9] As is well-documented,[10] Beccaria's influence in shaping French penal law and other European systems of criminal justice was profound, and it was he who gave concrete expression to the ideas of Montesquieu and Voltaire in detailing the principles of what became known as the liberal theory of criminal law.

One of the most enduring aspects of this philosophy was to assert that law's function is to serve the needs of society, rather than to enforce a particular set of moral values, religious or otherwise. Consequently, in developing principles for the justification and severity of punishment, Beccaria's approach was retributive, in advocating the use of punishment to re-assert rights infringed by crime, and utilitarian in accepting the need to limit retributive penalties to the extent necessary to protect society from future crimes being committed by the offender and to deter others.

As Radzinowicz points out,[11] the ideals of the liberal Enlightenment found their fullest expression in the French classical code of 1791– notably in its strong reaction against the use of judicial discretionary power to inflict arbitrary punishment on citizens. Yet the 1810 Code of Napoleon signalled a move away from undiluted liberalism by permitting the use of judicial discretion to allow sentencers to choose between fixed maximum and minimum penalties, and restored the prerogative of mercy. This move was both highly political and symbolic in re-asserting the constitutional authority of the Head of State. It also heralded a general increase in the severity of punishment and the increasing use of criminal justice as a means of social control and repression.[12]

---

8 For a detailed analysis of the issues, see Roberts (2008b).
9 For an overview of the historical foundations of French criminal justice, see Vogler (2005) 45–57. For a detailed account of the French system of criminal procedure, see Dervieux (2002).
10 See Radzinowicz (1966) ch. 1.
11 *Ibid.* 23.
12 This was also reflected in the new criminal procedure code of 1808 (the Code d'Instruction Criminelle); see Vogler (2005) 55.

It is important not to underestimate the impact of the neo-classical school of criminology on the use of judicial discretionary power during this period.[13] Stressing the moral responsibility of the individual signified an accommodation between the gravity of the crime and the culpability of the offender which was reflected in the increased individualisation of sentences. Paradoxically, as reflected in the more recent history of the relationship between penal policy and practice, it provided a context ripe for political exploitation, since the parameters (both moral and legal) within which the judiciary was asked to operate were increasingly characterised by a hegemonic and punitive ethic.

Additionally, in common with other European penal systems, the advent of more reliable criminal statistics in the mid-nineteenth century[14] and their use in penal policy-making, as well as the pervasive influence of positivist theories, such as those of Lombroso, Ferri and Garofalo in criminology, helped to pave the way for more discriminatory and socially divisive forms of penality which were variously justified in terms of their reductive[15] potential.

However, as Renout suggests,[16] the end of the Second World War saw the ascendancy of rehabilitative ideals such as re-education and resocialisation in the name of social defence and the development of alternatives to imprisonment.[17] Therefore, as in many other countries[18] the prevailing penal ideology until the 1970s was, according to Faugeron, a combination of 'rehabilitation, individualisation of the penalty and the dual approach of probation and imprisonment to avoid sending petty offenders and first offenders to prison'.[19]

Development in the post-modern era

Although a preventative rather than retributive emphasis continued to prevail into the 1980s, as in other countries, France's penal policy became increasingly bifurcated, with generally longer sentences being given for more serious forms of crime.[20] Moreover, as Cavadino and Dignan point out,[21] the strategy of encouraging the judiciary to use alternatives to custody has been unsuccessful, as in England and Wales. In common with other western justice systems, France gradually succumbed to the penality of 'law and order' during the

---

13 Especially scholars such as Guizot, Jouffroy, Rossi and Ortolan.
14 As a result of the pioneering work of Quetelet and Guerry.
15 See Walker (1972).
16 Renout (2009) 12.
17 See Ancel (1954).
18 This was certainly the case in England and Wales; see Thomas (1979) ch. 1. for a description of the difference between so-called 'tariff' sentencing and the individualised approach.
19 Faugeron (1991) 249.
20 See Galo (1995).
21 Cavadino and Dignan (2006) 134.

1990s, and this, through its accompanying rhetoric,[22] has been reflected in an exponential increase in sentencing severity.[23]

In terms of the perceived legitimacy of sentences, Cavadino and Dignan[24] raise the interesting issue of the apparent disconnect between public attitudes to punishment, as measured by opinion surveys, and the increasingly punitive stance on law and order taken by the political class. However, as Cavadino and Dignan caution:

> One cogent factor may well be the variable interrelationships that exist in different kinds of countries between ideological factors and attitudes on the one hand, and the institutional contexts within which these attitudes may be shaped, influenced and expressed on the other. Changes in punishment levels — or indeed lack of change – may again be largely explicable in terms of the interplay between rival sets of influences.[25]

The kinds of influences mentioned by Cavadino and Dignan include such things as the media, the degree of political populism regarding law and order issues, the opinions and values of the 'penal elite', as well as institutional differences which may affect leniency or stability within the system. However, the interrelationship between these sets of influences is by no means clear in the sentencing context, particularly in terms of the way in which the preferences expressed by the public are related to the sentencing practices of the courts.[26] Roberts and Hough's conclusions on this bear particular reflection in the case of France – so that further information would be required, for example, about the extent to which differences between public and court sentences varied according to offence seriousness and also regarding the amount of information available to the public about the sentencing options which may be imposed, and the background characteristics of offenders. Public support for community penalties not only tends to vary according to perceived offence seriousness, but also according to the extent to which they may include reparative and compensatory elements.

---

22 As elsewhere, it provides a convenient platform for extremism: in France, for example, the anti-immigration policies of nationalist politicians such as Jean-Marie Le Pen. In addition to a high number of remand prisoners, France's prison population is already characterised by a disproportionately large number of foreign nationals; Cavadino and Dignan (2006) 136.
23 See, generally, the discussion in Cavadino and Dignan (2006) 134–38.
24 *Ibid.* 139. The conclusion is based on a comparison between public attitudes favouring imprisonment and the actual imprisonment rate. For further discussion of the difficulties involved in drawing cross-national comparisons of such data, see Mayhew and van Kesteren (2002).
25 Cavadino and Dignan (2006) 38.
26 See Roberts and Hough (2005) 79.

The accountability of the judiciary in matters of punishment and sentencing

The influence of the prosecution

The French public prosecution service, or *ministère public* is a constitutionally independent authority founded in 1808.[27] This reflects the importance attached to a fundamental tenet of the social contract; that the administration of justice exists to uphold the rights and freedoms of citizens. However, there is an apparent paradox in that, although the Minister of Justice is responsible for formulating criminal policy, he may also issue general and specific instructions to the *ministère public* regarding its implementation. Whilst citizens entrust the state to prosecute cases on behalf of citizens in a fair and impartial[28] manner, victims retain important prosecutorial rights. However, the *ministère public* has primary responsibility for the execution of sentences.[29]

As far as sentencing proper is concerned, as Verrest points out,[30] the offender may not be punished without the intervention of a judge; an important constitutional protection against the possibility of punitive penal policies being forced by a repressive political state. Nevertheless, the principle of expediency, *opportunité des poursuites*, has assumed increasing significance since the 1990s as pressure grows for the more efficient disposal of cases. Therefore, prosecutorial decisions regarding alternative procedures such as mediation and the *composition pénale* have come under greater scrutiny.[31]

Although the French system of justice allows considerable involvement in the criminal process by the victim, the potential exists for the inherent flexibility of the expediency principle to be exploited by the Ministry of Justice if, for example, the legislature were to come under increasing political pressure to respond more effectively to public demands for dealing with offending behaviour. As Verrest puts it:

> ... legislators appear to be ignoring the real challenges the *ministère public* is confronted with: having to deal with the influx of criminal offences, the development of local security policies and internationalisation of justice.[32]

The reason for this is that, despite the legality of the expediency principle, its public acceptance as morally correct, especially in decisions not to proceed to trial, depend upon its capacity to strike the appropriate balance between facilitating the smooth functioning of the criminal process and

---

27 For a detailed description of the origins and functions of this office, see Verrest (2000).
28 See Art. 66 of the French Constitution.
29 Art. 707, CPP.
30 Verrest (2000) 245.
31 See, for example, Leblois-Happe (2000).
32 Verrest (2000) 245.

254 *Sentencing and legitimacy in France and Italy*

satisfying the expectations for 'justice' of the 'community' in a situation of value-pluralism.

Despite the clear differences in penal history and culture, the broader implications of Rogers's[33] suggestions (discussed in chapter 1) are significant when comparing the French and English context, particularly the point that distinguishing between the harms of punishment and prosecution can help delineate prosecutorial responsibility. A crucial issue in determining the nature of this relationship is the status of the victim *qua* citizen, especially the fact that the role of the victim in the French criminal process is not only more clearly defined, but also potentially interventionist. This reflects the contingent nature of the state in the administration of justice and provides a constant reminder of the fragility of the state's mandate to prosecute crimes.[34]

This systemic tension differs from that which pervades the English penal context, which has developed more organically over many centuries. However, this very flexibility belies where penal responsibility actually does lie, and the constant blurring of penal accountability is reflected in how trial participants have perceived their roles. The contested territory of judicial discretionary power (discussed in chapter 4) provides a clear example, whilst the acceptable parameters of prosecutorial responsibility represent another. One aspect of the latter is a failure to consider the relationship between pre-trial disposals and trial outcomes in terms of the overall purposes set for the criminal process. This obfuscation is exacerbated where penal accountability is not tied to a clear vision of where the state stands if it fails to satisfy the legitimate demands for justice of its citizens.

The rationale and framework for sentencing

The individualisation of penalties is of central importance to sentencing in France,[35] and it has considerable effect in broadening the range of sentences where judicial discretion can be exercised. Article 132–34, para. 1 states that the principle of individualisation depends on the circumstances of the offence and the personality of the accused. However, the judicial individualisation of sentences is constrained by the principle of legality, so that judges cannot impose penalties which exceed the maximum established by law. Respect for the principle of proportionality also ensures that the penalty is related to the seriousness of the offence and the offender's personality.[36] In addition, because there is no longer a minimum penalty applicable for each offence,

---

33 Rogers (2006) 778.
34 As evidenced by the ongoing debate about how best to deal with those who collaborated with the Vichy Regime. See, for example,Wexler (1995), Fournet (2007) ch. 17.
35 See the French Criminal Code of 1994, Chapter II, Section II, Title III.
36 Although not directly mentioned in the French Constitution, the principle of individualisation of the penalty has been recognised as having some sort of constitutional validity by the *Conseil Constitutionnel*; CC 13 août 1993, DC n 93–325, 11725.

judges are now able to exercise their discretion in choosing the sentence which they regard as just and appropriate according to the circumstances of the case. Following on from the determination of responsibility, it is the judge's duty to consider the specific circumstances of each case and those of the offender and to ensure that the chosen penalty is that which is most suitable within the limits imposed by law; *individualisation ou personnalisation judiciaire de la peine.*

Nevertheless, as Lelieur-Fischer points out,[37] since there is no obligation on French courts to provide reasons for their decisions regarding the determination of sentencing, there is no effective regulation of the correctness of such decisions by the *Cour de Cassation.*[38] Leblois-Happe describes the application of the wide measure of discretion available to the French judge when sentencing as something akin to the notion of 'sentencing as an art'; an epithet which was applied extensively to English sentencing during the 1970s and 80s when individualised sentencing was at its height:

> la détermination de la peine par le juge relève de l'exercice d'une *'faculté'* que lui octroie la loi.

She also draws attention to the enormous range of sentencing decisions over which the discretionary power of the judge may be exercised:

> … entre les peines principales prévues par le texte d'incrimination, les peines qui sont susceptibles d'y être substituées, et les peines complémentaires que le juge peut, à son gré, prononcer en plus ou à la place de la sanction principale.

However, she also argues that over the last ten years or so sentencing has become much more complex with, for example, some thirty possible combinations available for the punishment of theft, including imprisonment, fines, day fines, community work and other general deprivations or restriction of rights. To this may now be added citizenship requirements (Article 311–14–6 CP) and the relatively new sanction of reparation (Article 131–8–1 CP).

Yet the incursion of such legislative complexity into sentencing has not been without its drawbacks. As Leblois-Happe notes, the discretionary power afforded to judges has given rise to large disparities in the distribution of sanctions. For example, a study conducted by the Ministry of Justice in 1998 showed that driving while under the influence of alcohol was punishable by imprisonment in more than 80 per cent of cases in Finistère, as against only

---

37 Lelieur-Fischer (2004).

38 See, further, Leblois-Happe (2003). Leblois-Happe argues that French judges are effectively free to impose whatever sentence they feel appropriate in the individual case within the constraints of the legally permissible range.

30 per cent in the Côtes d'Armor, while the incidence of the offence was equal in both Breton departments.[39]

We now turn to consider more closely the reasons for the increasing degree of legislative constraint in France on the flexible use of sentencing discretion. Leblois-Happe categorises this as falling into two categories: the first concerned with choosing the nature of the punishment, and the second with determining its extent.

A good example of the second is the recent introduction of mandatory minimums for certain recidivist offenders. Law No. 2007–1198 of 10 August 2007 strengthened the fight against the recurrence of recidivism by introducing a 'special minimum' applicable when fixing the penalties for such crimes. The judge must impose a sentence on the offender at least equal to one-third of the sentence. However, in the case of the first repeat offence, the court may impose a lower sentence in consideration of the circumstances of the offence, the personality of the offender or the offender's prospects for integration or re-integration into society. As from the second repetition, the judge may only impose a lower sentence if the offender's prospects for integration or rehabilitation are exceptional. (Art. 132-18-1, 132-19-1 CP).

Reductions are also available based on having informed the authorities, and so averted further criminality; mitigated the damage; or identified accomplices. Drug-traffickers, kidnappers and offenders involved in organised criminal theft may be dealt with in this fashion.

There is clearly limited guidance in French law on which objectives should motivate the choice of penalty, and when, exceptionally, the law requires justification for the penalty, the *Cour de cassation* appears content with the minimum possible justification being provided by the sentencing judge. The rule confirming the lack of any need for the judge to give reasons for the sentence imposed has been in existence since a ruling of the *Cour de cassation* delivered on 11 October 1960. The court stated that in deciding the nature and extent of the penalty the court took little account of how the judge should use his discretionary power. Regrettably, reform of the French Penal Code has produced no change in this respect.

The adoption of Article 132–24, however, had raised hopes that the judicial determination of the sentence would be more regulated by law, since the first paragraph of the text refers to the fact that, within the limits set by law, the court must fix and pronounce the sentence according to the circumstances of the offence and the personality of the offender. From this, Leblois-Happe argues, one might therefore have expected that judges would be required to justify their sentences in terms of the 'circumstances of the offence' and the 'personality of the offender'.

The highest court has simply confirmed the status quo. By a ruling of 19 December 1996, the Supreme Court clearly indicated that it did not amend

---

39 Rizk and Salle (1998).

its law.[40] It appears from this ruling that 'sentencing by judges within the limits prescribed by law is an option for which they do not account, and to which section 132–24 of the new Penal Code does not make any restriction'. This approach has remained constant ever since. Such jurisprudence as there is supports the discretionary liberty of the judge.

Therefore, French judges do not have to justify their discretionary decision as to penalty, except where the code requires it. The focus is more on defending the freedom of the judge to ensure compliance with the law. Such case law as there is supports the discretionary liberty of the judge. For example, Article 132–19, paragraph 2 of the Penal Code requires the judge to give reasons when imposing a prison sentence, unless the offender is a recidivist. However, the Court of Cassation has exhibited a degree of flexibility in interpreting the text. It appears content with fairly superficial reasoning on the part of the judge, rejecting appeals against decisions to imprison on the grounds of the gravity of the offence and the personality of the offender.

Leblois-Happe suggests that in such cases the Court of Cassation has effectively ceded its role as guardian of the rule of law to the judge. The main negative consequence of this is the absence of any quality control over the exercise of discretionary power and resultant disparities in sentencing. She argues that the adoption of some form of sentencing guidelines, perhaps along the lines of those prevalent in some US states, may provide a constructive way forward, but, in the final analysis, the objective is not just about achieving greater consistency in sentencing, it is also about ensuring quality in the interpretation and application of the criminal code.

Although issues of law, fact or sentencing relating to cases tried in French courts may be appealed by both the defendant and the prosecution, the limited number of such appeals suggests that these forms of appellate review do not play a particularly significant role in French criminal justice.

Judicial discretionary power and sentencing

Before 1994, the use of judicial discretionary power was most relevant in connection with the determination of *circonstances atténuantes*, whilst aggravating circumstances (*circonstances aggravantes* or *causes d'aggravation*) were legally prescribed and mandatory, to the extent of producing a precise increase in the penalty. However, significant changes were introduced by the 1994 French Criminal Code which abolished the category of *circonstances atténuantes* and replaced it by an entirely new category of *causes d'atténuation de la responsabilité* as well as extending that of *circonstances aggravantes*. Regarding the latter, the changes widened the range of circumstances and their effects, and also drew a distinction between general and specific aggravating factors.[41]

---

40 Cass. crim. 19 déc. 1996 préc.
41 See Articles 132–71 to 132–75 of the 1994 French Criminal Code.

An interesting aspect of the special aggravating circumstances regime is that, in addition to pointing to a varied range of circumstances relevant to both the offender and the victim, they are also explicit in enumerating factors going to the relationship between the offender and the victim, especially as to motivation. Subjective or personal circumstances as regards the offender are distinguished from objective material circumstances which may relate to conditions surrounding the commission of the offence.[42]

The new category of *causes d'atténuation de la responsabilité* is more flexible than its predecessor *excuses atténuantes* in the sense that the discretion of judges is not constrained by the parameters of minimum terms, although this remains at two years imprisonment where the penalty provided is criminal imprisonment or criminal detention for life, and one year's imprisonment where the penalty provided for is criminal imprisonment for a specific term.[43] Apart from some specified causes of mitigation,[44] judges retain a wide measure of discretion in the sentencing of offenders. As Renout suggests:

> En absence d'une cause légale d'exemption de peine et s'il estime devoir prononcer une peine, le juge dispose d'une grande latitude pour adapter et moduler la peine encourue dans la limite du maximum légal, déterminé après avoir fait jouer; le cas échéant, les causes légales d'aggravation ou de diminution de la peine.[45]

In common with Italian penal law, French penal law gives judges considerable discretionary power in determining the both the content and method of execution of sentences and also their subsequent enforcement. For example, Articles 132–25 and 136–26 of the French Penal Code allow the judge to impose a sentence of imprisonment with a provision that the offender should serve part of the sentence in 'semi-liberty'.[46] The content and execution of such sentences is settled by *le judge de l'application des peines* under the supervisory jurisdiction of the regional *tribunal de l'application des peines*,[47] with the possibility of further appeal on specified matters to the *chambre de l'application des peines de la cour d'appel.*

---

42 See Renout (2009) 303–7 for a detailed account.
43 Article 132–18 of the 1994 French Criminal Code.
44 Namely, the youth of the accused and individual circumstances or behaviour during and/or after the commission of the crime and, the behaviour of the victim. Other mitigation is linked specifically to the specific crimes, such as murder and poisoning (Article 221-5-3), torture and inhumane acts (Article 222-6-2), drug trafficking (Article 222–43), kidnapping (Article 224-5-1) and, robbery, extortion and organised gangs (Articles 331-9-1 and 312-6-1).
45 Renout (2009) 307.
46 For further analysis, see Leblois-Happe (2008), Herzog-Evans (2009).
47 See Renout (2009) 344 *et seq.*

These broad judicial powers extend far beyond the parameters of sentence decision-making conventionally associated with adversarial forms of trial. In the case of England and Wales, for example, the functions attributed to the French *juge de l'application des peines* are by convention exercised by administrative authority under executive control. Indeed, it may be argued that the judicial function should not extend beyond giving particular effect to the declared purposes for punishment following conviction and sentence. Where imprisonment is appropriate, the sentencing function will normally consist of a proportionate prison sentence based on the principle of just deserts, although conditions attaching to subsidiary objectives such as rehabilitation may be applicable.[48] Beyond having the power to specify minimum terms of imprisonment where life sentences are imposed, English judges have until recently[49] remained relatively unconcerned with administrative contingencies such as early release or the appropriateness of particular rehabilitative regimes, or with any appeals relating to their operation.

The reasons for these differences of approach in the judicial function between adversarial and inquisitorial forms of trial are firmly rooted in social and political history.[50] In France, following the 1789 revolution, the impact of classical criminology on the administration of justice, with its strict regulation of the judicial role, was based on widespread fear of a return to the pre-revolutionary repression caused by a politicised judiciary having unregulated discretionary power. This was reflected in the Penal Code of 1791, which, as Leblois-Happe[51] states:

> ... a donc prévu des *peines fixes*, susceptibles de varier uniquement en fonction des circonstances prévues par la loi et dans la proportion déterminée par elle. Le juge a perdu tout pouvoir de modulation; il est devenu 'une simple machine à appliquer un tarif' [emphasis in original].

As noted earlier, the gradual softening of this hard-line approach to controlling judicial discretion by neo-classical thinkers such as Garofalo and Ferri, with their positivist emphasis on the virtues of individualisation in sentencing, facilitated the re-introduction of a limited amount of judicial discretion in sentencing in the Code Napoleon of 1810. The Code merely permitted the individualisation of sentences; it did not make this a mandatory feature of the sentencing regime – this was only achieved by the law of 28 April 1832, which legally enshrined the principle of individualisation by introducing the concept of *circonstances atténuantes*, subsequently abolished in 1994. The notion of individualisation itself received renewed emphasis after

48 See S142 of the Criminal Justice Act (2003).
49 Note the obligations of the new Sentencing Council in this respect when framing sentencing guidelines; see S131 of the Coroners and Justice Act (2009).
50 See Radzinowicz (1966) ch. 1.
51 Leblois-Happe (2008) 3.

the Second World War, although in a reconceptualised form, through the penal reforms inspired by social defence theorist Marc Ancel,[52] eventually emerging as *le principe de la personnalisation de la répression* in Article 132–24 of the Penal Code.

It may be argued that this incremental expansion of French judicial discretionary power after its virtual extinction by the Penal Code of 1791 has increased the potential for politicisation of the penal process. Alternatively, one could also argue that this tendency is more effectively resisted where there is a strong and independent judicial culture operating against a normative framework of entrenched processual rights for citizens. Certainly, the implications of Leblois-Happe's observations are that the absence of any effective regulation of judicial discretionary power in the individualisation of sentences carries with it a potential threat to the moral integrity of the French criminal justice system as a bulwark of the state in defending the rights and liberties of citizens.

Correspondingly, if such unregulated judicial discretionary power were to extend to its pivotal role in regulating the content and enforcement of sentences, this might further hinder executive attempts to react *effectively* to the legitimate demands of citizens for penal reform. At worst, far from protecting the rights of citizens, a weakening in the legitimacy accorded to judicial discretionary decisions about punishment and sentencing might facilitate unwarranted repression by a politicised state bent on fostering diversity and social exclusion.

Accordingly, the unregulated nature of judicial discretionary power may prove to be an obstacle in the development of more communitarian forms of justice. As Crawford suggests,[53] the paradox in French society between universal notions of the state as a 'community' (commonly associated with the idea of a *justice de proximité*) and that of the diverse social reality of actual 'communities' produces a tension in the political discourse about 'community' which penal policy in France has continually struggled to overcome. Far from being portrayed as detached from the interests of citizens, as is the common perception in England and Wales, the powers given to the French state by citizens are fundamentally symbolic of the social contract between citizen and state, and its institutions therefore carry both an ideological and normative mandate to discharge this essentially communitarian obligation.

The development of more restorative and socially inclusive forms of sentencing practice, including practices such as mediation, depend essentially on the development of judicial discretionary power within an appropriately sympathetic ideological and normative context. Therefore, it would seem incumbent on the French penal state to engage effectively with the issue of regulating judicial discretion in sentencing by imposing new normative

---

52 Ancel (1954).
53 Crawford (2000) 209.

parameters for sentence individualisation that are both consistent with the symbolic aspirations of the social contract and the social reality of achieving those of its increasingly diverse moral 'community'.

Procedural justice and due process

Technically, there is no 'plea' bargaining in France, because there are no 'pleas' as such by the accused. In addition, there appears to be very little by way of any explicit trading of leniency made in return for admissions of guilt, at least in the most serious cases. From this perspective, it is worth noting that French trials are comparatively speedy affairs, thereby reducing the need to minimise trial adjudication through such mechanisms as plea bargaining for reasons related to administrative and resource savings. Furthermore, although French prosecutors have less control over charges than those coming from a purely adversarial common-law tradition such as the United States, it is significant that French courts and prosecutors retain substantial unregulated discretion to be lenient with those defendants who do co-operate.

Therefore, in general terms, the French system has neither a formal charge nor a sentence bargaining mechanism in place. However, several forms of tacit bargaining do appear to exist, and, particularly in correctional and police courts, basic issues are frequently uncontested, so that a confession from the accused during somewhat cursory proceedings at the outset of the trial facilitates a comparatively speedy 'finding' of guilt.

As far as *délits* are concerned, Law no. 2004–204 of 9 March 2004 introduced a new procedure into the French system; the *comparution sur reconnaissance préalable de culpabilité*, which bears some resemblance to common-law models of plea bargaining. The procedure is limited to those *délits* punishable by a term of five years imprisonment or less and is initiated by the prosecution, or the accused following an admission of guilt. The prosecution may propose a sentence not exceeding one year's imprisonment, or half the normally applicable penalty. Legal representation is mandatory for the accused (Article 495–98), and the judge is under a duty to verify the factual basis which underpins the admission of guilt.

According to Article 495–99, para. 2, the judge has complete discretion to grant or deny the penalty which is proposed by the parties under the *comparution* procedure and could, for example, reject it on the basis that he or she feels that further factual information might place the offence outside the five year limit. In any event, refusal by the judge to accept the request triggers a return of the case to the normal criminal process (Article 495–12). Correspondingly, once accepted, the penalty cannot subsequently be modernised.[54]

---

54 See, further, Langer (2004) 60 and his description of this procedure as an example of depenalization.

Two other aspects of French criminal procedure bear some resemblance to plea and sentence bargaining.[55] The first, which applies to specific crimes such as tax offences, occurs where a specific settlement is proposed before the commencement of legal proceedings. In such a case, the competent administrative authority proposes that the charges be dropped where the suspect admits the facts and pays a nominated sum. The second example, which is similar to sentence bargaining, occurs where a drug offender agrees to undergo treatment in return for the exclusion of a criminal trial.[56]

Another form of settlement procedure, the *injonction pénale*, was declared unconstitutional by the French Constitutional Tribunal in 1995, since it lacked any judicial authorisation.[57] It was re-introduced in 1999 in a reconstituted form as the *composition pénale* and requires the approval of the President of the District Tribunal.[58] Whilst the procedure involves a punitive measure, it focuses on redress to the victim, the restoration of order, or the inducement of the offender to accept social or medical treatment.[59] It is only available for a restricted number of offences, all of which are subject to a maximum of three years imprisonment, and normally only where the offender has confessed. The most interesting aspects of this process concern the public prosecutor's obligations with respect to the victim. Compliance by the offender with the terms of the *composition* results in waiver of the *action publique*, although this does not affect the victim's rights to pursue compensation through an *action civile*.[60]

Victims and sentencing

The position of the victim where the offender pleads guilty under the *comparution sur reconnaissance préalable de culpabilité* procedure is worthy of comment. In such a case, Article 495–13 of the 1994 French Criminal Code states that the victim (if known) must be informed of the offender's decision and be invited to the hearing before the judge. The victim may also file a *partie civile* action which may be decided upon by the judge at the same time as the *action publique*.[61]

Deconstructing evidence for sentencing

The burden of proof falling upon the prosecution is relieved by the fact that there is a legal presumption of guilt in the case of *contraventions* and *délits*; the accused is obliged to prove certain facts relating to justifications and excuses; and, the *juge d'instruction* is charged with collecting evidence on behalf of both

---

55 Articles L 248–49, *Livres des procédures fiscales.*
56 Article L 628-I, *Code de santé publique.*
57 *Conseil constitutionnel,* nr 95–360 DC, 2 February 1995.
58 Law no 99–515, 23 June 1999.
59 Leblois-Happe (2000) 67.
60 Note also the practice of *correctionnalisation* in relation to minor offences and that of *comparution immédiate,* available where the accused has been caught red-handed; see, further, Tulkens (2002) 672.
61 See, further, Pradel (2008).

the prosecution and the defence. Also significant is the reduced role of the defence, since the accused has an absolute right to inspect the full dossier of the case prior to the trial and also at certain specified stages in the pre-trial procedure,[62] as well as the right to ask the judge to acquire more pre-trial material.[63]

As far as the trial itself is concerned, judges are free to determine the weight to be given to any piece of evidence and, applying the principle of *intime conviction*, reach a decision on the basis of the evidence revealed to the court during the course of the trial. In addition to the dossier, this approach relies heavily on the principle of orality, implying the use of live testimony from the accused, witnesses and experts. There are also principles of publicity and contradiction which are designed to ensure, firstly, that proceedings are public, and, secondly, that judges articulate extremely cogent reasons for refusing to allow the admission of defence testimony.

As in Italy, the absence of a separate sentencing hearing in France is significant because it arguably forces many defendants to expose themselves to questions concerning guilt in order to ensure that they will be heard on issues of punishment. All the same, if the accused refuses to answer questions during the initial trial interrogation, he or she can still present mitigating evidence through other witness testimony, or after all the evidence and final arguments have been made. Overall, however, it may be argued that fundamental problems may arise in trying to reconcile a trial structure which has adopted adversarial elements with a unitary form of trial combining verdict and sentence phases. More particularly, unless such procedural changes are accommodated within a changed rationale for the trial, there is a danger that crime control values will tend to outweigh any intended due process considerations and the impact of associated rights.

Punishment and sentencing as governance

It is significant that, following the abolition of the criminal procedure reforms instituted in 1993 as a result of the *Commission Delmas-Marty*,[64] in common with Italy, the impetus for change was the politically explosive issue of the corrupt relationship between the exercise of political discretion and the administration of criminal justice. This concerned the revelation that since the late 1980s there had been significant use of public funds and corruption in the funding of MPs electoral campaigns, and that the discretion over criminal prosecutions exercised by the *ministère public* was being abused to protect electoral campaign funding sources.[65] A special commission, the *Commission Truche*, was

---

62 See *ibid.* and Pradel (1993) 117–18. There is no reciprocal right to defence disclosure, although in practice exculpatory material is normally disclosed to the *juge d'instruction* as soon as it becomes available; see, generally, Hodgson (2001), Hodgson (2002b), Hodgson (2002a).
63 In general, there are no restrictions as to the forms of evidence which may be used as proof, such as hearsay.
64 Commission Justice pénale et Droits de l'homme (1991).
65 See Verrest (2000).

established in another attempt at reforming the pre-trial phase, especially the relationship between the Minister of Justice and the *ministère public*. Among its recommendations, the *Commission Truche* proposed a number of important changes, including removing the *juge d'instruction*'s powers of preliminary detention and the examining judge's power to place suspects in preliminary detention.[66]

Verrest argues[67] that the changes in practice which followed the *Commission Truche* are important in understanding how recent reforms in French criminal procedure impacted on the role of the trial. In particular, they facilitated improved communication between public prosecutors and the police, thereby allowing more efficient anticipation and planning of cases for later referral to the public prosecutor, and, secondly, expedited trial proceedings and trial alternatives began to be developed. Consequently, trials became increasingly reserved for the most serious cases, and larger numbers of those accused were exposed to expedited trial processes rather than a full trial. This phenomenon has parallels with the process of informalisation of justice witnessed in Italy over recent years, with the expansion of such services as victim aid and mediation between victim and perpetrators.[68]

The *Commission Truche* in fact precipitated a significant legislative reform programme known as the *Réforme de la Justice*, which had the central objectives of improving the protection of civil liberties, enhancing prosecutorial independence and increasing accessibility to justice. In the event, the reform programme included *inter alia* reforms in the areas of pre-trial investigation and judicial competency, transferring the *juge d'instuction*'s powers of pre-trial detention to a newly created *juge des libertés et de la détention*; provision of another appeal mechanism from decisions of the *cours d'assises*; and the reconstituted *composition pénale* mechanism referred to earlier.

To conclude, it is important to note that international laws and principles have, in common with most systems of criminal justice, increasingly had a major impact on French penal law and criminal procedure. The main sources for this process of internationalisation range from the European Convention on Human Rights and ICCPR to instruments such as UN General Assembly Resolutions. The strongest of these influences has undoubtedly been the ECHR.[69]

Sentencing and Legitimacy in Italy

General overview

The Italian sentencing process begins immediately the court has reached its decision on verdict. The announcement of the verdict and the process of sentencing is a continuous component of the trial. The judges reach their

---

66 See, further, Hodgson (2001).
67 Verrest (2000) 217.
68 For further analysis, see Crawford (2000).
69 Cockayne (2002).

decisions on verdict immediately after the trial phase ends,[70] following collegial deliberations *in camera* directed by the President of the court.[71] The obligation on the court is then to announce its judgement (*sentenza*) and give reasons for its decisions. Where a conviction has resulted, the court is obliged to consider relevant aggravating and mitigating circumstances,[72] before detailing the sanctions to be imposed.[73] Any associated civil action order is also determined and announced at this stage.[74] The President delivers his remarks to the body of the court, and there is no interaction (procedural or otherwise) with anyone else present at this stage.

The final part of the judgement deals with consequential matters such as costs and the outcome of the civil claim, before the final stage dealing with the nature of the sanctions to be imposed. The judges adopt a declaratory tone according to the formula prescribed by the Code of Criminal Procedure.[75]

At the legal level, the Italian sentencing paradigm reflects the role of judicial discretion in sentencing decisions following the introduction of the new Code of Criminal Procedure in 1988. However, it is important to note that the current sentencing model derives not from the 1988 procedural revisions but from Articles 132 and 133[76] of the 1930 Criminal Code, which established the principle that the judge both determines the sentence and

---

70 C.P.P. Art. 525.

71 *Ibid.* Art. 527.

72 It is significant that aggravating and mitigating factors relating to determination of both crime severity and sentence severity are classified in the Italian Criminal Code (Codice Rocco, enacted in 1930).

73 C.P.P. Arts. 533–37.

74 *Ibid.* Arts. 538–43.

75 C.P.P. Arts. 533 and 535.

76 **Article 133**

Discretionary power of the judge in applying the sentence – Within the limits set by law, the judge must apply the sentence discretionally; it must indicate the reasons that justify the use of such discretionary power.

In increasing or reducing the sentence the limits set for each type of sentence must not be exceeded excepting where otherwise specified by law.

Article 133

Gravity of the crime: evaluation for fixing the sentence – In the exercise of his/her discretionary powers indicated in the preceding article, the judge must take into consideration the gravity of the crime deduced from:

• the nature, the type, the means, the object, the times, the place and each and every other modality of action;

• the gravity of damage or danger caused by the person hurt by the crime;

• the intensity of the *mens rea* and the degree of guilt.

The judge must also take into consideration the capacity to commit crimes of the offender, derived from:

• the reasons for committing the crime and the character of the offender;

• previous criminal record and generally the behaviour and life of the offender, before the fact;

• the conduct of the offender during or successive to the crime;

• the lifestyle of the offender, his/her family and social environment.

sets the punishment.[77] Article 132, in particular, provides that judicial discretion[78] must be exercised within the legally permissible penalty range, and imposes an obligation to justify the sentence by relating the facts to the severity and nature of the punishment.[79] The model is, therefore, essentially retributive in character. Article 133 sets out the criteria that guide judges in exercising their discretionary powers under Article 132. The fundamental guiding criteria are:

1. the gravity of the behaviour;
2. the offender's propensity to commit crime.

The first criterion is derived from an evaluation of objective and subjective factors, whilst the second is implicitly concerned with formulating a predictive judgement regarding the offender's likely recidivism.

Although most judges allude briefly to matters relevant to the criteria in Article 133, it is mainly significant for its failure to elaborate on the justification for punishment beyond mere retribution and denunciation.[80] The mechanical rigidity of the legislative formula, and the absence of any jurisprudential guidance[81] to develop sentencing practice, is reflected in the absence of any reference to similar judicial practice or concerns relating to the proper grading of punishment for the crime.[82]

Nevertheless, the court's obligations are further circumscribed by the constitutional requirement that any dispositive judicial decision must be 'reasoned'

---

77 For further discussion, see Girling (2006).
78 See Bellavista (1939), Bricola (1965), Dolcini (1979).
79 As Grande suggests, the problem lies in the fact that both minimum and maximum sentences are fixed at such a high level so that judges have since 1974 consistently used their wide discretionary powers to pass sentences well below the statutory minimum. However, this is achieved in many different ways and without principled guidance; Grande (2002).
80 As Mannozzi (1999) 3 points out, this reflects the lack of any indications in the code regarding the objectives of punishment, and has led to an inability to exercise control over judicial discretionary powers in sentencing, and more or less hidden forms of sentencing disparity.
81 It should be noted that Article 27 of the Italian Constitution explicitly mentions the rehabilitative ideal, and decisions of the Constitutional Court have consistently emphasised the 'polyfunctional' concept of punishment, whereby judges may determine the correct degree of punishment in the light of the characteristics of each case against retributive, rehabilitative and deterrent criteria. Mannozzi (1999) 4 suggests that the so-called polyfunctional theory is 'nothing more than an attempt to give the "ideological vagueness" afflicting those who drafted Art. 133 of the Code some kind of coherence.'
82 The crime of murder is punishable by a sentence of no less than 21 years imprisonment (C.C. Art. 575). However, if more than one mitigating circumstance pertains, the term of imprisonment may be reduced to five years and six months. A variety of aggravating circumstances specified in the Code may permit a sentence of life imprisonment (i.e. premeditation, parental murder or infanticide).

and that this reasoning must be explicit, so that the basis of the decision can be scrutinised by public opinion or by an appellate court.[83]

Despite the reforms in criminal procedure of 1988, the pre-existing discretionary model of retributive sentencing[84] has failed to develop coherently within the adversarial atmosphere that now characterises the Italian criminal trial process. This is evidenced by the absence of any apparent requirement to relate the reasons for sentence to anything beyond the criteria specified in Article 133 of the 1930 Criminal Code. With its contemporary emphasis on expediency, the adversarial influence is felt throughout the Italian sentencing process, with counsel being more openly interventionist in mitigation. However, most judgements, although alluding to mitigating circumstances indirectly through the application of the Article 133 criteria as they relate to the capacity of the offender, are devoid of any substantive debate or deliberation amongst the legal participants.

Formal verdict delivery and the pronouncement of sentence is normally differentiated by means of its somewhat flat tone and solemn, mechanistic delivery. Notwithstanding, its brevity reflects the key symbolic and ceremonial role attributed to the formal public enunciation of punishment. The sentencing phase is therefore typified by legal formalism and particular procedural constraints on the information deemed relevant for discretionary decisions and its appropriation in sentencing. The restrictive and underdeveloped ideology of the Italian sentencing paradigm consequently delimits the terrain in terms of due process and restorative justice beyond any communitarian purposes attributed to the ritualism of denunciation.

Thus, at the organisational level, the context of the sentencing stage of the trial remains symbolic rather than interactive, and sits uncomfortably with the adversarial requirements imposed on the trial proper by the 1988 criminal procedure reforms. Sentencing is not an integrated process, despite the conceptual link made between the determination of crime and sentence severity through the provisions of the Criminal Code. Delivery of verdict and sentence remains firmly in judicial hands.

At the interactive level, judicial style is typified by its authoritarian approach reflective of the hierarchical status of the President and the solemn process of the sentencing ritual. Here, the emphasis is on public delivery without deference to principle (legal or otherwise) or wider communitarian concerns. The enabled outcome of the structural constraints on sentencing is a formalised, mechanistic sentencing process, which conceals the exercise of significant judicial discretionary power, delivered with minimum justification[85] and maximum rhetorical force.

---

83 Italian Constitution, Article 111, and see Certoma (1985) 223.
84 Strictly speaking, Italian sentencing was not totally oriented towards retribution before 1988, as the 1948 Italian Constitution referred to the aim of rehabilitation.
85 On the problem of sentencing justification, see, for example, Cassazione Penale, 14 January 1987, *Rivista Penale* 1987, 631.

Challenges to existing paradigms

Grande[86] has described the connection between Enlightenment liberalism and the foundations of the adversarial mode of trial, yet the paradox is that by adopting measures designed to protect the individual against state abuse, Italy appears to have achieved the opposite effect.[87]

As Cavadino and Dignan point out,[88] the influence of the Italian penal reformer Cesare Beccaria, one of the most significant figures of classical criminology, and that of the pioneering positivist criminologists Lombroso, Ferri and Garofalo, is reflected in the provisions of the 1930 CC, the latter being chiefly responsible for the introduction of indeterminate sentencing and more 'flexible' forms of early release. The high tariffs contained in the 1930 CC, especially the fixed minimum sentences, have been mitigated to some extent by the exercise of judicial discretionary power. This has tended to counteract some of the worst aspects of the Code and, as Pavarini suggests,[89] provided a degree of legitimacy to a penal system which is perceived by many to be inherently partisan and socially divisive.

In this regard, Ruggiero attributes many of the fluctuations in the Italian incarceration rate to media-driven 'moral panics' and the demonisation of particular categories of offender who may suddenly be deemed 'dangerous', or otherwise socially 'undesirable' by the political elite. In the past, such 'emergencies' have included armed robbers and political terrorists, but the most significant recent example has been the issue of Mafia corruption.[90]

The demonisation of Romanian immigrant workers in Italy provides a further example of how easy it is for partisan ideologies to exploit the lack of moral legitimacy attached to the penal framework and the foundational values of the 1930 CC.[91] Despite fierce criticism from human rights organisations and the Vatican, fuelled by a concerted media-led campaign, the

---

86 Grande (2000) 231. See also Radzinowicz (1966).
87 For an overview of the origins and principles underlying the Italian system of criminal procedure, see Perrodet (2002b), van den Wyngaert *et al.* (eds) (1993) ch. 8. As Ricci points out (Perrodet 2002b 348), the Italian system has developed from its origins as a predominantly post-Enlightenment inquisitorial system based on the Napoleonic Code to reflect a range of political ideologies. These include the liberalism of the 1913 Code, the fascist totalitarianism of the 1930 Code and, more recently, the democratic values which informed the 1988 reforms.
88 Cavadino and Dignan (2006) 141.
89 Pavarini (2001).
90 See Ruggiero (1998). Ruggiero also notes the adverse consequences for Italian penality of the ambivalent relationship between consequentialist and retributive forms of penal ideology that has persisted since the Enlightenment; *ibid.* 211. The context surrounding the introduction of Law n 663 of 10 October 1986, discussed *post*, provides a good illustration of this issue.
    As regards Mafia corruption, attention has focused particularly on a previously unexplained reduction in convictions following the conclusion of the so-called 'Clean Hands' investigation in the early 1990s; see Piercamillo and Mannozzi (2007) ch. 5. For an English summary, see Sisti (2007).
91 See Masera (2009), Ruga Riva (2009).

Senate passed a law making illegal immigration an offence punishable with a fine of between 5,000 and 10,000 euros, in addition to approving mandatory life sentences for deaths from rape, fast-track sentences for existing sex offenders, and mandatory life sentences for the rape of minors. The new law also permitted mayoral approval of unarmed and unpaid citizens' patrols.

Facing an estimated total of 36,000 illegal immigrants in 2008, the then Prime Minister Silvio Berlusconi focused on the issue as part of his electoral campaign, seeking to exploit a spurious link between immigration and increasing levels of sexual assault, particularly rape. Although statistical data for 2008 revealed a fall in the number of sexual assaults, the media (a large proportion of it controlled by Berlusconi) became increasingly vociferous in their calls for tougher measures by the legislature against immigrants, and Roma in particular, who were singled out as bearing primary responsibility for such crimes, thereby stigmatising Romanian immigrants as a whole.[92]

In conclusion, it is worth repeating those factors in Italian culture identified by Pavarini that produce feelings of 'suspicion and diffidence' on the part of citizens about the politicised relationship between crime and penality:[93]

- a deep-seated, widespread social perception of crime as a political matter;
- an equally entrenched and widespread social perception, particularly among the subaltern classes, of the criminal justice system as a violent means of preserving social inequality;
- the fact that in Italy the crime issue has long been identified with the 'southern question', a political issue *par excellence*; and
- the decisive role played by political terrorism and by the long struggle against repression in the 1970s and early 1980s, both of which have bolstered Italian society's perception of the crime issue and the criminal justice system as being political.

The constitutional position of the judiciary in matters of punishment and sentencing

The Italian Constitution expresses the principles that the judiciary must follow in matters of punishment and sentencing. Article 25 of the Constitution prohibits judges from punishing someone for an act which is not deemed a crime by Statute. In addition, judges cannot deliver a penalty which is not laid down by law for a given crime, nor can they decide upon a different term. Article 111 of the Constitution establishes the principle of 'due process' and

---

92 For a useful overview, see EurActiv (2009) and, more generally, Bianchi, Buonanno and Pinotti (2008).
93 Pavarini (2001) 415.

provides guidelines for the conduct of criminal trials, including a list of guarantees for the defendant. It also mandates judges to state the rationale for sentencing decisions, explaining in terms of fact and law the reasons for their judgment. The Constitution also makes clear that it is the judge deciding the culpability of the offender who sets the punishment during the sentencing phase. In both instances there is a requirement to justify his or her discretionary power.

Article 101 of the Constitution provides that the judiciary is subject only to the law and affirms its independence. In addition, Article 104 of the Constitution states that the judiciary is self-governing and independent of any other authority. These two provisions make it clear that the whole body of the judiciary is governed by this principle, not just each judge in isolation, and it is a clear expression of the fundamental principle of the separation of powers. The judiciary's independence from the executive is strongly guaranteed, since members of the judiciary are selected through a competitive state examination. Furthermore, penal action is mandatory, so that the public prosecutor cannot choose which crimes are worthy of judgment by the state.

Hence, judges are only accountable to the law, and their independence and autonomy are guaranteed by special legal provisions, the fact they are appointed for life, and the *Consiglio Superiore della Magistratura*.[94] In theory, the guarantee of impartiality comes from the fact that there is a clear distinction drawn between those who investigate and those who judge, especially since the role of the investigating judge was abolished by the 1988 procedural reforms. Possible situations of incompatibility between judicial and other functions are elaborated in the 1988 Code.

Grande[95] describes how the judiciary is appointed and Italian legal culture. Since the 1988 reforms the prosecutor's truth-finding function has narrowed from one of collecting evidence both for and against the accused, as the official in charge of discovering the 'truth', to simply the latter. Grande suggests that a fair trial is impossible because the judge who is the trier of fact is effectively part of the same judiciary; there is a lack of separation between the adjudicating and prosecuting members of the judiciary.[96]

Since relinquishing the investigative function the Italian judiciary has assumed more of a neutral stance in the context of the adversarial contest between the prosecution and the defence which has gradually come to replace the inquisitorial framework following the procedural reforms of 1988.[97]

---

94 Van den Wyngaert *et al.* (eds) (1993) 229.
95 Grande (2000) 236.
96 See, further, Perrodet (2002a) 438, 447.
97 Salas (2002).

The accountability of the judiciary to the legislature

The operation of the doctrine of separation of powers applies equally to legislative power, so the Italian judiciary is not subject to Parliament, and there is no direct relationship between the two bodies. This means that, although the judiciary is not accountable to the legislature, it is, as already stated, subject to the law, and therefore punishment may ensue if judges commit an illegal act, or to civil liability, where damage ensues.

Constitutional provisions therefore guarantee the judiciary's independence and prevent any form of subordination, or any kind of liability towards the legislature. The notion of compulsory prosecution is also there as a direct reminder of the Enlightenment reformers' desire to control the use of discretionary power in the administration of justice. In particular, it lessens the possibility that the prosecutor will support undesirable forms of political power, thereby ensuring greater equality before the law.[98] The danger however is that there has been a distinct absence of accountability underpinning the operation of this principle, so that the way in which the Prosecutor's office chooses to exercise its function in choosing who (and who not) to prosecute, is subject to insufficient scrutiny.[99] As Grande[100] concludes, giving the prosecutor a greater sense of responsibility for the outcome of cases may help.

Comparing the English and Italian sentencing systems

The English and Italian jurisdictions reflect different and innovative approaches to integrated sentencing. In particular, they demonstrate recent initiatives in victim involvement, and peculiarities in judicial discretion and intervention in the sentencing process in the context of various procedural traditions, for example:

- Verdict deliberations in the Italian process are judicial, collegiate and secret, with the result subsequently announced by the court. This is in marked contrast to the often protracted nature of English jury trial.
- The sentencing phase of the English trial process (in contrast to Italy) is separate from that which determines guilt or innocence. Its form is determined by conventions, principles, relationships and interactions which differ from the main body of the trial.

---

98 Grande (2000) 241.
99 As Perrodet (2002a) 429 argues, executive control of the prosecution service has gradually dissipated as a result of the assimilation of the status of prosecutor with cannot be subordinated to executive control; *ibid.* 431, 447. However, the complex relationship between the prosecutorial and the judicial function serves to obfuscate the public perception of the judicial role; see Salas (2002) 496.
100 Grande (2000) 256.

- There are considerable differences of approach between the English and Italian systems in establishing the criteria necessary to determine the seriousness of the offence for the purposes of sentencing.
- The overriding failure of the Italian system to rationalise the purposes of sentencing means that judicial discretion operates in an ideological vacuum which appears incapable of promoting principles for the rational variation of cases. In England judicial ideology and instrumental rationality are grounded in a substantial body of sentencing principle.
- The more proactive and confrontational aspects of judicial behaviour typified by the adversarial paradigm are present in the English sentencing phase.

The rationale and framework for sentencing

As described earlier, the theoretical framework which informs Italian sentencing is a mixture of jurisprudence and law (see Article 133 CC and Article 27 of the Constitution). In particular, Article 27(3) of the Italian Constitution establishes two important principles; that punishment must be both humane and aimed towards the rehabilitation of the offender.[101] However, in order not to contravene Article 27, a penalty cannot be made indefinite until rehabilitation is achieved.

Grande[102] makes the point that the introduction of adversarial elements into the old non-adversarial system has produced effects diametrically opposed to those expected. In particular, Grande asserts that the accused is less protected against abuse of power than before the introduction of the common law adversarial elements.

The relationship between the aims of punishment and the principles of distributive justice

Although the Italian Constitution states that the main goal of punishment should be the rehabilitation of the offender, this is not its only purpose, since the Constitutional Court[103] has endorsed the notion of a polyfunctional theory of punishment, according to which punishment may have different goals.[104] Accordingly, the aims which may inform Italian sentencing are retribution, general prevention, deterrence and special prevention (even neutralisation), flexibility being permitted in terms of their practical application. According to the theory elaborated by Roxin,[105] retribution and general

---

101 See Fiandaca (1994).
102 Grande (2000) 232.
103 Corte Constituzionale, judgement n 107/1980.
104 See Vassalli (ed.) (1982).
105 Roxin (1994).

prevention should inform the legislative phase, retribution the sentencing phase, and special prevention should be the primary focus during the sentence enforcement phase of the criminal process.

In discussing what kind of rationale framework might be developed in Italy, Grazia Mannozzi[106] favours an approach which adopts dominant criminal policy aims for each phase of punishment: namely threat, infliction and enforcement, balancing these against so-called recessive aims, whose function is to limit the achievement of the other aims:

- The threat of punishment phase is generally guided by considerations of general prevention.
- The sentencing phase, in contrast, is guided by the principle of special prevention (and by rehabilitation), but within the bounds of punishment proportionate to the liability of the offender.
- The enforcement phase, should strive towards the 'rehabilitation' of the offender, wherever possible and on a voluntary basis only.[107]

This suggests a progressive integrated framework for rationalising the notion of punishment and sentencing through all its phases, both pre- and post-trial. As such, it provides rational parameters for developing both the system of criminal justice and for establishing the liability of those individuals subjected to punishment, but with the added dimension of taking account of the capacity of the system to achieve punishment objectives.

The aims of punishment and sentencing and shared values about justice

This is difficult question to address, since, as Mannozzi[108] points out, there are few empirical studies dealing with the perception of fairness in punishment in Italy. The media tend to emphasise the lack of penal effectiveness and that, given current levels of prison overcrowding, sanctions appear to be relatively effective. Criminal sanctions appear to be effective only for selected categories of offenders and crimes (mainly crimes against property, homicide, organised crime and drug trafficking) and not for white-collar crimes.

At the same time, the media tends to focus on crimes committed by recidivists; either on probation, parole or following 'early release'. Public perceptions of the appropriateness of sentence severity are disproportionately influenced by media coverage, especially since the public have no parameters by which to evaluate the correctness of sentencing options. Consequently, Mannozzi concludes that the general public perception is that punishment and sentencing is excessively lenient.

---

106 Mannozzi (2002). See also Mannozzi (1996) 389–416.
107 *Ibid.*
108 Private communication, July 2009.

Discretionary power and sentencing

General overview

As suggested earlier, the so-called mono-phase or unitary sentencing model for adult sentencing in Italian criminal procedure is especially significant in determining the boundaries of judicial discretion, since there is effectively no distinction in processual terms made between the delivery of the verdict and the sentence. The effect of such a paradigm is potentially of great significance in terms of the factual basis for sentencing, since it is essentially trial norms and the forces that shape their implementation which determine what counts as fact, rather then the rationale and normative framework for sentencing.

In summary, judges reach their verdict immediately after the close of the trial (Article 525 CCP) following collegial deliberations *in camera* directed by the President of the court (Article 527 CCP). The obligation on the court is then to announce its judgement (*sentenza*) and give reasons for its decisions, usually within 30–90 days. Where a conviction results, the court is obliged to consider relevant aggravating and mitigating circumstances as specified in Article 133 CC before dealing with the sanctions to be imposed (Articles 533–37 CCP).

Unlike the English adversarial form of jury trial, there is no independent procedural structure provided for sentencing, and therefore no conceptual distinction made between the procedural contexts for receiving information relevant to sentence which might serve to differentiate the qualitative nature of the evidence for the purposes of either verdict or sentence.[109] The sentencing phase of the Italian trial is characterised by form (Articles 533 and 535 CCP), with any allusions to sentence justification being merely declaratory of the court's considered view without further justification. This suggests that the potential for contexts of influence to impact upon sentencing outcomes is constrained by the fact that the paradigm for decision-making is essentially governed by the requirements of the trial. Hence, the potential for flexibility and the constructive use of discretion is seriously limited. Furthermore, since the normative framework itself is chiefly concerned with form and regulation, this restricts the nature and extent of substantive evidence admitted to trial.

These apparent differences in structure and form between Italian and English sentencing are paradoxical for victims, in the sense that Italian law imposes no substantive limits on the possible extent of victim participation in sentencing, whilst English sentencing law envisages no substantive rights at all, and has only recently succumbed to the notion of victim personal statements which aim to satisfy purely procedural or 'service' rights

An important structural judicial influence on the sentencing process in Italian trials which illustrates the last point is the judicial supervision and

---

109 Note the significance of 'Newton' hearings in English sentencing law; see Ashworth (2010) 375.

enforcement of sentences. As Mannozzi[110] explains, an offender who receives a sentence of imprisonment from the sentencing judge may have this modified either qualitatively or quantitatively, even by a different judge. The sentence can be changed *qualitatively* either by the sentencing judge through the use of substitutive sanctions consisting of non-custodial or semi-custodial penalties for short periods of imprisonment of up to one year (e.g. a suspended sentence for up to two years; Article 162 CC), or by the supervisory judge, who may substitute various alternative measures (such as house arrest; Article 47, Act no.354/1975). Further, *quantitative* changes to the prison term and its application may be ordered by the enforcement judge; the judge who previously issued the sentence. Mannozzi illustrates how the availability of these procedures to avoid imprisonment have contributed to the so-called crisis in the mono-phase (or unitary) model of sentencing, in effect, helping to perpetuate a sentencing paradigm with endosystematic aims (i.e. internal to the system).

The Italian experience shows us that the reasons for increasing penal obfuscation, and the 'labyrinthine' effect[111] produced by the alternative effects of the supervisory and enforcement judges are intimately related to the problems inherent in the rationale and operation of the main sentencing provisions included in Articles 132 and 133 of the Criminal Code. In other words, these procedures exacerbated an already increasingly unworkable system lacking in rationality, coherence and transparency.[112]

Executive control over the exercise of judicial discretion

In general terms, because Article 101 of the Constitution states that judges are subject only to the law, there is a direct connection between judges and the law which in effect means that they are completely free to interpret the law. From this perspective, therefore, the executive cannot interfere with decisions, nor control the exercise of judicial discretion. However, since the executive controls the resources and the staff of the department with responsibility for the administration of justice, practical constraints may affect judicial discretion.

In addition, the Ministry of Justice may intervene in the application of Article 41 *bis* Act 335/1975 which establishes the principle of so-called 'hard-line imprisonment' and its strict enforcement as solitary confinement. Furthermore, there have been several politically charged changes to the rules for criminal trials, most notably following the so-called 'Clean Hands' investigations against corruption and investigations into the activities of Italian Prime Minister Silvio Berlusconi.

---

110 Mannozzi (2002) 113.
111 See Mannozzi (2000) 69–94.
112 Alternatively, it may be argued that the flexibility of the system promotes the goal of rehabilitation.

Penal policy and political objectives

More recently, Italian penal policy has been strongly dictated by political aims. As stated, the legislature increasingly resorts to the criminal law to appease perceived public anxieties inflamed by the media, especially regarding security issues, or focusing on certain crimes and certain types of offender.

The issue of prison overcrowding has also become increasingly politicised. As Grande suggests,[113] the crisis of prison overcrowding prompted the government through the law of 10 October 1986, n 663 to transform the rehabilitative aims underpinning alternative measures into instruments for controlling the prison population by making them 'instruments of prison governance'. This was achieved mainly by expanding the powers of the surveillance tribunal (*tribunale di surveglianza*) to permit alternative measures based on rehabilitative considerations. However, the credibility of all these sanctions was critically undermined by a serious reduction in the capacity of the prison infrastructure to carry out rehabilitative programmes and assessments. As Grande explains,[114] this led to the invidious situation of decisions relating to the so-called 'social dangerousness' of offenders being based on largely subjective evaluations of their social and personal circumstances.

The politicisation of these decisions was made more explicit by amendments made to the legislation in 1991 and 1992 linking the basis for them to the giving of information leading to the prosecution of members of criminal organisations; in other words, the changes were directed at obtaining testimony directly against accomplices in Mafia cases.

The political strategy of supporting surveillance rather than rehabilitation was also sustained by the legal culture. The high turnover of supervisory judges tended to militate against the development of rights protection, instead facilitating the expansion of discriminatory and arbitrary forms of decision-making. However, for reasons described by Mannozzi,[115] the development of appropriate forms of discretionary control underpinned by a coherent set of aims; the so-called polycentric approach, coupled with shifting flexibility from the execution to the sentencing phase, although supported by Grande and others, has failed to materialise because of the pervasive influence of the unitary sentencing framework based on retribution and deterrence established by the 1930 CC. and its continued support by the Constitutional Court.

The influence of legal and social constraints on judicial sentencing

Since Italy is a civil law country its criminal law and procedure is firmly constrained by the rule of law, both in terms of its underlying philosophical foundations and its normative characteristics and practice. Criminal law fixes the

---

113 Grande (2002) 6.
114 *Ibid.* 8.
115 Mannozzi (2002).

type of punishment, the range of criminal sanctions, the list of mitigating and aggravating factors, and provides narrow guidelines for sentencing. It also regulates the stages of the enforcement of sanctions which is supervised by judges.

However, there is a strong sense in which this legal and philosophical paradigm has been undermined in recent years. The move towards a more adversarial trial procedure in Italy has had serious implications for trial process and judicial culture in particular. For example, the principle of orality and the nature and order of permissible testimony resemble common law trials.[116] Yet, significantly, inquisitorial elements remain; judges may direct the further exploration of issues on their own initiative (Article 506(1) CCP), intervene with their own questions during the examination of witnesses (Article 506(2) CCP), subpoena experts (Article 508 CCP), and require the acquisition of further evidence where absolutely necessary (Article 507 CCP).

The principle of immediacy also means that the judge who collects the evidence is also the one who decides on the merits of the case, further pressure coming from the fact that the trial must be held within a reasonable time to permit clear recollection of the evidence at the time of its evaluation.[117]

For these reasons, there may be even greater restraint on the part of victims in exercising their procedural rights under Article 90, or exposing themselves unduly to the rigours of adversarial evidential procedure and possible further questioning at the discretion of the judge, because the potential to develop a relationship of inclusion between judge and victim remains circumscribed and critically weakened by the pre-existing inquisitorial culture of minimal involvement and adherence to form.

As regards the procedural aspects of sentencing, Italian judges also have a considerable amount of discretion relating to decisions about aggravating and mitigating circumstances, despite the fact that the criteria to be applied appear to be much more closely circumscribed than in common law countries, such as England and Wales. In Italy, the concept of the 'circumstances of the crime' is a significant factor in sentencing, despite the fact that it remains undefined in the relevant legal instruments.[118] Although the 1930 CC appeared to accept that the circumstances of crime should be seen in terms of accessory elements to the offence, the fact that there is no definitive understanding beyond this general notion opens up the possibility for extensive judicial interpretation. Nevertheless, some broad indications are provided by Articles 70 and 61of the 1930 CC.; the former distinguishes between

---

116 Spencer suggests that since the 1988 reforms the Italian courts must decide the case on the basis of oral testimony rather than written statements contained in a dossier compiled by others; see Spencer (2002).

117 Corso (1993).

118 Thus, it remains unclear whether such circumstances relate more specifically to the process of individualisation, or in determining the accused's culpability, or in assessing the potential danger posed by an accused, although in practice they are treated as relevant to the severity of sanctions rather than the culpability of the offender.

'objective' and 'subjective circumstances, including such matters as the nature, type, modality, time and place of the crime, gravity of the damage caused and the personal characteristics of victims, whilst the latter focus on such matters as the degree of *mens rea*, personal circumstances of the offender and the relationship between the offender and the victim. Article 61 CC lists a great many factors which may be considered as aggravating factors, where these are not already taken into account as constituent elements of the substantive offence. Among them are the use of torture or cruelty in the commission of the crime, and the abuse of power or trust, or crime committed against a public servant.

The issue of general mitigating circumstances (*circostanze attenuanti comuni*) is dealt within Article 62, which, as with aggravating circumstances under Article 61, cannot be taken into account where they form constitutive elements of the offence.[119] These include the fact of having acted for particular moral or social reasons; or in a state of anger caused by an injustice; or having caused minimal damage where fiscal or property crimes are involved; or having before the trial fully repaired the damage through compensation. However, Article 62 *bis*, harbours a broad discretionary potential as regards general mitigating circumstances (*circostanze attenuanti generiche*) since this enables judges to take into account other mitigating factors which are not explicitly referred to nor defined by law when passing sentence, especially in terms of their identification and evaluation.[120]

Judicial reaction to increased regulation

As regards the role of judicial discretion[121] and the prospects for process and victim integration, the 2000 reforms have in a sense democratised the Italian criminal process by restoring aspects of penal resolution to citizens, yet this weakening of judicial and state authority has been reversed by the pivotal role accorded to judicial discretion in ordinary criminal proceedings following the 1988 reforms, and an absence of rights protection. These reforms have

---

119 This raises an interesting contrast with the position in England and Wales where certain evidence may have been deliberately omitted from consideration during the trial because of its potentially prejudicial effect on the party introducing it. Such an effect is much less likely to arise in the inquisitorial context because evidence is not selected by the prosecution or the defence solely for the purposes of winning the adversarial contest. Rather, a judicial determination of what evidence should be admitted and selected is made to serve the truth-finding function of the trial. Consequently, it is much more likely that there is a potential overlap between the trial and sentencing phases regarding evidence of aggravating or mitigating factors.

120 Articles 63–69 CC provide detailed indications for increasing or decreasing the penalty where one or more circumstances exist, and sets out the highest and lowest possible adjustments of the penalty so permitted.

121 Acknowledging its potential as a vehicle for overcoming limitations of principle and procedure.

gone far beyond those experienced in England, or in fact in the notion of victim participation evident in the norms and practices of international criminal tribunals, such as the International Criminal Court (ICC).[122]

The general effect of the Italian reforms is, of course, to reduce the overall significance of the new adversarial model through the introduction of alternative models which provide significant derogations from the accusatorial approach. For example, the novel penal jurisdiction of the Justice of the Peace[123] created a new sanctioning 'microcosm' (new sanctions and alternative mechanisms for resolving conflicts) that functions independently of the ordinary criminal justice system for adult offenders. Structurally, it is a mixed model that combines retributive and reparative aspects. The basic objectives of the reform were administrative and bureaucratic; to lighten the workload of the system of ordinary justice, thereby minimising recourse to criminal sanctions and favouring reparative conduct and reconciliation between the parties in a dispute. The implantation of this alternative paradigm was forced into the existing hybridised trial context without any attempt being made to rationalise the overall framework of penal justice. Consequently, the adversarial reforms designed (in part) to promote the adult trial as *the* context for determining truth, guilt and justice have been undermined by initiatives such as this designed to democratise justice, by giving the power to victims to drive the process and have a definitive role in the determination of the sanction.

Procedural justice and due process

The theory and practice of plea bargaining

It is generally agreed that plea bargaining,[124] first introduced in 1988 with the reform of the Italian code of criminal procedure, revolutionised its criminal justice system. However, despite the legislature's aim that the great majority of the trials should be concluded through sentence negotiation, relatively few trials are concluded by such means in practice (only forty per cent).[125] The possibility of the case against the accused being extinguished through effluxion of time encourages many defendants to favour ordinary trial over sentence negotiation.

To be sure, plea bargaining is a procedure much preferred by the prosecutor because of its simplicity and speed, as well as by the defence, thanks to the sentence reductions imposed by law. However, doubts remain about the true nature of plea bargaining, especially the consequences of accepting a guilty

---

122 Ashworth (2010) 385. See also, Ashworth (2000d) ch. 9; Ashworth (2002b).
123 Although introduced on 28 August, 2000 by law n. 274, the justice of the peace paradigm only became operative on 2 January, 2002. See, generally, Picotti and Spangher (2003).
124 More accurately, negotiation of the sentence.
125 See, further, Caputo (2009).

plea. In particular, it is unclear whether the latter can produce a conviction because a guilty plea cannot be taken as proof of penal responsibility on the part of the accused.[126] Furthermore, a finding of guilt following a plea bargain cannot be used in a civil trial to prove the merit of a compensatory claim for damages.

Plea bargaining is not institutionalised in Italy because the Italian legal system is based on the principle of mandatory prosecution, meaning that only sentence bargaining is possible and *not* charge bargaining. The importance of plea bargaining to the Prosecutor in Italy is less important than in the US or UK because he or she has virtually nothing to gain, given that the reduction in punishment is not exchanged for a *plea of guilty*.[127] This is because the sentence which concludes the trial, whilst a punishment, does not equate with an admission of guilt. In Italy the basic principle is that a guilty plea does *not* mean an individual can consent to be found guilty in the absence of evidence that he or she did in fact commit a crime. The only advantage to the Prosecutor may be in shortening the trial and in simplifying the gathering of evidence.[128]

The 1988 CCP introduced two procedures based on negotiation between the prosecution and the accused. Although in theory still dominated by the legality principle, these procedures depend upon the consent of the parties. However, the decision relates not to the decision to prosecute but to the size of the penalty, and/or the form of the procedure. The objective apprears to be speed, since Italy has frequently been condemned by the ECHR for violation of the requirement of trial within a reasonable length of time (Article 6(1) ECHR).

PATTEGGIAMENTO

This is an application relating to the penalty which is made at the request of the parties (*applicazione della pena su richiesta della parti*).[129] For offences with a maximum penalty of five years imprisonment,[130] the accused and the

---

126 The most recent Supreme Court decisions on sentencing are gradually attributing the character of a true conviction to the outcomes of plea bargains primarily because: (i) they constitute the basis for handing down punishment, requiring, at least implicitly, a recognition of criminal responsibility; and (ii) the judge is asked to evaluate the proportionality between the facts realised and the punishment agreed by prosecutor and lawyer.

127 For comparative analysis within Europe, see Tulkens (2002).

128 However, the pre-trial summary trial procedure available under Article 442 CCP is not dissimilar to the English 'plea before venue procedure'. According to Pizzi and Marafioti (1992) 1–40, the guilty plea requirement was omitted because the Code's drafters feared an admission of guilt would undermine the presumption of innocence guaranteed to all defendants by the Italian Constitution.

129 Articles 444–48 CCP.

130 Originally two years, but extended to five years imprisonment by Law n. 134 of 12 June 2003. Note that this refers to the negotiated sanction and not the maximum provided by law for the crime committed.

public prosecutor may ask the judge to apply the penalty on which they have agreed. In other words, the judge is asked to formally approve their agreed choice of a reduced penalty

The procedure may be used either during the preliminary stage or during the trial stage. If accepted, it leads to a judgement which could (in theory) result in acquittal of the accused. Where there is a guilty verdict, then, subject to the judge's duty to monitor the lawfulness of the procedure, and subject to the provisions of the Constitution[131] which require sentencers to promote reform of the offender, the judge pronounces a reduced penalty. However, the reduction may be no greater than one-third.

No further penalty may be imposed on the accused, who is, furthermore, not liable for the expenses of the proceedings. In return, the accused forgoes his or her right to contest the charges and to lodge an appeal. In other words, there is an implicit admission of guilt,[132] rather than a conviction equivalent to an admission of guilt. However, if the judge refuses to seal the agreement of the parties, and proceedings are continued, the accused's request may not be treated as a confession. This is difficult to maintain in reality

GIUDIZIO ABBREVIATO

Again introduced by the 1988 CCP, this procedure may be applied for in respect of all offences, however serious, and without limit as to the extent of the penalty, with the exception of life imprisonment. Here agreement is based on the choice of shortened procedure as against the ordinary trial procedure. From the preliminary stage the judge may agree to the accused's request to be judged 'according to the current state of the case'. If the prosecution agrees (which prevents it from later modifying the charges), the case will be judged not by the trial judge but by the *giudice dell'udienza preliminare* (GUP), according to the current state of the case (*allo stato degli atti*), on the basis of the dossier and without the trial being public.

The outcome of the 'abbreviated' judgement is either an acquittal or a guilty verdict, with a penalty which is normally reduced by one-third. Moreover, the conviction will not figure in the accused's criminal record. The accused renounces his or her right to appeal, but not to take the case to the Court of Cassation. However, he avoids a more detailed search for evidence, which might lead to new charges.

In 1999 the rules of 'abbreviated judgement' were significantly altered, and so was its consensual character (Law no. 479/99). Where the accused requests, the judge no longer has to obtain the prosecutor's agreement, and is obliged to deal with the case by abbreviated judgement. The procedure was extended to

---

131 Article 27 of the Italian Constitution guarantees the presumption of innocence.
132 Article 447, para. 1 *bis.* This article also prohibits use of the sentence in civil or administrative proceedings.

make it potentially available in cases where a life sentence was a possibility. In addition, where the accused makes the request conditional on the collection of evidence relating to the essence of the case, the judge may agree to this, provided hearing the requested evidence seems necessary and is compatible with the general aim of economy that underlies this type of judgement. Thus, the procedure is no longer one that judges the cases 'as the file now stands', because it is now possible for further evidence to be collected as the basis for the eventual decision.

Whilst these so-called consensual forms of justice have reduced the burden on the courts, opinion varies as to their effect in terms of expediting justice. Others feel that they have damaged the basic principles underlying criminal procedure in Italy. For instance, some commentators argue that the *patteggiamento* is an opportunity for lawyers to ditch less profitable cases. Chiavario[133] suggests that the development of such simplified procedures waters down, or even abandons, fundamental tenets of adversarial justice.

At the same time as Italy has been developing adversarial elements in criminal procedure, an increasing number of special procedures have been designed to bypass them. For instance, the *decreto penale*, already present in the 1930 CC, allows the judge in minor cases to convict the accused merely on the basis of a dossier put together by the police, and in exchange for a one-half sentence reduction (Article 459, CCP). The accused may enter an objection to a conviction resulting from this procedure and require the case to be heard under the ordinary rules. However, if he does, he renounces his claim to a reduced penalty.[134]

Grande[135] adds a cautionary note with regard to the operation of Italy's 'summary proceedings'. She observes that the accused can never be sure of the promised reduction, due to the unresolved contradictions between adversarial and inquisitorial concepts of due process that face judges exercising their discretion in 'plea bargaining' cases:

> ... one may note how difficult it is to reconcile the ideal of an efficient justice system with the continental ideal of justice that hands the truth-finding role over to the judge and requires him to properly and uniformely [sic] sentence convicted offenders. The civil law's inherent distrust of any formal plea bargaining and negotiation between the parties that is apt to prevent the judge from perfoming his fact-finding and sentencing functions runs counter to a quick disposition of criminal cases.[136]

---

133 Chiavario (1994).
134 See, further, Perrodet (2002a).
135 Grande (2000) 251–56.
136 *Ibid.* 256.

Victimisation and sentencing

Cultural perceptions about the role of victims in the trial process and sentencing

Legal culture and the broader context of the criminal process have determined the response of the Italian courts to victim conceptualisation. These factors condition the circumspection with which victim evidence is received and treated by the Italian judiciary. As pointed out earlier, there are no substantive legal reasons for excluding or restricting victim participation in decisions which inform the basis for sentencing under Article 133 CC. The position is further complicated where a civil claim is being simultaneously pursued by the injured party. Not only does this tend to reinforce the potentially prejudicial nature of victim/witness testimony for the judiciary, it also sets *state* and *individual* interests at odds

Mannozzi[137] suggests that the victim in the Italian penal system has a minimal influence on decisions regarding length of sentence. However, victims do not have a real interest in supplying relevant information spontaneously during the course of the trial. In their civil role, victims participate in the criminal trial as 'plaintiffs' with limited capacity to protect their interest in obtaining damages. The plaintiff does not have an independent right to contest the accused's acquittal, and is excluded from any sentence bargaining procedure. Furthermore, Mannozzi[138] argues that, from the perspective of the penal process, the act of compensation through damages arising from the offence is viewed as a possible source of distortion of the formal procedure. The latter is almost totally dominated by the public interest of punishing the guilty party and restoring social tranquility, not the private interest of compensating an individual for economic loss.

During the Italian trial victims provide their account almost exclusively through oral testimony. Although the injured party has status as a witness, and as such is examined during the hearing, such a witness is regarded by the judiciary with particular circumspection as substantially different from other possible witnesses, since the injured party is implicated in the criminal act (often dramatically so) and usually makes the accusation or initiates the private prosecution. Mannozzi[139] makes the point that such suspicion can be considered institutionalized, since it derives from well-entrenched judicial practice in Italy.

On the basis of these observations it may be argued that the treatment of victims in the Italian trial process and its implications for sentencing reflects the traditionally circumspect and formal way in which the inquisitorial trial has proceeded in the past; a culture which continues to pervade the approach of the Italian judiciary to victims' concerns. Furthermore, as indicated earlier, the

---

137 See Henham and Mannozzi (2003).
138 *Ibid.*
139 *Ibid.*

Italian sentencing narrative tends towards a narrower representation of the wider symbolic force of judicial discretionary power, perhaps because of the conceptual and practical uncertainties which pervade the Italian sentencing system.

The dynamics of trial interaction appear constrained by process to the extent that the symbolic aspects of sentencing relate directly to the denunciatory and retributive themes evinced by the 1930 CC. Beyond dramatisation, there is no overt judicial attempt to connect with the wider audience outside the court-room, it being implicit that what is said and described by the judges is equally well reflected in the moral values held by the general public. In other words, the legitimacy of all that is said and done by the judiciary in the name of the state remains unchallenged, as therefore is the moral authority of the judiciary.

Thus, from a legal perspective, the Italian sentencing process is typified by formalism and the restrictive judicial interpretation of procedural constraints on the appropriation of information deemed relevant to victim participation in sentencing decisions. This narrow ideology consequently delimits the appropriate terrain for victim participation in sentencing in terms of due process as well as the potential for restorative justice themes to be developed beyond any communitarian function that might be attributed to denunciation, as an aspect of retribution. The position of victims has therefore been weakened through the introduction of particular procedural reforms (some designed to further restorative concerns) within a penal context focused primarily on blame allocation, censure and proportionate punishment.[140]

In Italy such reforms are exemplified by the introduction of summary trial and sentence bargaining described earlier.[141] The primary rationale for the special proceedings introduced by the 1988 CPP appears to have been bureaucratic and managerial efficiency, since it was envisaged that the movement towards a more adversarial form of trial would make greater demands on already scarce resources.[142]

The more radical innovation of sentence bargaining under Article 444 CCP envisaged a considerable role for judicial discretion in that the accused and the prosecutor must present their negotiated sentence to the preliminary investigations judge who (in turn) must verify that the parties' determination of the applicable charge and penalty is correct. In an important decision of the Constitutional Court[143] it was held that the CCP's plea bargaining provisions were unconstitutional as a violation of the presumption of innocence, to the extent that no provision exists for judicial review of the bargain to ensure

---

140 For current perspectives on victims in the criminal process, see Del Tufo (2009) and, from the perspective of criminal procedure, Di Chiara (2009).
141 The Italian possibility of reflecting reparative concerns during the enforcement phase of the sentence has no comparable process in England, where sentence enforcement is strictly an administrative function under executive control.
142 Freccero (1994).
143 Judgment No 313, July 3, 1990, Corte cost. 35 *Giurisprudenza constituzionale* 1981 (1990).

proper balance between the crime and the bargained sentence. This decision effectively increased the judicial role in reviewing negotiated sentences in special proceedings and, as Cockayne suggests,[144] indicated an unwillingness to see sentencing discretion pass from the judge, as under the traditional inquisitorial system, to the parties themselves under the new system.[145]

As suggested, an important recent development in Italian penality has been the extension of victim–offender mediation to cases of adult crime.[146] Mannozzi discusses the theoretical justifications for this, emphasising in particular how the fundamental principles of certainty and immediacy of punishment have been systematically eroded. For example, she cites the paradox of mandatory prosecution, where, despite the fact that both the law and the Constitution provide for this, in practice public prosecutors have enormous discretionary powers. Other examples are the notoriously excessive length of many trials and the immense discretionary powers in sentencing of both the sentencing and supervisory judges, which has a destabilising effect on the perceived legitimacy of punishment.

In developing the argument that retributive and deterrent forms of punishment simply alleviate the symptoms rather than the causes of crime, and so fuel the development of more repressive forms of penality, Mannozzi points to the peculiarly paradoxical nature of the Italian experience.[147] Increasingly repressive penal laws have been accompanied by an increasing leniency in the sentencing of offenders, due to the combined effect of judges in less serious cases mitigating the effect of the harsh penalties the law provides and the problems of concluding trials within a reasonable time.

Mannozzi makes the important point that it is necessary to understand how the traditional model of the criminal law and its function has been constructed in Italian society from a historical perspective in order to appreciate the development and perception of mediatory approaches in the penal system, and more particularly how the existing office of the 'justice of the peace' came to be extended to deal with mediation and reparation for specified offences.[148] The most significant aspect of the role of the justice of the peace is the broad range of disposals available, which include mediatory and/or reparative measures, deflective solutions or punitive measures. However, as Mannozzi suggests,[149] the justification for reparative measures in terms of censure and

---

144 Cockayne (2002).
145 This trend is exemplified by the reforms instituted on 28 August 2000 (effective from 2 January 2002) which awarded a new penal competence to the Justice of the Peace. However, in this case the shift in discretionary power is more towards the police of penal prosecution governed by the principle of legality; Cockayne (2002).
146 See Mannozzi (2003).
147 *Ibid.* 286.
148 *Ibid.* 287. Article 274 of 28 August 2000, which came into effect in January 2002. It is important to note that justices of the peace are not professional career judges but honorary members of the judiciary whose civil jurisdiction has been extended to the criminal sphere as part of the strategy to reduce the backlog of cases.
149 *Ibid.* 291.

prevention, and the use of the power to temporarily suspend the trial to facilitate reparative conduct on the part of the offender, has proved problematic because of the unverifiable nature of the discretionary powers given to the judges and the absence of any agreement as to the meaning of these two concepts. Similarly, the use of deflective measures under Article 273 is severely constrained by the justificatory criteria contained in the sentencing model provided by Articles 132 and 133 of the 1930 Penal Code.[150]

Despite the operational problems associated with mediation, especially in terms of monitoring and control, Mannozzi highlights the ambivalence surrounding the underlying purpose of these processes, especially the fact that mediation can be seen both in punitive and rehabilitative terms.[151] Referring to Picotti's[152] description of mediation as an expression of the need to promote the 'rehabilitation of a correct model of social relationships', Mannozzi raises the fundamental issue of legitimacy; more particularly, the extent to which, as Cohen has argued,[153] measures which appear to support rehabilitative and restorative objectives are in fact a thinly disguised way of extending the reach of criminal justice for hegemonic purposes of social control.

Deconstructing evidence for sentencing

The pre-trial stage

One significant change from the former code is the separation between the investigative and the judicial function during the preliminary phase, the former being carried out by the public prosecutor and the latter by a judge appointed for the purpose. This has had an important impact on the evidence collected for trial. It is interesting to note that if the judge is unhappy with the Prosecutor's decision to ask for a dismissal, the victim may intervene at this stage and request the Prosecutor to carry out further investigations.

However, more significant is the change that has occurred in the way the Prosecutor collects evidence. Instead of gathering both inculpatory and exculpatory evidence in an impartial way, as under the old code, the Prosecutor is no longer tasked to pursue the search for 'truth' in his investigations but is made a partisan party to the proceedings. In other words, he is no longer collecting evidence 'on behalf of the person under investigation'.[154] Consequently, once satisfied there is a case to answer, the Prosecutor is not obliged to look for any exculpatory evidence.

---

150 This provision is progressive, to the extent that the victim has a participatory role through the ability to veto the decision not to impose a sanction made at the beginning of the sentencing phase of the trial.
151 Mannozzi (2003) 293.
152 Picotti (1998) 312.
153 Cohen (1985).
154 Grande (2000) 234, at footnote 20.

As Grande points out,[155] however, in the Italian context the idea that the 'truth' will somehow emerge from two partisan accounts through the adversarial contest where both parties are equally matched is flawed. The reason is that the power disparity of the preliminary stage is reproduced at trial. Thanks to a decision of the Constitutional Court,[156] the probative value of the preliminary stage evidence has been widened instead of narrowed, as originally intended. Hence, secretly gathered and partial evidence can find its way before the trial court.[157] Furthermore, the grounds for allowing out-of-court witness statements to be admitted have been widened where the witness has been the object of violence, threats or undue influence, so making witnesses reluctant to testify at trial. Finally, the fact of the suspect's silence in response to the Prosecutor's request to submit to an interrogation will be entered on the preliminary interrogation record and so may, upon a party's request, find its way before the trial proper, since it will be admitted as having full probative value.

The preliminary hearing is essentially document-based and takes place in camera (its purpose being to select cases for trial), thereby allowing the accused to adduce any exculpatory evidence relevant to that, and facilitate possible trial alternatives (such as sentence bargains). The latter receive full disclosure, unlike what generally occurs in the common law world.[158]

The trial stage

The combined effect of Articles 111 and 27, paragraph 2 of the Italian Constitution and Article 533 of the CCP is to impose very stringent controls on the judge as regards the evidence. The first two articles provide that the accused is considered not guilty until the pronunciation of a definitive conviction based upon evidence produced in a cross-examination between the parties. Correspondingly, Article 533 provides that the judge must convict the accused only when he or she is found criminally responsible beyond all reasonable doubt.

These elements of construction and evaluation of the evidence ensure that the accused may participate personally in the formation of the proofs of evidence and be protected from possible irregularities which may have occurred in the previous phase. However, these elements also make the trial very slow and lengthy,[159] thereby exposing the whole system to censorship from the European Court of Human Rights and to doubts of constitutionality. In particular, this may produce conflict between Article 6 of the ECHR and

---

155 *Ibid.*, 235.
156 *Ibid.*, 238.
157 See, further, Salas (2002) 514–15.
158 Grande (2000) 243.
159 Moretti's analysis of the 1998 ISTAT (Italian National Institute for Statistics) data for cases of sexual assault noted that the average length of time between commission of the crime and sentence was 34 months (with 29.8 per cent of cases taking over 3 years), with further extensions for appeals of 60 months from the date of the crime; see Moretti (2002).

Article 111 of the Italian Constitution, which provides that the law has to define reasonable time limits for proceedings.

Generally, it is important to remember that there is no distinction made between issues of guilt and sentencing, so, unlike in common law systems, there is no bifurcated hearing. In more serious cases, there is a single body of adjudicators consisting of professional judges and lay assessors because there is no need for any distinction to be made between judge and jury

The factual basis for sentencing

Unlike the previous model, the Prosecutor's pre-trial dossier is not available to the trial judge, who receives all evidence in its original form to satisfy the 'immediacy' principle. The only files the judge receives (Article 431 CCP) are the charging documents, physical evidence connected with the crime, the *incidente probatorio* record, the accused's prior criminal record, civil claim documents, and any police or prosecutorial evidence it is impossible to replicate.

The previous inquisitorial system ensured that matters of fact and proof were officially controlled, with the evidence being assembled by judges and other impartial officials and produced in court by the trial judge; under the new adversarial system the parties present the evidence through the process of calling witnesses and examining them. Because there is no bifurcated trial process, and so no separate jury tasked to determine what counts as facts, the order of evidence production is more flexible than in an adversarial trial. As stated, the victim's potential status and possible participation as *partie civile* is important from an evidential perspective, especially since, as an injured party, the victim can apply to become a co-plaintiff together with the Prosecutor.

Also significant is the trial judge's capacity to examine proof *sua sponte* if not completely satisfied. As Grande explains,[160] the Constitutional Court has widened the ambit of this originally narrow exception, which existed to prevent the partisan use of evidence and was only to be used 'whenever absolutely necessary'. This encouragement of judicial activism has been widely criticised, since the official adducing of evidence is likely to upset the principle of equality between the parties if subject to abuse. Others have argued that this kind of judicial discretion is necessary to protect the interests of the parties where prosecutors may be unjustifiably tempted to drop cases with weak evidence. Grande makes the interesting point that it was the Italian inquisitorial attitude of hostility to officially manufactured 'truth' which transformed what was really meant as an exceptional judicial power into a springboard for wider and unfettered judicial activism.

There are several additional important evidential points made by Grande.[161] One is that exclusionary rules are not designed to insulate triers of

---

160 Grande (2000) 245.
161 *Ibid.* 247–48.

fact from the impact of admissible evidence, as in common law jurisdictions, where there is a jury. There is no bifurcated trial in Italy. Secondly, in Italy the parties have little control over the rules of evidence. Whereas in common law trials they can object if they feel adversely affected by the application of the rules, through objecting to the judge, who rules in an impartial manner, the Italian principle preventing the partisan presentation of evidence means that objections require official sanction and can be raised at any stage in the proceedings. Therefore, the parties may not use the rules to play the adversarial contest (Article 191 CCP).

Significantly, unless inadmissible or clearly superfluous, Article 190 CCP stipulates that the trial judge *must* admit all evidence presented to the parties. This has interesting implications for determining the factual basis for sentencing, which should be read in the context of Articles 132 and 133 CCP. Certainly, Grande concludes[162] that judicial control over the evidential process is considerable. She refers to their greater sense of personal responsibility as triers of law and fact, which, together with Italy's long civil law tradition, accounts for the extensive judicial activism of Italian courts and judges.

One of the most significant practical implications of the separation of verdict and sentence for victim integration concerns the need for evidence to be reconstructed to serve the purposes of the sentencing phase.[163] However, this phenomenon may also take place within any integrated model. In Italy, for example, specific criteria establish the boundaries for the exercise of discretionary power relevant to sentence, but it is witness testimony elicited during the trial phase that is evaluated against these legal constraints.[164]

Similarly, the rights accorded to victims under Article 90 CCP are directed towards the trial (verdict and sentence) rather than to sentence. Such a model should also be integrated in the sense that the rationale, policy and procedure governing the exercise of judicial discretion for the purposes of verdict and sentence should reflect and relate to one another. As suggested, this has not occurred with Italian sentencing. In a sense, what has transpired in Italy reflects the fundamental tensions which occur in purely adversarial systems; ultimately, the ideology of traditional criminal law theory and its core principles of certainty, predictability and consistency are problematic where

---

162 *Ibid.* 249.

163 In England, the difficulties caused by the need to establish the factual basis for sentencing are a direct result of the division of the trial into two distinct phases. In particular, evidence relevant to sentence (such as provocation) may not be sufficiently explored, even during a full trial. Where the offender pleads guilty these difficulties are exacerbated, since the prosecution and defence accounts of the facts may differ considerably.

164 Judicial deliberations follow immediately after the close of the trial and, after considering any unresolved preliminary matter and/or procedural issues, judges must consider each issue of fact or law, *as well as the proper sentence*. Needless to say, abbreviated proceedings and procedures that facilitate sentence bargaining distort the extent to which the facts upon which sentence is based actually correspond with those that occurred.

consequentialist and utilitarian justifications also constitute primary rationales for punishment. The failure of adversarial systems to integrate these
diverse purposes within trial ideology and practice has meant that questions
of procedural fairness and rights protection have assumed particular (and
possibly disproportionate) significance and deflected attention away from
what is a fundamental underlying weakness.

*How the requirements relating to verdict, previous convictions and evidential
disputes affect sentencing*

To summarise, the conviction must prove the responsibility of the accused
beyond any reasonable doubt. This principle implies that the judge must
explain why he or she thinks that the evidence against the accused is well
founded or not. The evaluation of evidence is governed by the principle of so
called 'free evaluation' of evidence by the judge. This means that the judge
does not have to follow specific rules in the evaluation of the evidence; any
piece of evidence can be chosen as the basis of the decision, as long as its
evaluation is supported by logical reasons.

As for the relevance of the previous convictions, recent reforms[165] have
imposed stricter bounds on the judge's discretionary power in the choice of
the sentence. In particular, the existence of previous convictions can:

(i)   result in a higher sentence;
(ii)   prevent access by the offender to alternative measures than imprison-
       ment; and
(iii) prevent the judge from suspending the sentence and from taking
       account of mitigating and aggravating circumstances.

Access to justice, rights and accountability

The victim plays a very limited role in the Italian criminal process. Before the
institution of criminal proceeding, a victim's rights are limited to soliciting an
investigation, producing documents, challenging the prosecutor's decision to
dismiss a case, and supplying new evidence, thereby obliging the prosecution
to investigate further to establish whether the new evidence is factually accurate.

During the trial proper the victim plays an ancillary role to the prosecution,
since the latter is the only subject who can instigate criminal action against an
individual. A somewhat different system has recently been introduced for
some minor offences. In such cases the victim plays a great role in deciding
whether to prosecute the offender. However, the victim is also mandated to
take part in any attempt at judicial conciliation, which takes place before the
prosecution brings proceedings against the offender.

---

165 For a comparative survey, see Roberts (2008b) ch. 5.

Punishment and sentencing as governance

More recently, pubic opinion has been oriented towards demanding greater severity of punishment and a more effective application of sentences. However, most public concern appears to be directed, not so much at the excessive severity of punishments inflicted on offenders, but rather at the perceived excessive leniency of certain sentences.[166] The legislature has responded to this demand by imposing limits on judicial discretionary power in cases where public opinion appears more sensitive, such as those involving minor offences committed by immigrants or recidivists, and in cases of organised crime. Chiavario's point about the significance of the large numbers of appeals against conviction in Italy when compared to England is relevant here, in the sense that it to some extent overcompensates for the perceived severity of the Italian penal system and an absence of trust in the guarantees underpinning the trial.[167]

Conclusion

A significant measure of legitimacy, particularly in France and Italy, is the degree to which Enlightenment philosophy continues to exert its influence on penal ideology.[168] Its fundamental tenets for the administration of penal justice may be summarised in the following principles:

- The function of penal law should be to re-assert through punishment the 'appropriate' balance where citizens' rights have been infringed by 'crime'.
- It should also be utilitarian in accepting the need to limit retributive penalties to the extent necessary to protect society from future crimes being committed by the offender and to deter others.

The rationale for attaching such significance to the moral foundations of Enlightenment penality is rooted in the notion of the social contract. This emphasised the need for the criminal process to serve the interests of all citizens, rather than the partisan objectives of a small powerful elite, as hitherto.

---

166 In this connection, Pavarini (2001) 414, 415 makes the following important observations:

> The interesting phenomenon to grasp is not the antinomy between severe legislation and lenient sentencing, but the social conditions responsible for an excessive severity 'in words' and a paternalistic clemency in practice ... A culture of suspicion and diffidence has [thus] been far more resistant to the dangers of repressive agencies than the dangers of crime ... collective feelings of insecurity have been expressed as a political demand for change and more intense democratic participation ... In other words, social communication via the language of politics has fostered a social construct of insecurity and conflict outside the moral categories of guilt and punishment.

167 Chiavario (2002).
168 The reason is that the Englightenment reforms reflected a clear consensus about the role of criminal justice and the normative framework needed to facilitate it.

Its communitarian morality was entrenched in the social contract's broad-based agreement about the nature of democratic values and how structures of governance should be configured in order to facilitate them. Despite ignoring the social causes of inequality and its impact on free will, Enlightenment philosophy produced a clear framework of principles for distributive justice based on universally accepted moral values about the purposes of punishment and how they should be implemented.

The unfettered use of judicial discretionary power, especially in sentencing, was deemed to pose a direct threat to citizens' rights of 'equality' before the law, yet, paradoxically, such discretion also provided the means for recognising different levels of accountability for crime by citizens. The exploitation by successive governments of the state's function to reflect this accountability in fair and equitable principles for punishment has become commonplace and disguises a more fundamental failure to remedy the causes of criminality. In other words, the sentencing process perpetuates a narrow conception of moral culpability that is circumscribed by retributive and deterrent concerns. This has come to define the social reality of citizens' 'rights' to penal equality, yet it ignores social context, especially the relationship between individual and collective notions of responsibility and how this should be mirrored in penal ideology and practice.

Beginning with the Code Napoleon of 1810, the increasing influence of judicial discretionary power in France has reflected the hegemony of penal law. This has been characterised by greater sentencing severity, the increased use of custody, and the identification and repression of minorities. Correspondingly, there has been a greater focus on moral responsibility, evidenced in the notion of culpability and its realisation through the individualisation of punishments.

The relationship between offence gravity and individual moral culpability is still framed by a retributive dynamic in both France and Italy, and, therefore, so is the ideological context for exercising sentencing discretion. Constitutional imperatives for penalties to engage with rehabilitation are marginalised by a persistent failure to develop more contemporary rationalisations for imposing punishment.

In France, the ideological context for individualisation was broadened in the post-war rehabilitative era by arguments that reform and rehabilitation were appropriate social responses to criminality. However, the moral basis for this justification, as elsewhere, was severely undermined when the effectiveness of the response was exposed as weak. However, the concept of social response remains firmly rooted in the justificatory language of punishment. Unfortunately, the politics of social control have become increasingly out of step with communitarian notions of social defence through moral diversification and diverging expectations of the penal system. In addition, politicians have increasingly relied on surveys and public opinion polls to provide them with an impression of what citizens need and expect, and have consequently become unable or unwilling to establish a coherent ideology for 'rights' in terms of what citizens 'really' need and expect from the state.

Paradoxically, in inquisitorial systems, a further latent threat to penal legitimacy stems from a weakening in the constitutional independence of the prosecutor, through political compromise of prosecutorial control over crucial decision-making sites before, during and after the trial. In the post-modern era the intended social function of prosecutorial independence has become increasingly opaque in consequence of the growing distance between state and citizen. This social distance may be measured in terms of the divide that exists between the rhetoric of social egalitarianism extolled by the political elite and the social reality of everyday life in terms of criminal victimisation and its disproportionate experience within specific communities. Hence, clear notions of 'rights' and 'freedoms' for citizens that the independent prosecutorial function was established to defend against political hegemony are no longer meaningful in terms of the social realities of citizens' lives.

In both France and Italy, for example, implicating the victim in the drive for trial expediency has given such procedures a false validity, since in neither case have these so-called innovations been underpinned by linking their use to what victims and diverse communities need and expect in terms of trial justice. The adverse consequences of the failure to integrate such 'reforms' within the existing penal framework have been felt most keenly in Italy.

The traditionally limited requirements for justifying the sentence are a characteristic of inquisitorial systems that militates against the development of a coherent set of principles for distributive justice. In particular, it obscures the need for clarity about the criteria that should distinguish between offence and offender circumstances, and the appropriate balance that should be drawn between them for sentencing purposes. The continuation of this tendency emphasises the controlling influence of the judiciary and its reluctance to cede discretionary power in accordance with the foundation ideals of the social contract. Hence, the fact that there may be a constitutional obligation on the part of judges to justify the exercise of their discretionary powers when sentencing is no guarantee that they can engage with the social reality of crime and punishment.

As in England and Wales, it may be argued that the strengthening of judicial discretionary power in France provides a bulwark against the excessive politicisation of punishment. However, it is equally true to say that the widening of judicial discretionary power may be self-serving[169] and counter-productive to the development of more inclusive forms of penalty, unless such power is able to engage with communitarian conceptions of 'justice' in ways that the 'responsible' and 'protective' state has manifestly failed to achieve.

The inquisitorial judge's power to direct and shape the trial process within an appropriately communitarian penal framework has greater potential for achieving this goal that its adversarial counterpart. As the hybridisation of trial styles has illustrated, especially in the context of international structures

---

169 As Pavarini (2001) suggests, in the case of Italy the legitimacy of this is perceived by many to be inherently partisan and socially divisive.

such as the ICC, there must first be an agreed non-partisan strategy for identifying 'interests' and a normative framework for trial and sentence that is capable of responding effectively to them.

Regrettably, the capacity of trial and sentence to engage fully with communitarian interests has narrowed in both common and civil law systems. In France and Italy the ubiquity of the trial has been reduced through crime control considerations designed to expedite the criminal process, whilst the trial itself has been primarily reserved for the most serious cases. The so-called informalisation of justice has also resulted in the expansion of alternative resolution mechanisms, such as mediation. Increasing the responsibilities of the Prosecutor with regard to the trial's broader social function, particularly the impact of punishment, may serve to secure the trial's legitimacy more effectively in the eyes of citizens in the light of these developments.

Nonetheless, the overriding threat to penal legitimacy in England and Wales, France and Italy remains the overt politicisation of penal policy, especially through the stigmatisation and oppression of demonised categories of offender,[170] or particular groups and communities.[171] Arguably, the danger with this trend is that states which have become detached from democratic values, where the moral foundations of the rule of law have been weakened, may increasingly come to regard penal policy as a suitable vehicle for social engineering, by legitimating socially divisive and repressive policies. In addition, media portrayal of certain social groups as inadequate, socially unstable or otherwise diverging from so-called 'mainstream' social values, may feed into the negative public perception of these groups and subsequently into sentencing decisions. A drift towards the social reality of the quasi-totalitarian state may be facilitated through penal justice where a state distorts the rationales for punishment to divert attention from the fact that it no longer has a moral mandate for enforcing the rule of law.

---

170 Such as so-called 'dangerous' offenders.
171 A significant recent example concerns the Roma of Italy; see EurActiv (2009);   Bianchi, Buonanno and Pinotti (2008); and BBC News (2009).

9 Punishment and Sentencing as Governance

The pervading theme of this book has been the development of a more normative perspective for conceptualising criminal justice that will enable us to comprehend the significance of punishment and sentencing more effectively in an increasingly pluralistic world. I have argued that this is necessary in order that penal policy-makers can respond more effectively to questions about the legitimacy of trial justice and its relevance as a pivotal aspect of criminal justice governance. In consequence, it is hoped the ideologies and structures of penal law will take greater account of the increasingly diverse views about the legitimacy of trial justice that pervade societies in the late post-modern period, and so enable sentence decision-makers to respond more appropriately to the expectations they engender.

The discussion has sought to explain why it is becoming increasingly difficult for sentencing to engage with the justice aspirations and expectations of such competing moral constituencies at the global and local level, and also considered the extent to which existing justifications and structures for the delivery of trial justice are equipped to do this. In short, my objective has been to establish that lack of 'legitimacy' is an emerging and significant problem for sentencing which requires new forms of theorising and evaluation.

The preceding chapters have explored this issue in detail by focusing on core aspects of sentencing, particularly how the relationship between sentencing decisions and perceptions of justice impacts on social reality. In addition, the conceptual model developed in chapter 2 has emphasised the recursive nature of trial justice and its relationship to the governance role of criminal justice, especially the capacity of trial outcomes to change perceptions and behaviour and its subsequent impact on penal ideology and policy.

However, the challenge has not simply been one of conceptualising this process. The focus has been on developing a greater understanding of the connections between trial justice and its *actual* effects. This is seen as crucial if we are to come to terms with explaining the social consequences of criminal justice. This is essentially a normative question. For this reason, the book has argued strongly that the development of a more normative perspective for theory should be co-extensive with the development of appropriate methodologies, such as comparative contextual analysis, which facilitate contextualised accounts of the social reality of such processes across time and space. Since the phenomenon of penal legitimacy is essentially relative, this book has suggested how current conceptualisations of punishment and sentencing might be strengthened to provide a normative framework for its understanding within different jurisdictional settings.

Relative justice and governance

Commonality in sentencing

Sentencing is concerned with deciding what to do with those who have infringed legal norms. Although the latter do not necessarily reflect moral norms, they may overlap. The common factor is that the infringement of behavioural norms is punished in some way.

Theories and methodologies of criminal justice tend to essentialise human beings.[1] This affects our understandings of how they live and how their behaviours are responded to. However, comparison is a matter of acknowledging relativity: understanding its effects, and then seeking commonality. Stripping away those things that constitute relativity (those factors that vary according to context), such as culture, society, history, and appreciating their meaning, may help us to identify and comprehend the essentials of any particular human activity.[2]

For criminal justice, research may include exploring the social construction of deviance[3] and collective responses to it, how deviance is particularised through jurisdictional forms, and the extent to which those forms have commonality. In the case of sentencing, it may be argued that commonalities arise from the fact that similar behaviours are criminalised and punished for similar reasons, and that similar effects occur wherever and whenever this takes place. These are essentially problems of justification and response. However, such generalisations fail to take into account the influence of context in shaping social reality.

Therefore, provided the inherent difficulties of comparative analysis can be addressed satisfactorily, structural processes such as sentencing, which are jurisdictionally specific and diverse, and the rationalisations which underpin

---

1 This tendency has been noted especially in the context of seeking accountability for mass atrocity; see, for example, Clark (2008).
2 As Simon also points out, it is often imagined risk – the possibility of victimisation – that shapes the response of the political community and the terrain of governable interests. The creation of the 'crime victim' has provided states with a metaphor justifying the territorialisation of communities where retributive rationality can be given its full effect; Simon (2002) 1042–43.
3 Cf. Becker's argument that an act only becomes deviant if reacted to; Becker (1973).

them, may be evaluated in terms of their comparability and influence, whether as vertical, horizontal or hybridised systems of social control.[4]

Dispelling myths

Recognising relationships of influence

I suggest that in order to grasp the significance of criminal justice as elemental to governance it is necessary to appreciate vertical and horizontal relationships of influence as between systems. Although there will necessarily be system differences, my argument for focusing on synergy rather than diversity transcends debates concerning differences of form and process, or their particularly exclusive cultural manifestations. As I have indicated, the drive for synergy and the unifying force for governance is the belief that, for criminal justice to be effective beyond mere symbolism (at whatever level), depends upon recognising the need for a new kind of penal ideology, where the rationality for action is achieving a greater measure of social legitimacy – for sentencing outcomes especially.

The synergy between localised and internationalised forms of criminal justice cannot easily be dismissed. It is also important to note that currently the implications of such relationships, whether in terms of form, process or influence, are not necessarily beneficial. The reasons for this are complex, but I would argue that the question of legitimacy, in terms of how justice is perceived as fair and appropriate, is a crucial factor. However, the fundamental point to recognise at the outset is that such links do in fact exist.

A useful illustration of how the relationship between local and internationalised criminal justice agendas could compromise legitimacy is provided by European Union laws on counter terrorism and international crime under its third pillar, which include the power for the European Union to force

---

4 The crucial point is to devise credible methodologies that allow us to recognise and understand the meaning of those factors that particularise the definition of behaviours as deviance/crime, and the response of law and process. These issues are explored in greater depth in Findlay and Henham (2005). The authors' methodology of comparative contextual analysis focuses on the form and reasons for influence on sentencing decisions in different jurisdictional contexts, depending on judge and court level. It aims to facilitate our understanding of the forces that are at work in the relationship and how they relate to (or work against) each other. In this way it becomes possible to identify how different pathways of influence produce different configurations of fact/value whose practical effects are manifested in greater or lesser participation for victims in those aspects of the trial process that are relevant for victims and sentence. Accepting the possibility of meaningful comparative contextual analysis does not, of course, deal with the manifold objections that could conceivably be raised against the virtue of such comparisons. These concern particularly questions relating to the appropriateness of vertical comparisons between local and global forms of criminal justice. Such objections typically rely on the argument that doctrinal and cultural differences render futile any comparison of punishment rationales and sentencing practice. See, for example, Sloane (2007).

member states to impose mandatory minimum sentences for various offence of terrorism, as defined.[5] Leaving aside the political ramifications of these developments, their significance for criminal justice governance and judicial sentencing in particular cannot be overstated. In the English context, the external imposition of what amounts to criminal sentencing guidelines would not only breach the principle of state sovereignty in matters of punishment, it would also constitute a direct interference with the constitutional convention of judicial independence, amounting to another significant restriction on the ability of the English judiciary to exercise their discretionary powers in sentencing.

No doubt it may be argued that the need for political solidarity in the face of the 'war on terror' and the perceived collective threat to the security of European Union member states requires such overt control of sentence decision-making. However, the implications for sentencing, and the governance of criminal justice more generally, are potentially much more sinister, since behind the symbolism of the collective condemnatory messages such sentences would purportedly deliver there is little, if any, evidence that such politically centralised manipulation of state penality is necessary[6] in the face of what amounts to an unquantifiable risk.[7]

It is equally important to consider the reciprocal nature of relationships of influence within systems, whether horizontal or vertical. Whilst much of the focus is on how sentencers should or could respond more effectively to victims or communitarian expectations for justice, less attention is devoted to the ways in which issues of immediate and broader social concern actually impact on the approach to decision-making.[8] In the domestic context, for example, research by Parker, Sumner and Jarvis in 1989[9] illustrated clearly that

---

5 Sections 111 and 112 of the Anti-Terrorism, Crime and Security Act 2001 enables the UK Government to give effect to the third pillar through passing secondary legislation. See, more generally, Baker (2009), and Henham (2000b) for a discussion of similar difficulties in the context of sentencing dangerous offenders.

6 Significantly, paragraph IV.49.26 of the Consolidated Criminal Practice Direction (Life Sentences) suggests a higher starting point of 15/16 years where the offender's culpability is high or the victim particularly vulnerable, such cases being characterised by a number of features, such as the fact that the killing was politically motivated (undefined). Further, by virtue of paragraph IV.49.32, so-called 'very serious cases' involving, for example, multiple murders, might attract a minimum term of 30 years, or life if of exceptional depravity. The most important guidance concerning judicial discretion is to be found in paragraphs IV.49.27–31 which detail relevant aggravating and mitigating factors that might allow the sentencing judge to vary the suggested starting point upwards or downwards; these relate to either the offender or the offence in each particular case. The Consolidated Criminal Practice Direction may be accessed at http://www.justice. gov.uk/criminal/procrules_fin/contents/practice_direction/pd_consolidated.htm (accessed 2011).

7 See, in particular, Lucia Zedner's discussion about the balance between security and liberty; Zedner (2005); Mythen and Walklate (2005) 389, suggesting that 'understandings of terrorism are being discursively shaped by the agencies involved in risk definition'; Findlay (2007).

8 A notable exception is Hogarth's early work on the relationship between the penal philosophies of Canadian magistrates and community characteristics; Hogarth (1971).

9 Parker, Sumner and Jarvis (1989).

magistrates were highly sensitive to 'public opinion' and media representations of so-called 'crime problems'. Whilst they constructed their own perceptions, these tended to justify particular patterns of sentencing, rather than constituting a particular explanation of individual sentencing decisions.[10] Different perceptions of crime were also more likely to be associated with the social characteristics of an area, rather than any objective considerations regarding the extent and character of crime.[11] Consequently, magistrates saw themselves as maintaining the 'balance' between public interests and those of the offender as perceived. Although this appeared to be linked to the pattern of custodial sentencing, it was not necessarily associated with local or national sentencing policy.[12]

Arguably, the influence of the media in shaping perceptions of crime and crime problems has increased significantly in recent years, alongside the increasingly morally pluralistic society of the post-modern state. Correspondingly, the alleged inability of judges and magistrates to provide an appropriately 'balanced' response to crime has been more easily exploited by politicians in framing penal policy, especially where, as Tonry, points out,[13] the dangers to liberty represented by excessive judicial discretion are substantial. Instead, I have argued that the key should lie in turning these relationships of influence into relationships of trust. Ideally, this process should be informed by principles of equality and tolerance and founded upon commonly accepted communitarian values of individual and social responsibility. Relationships of trust will not necessarily be achieved through steps aimed at ensuring that sentencers are more socially representative, desirable though this may be, or through the incremental reduction of sentencing discretion. Rather, it will depend upon a broadening of the moral discourse that informs penal ideology towards objectives aimed at fostering social cohesion, so providing a more constructive role for punishment and sentencing in criminal justice governance.

Recognising commonality

As regards international criminal justice, I would argue that the notion that it is a phenomenon that has emerged *de novo*, and so is completely unrelated to localised forms of justice, is fallacious. For example, the foundation instruments of the United Nations International Criminal Tribunals for the Former Yugoslavia (ICTY) and Rwanda (ICTR) represent a long process of compromise and the hybridisation of adversarial and inquisitorial criminal process and procedure. In addition, both the ICTY and ICTR have to refer to local penal laws;[14] and,

---

10 *Ibid.* 79.
11 *Ibid.* 82.
12 *Ibid.* 85.
13 Tonry (2002).
14 See Schabas (2006) ch. 11.

their international judiciary are drawn from across a wide spectrum representing all shades of trial tradition.[15]

As far as the International Criminal Court (ICC) is concerned, the principle of complementarity operates to regulate its jurisdiction through strict conditions of admissibility,[16] which, if unfulfilled, leave national systems free to investigate and prosecute offences over which the Court would otherwise have jurisdiction. McGoldrick suggests[17] that the structural relationship between the ICC and national courts is best conceived at a horizontal level. In consequence, he argues that the potential for further obfuscation of the purposes and normative principles which will in future govern the sentencing of those convicted of 'the most serious crimes of international concern' will be even greater than currently exists with the *ad hoc* tribunals.[18]

The fact that international criminal justice deals with crimes of a different order from localised or state-administered systems of criminal justice is another argument frequently deployed against the desirability of drawing comparisons between the two.[19] After all, international crimes are defined collectively; are much more serious; and, are more to do with ensuring that those who are responsible for perpetrating gross violations of human rights are punished. International courts are generally not concerned with the typical

---

15 See Pakes (2004) ch. 8. Interestingly, Pakes supports the moral injunction to 'truth-finding', implicit in the inquisitorial-style tradition, as a desirable force for the gradual transformation of ICTY trial procedure that would not threaten impartiality. However, there is a broader dimension to the analysis of judicial discretionary behaviour that needs to be taken into account. This is the implicit notion that the variation and transformation of trial style is an autonomous process. In other words, Pakes treats the legal and social characteristics of sentencers and their impact on discretionary decision-making as independent rather than dependant variables. However, sentencers (as do all trial actors) utilise normative codes instrumentally as negotiatiors and transformers of factual information, attributing value to factual assertions at various decision-making sites integral to the trial process. They do not operate in an ideological or normative vacuum. Consequently, it is necessary to consider the nature of the decision-making process and its significance for sentencing. Firstly, discretionary decision-making is a product of the interaction of many complex variables – a unique experience, the description and explanation of which, and the extent to which conclusions can be generalised, being dependant upon the epistemological persuasion of the observer. Secondly, as soon as we accept the notion of discretionary decision-making as being instrumental (as Pakes does), it must be recognised that we are investing the notion of 'truth' with some legitimacy; we are saying that not only is the pursuit of 'truth' a desirable objective for international trial process to move towards, but also that there must exist some measure(s) whereby the 'legitimacy' of what is accepted as 'truth' can be measured. If so, it must then be asked whose 'truth' is being negotiated and manufactured within the wide discretionary parameters provided by the normative codes of international trial instruments.

16 Article 17, ICC Statute.

17 McGoldrick (1999).

18 This is due to the fact that both the ICTY (Article 9) and ICTR (Article 8) assert the primacy of their respective tribunals over national jurisdictions.

19 Fletcher and Weinstein (2002), Tallgren (2002) 561.

criminal activity of state criminal justice, and therefore the same kinds of justifications for punishment cannot be relevant.[20]

Drumbl argues[21] further that states or powerful groups within states may be inherently undemocratic, so that transitional justice cannot necessarily be expected to correct power imbalances; for example, those in Rwanda, having their roots in tribal cultures that have persisted over centuries.[22] Nevertheless, it may be possible to strengthen institutional structures and process by developing ties of horizontal and vertical trust among citizens, so that there gradually emerges a willingness on the part of all citizens to place trust in achieving common political objectives, protected by a strengthened framework of fundamental rights.[23]

Absence of trust, resulting from a failure of the democratic process to meet the legitimate aspirations of citizens is of equal concern in the context of local criminal justice. As argued, in such circumstances criminal justice governance merely reinforces the social differentiation and exclusory policies of partisan political power. Such divisions can far too readily find their way into the cultural and social fabric of a society, becoming so deeply ingrained as to provide a cause of war and social conflict for decades into the future. Building relationships of trust with excluded and alienated social groups is a necessary precursor to restoring legitimacy to criminal justice, as is the need for effective participative rights, where regarded as necessary to promote this objective.

Of course, there are significant differences in the nature of criminalised activity dealt with by international and local forms of criminal justice, but that is not the point. All criminalised activity represents behaviour that has been identified and labelled as a form of deviance. Whatever the behaviour in question, the ideologies, structures and outcomes which together constitute the penal apparatus of criminal justice reflect moral judgements about that

---

20 Cockayne (2001) proposes two models of trial process suggesting differences between in the social reality of international trial justice in terms of victim participation and its symbolism:

> In one [model], represented through the rhetoric of the Prosecutor and the official spokespeople of the Tribunals, victims and witnesses are central actors in the trial process. The Tribunal is, according to this model, there as a mouthpiece, a chance for their voices to be heard, for them to participate in the formation of the historical record and to ensure that these crimes are not forgotten. This model suggests a sociological role for the trial process which is not often ascribed to domestic criminal trials. The Tribunals are a tool for the *construction* of an international civil order ... In contrast, domestic criminal trials are rarely justified in these terms, as contributing to the construction of the domestic public order. Instead, they are conceived as enforcing that order. The second model for the Tribunals' trial process is more like that. It treats victims and witnesses as instruments in the Prosecutor's quest for a conviction. Protective and rehabilitative measures are not conceived as an integral part of the Tribunals' performance of their mandates, reconstructing civil order, but as instrumental measures designed to ensure victim participation and the ability of the Tribunal to function [emphasis in original].

21 Drumbl (2005) 598
22 See Alvarez (1999), Aukerman (2002).
23 See International Centre for Transitional Justice (2006).

behaviour. They address fundamental questions about why behaviour should be punished; how punishment should be inflicted; and, what objectives it is hoped punishment will achieve.

As abstract principles, justifications for punishment may claim universal moral validity. They embody values that are conceptually distinct from their actual manifestation in the 'real' world. The argument about legitimacy in criminal justice is therefore one that is conducted at the intersection of value and fact. It exists in punishment at the precise moment where law and morality meet. Legitimacy and penal law's consequent claim to authority is therefore derived from the extent to which individuals and entities claiming dominion over them (such as sovereign states) *effectively* promote civil society by protecting individuals against those behaviours which threaten them.

Conceptualising justice

Identifying the fundamentals of legitimacy

The legitimacy of criminal justice, whether global or local, depends upon the validity of its moral claim to dominion. This is not simply a truism or tautology, because, as argued earlier, the nexus for scrutinising the link between the morality of punishment and its social reality – where fact and value is negotiated on behalf of (and for) individuals and communities – is the criminal process itself, and the sentencing decisions it produces.

Elsewhere Mark Findlay and I have argued[24] that the moral value of the criminal process lies in its capacity to deliver what are perceived to be 'legitimate' outcomes by those who demand 'justice' and have a recognised 'interest' in doing so. Since the need to resolve social conflict is intrinsic to the human condition, it imbues penal rationality with a communitarian purpose. Hence, judicial discretionary power could be mobilised within such a context to pursue outcomes aimed at restoring the autonomy of individuals within societies or social groups by recognising and working towards their aspirations for justice. Such aspirations may be individual or collective, in the sense that trial outcomes are morally relevant to both victimised individuals and groups within civil society. Conceptualising justice as humanitarian in this way provides a moral foundation for transforming the criminal trial and increasing its capacity for justice delivery. It emphasises those values that promote peace and social solidarity within communities, such as respect for human dignity, compassion and adherence to social norms.

Of course, these arguments run counter to those who, like Sloane,[25] envisage a somewhat diminished role for international sentencing in post-conflict justice. In advocating the virtues of expressivism as the rationale for international

---

24 Findlay and Henham (2005).
25 Sloane (2007).

punishment, Sloane provides a very restricted interpretation of the significance of 'legitimacy' in the context of international sentencing outcomes:

> The expressive value of a sentence, its *legitimacy and authority*, depends on the extent to which it both embodies the moral and legal norms of the *authorising* community and fits the circumstances of the offender in light of those norms [emphasis added].[26]

Sloane[27] goes on to suggest that there is general cross-cultural consensus about the expressive value of incarceration and the ability of the sentencing process to express 'an extraordinarily high level of international condemnation' for international crimes. He regards improved communication as the key to ensuring that the 'right meaning' is conveyed to those seeking justice, invoking a Durkheimian analogy by stressing expressivism's function of emphasising the value of punishment to the 'figurative international community'.

Sloane's willingness to rely on 'a common commitment' to human rights and the international community's capacity to mobilise some kind of moral consensus in this regard is surely naive. His affirmation[28] that sentencing, at whatever level, should be 'a ritual of manifest moral significance' is meaningless unless and until international sentencing outcomes really do have the 'legitimacy and authority' which Sloane claims. As I have argued, there can be no presumed consensus, or 'authorising' community in the absence of further attempts to engage and reflect the aspirations for justice of victims and communities seeking justice in the aftermath of war and social conflict. The 'authority' of international penal law as presently constituted is undoubtedly partial; the presumed moral consensus, illusory.

There needs to be something more than mere condemnation, symbolic and partial as it is, to give 'legitimacy' to the outcomes of criminal trials, at whatever level. Whilst the morality of trial outcomes will always be relative, punishment must have the capacity to be perceived as moral by individuals and groups. Moral judgements subjectively held may thus be generalised within groups or communities. As has been argued, it is the criminal process itself that bears the responsibility and capacity for transforming abstract moral values into outcomes having 'real' moral significance, in that they can influence behaviour. For those individuals or groups who are (were) not involved in the conflict (criminality), the perception of *moral* punishment is equally relevant.

For those beyond the conflict, mere condemnatory (expressive) punishment should not suffice. As with all trial outcomes, a level of moral engagement for humanity at large should exist – after all, we can all recognise a fundamental breach of human rights. It is the context in which rights are breached which

---

26 *Ibid.* 53.
27 *Ibid.* 53, 55.
28 *Ibid.* 61.

304 Punishment and sentencing as governance

provokes conjecture. The difficult question to answer is how to realise whatever consensus exists through the processes and outcomes of international criminal trials.[29]

Responsibility and governance

The aim of establishing responsibility for criminalised behaviour is central to the liberal consensus trial paradigm and fundamental for any legal framework designed to establish guilt or innocence according to due process. However, where behaviour is not even classed as deviant by particular individuals, social groups or cultures, the concept of responsibility has little significance beyond its embodiment in law. Indeed, its imposition through 'rule of law' processes and institutions lacking legitimacy may well serve to engender conflict and deepen extant cultural divides; in other words, it may possibly weaken and even fragment societies where moral consensus is already fragile.

The downgrading of offences (and behaviours) through penalties which have the effect of diminishing perceptions of seriousness and denying justice for offenders and victims also diminishes responsibility as a determining feature of criminal liability. The result of this is to deny responsibility as relevant, thereby contributing to the breakdown of a system of criminal justice governance based on the maintenance of social cohesion and consensus. Such an approach fails to consider crime causation, since it ignores offender-related and social factors, and marginalises the individualisation of penalties through the use of judicial discretion. Instead, it has the effect of tolerating social divisions and inequalities, engendering the fear of crime and failing victims.

Measures in England and Wales to increase significantly the range of offences where fixed penalties are imposed,[30] and the extended use of conditional cautions,[31] have led to a shifting downwards in the threshold of behaviours deemed deviant and their criminalisation. This narrows the terrain of governance. In addition to trivialising and curtailing due process, such proposals may contribute to value breakdown and social conflict. As a form of penal policy, the politically pragmatic expedient of increasing the scope of strict-liability offences personifies what Blumberg[32] termed the 'assembly-line' or 'bargain-counter' approach to criminal justice. Such strategies may be viewed merely as a cynical exercise in resource manipulation, whereby the chief object of government penal policy is reduced to that of implementing measures to control the supply of potential offenders, depending upon how critical the crisis in police resources and prison overcrowding becomes.

---

29 See Findlay and Henham (2010).
30 See Home Office (2004).
31 Introduced by Sections 22–27 Criminal Justice Act 2003.
32 Blumberg (1970).

Further examples of the impact of cost and resource management on the delivery of criminal justice are not difficult to find. In addition to the strong criticisms directed at mechanisms such as plea bargaining,[33] there is now evidence from the United States of cost considerations being introduced directly into the sentence decision-making process.[34] This suggests that there may be a moral as well as a legal responsibility on judges and magistrates to balance perceived demands for 'justice' against what the state can afford. Too often, this imperative is perceived as that which is most likely to produce the desired outcome for the minimum cost. The difficulty with such an approach is that the normative framework for delivering this kind of output is essentially inspired by political considerations, rather than values of a communitarian nature.[35] Beyond the hitherto conventional retort,[36] that issues of cost have no place in determining what should be the appropriate sentence in any particular case, there is a strong argument for suggesting that criminal justice resource management should be informed more directly by factors relating to local crime and crime problems. This includes how offenders are punished and the cost implications for citizens locally and their communities. For sentencing, it suggests that greater 'legitimacy' can be achieved by ensuring that decision-makers are made aware of community views and expectations regarding punishment and its cost effectiveness. In this sense, cost becomes an element by which the moral value of punishment is judged from a communitarian perspective. Arguably, however, it should not assume undue significance as a measure of the moral value of punishment. The latter should focus on the nature of the harm caused and its impact on the community, so that the penal response reflects as far as possible what sentencers guage to be appropriate for redressing the balance of 'legitimate interests' towards the maintenance of 'civil society'.

If the framework for delivering criminal justice is generally perceived as lacking legitimacy or subverting civil society, then its credibility as a pillar of governance may eventually be eroded to the point where the entire panoply of ideologies and practices which constitute state penality collapses, so becoming implicated in society's self-destruction.[37] Criminal justice may thus be perceived

---

33 See chapter 5 for further discussion.
34 See; http://blog.lawinfo.com/2010/09/20/new-missouri-sentencing-guidelines-tell-judges-how-much-it-costs-to-punish-an-offender/ (accessed 2010). Similar considerations were introduced by Section 170(5)(c) of the Criminal Justice Act 2003 which mandated the Sentencing Guidelines Council to take the cost of different sentences and their relative effectiveness in preventing re-offending into account when framing sentencing guidelines. This injunction was repeated with respect to the Sentencing Council by Section 120(11)(e) of the Coroners and Justice Act 2009, with specific duties imposed as to resource implications under Section 127.
35 Such arguments have been deployed to counter the drastic reduction in Legal Aid in England and Wales for certain family cases and its likely disproportionate impact on those living in socially deprived areas.
36 Until recently, this was the convention adopted by the judiciary of England and Wales.
37 As occurred in pre-Revolutionary France.

as a divisive force, driven by the hegemonic aspirations of those who wish to subjugate particular groups or symbolising something that is meaningless to citizens because it fails to engage with the justice aspirations of individuals, groups or society at large. Where the social responsibility for responding to behaviour that contravenes 'socially accepted' norms in any meaningful way is abandoned by the state, or the international community, the likely result will be some form of anarchy,[38] possibly leading to the eventual collapse of civil society. Whether this takes place within states, or as a result of international rulings that impact upon states is irrelevant; the important lesson to draw from both global and local contexts is that the foundations of criminal justice governance may be eroded where the legitimacy of its outcomes are suspect.

Turning now to the nature of responsibility, and professed differences between international criminal justice and criminal justice more generally, there is no doubt that the former has consistently focused on the establishment of individual responsibility[39] in the context of collective violence and mass atrocity.[40] Nevertheless, the principles of international criminal law have been developed from basic concepts of criminal law[41] adapted to suit the circumstances of international crimes and their constituent parts. However, there is no denying the basic differences in the conceptual foundations of liability in singling out individual perpetrators for justice when responsibility itself is collective and behaviours are often culturally approved by particular factions or groups within society. Paradoxically, although state-sponsored, the focus of responsibility for local criminal justice *is* individual, with outcomes possibly engaging with victims or communities more generally, depending upon the exercise of sentencing discretion and the extent to which restorative themes have been embraced as elemental to criminal justice governance.

For all that, individualised notions of criminal responsibility as they relate to trial outcomes may be misplaced.[42] This suggests that there needs to be a reconceptualisation of the notion of responsibility in all forms of criminal trial (whether international, regional or local) towards a greater recognition of the community's role in defining its meaning and significance, consistent with Norrie's notion of relational justice.[43] Ironically, however, in sharp contrast to extant political rhetoric, victim and community participation in the processes of decision-making at the post-conviction stage of criminal justice is

---

38 For Durkheim, such an outcome would be perceived as having a positive impact in reinforcing the 'collective sentiments'. Evidently, the moral cohesion underpinning law that Durkheim envisaged no longer exists.

39 One obvious reason being jurisdictional limitation.

40 On the social function of guilt, see Meierhenrich (2006).

41 Note, however, Sloane's caveat on the more benign influence of international law; Sloane (2007).

42 As Lacey suggests, such questions cannot usefully be explored solely within the confines of traditional criminal law theory; Lacey (1987) 229–31.

43 Norrie (1996a).

weaker than required. Although greater emphasis is placed on community punishments, including a broader menu of ingredients which might include more restorative and community-based options, in reality these developments continue to be seriously compromised by the all-pervading influence of retributive justice ideology, driven forward by the populism of thinly-disguised political agendas.[44]

Justice as transitional

It has been argued that the relational context of penality has increasing relevance for both global and local conceptualisations of criminal justice, albeit that the particular dimensions of criminalisation, criminal responsibility and penal outcome may differ.

On the face of it, a clear distinction exists between local and international forms of criminal justice regarding their significance for governance. As Cockayne suggests;[45] international criminal justice is more to do with notions of societal transition: namely, what to do in the aftermath of social conflict, and how to facilitate the return to civil society.

However, at the local level, it may correspondingly be argued that the failure of much state penality to engage with communitarian notions of justice, perhaps through alienation, repression or social exclusion, reflects a breakdown of political accountability, and so diminishes the relevance of criminal justice as a form of governance. Consequently, establishing structures which can promote relational forms of penal accountability that are responsive to the aspirations of citizens is a mission common to both international and local criminal justice systems. For criminal justice administered locally, such communicative aspects of penality might also be conceived as 'transitional' – in the sense of providing a bridge between citizens and the state to facilitate the re-engagement of excluded, divided, or deprived communities – suggesting a way for them to participate more fully in the reinstatement of civil society through the restoration of common values.[46]

---

44 It remains to be seen whether this state of affairs continues in England and Wales following the new coalition government's renewed emphasis on rehabilitation and the publication of a Green Paper that will propose major structural changes to the sentencing regime; see Clarke, K. (2010).

45 Cockayne (2001).

46 There are cogent arguments for suggesting that issues of race, gender and poverty need to be addressed more profoundly in their impact on criminal justice governance. Wacquant, for example, has suggested that successive governments across the western industrialised world have validated a new form of punitive ideology as a response to increased urban social inequality and used it to disguise an agenda for dismantling core components of the welfare state, and so effectively criminalise poverty. Wacquant implicates right-wing conservative politicians and policy institutes as well as academics in perpetuating this trend; see Wacquant (2009). Such arguments invite comparison with Foucault's attribution of punishment as a technology of power and Mathiesen's observations regarding the socio-historical function of imprisonment as affirming the use by powerful classes of state penal machinery to systematically stigmatise, oppress and exclude minorities perceived as threatening. For the sentencing implications of taking issues of social differentiation and deprivation into account, see Easton and Piper (2008) ch. 10; von Hirsch and Ashworth (2005) ch. 5.

In both international and domestic settings, the capacity for trial justice to engage with social context depends upon it being conceptualised as fundamental to the governance role of criminal justice in civil society, and not merely as subservient to the power relations of domination. This is to say that the idealism and reality of justice should merge conceptually and practically in envisaging how justice itself can best serve the interests of what citizens regard as moral (and, therefore, legitimate). I would argue that such a vision is necessary in order to invest the notion of justice with its greater potential for governance, and certainly one which might set itself against the constraints imposed by the forces of hegemony.

Justice as universal

International criminal trials are concerned with the application of principles of international criminal law claiming universal authority – as do the principles of justice they espouse. Paradoxically, although the basic human rights and freedoms underpinning international humanitarian law are universally recognised, the rights themselves are relative in their practical effect.

Rights both reflect and constrain freedom and access. As with the notion of justice itself, the ideology and the reality of rights differs for criminal justice, whether at the global or local level. This is evident, more particularly, in the extent to which 'real' participative rights can be seen to exist. It is within the specific contexts of access to justice and victim participation that the reality of the failure of so-called inclusive justice (or inclusivity) is brought home. Within England and Wales, for example, participation remains largely symbolic and circumspect,[47] even though restricted rights of victim allocution have recently been introduced.[48] Therefore, there is scant possibility of victims or victimised communities taking a more active role in *actual* decision-making at the present time.

Consequently, it may be argued that the answer lies in constructing a system where participation (and its principled enforcement through a framework of rights) is not seen as a systemic weakness, but rather as an essential buttress for criminal justice governance. As Norrie indicates,[49] this could come about if principles and purposes for criminal justice were designed to be more inclusive, and the possibility existed for such participation without it destroying cherished ideals of consistency and proportionality. Surely, the possibility of compromise must exist, between constructing a system which is rigidly consistent but essentially backward looking, non-inclusive and disconnected from the social reality of everyday life, and one in which the idea of consistency fuels a principled commitment towards achieving a more egalitarian form of criminal justice by increasing participation and, crucially, by providing the rights framework to make that work.

---

47 See Ashworth (2000d) ch. 9.
48 For commentary, see Doak, Henham, and Mitchell (2009).
49 Norrie (1996a).

Sentencing and governance

Subverting governance

As I have argued, the undermining influence of structural mechanisms such as plea bargains and sentence discounts, the evidential repercussions of the division between verdict and sentence, and the problems caused by the failure to clearly delineate offence gravity and link this to penal severity – all serve to weaken the credibility of international criminal justice as a form of governance.[50] However, such subversion is equally damaging to the perceived legitimacy of criminal trial justice in domestic jurisdictions. Not only is due process undermined, so is the establishment of consistent principles of procedural penal law. Nevertheless, for international criminal justice, the anarchic potential of procedures anomalous to due process is multiplied through the obfuscation in penal rationality so evident in the sentencing judgements of the ICTY and ICTR.[51]

It may be argued that international criminal justice is chiefly concerned with the resolution of disputes borne out of the politics of international relations; that it is really about state supremacy, global hegemony and ideological dominion – above all, securing economic advantage.[52] Local systems of criminal justice are surely similar in reflecting relationships of power, authority and subjugation; it is simply that the social context for governance is different. For international criminal justice, state sovereignty may be supplanted by structural relationships that are global and driven by economic or political forces pursuing ideologies that are essentially independent of state interests, or those of supranational corporations.

Ultimately, however, relationships of governance in criminal justice require structures to support them which are driven instrumentally by ideologies that are inclusive and non-discriminatory. Following the Nuremberg trials, for example, retributive ideology came to symbolise victor's justice and the appropriate form of condemnation for perpetrators of mass atrocity. However, that response may also be seen as responsible for perpetuating existing social divisions; as vindicating the rationale for conflict; and, as confirming the victor's propaganda and myths.[53] Similar parallels may be drawn in the context of local forms of criminal justice delivery.[54]

Restorative ideology, on the other hand, is typified by the ideals of participative engagement and relational justice, symbolising healing and

---

50 See Henham (2005b) ch. 2, Henham and Drumbl (2005).
51 See Henham (2005b).
52 Notwithstanding that inter-state disputes are (with agreement) regulated by the International Court of Justice.
53 See Schabas (1997), Wexler (1996).
54 See, for example, Stuart Hall's work signifying criminal justice as a structure for diverting attention away from politically sensitive debates about crime causation, such as social exclusion through poverty, education and discrimination; Hall *et al.* (1978).

reconciliation. The deployment of restorative justice as a smoke screen for perpetuating the retributive hegemony of international criminal justice poses a consummate threat to the delivery of a more inclusive form of justice. However, I suggest that this is exactly what will happen if there is no departure from the symbolic underpinning of international criminal justice by the rationales of retribution and deterrence. A similar result may follow the piecemeal unprincipled adoption at the domestic level of restorative initiatives in many western criminal justice systems.

Re-asserting governance

The outcomes of international trials can be seen as fundamentally concerned with the role of justice in making the transition from war to peace. Some commentators view the rationale for international trials as preventing impunity by facilitating the delivery of retributive justice and deterrence,[55] while others, such as Braithwaite,[56] are more likely to regard trial justice (and international criminal justice more broadly conceived) as an important element in a complex and unique jigsaw for moving forward from war to peace. Similarly, local criminal justice, freed from the constraining reactive influence of the retributive dynamic, may be viewed as essential to the maintenance of civil society, and, therefore, as a potential force for social cohesion and peace. In either case, the ideology which sustains the impetus for penal change may be viewed as forming part of a wider moral foundation advocating social reconstruction.

Ultimately, even retributive ideology, and its more recent limited manifestation as just deserts, needs to be evaluated against a context of moral accountability. If retributive justice fails deliver what is perceived as legitimate punishment in any particular jurisdictional context, even if retribution is justifiable as a categorical imperative, the social consequences will be to diminish the moral value of that justification.

Arguably, this effect has been observed more recently with regard to sentencing in England and Wales, where concepts of just deserts and proportionality and their judicial interpretation have come under increasing scrutiny from the media and its characterisation of public opinion.[57] Subsequently, the media-led campaign became personalised to the judiciary, with politicians being accused of resorting to 'knee-jerk' penal responses and tokenism, and political pragmatism replacing a principled balancing of the moral claims of citizens for justifying penal intervention. Such populism has tended to undermine long-established constitutional convention for short-term political advantage, more especially in the gradual diminution of the hitherto largely unfettered

---

55 Bagaric and Morss (2006).
56 Braithwaite (2002).
57 Consistent with Young's 'consensual' paradigm, knowledge is presented as 'public opinion' thereby giving the appearance of consensus regarding the perceived 'leniency' of judicial sentencing; Young (1972).

sentencing discretion of the judiciary. More significantly, it has diverted attention from the fact that particular social policies have failed to deliver crucial change in the causal patterns of crime.

Arguably, the practice of penal politics as the principal facilitator of criminal justice governance has become a more overtly cynical and manipulative exercise.[58] In Foucaultian terms,[59] such political pragmatism deliberately sustains social diversity and value-pluralism by facilitating the polarisation of power and its technologies. Furthermore, this constant re-alignment of power is effectively concealed through the duplicity of penal policy-making, which incrementally lessens accountability,[60] whilst appearing to assert the opposite through policy and legislation. Some may argue that the objective is to divert attention away from the ideological and moral failure of the liberal-consensus model of the rule of law and its dependant structures of criminal justice.[61]

Promoting governance

The preceding discussion suggests that the link between sentencing and governance is unclear where the role of criminal justice as a form of governance is itself uncertain and obfuscated by political ideology. On the one hand, it may be argued that the institutions of criminal justice are essential to sustain civil society, while the alternative perspective suggests that such structures are merely instrumental in perpetuating the power relations of hegemony.

Of course, both arguments may be correct – the real point being that, although the purposes of criminal justice governance are moral questions, their meaning and effect depend upon social context. Ultimately, it is social reality that determines the moral authority of penal law and process, so imbuing criminal justice with its sense of moral purpose and legitimacy. Governance in the field of criminal justice therefore represents a distinct moral compromise about the desirability of criminalising certain behaviours and the appropriateness of inflicting particular punishments in respect of them. It is usually distilled through the democratic process by moral negotiation between citizens and representative forms of authority, whose mandate is to balance the rights and duties of individuals and groups.

In England and the Wales, the shifting boundaries of penal responsibility, so eloquently described by Garland,[62] and the increasing desire of the executive to centralise and control the discretionary powers of the judiciary in

---

58 This might be characterised somewhat cynically as follows: election promises; ideological brief; institutional assessment; new penal policy; new targets; inadequate resources; inspection; deemed failure; remedial plan; repeated failure; failure of policy; scapegoating by executive; blurring of responsibilities; failure of governance.
59 See Pratt (1998).
60 As Sparks suggests in his notion of 'less eligibility'; Sparks (1996).
61 See Mathiesen (1990).
62 Garland (2001).

matters of sentencing, have exposed the practice of sentencing as somehow lacking in moral legitimacy, with the judges appearing to bear greater public responsibility for its perceived failings than the policy-makers. The capacity of the executive to deliver a criminal justice system which can satisfy the justice demands of a society increasingly characterised by value-pluralism and fragmented communities depends upon its ability to address the macro-social problems of exclusion and relative deprivation. Nevertheless, it may not be unrealistic to argue that the structures of criminal justice, and its human agents, could be tasked to deliver more inclusive forms of justice which engage with notions of what are regarded as 'morally appropriate' responses to criminalised behaviour within the existing frameworks for governance of particular societies.

Correspondingly, the social fragmentation of states and communities and its causes receive scant attention in the penal rationales and sentencing practices of international criminal trials. Yet, as has been argued, the challenges faced by judges in sentencing the perpetrators of international crimes are in many ways similar to those persisting in local systems of criminal justice, since (for both) it is becoming increasingly necessary to justify penal interventions on moral as well as legal grounds, albeit retrospectively.[63] Hence, I would argue that choices to invoke particular penal responses through sentencing should increasingly be made with broader considerations in mind than those which simply continue to draw on the liberal consensus model of punishment.

The continued relevance of the idea that there is some kind of moral consensus that underpins the normative framework of penal law and acts as a rationale for criminal justice governance, more generally, is highly suspect. Notions of moral accountability and maintenance of the rule of law are no longer co-extensive in the penal domain, nor do they remain the exclusive prerogative of sovereign states or international organisations. Accountability and responsibility for behaviour which infringes legal norms have become diffused in the administration of penal law because criminal justice governance is now more to do with controlling risk than defending shared moral values.[64] In this members of the judiciary at all levels have a pivotal role to play,[65] and it is for this reason that their perceived failure to do so in certain key areas of governance receives such high-profile coverage and criticism.

---

63 Note the interventions of the ICC in Uganda; see Volqvartz (2005).
64 See Shearing and Johnston (2005).
65 The sentencing of so-called 'dangerous' offenders in England and Wales provides a useful example and, as argued earlier, where policy and legislature are ill-thought-through, the judiciary is left with the unenviable task of justifying decisions made in compliance with a normative framework that is inadequate and morally suspect. This dilemma is well summarised in a recent report on the operation of IPP sentences made for the Prison Reform Trust; See Jacobson and Hough (2010), 31.

> ... the limitations of risk assessment are so evident that if the courts have extensive powers to lock up individuals to pre-empt violent or sexual offending, these powers will often be used in ways that are neither effective nor just. Again, this viewpoint was expressed by many

It may be argued that a more obvious solution, although administratively and politically problematic, would be to establish a structure for monitoring the values and norms of penal law in the face of changing social conditions and ensuring that findings are reflected in sentencing praxis.[66] This would ensure that the justifications that underpin penal governance engage more directly with the diverse and changing moral values and aspirations for punishment held by citizens. Hence, a more flexible model of penal accountability is required; one which recognises that more transparency and ensuring a wider range of social factors are taken into account in penal policy do not guarantee *per se* the impartiality and legitimacy of trial justice for all groups in society.[67]

Although Norrie's emphasis on relational justice suggests a greater engagement with notions of popular justice, at the local level such aspirations remain largely unfulfilled. Despite the fact that community punishments have continually been rebranded[68] to include more restorative and community-based options, the reality is that these much-heralded changes in penal direction have been accommodated by constantly modifying the existing retributive justice paradigm and have increasingly been driven by the politically pragmatic demands of responding quickly to perceived risk and security concerns.[69]

Therefore, for local contexts, the relationship between sentencing and criminal justice governance might be conceived in terms which focus on the extent to which punishment is able to engage with broader notions of social responsibility. This does not simply mean delivering justice which is perceived as relevant to the social needs of recognised communities of interest. It also suggests that penal outcomes should be informed by a more coherent ideology for political and social life – one that promotes social responsibility *and* accountability as twin rationales for governance.

The legitimacy of international criminal justice similarly depends upon developing notions of governance as relational contexts which provide meaningful links between individual and collective aspirations for justice within a framework of responsibility designed to build trust in the institutions of civil

---

of our lawyer respondents (as well as some others), such as one who commented, in an email submission, that the IPP *requires the sentencing court to engage in a wholly speculative predictive exercise about future dangerousness when there is no reliable measure of such dangerousness. … The task of predicting whether particular types of offending might escalate to cause serious harm and then whether the person might pose a risk of harm in the future is simply too speculative and subjective to form the basis for indefinite detention.*

66 The extended remit of the newly-created Sentencing Council for England and Wales does not provide this, having been created to advance sentencing guidance within the normative framework of existing penal ideology.

67 Practical steps in England and Wales include inter-agency community projects aimed at establishing clear parameters of institutional responsibility; Allen and Hough (2008) 236.

68 As a consequence of the continuing 'bifurcation' in penal policy-making; see Bottoms (1977).

69 The sentencing of 'terrorists' presents particular difficulties in this respect. See Findlay (2007).

society. In this sense, all forms of criminal justice governance should be regarded as transitional and contingent – capable of responding to changing social needs, with accountability developing as a bi-partisan endeavour, whereby criminal justice policy and practice reflect an ongoing dialogue between those who seek justice and those tasked with delivering it.

Consequently, reciprocal notions of rights should also be broadened and interpreted within a democratised framework for accountability, so that rights themselves are conceived as essential components for maintaining the dialogue of justice with victims and communities. In this way, accountability can move beyond its conventional role of ensuring the principled enforcement of penal norms by enabling rights to become more socially responsive.

I have suggested that judicial discretionary power is the key variable for mobilising such a notion of accountability by ensuring that it engages practically with acknowledged justice demands and supports rights which are consistent with their achievement. Consequently, at all levels, access to justice should become a core value for criminal justice governance; one equated with a participative role for victims and community representatives in the sentencing decision-making process. In consequence, and in order to facilitate change in the context of justice delivery, the instrumental power of sentencing discretion should be mobilised more effectively, with judges becoming central figures in determining the *actual* parameters of penal accountability, and ensuring their sensitive interpretation and future development.

Thus, the exact parameters of access and rights should reflect a compromise between relevant interests and demands derived from an ongoing process of dialogue and representation with all interested parties, especially those of victims and communities. It has been argued that, as a cornerstone of criminal justice governance, sentencing should provide a context where the ideological and philosophical rationales that inform penal policy and its structures are negotiated in ways that reflect meaningful connections between the institutions of punishment and those individuals and communities affected by them, whether global or local.

The mobilisation of judicial discretion towards a more restorative and inclusive justice paradigm will depend on the development of appropriate normative structures underpinned by strong ideological foundations committed to the integration of the diverse attitudes, beliefs and values within relevant social contexts of community. Such a sentencing framework will then be driven by the need to reconcile the moral justifications for punishment with the perceived moral legitimacy of sentencing and its outcomes within communities. Consequently, the sentencing context is conceived through moving beyond conventional conceptualisations that envisage 'communities' purely in terms of victimisation towards one that regards sentencing as a context for their holistic restoration.

The acknowledgement of repeat victimisation within cultures and communities is significant in attributing meaningful victim status, as is recognition of the political motivations that validate that status through selective criminalisation of opponents and resistant groups. As Findlay argues,[70] a significant element of this form of legitimisation model is to neutralise value-plurality by supporting alternative favoured victim constituencies, so providing a single overriding justification for discriminatory and oppressive justice responses that tend to alienate resistant victim communities. However, establishing the contextual relativity of victimisation without an accompanying ideological repositioning for justice delivery will not deliver an identifiable shared moral perspective for criminal justice governance.

Enhancing the legitimacy of trial justice

Recognising core relationships

To assert that penality fulfils an overarching criminal justice role is controversial because, arguably, it fails to recognise different kinds of criminality and the power structures that define them. Within the state context, therefore, as Garland argues,[71] crime and its definition serve the interests of the polity; Foucault[72] meanwhile describes how this controlling function subjugates citizens and rails against social justice. Superficially, accountability for penal policy is transparent and democratic, but this paradigm is not reflected in the subjective experiences of individual citizens. For individuals, accountability is a relative concept, one that is essentially relational, in that it varies according to the vagaries of personal experience and social interaction. It is a matter of perception, so that the legitimacy of penal policy is judged according to its perceived effects.[73]

It may be argued that local criminal justice impacts daily on the lives of individual citizens everywhere, whereas international criminal justice does not – the criminality and the justice responses required being of a different order, both temporal and spatial. Furthermore, local criminal justice envisions punishment as a crucial bastion against the fragmentation of civil society; vital for the maintenance of states as functioning, holistic, social entities, with their own structural space.

In similar vein, international criminal justice may be said to contribute to the maintenance of global peace, thereby helping to protect the integrity of social entities, or social groups. It may also be perceived as helping to preserve the dignity of human life and protecting the integrity of individuals everywhere because of its humanitarian focus. This perceived commonality is reinforced through the ubiquitous notion of 'international' criminal justice, and its implicit claims of consistency and equality of treatment. Although, as Matza implies,[74] such notions of universal justice may be judged objectively

---

70 Findlay (2009).
71 Garland (2001).
72 Foucault (1977).
73 For an example, see Rogers and Erez (1999).
74 Matza (1964).

through principled evaluation, such paradigms do not help us to ensure the viability of criminal justice as a system of governance. What matters is the degree of engagement with the moral values that underpin notions of justice within any particular context.

If, as Durkheim suggests,[75] deviance is a necessary aspect of the human condition, the instrumental value of punishment for contemporary society may depend on its ability to reinforce the collective consciousness in its post-modern manifestation. Consequently, if there is no collective moral consciousness, the response to deviance is likely to depend upon what is *deemed* necessary in order to facilitate a state of civil society.[76] This may be conceived in terms of the state's function to reflect the interests of individuals sharing common values of culture and community; a 'shared context' for living. In the post-modern state, such contexts are fluid and often fragmented. They may be contexts of emotion and sentiment, or virtual in the sense of not being grounded by conventional parameters of time and space.[77] The relentless merging of global and local influences in social life ensures that shared contexts can no longer be delineated solely by the commonalities of community, peer group or family.

It may, of course, be countered that, ultimately, all contexts for living, shared or otherwise, depend upon a principled exercise of power for their legitimacy. Otherwise, as Foucault argues,[78] punishment becomes a pure technology of power. Whilst this is a truism, it ignores the power of free will and the human capacity for moral reasoning. The capacity for human beings to assert their identity as individuals extends far beyond the physical. Although physical subjugation and persecution may crush the physical body, it will not extinguish universal human values of life and liberty.[79] Penal values and norms should therefore be sensitive to maintaining the appropriate balance between social control and subjugation, and how this balance is perceived by different social groups and communities.

Reflecting shared values

The legitimacy of trial justice is attributed within a framework of values that influence our perception of punishment. As I have suggested, any commonality in this perceived legitimacy implies two things:

---

75 Durkheim (1968), Cotterrell (1999).
76 What is 'deemed' necessary in practice depends upon the political process and the power relationships that exist within particular states. The uncertain morality underpinning criminal justice in England and Wales was recently emphasised by the polarised public and media reaction to the suicide of the murder fugitive Raoul Moat; see, for example, Watson (2010).
77 For further discussion, see Girling (2006).
78 Foucault (1977). Technologies of control operating beyond the reach of conventional forms of political accountability are increasing, whereas paradoxically democratic accountability is decreasing in local contexts; Mathiesen (2006).
79 Of course, crimes of mass atrocity aim to achieve both objectives.

1) There must be a sharing of values about how we can live together as 'civil society', however defined.

2) Such sharing must include some consensus about the role of punishment and sentencing and the system of criminal justice necessary to sustain it.

It may, therefore, be argued that the present disjunction between the rhetoric and reality of criminal justice in Western jurisdictions reflects a moral fragmentation of society in general.[80] This has produced plural understandings of what is entailed morally in the concept of 'responsibility', and a consequent unwillingness on the part of individuals to accept authoritarian definitions of responsibility for their own and others' behaviour. The effect is a moral detachment between actions and consequences, in that individuals may not perceive it as *their* responsibility to exercise control over certain forms of behaviour. In this sense, as Armstrong suggests,[81] a conceptual distinction may be drawn between citizens' perceptions of the regulatory nature of criminal justice and the normative claims apparent in the politicised rhetoric of crime control.

Consequently, individuals may not attach any moral value to rationales attributing responsibility to them, or to the institutional power bases from which they emanate.[82] Such subliminal responses parody Matza's techniques of neutralisation,[83] in suggesting reasons why individuals are able to disavow responsibility by denying the value of existing rationales and structures for punishment. Although the distinctions between local and global notions of criminal justice are important in this context,[84] the unifying force of such excuses is derived from a single desire to absolve perpetrators of any moral responsibility for their actions.

Judged against this background, gauging the significance of penality for governance at either the global or local level will require a profound analysis of the complex relationships that exist between the ideologies which inform institutionalised punishment and what is perceived as 'justice' as a matter of subjective perception, commonly shared. In other words, the question is not so much one of asserting that penality *is* a technology of power, but rather of extending the question by positing whether it can become a *constructive* technology – not in the sense of being supportive of secular hegemonic aspirations, but rather as a force for positive change and social justice, perceived as such by individual human beings sharing common values. In short, a shared context which attaches legitimacy to penal outcomes and their ideological foundations is envisaged.

---

80 For further discussion in the context of crime and its control, see O'Malley (1999), Rose (2000), Hutchinson (2006).
81 Armstrong (2007).
82 See, further, Tyler (2003), Tyler and Darley (2000).
83 Matza (1964).
84 Cohen (1993).

The accuracy of these assertions can only be verified empirically by drawing theoretically and methodologically informed comparisons between different manifestations of criminal justice.[85] I would argue that such insights are best achieved through comparative contextual analyses.[86] This methodological approach is designed to examine how processes of evolution, adaptation and change characterise individual perceptions of punishment and sentencing, and the extent to which common perceptions may be generalised. Drawing common understandings in this way facilitates the theorisation of such developments and evaluates the praxis of punishment and sentencing as crucial pillars of criminal justice governance.

Global and local forms of criminal justice may suggest different parameters of power, social control and accountability, involve crimes of a different magnitude in terms of gravity, and appear to implement diverse punishment objectives. However, their perception as legitimate forms of penalty depends upon the morality attached to them by individuals and social groups, irrespective of time and space. This characterisation allocates moral responsibility for actions deemed deviant and decides whether any consequential punishment should be perceived as attributed legitimately. Hence, the two crucial elements against which the legitimacy of punishment and sentencing are judged involve:

(a)   the attribution of responsibility; and
(b)   consequential accountability.[87]

The fact that actions are evaluated against moral values individuals and communities hold about crime and punishment is not surprising. However, it is, and always has been, a fundamental issue for the credibility of criminal justice. This book has examined the implications of such an observation for the future legitimacy of trial justice. Essentially, it has been argued that moral values commonly held about crime and punishment are reflected in shared

---

85 For an example of cross-jurisdictional comparison, see Henham and Mannozzi (2003).
86 For further elaboration, see Findlay and Henham (2005) chs 1 and 2.
87 This is not to deny that accountability can be conceptualised and measured in many different ways. For example, in the context of international criminal justice, we might measure accountability for practices such as plea bargaining against purely bureaucratic or economic criteria – as a discrete regulatory context that may be justified as such, conceptually distinct from the normative framework underpinning the structural arrangements of which it forms part. By contrast, the interpretation adopted here focuses on 'responsibility' as the core for governance in a broader, morally inclusive sense, rather than the narrow perspective of doctrinal criminal law, or crime control and due process modelling. The reasoning for this is tied to the linkage between the morality and the legitimacy of punishment and its recursive manufacture through the processual activity of trial justice. Hence, this book adopts a more relational and communitarian notion of 'responsibility', mirrored in the view that accountability is both individual and collective, so that the legitimacy of trial outcomes must be evaluated against a holistic ('shared') vision of the individual *in* the community.

perceptions about the legitimacy of sentencing. It is the recognition of, and response to, such shared values for punishment in morally pluralistic societies that poses a fundamental challenge for policy-makers. Upon this hinges the viability of criminal justice as a system of governance. I have argued further that the capacity for realising this aspiration lies in developing the discretionary power of sentencing, which is conceived as a structural process capable of transforming moral values through the delivery of normatively significant outcomes.

Thus, I have suggested that the legitimacy of trial justice should be judged primarily in terms of how penal norms and practices respond to issues of responsibility and accountability as seen from a shared moral perspective, whether the social context in question is global or local. The adoption of such an approach should be preceded by a profound contextual analysis of the trial process and its social context. It is only by developing a deeper understanding of the reasons why penal values and norms exist, and of their meaning and function, that will we be able to identify points of commonality and difference and judge the normative significance of trial justice for particular communities as shared aspects of moral experience.

References

Albrecht, H.-J. (2001), 'Post-Adjudication Dispositions in Comparative Perspective' in M. Tonry and R. Frase (eds) *Sentencing and Sanctions in Western Countries* (Oxford: Oxford University Press), 293.

Allan, T.R.S. (2006) 'The Rule of Law as Liberal Justice', 56 *University of Toronto Law Journal*, 283.

Allen, R., and Hough, M. (2008)'Does it Matter? Reflections on the Effectiveness of Institutionalised Public Participation in the Development of Sentencing Policy' in A. Freiberg and K. Gelb *Penal Populism, Sentencing Councils and Sentencing Policy* (Cullompton: Willan Publishing), 224.

Alvarez, J.E. (1998) 'Rush to Closure: Lessons of the Tadić Judgment', 96 *Michigan Law Review* 2031.

——(1999) 'Crimes of States/Crimes of Hate: Lessons from Rwanda', 24 *Yale Journal of International Law*, 365.

Amann, D.M. (2002) 'Group Mentality, Expressivism and Genocide', 2 *International Criminal Law Review*, 93.

Ancel, M. (1954) *La défense sociale nouvelle* (Paris: Editions Cujas).

Armstrong, S. (2007)'Accountability in Criminal Justice: From Judgement to Measurement', Paper presented at Oxford Centre for Criminology Seminar, 25 April.

Armstrong, S. and McAra, L. (2006) 'Audiences, Borders and Architecture' in S. Armstrong and L. McAra (eds) *Perspectives on Punishment: The Contours of Control* (Oxford: Oxford University Press).

Ashworth, A. (1983) *Sentencing and Penal Policy* (London: Weidenfeld and Nicolson).

——(1986) 'Punishment and Compensation: Victims, Offenders and the State', 6 *Oxford Journal of Legal Studies*, 86.

——(1993) 'Victim Impact Statements and Sentencing', *Criminal Law Review*, 498.

——(1991) *Sentencing and Criminal Justice* (London: Weidenfeld and Nicolson).

——(1994)*The Criminal Process: An Evaluative Study* (Oxford: Oxford University Press, 1st ed.).

——(1996a) 'Crime, Community and Creeping Consequentialism', 43 *Criminal Law Review*, 220.

——(1996b) 'Proposals for Major Sentencing Changes', *Criminal Law Review*, 365.

——(2000a) 'Developments in the Public Prosecutor's Office in England and Wales', 8 *European Journal of Crime, Criminal Law and Criminal Justice*, 257.

——(2000b) 'The Roles of Legislature and Judiciary in English Sentencing' in S. Doran and J.D. Jackson (eds) *The Judicial Role in Criminal Proceedings* (Oxford: Hart Publishing).

——(2000c) *Sentencing and Criminal Justice* (London: Butterworth, 3rd ed.).

——(2000d) 'Victims' Rights, Defendants' Rights and Criminal Procedure' in A. Crawford and J. Goodey (eds) *Integrating a Victim Perspective Within Criminal Justice* (Aldershot: Ashgate).

——(2001) 'The Decline of English Sentencing' in M. Tonry and R. Frase (eds) *Sentencing and Sanctions in Western Countries* (Oxford: Oxford University Press).

——(2002a) *Human Rights, Serious Crimes and Criminal Procedure* (London: Sweet & Maxwell).

——(2002b) 'Responsibilities, Rights and Restorative Justice', 42 *British Journal of Criminology*, 578.

——(2004) 'Criminal Justice Act 2003 – (2) Criminal Justice Reform: Principles, Human Rights and Public Protection', *Criminal Law Review*, 516.

——(2005) *Sentencing and Criminal Justice* (Cambridge: Cambridge University Press, 4th ed.).

——(2006) *Principles of Criminal Law* (Oxford: Oxford University Press, 5th ed.).

——(2010) *Sentencing and Criminal Justice* (Cambridge: Cambridge University Press, 5th ed.).

Ashworth, A., and Player, E. (2005) 'Criminal Justice Act 2003: The Sentencing Provisions', 68 *Modern Law Review*, 822.

Ashworth, A., and Redmayne, M. (2005) *The Criminal Process* (Oxford: Oxford University Press, 3rd ed.).

Aukerman, M.J. (2002) 'Extraordinary Evil, Ordinary Crime: A Framework for Understanding Transitional Justice', 15 *Harvard Human Rights Journal*, 39.

Auld, R. (LJ) (2001) *Review of the Criminal Courts* (London: The Stationery Office).

Bagaric, M., and Amarasekara, K. (2001) 'Feeling Sorry? – Tell Someone who Cares: The Irrelevance of Remorse in Sentencing', 40 *Howard Journal of Criminal Justice*, 364.

Bagaric, M., and Morss, J. (2006) 'International Sentencing Law: In Search of a Justification and a Coherent Framework', 6 *International Criminal Law Review*, 191.

Baker, E. (2009) 'The European Union's "Area of Freedom, Security and (Criminal) Justice" Ten Years On', *Criminal Law Review*, 833.

Baker, E., and Clarkson, C.M.V. (2002) 'Making Punishments Work? An Evaluation of the Halliday Report on Sentencing in England and Wales', *Criminal Law Review*, 81.

Baldwin, J., and McConville, M. (1977) *Negotiated Justice: Pressures on Defendants to Plead Guilty* (London: Martin Robertson).

BBC News (2003) 'Woolf denies "charter for burglars"', 14 February, http://news.bbc.co.uk/1/hi/uk/2655883.stm (accessed 2010).

——(2005) 'Voters don't Trust Politicians', 18 March at http://news.bbc.co.uk/1/hi/uk_politics/4360597.stm (accessed 2011).

——(2006a) 'Judge breaks silence on sentences', 18 June, http://news.bbc.co.uk/1/hi/5091590.stm.

——(2006b) 'Rape judge slammed for 'leniency'' 13 September, http://news.bbc.co.uk/1/hi/england/humber/5343294.stm (accessed 2006).

——(2007a) 'Reid Hits Back in Sentencing Row' 26 Jan at http://news.bbc.co.uk/go/pr/fr/-/1/hi/uk_politics/6301125.stm (accessed 2007).

——(2007b) 'Some Murderers in Jail too Long' 9 March at http://news.bbc.co.uk/1/hi/uk/6433195.stm; (accessed 2007).

——(2009) 'Italy adopts law to curb migrants', 3 July http://news.bbc.co.uk/go/pr/fr/-/1/hi/world/europe/8132084.stm (accessed 2010).

BBC *Panorama* (2009) 'Cautions "deny victims justice"', 9 November, http://news.bbc.co.uk/panorama/hi/front_page/newsid_8346000/8346321.stm (accessed 2010).

Beccaria, C. (1995) *On Crimes and Punishments and Other Writings*, Cambridge Texts in the History of Political Thought, ed. R Bellamy (Cambridge: Cambridge University Press).

Becker, H. (1973) *Outsiders* (New York: Free Press, 2nd ed.).

Bell, J. (2001) *French Legal Cultures* (London: Butterworth).

Bellavista, G. (1939) *Il potere discrezionale del guidice nell'applicozione della pene* (Milan: Bocca).

Beresford, S. (2002) 'Unshackling the Paper Tiger: The Sentencing Practices of the Ad Hoc International Criminal Tribunals for the Former Yugoslavia and Rwanda', 1 *International Criminal Law Review*, 33.

Bianchi, M., Buonanno, P., and Pinotti, P. (2008)'Immigration and Crime: An Empirical Analysis' (12 December 2008), Bank of Italy Temi di Discussione (Working Paper) No. 698, available at Social Science Research Network: http://ssrn.com/abstract=1356568 (accessed 2010).

Blumberg, A.S. (1970) *Criminal Justice* (Chicago: Quadrangle Books).

Bohlander, M. (2004), Review of F. Pakes, 'Styles of Trial Procedure at the International Criminal Tribunal for the Former Yugoslavia' in P.J. van Koppen and S. Penrod (eds) *Adversarial versus Inquisitorial Justice, Psychological Perspectives on Criminal Justice Systems* (New York: Plenum Press, 2003), in 4 *International Criminal Law Review*, 125.

Bond, C.E.W. and Jeffries, S. (2010) 'Sentencing Indigenous and Non-Indigenous Women in Western Australia's Higher Courts', 17 *Psychiatry, Psychology and Law*, 70.

Bottoms, A.E. (1977) 'Reflections on the Renaissance of Dangerousness', 16 *Howard Journal of Penology and Crime Prevention*, 70.

——(1995) 'The Philosophy and Politics of Punishment and Sentencing' in C. Clarkson and R. Morgan *The Politics of Sentencing Reform* (Oxford: Clarendon Press).

——(2002) 'Morality, Crime, Compliance and Public Policy' in A. Bottoms and M. Tonry (eds) *Ideology, Crime and Criminal Justice* (Cullompton: Willan Publishing), 23.

Bottoms, A.E. and Brownsword, R. (1982) 'The Dangerousness Debate after the Floud Report', 22 *British Journal of Criminology*, 229.

Bottoms, A., and Roberts, J.V. (eds) (2009) *Victims in Contemporary Criminal Justice* (Cullompton, Willan Publishing).

Bourdieu, P. (1977) *Outline of a Theory of Practice* (Cambridge: Cambridge University Press).

Boutellier, H. (2000) *Crime and Morality: The Significance of Criminal Justice in Post-Modern Culture* (Dordrecht: Kluwer Academic).

——(2004) *The Safety Utopia: Contemporary Discontent and Desire as to Crime and Punishment* (Dordrecht, Kluwer Academic).

Braithwaite, J. (2002) *Restorative Justice and Responsive Regulation* (Oxford: Oxford University Press).

Bricola, F. (1965) *La discrezionalita nel diritto penale : Nozioni e aspetti costituzionali* (Milan: Guiffre).

Brown, M., and Pratt, J. (eds) (2000) *Dangerous Offenders: Punishment and Social Order* (London: Routledge).

Brownlee, I.D. (2007) 'Conditional Cautions and Fair Trial Rights: Form versus Substance in the Diversionary Agenda', *Criminal Law Review*, 129.

Buruma, Y. 2004 'Doubts on the Upsurge of the Victim's Role in Criminal Law' in H Kaptein and M Malsch (eds) *Crime, Victims, and Justice: Essays on Principles and Practice* (Aldershot: Ashgate).

Caputo, M. (2009) *Il diritto penale e il problema del patteggiamento* (Naples: Esselibri Simone).

Carcano, A. (2002) 'Sentencing and the Gravity of the Offence in International Criminal Law', 51 *International and Comparative Law Quarterly*, 583.

Carlen, P. (1976) *Magistrates' Justice* (London: Martin Robertson).

Carter Review (2007) *Securing the Future* (London: Ministry of Justice).

Casanovas, P. (1999) 'Pragmatic Legal Contexts' Paper presented at the International Pragmatics Conference on Pragmatics and Negotiation, Tel Aviv University/Hebrew University of Jerusalem, 13–16 June.

Cassese, A. 'Terrorism is also disputing some crucial legal categories of International Law' (2001) 12 *European Journal of International Law* 983.

Cavadino, M., and Dignan, J. (1997) 'Reparation, Retribution and Rights', 4 *International Review of Victimology*, 233.

——(2002) *The Penal System: An Introduction* (London: Sage, 3rd ed.).

——(2006) *Penal Systems: A Comparative Approach* (London: Sage).

Certoma, G.L. (1985) *The Italian Legal System* (London: Butterworth).

Chiavario, M. (1994) 'Aperçus sur la procedure d'audience en Italie entre reforme et "post-reforme"', *Revue de science criminelle et de droit pénal comparé*, 207.

——(2002) 'The Rights of the Defendant and the Victim' in M. Delmas-Marty and J.R. Spencer (eds) *European Criminal Procedures* (Cambridge: Cambridge University Press), 577.

Christodoulidis, E.A. (2000) 'Truth and Reconciliation as Risks', 9 *Social & Legal Studies*, 179.

Cicourel, A. (1968) *The Social Organisation of Juvenile Justice* (New York: John Wiley).

Clark, N.J. (2009) 'Plea Bargaining at the ICTY: Guilty Pleas and Reconciliation', 20 *European Journal of International Law*, 415.

Clark, P. (2008) 'Establishing a Conceptual Framework: Six Key Transitional Justice Themes' in P. Clark and Z. Kaufman (eds) *After Genocide: Transitional Justice, Post-Conflict Reconstruction and Reconciliation in Rwanda and Beyond* (London: Hurst).

Clarke, A., Moran-Ellis, J. and Sleney, J. (2002) *Attitudes to Date Rape and Relationship Rape: A Qualitative Study*, Sentencing Advisory Panel Research Report 2 (London: Sentencing Advisory Panel), http://www.sentencing-guidelines.gov.uk/docs/research.pdf (accessed 2009).

Clarke, K., Lord Chancellor and Secretary of State for Justice, (2010) 'The Government's Vision for Criminal Justice Reform', (London: Centre for Crime and Justice Studies, 30 June 2010), http://www.justice.gov.uk/sp300610a.htm (accessed 2010).

Clarkson, C.M.V. and Keating, H.M. (1994) *Criminal Law: Text and Materials* (London: Sweet & Maxwell, 3rd ed.).

Cockayne, J. (2001) 'Procedural and Processual Synthesis in the International Tribunals. Part 1: The Context of Synthesis' (unpublished paper prepared for the International Criminal Trial Project, Nottingham Law School).

——(2002) 'A Survey of Recent Criminal Procedure Reform in Italy, France and Spain: evidence of internationalisation?'(unpublished paper prepared for the International Criminal Trial Project, Nottingham Law School).

——(2005) 'Hybrids or Mongrels? Internationalized War Crimes Trials as Unsuccessful Degradation Ceremonies', 4 *Journal of Human Rights*, 455.

Cohen, S. (1985) *Visions of Social Control: Crime, Punishment and Classification* (Cambridge: Polity Press).

——(1993) 'Human Rights and Crimes of the State: The Culture of Denial', 26 *Australian and New Zealand Journal of Criminology*, 97.

——(1995) 'State Crimes of Previous Regimes: Knowledge, Accountability and the Policing of the Past', 20 *Law and Social Inquiry*, 7.

Cohen, S., and Young, J. (1981) *The Manufacture of News, Deviance, Social Problems and the Mass Media* (London: Constable, 2nd rev. ed.).

Combs, N.A. (2002) 'Copping a Plea to Genocide: The Plea Bargaining of International Crimes', 151 *University of Pennsylvania Law Review*, 1.

——(2007) *Guilty Pleas in International Criminal Law: Constructing a Restorative Justice Approach* (Stanford CA: Stanford University Press).

Comment to Art. 46 "Sentencing" Yearbook of the International Law Commission (1994).

Commission Justice pénale et Droits de l'homme, (1991) *La mise en état des affaires pénales*, rapport final (Paris: La Documentation Française).

Corbett, C., and Simon, F. (1991) 'Police and Public Perceptions of the Seriousness of Traffic Offences', 31 *British Journal of Criminology*, 153.

Corso, P. (1993) 'Italy' in C. Van Den Wyngaert *et al.* (eds) *Criminal Procedure Systems in the European Community* (London: Butterworth), 239.

Cotterrell, R.B.M. (1983) 'Legality and Political Legitimacy in the Sociology of Max Weber' in D. Sugarman (ed.) *Legality, Ideology and the State* (London and New York: Academic Press) 69–93.

——(1989) *The Politics of Jurisprudence: A Critical Introduction to Legal Philosophy* (London: Butterworth, 1st ed.) 146.

——(1992) *The Sociology of Law: An Introduction* (London: Butterworth, 2nd ed.).

——(1998) 'Why Must Legal Ideas Be Interpreted Sociologically?', 25 *Journal of Law and Society*, 171.

——(1999) *Emile Durkheim: Law in a Moral Domain* (Edinburgh: Edinburgh University Press).

——(2002) 'Seeking Similarity, Appreciating Difference: Comparative Law and Communities' in A. Harding and E. Orucu (eds) *Comparative Law in the 21st Century* (The Hague: Kluwer).

——(2006) *Law, Culture and Society* (Aldershot: Ashgate).

Crawford, A. (2000) 'Contrasts in Victim–Offender Mediation and Appeals to Community on France and England' in D. Nelken (ed.) *Contrasting Criminal Justice: Getting from Here to There* (Aldershot: Ashgate), 205.

Crocker, L. (1995) 'The Upper Limit of Just Punishment' (1995) 41 *Emory Law Journal*, 1059.

Crown Prosecution Service (2010) *The Code for Crown Prosecutors*, February 2010, http://www.cps.gov.uk/publications/docs/code2010english.pdf (accessed 2010).

Daems, T. (2008) *Making Sense of Penal Change* (Oxford: Oxford University Press).

Damaška, M. (1986) *The Faces of Justice and State Authority* (New Haven: Yale University Press).

——'What is the Point of International Criminal Justice?' (2008) 83 *Chicago Kent Law Review*, 329.

Dana, S. (2004) 'Revisiting the Blaškić Sentence: Some Reflections on the Sentencing Jurisprudence of the ICTY', 4 *International Criminal Law Review*, 321.

Darbyshire, P. (1997) 'For the New Lord Chancellor – Some Causes for Concern about Magistrates', *Criminal Law Review*, 861.

——(2000) 'The Mischief of Plea Bargaining and Sentence Rewards', *Criminal Law Review*, 894.

Davies, M. (2005) 'A New Training Initiative for the Lay Magistracy in England and Wales – A Further Step Towards Professionalisation?', 12 *International Journal of the Legal Profession*, 93.

Davis, K. (1969) *Discretionary Justice: A Preliminary Inquiry* (Baton Rouge LA: Louisiana State University).

de Boer, J., and Gernts, J. (2007) 'Learning from Holland: The TBS System', 6 *Psychiatry*, 459.

Delmas-Marty, M. (1995) 'Towards a European Model of the Criminal Trial' in M Delmas-Marty (ed.) *The Criminal Process and Human Rights: Towards a European Consciousness* (Dordrecht, Netherlands: Martinus Nijhoff), 194.

de Londras, F. (2007) 'Telling Stories and Hearing Truths: Providing an Effective Remedy to Genocidal Sexual Violence against Women' in R. Henham and P. Behrens (eds) *The Criminal Law of Genocide: International, Comparative and Contextual Aspects* (Aldershot: Ashgate).

Del Tufo, M.V. (2009) 'La vittima di fronte al reato nell'orizzonte europeo' in G. Fiandaca and C. Visconti (eds) *Punire, mediare, reconciliari* (Turin: Giappichelli), 107–19.

Dennis, I. (2001) 'The International Criminal Court Act 2001', 48 *Criminal Law Review*, 767.

Dervieux, V. (2002) 'The French System' in M. Delmas-Marty and J.R. Spencer (eds) *European Criminal Procedures* (Cambridge: Cambridge University Press) ch. 4.

Dhami, M.K. (2007) 'Sentencing Decisions' in B. Cutler (ed.) *Encyclopaedia of Law and Psychology* (Thousand Oaks CA: Sage).

Dhami, M.K., and Souza, K.A. (2009) Study of Sentencing and its Outcomes: Pilot Report, Ministry of Justice Research Series 2/09 (London: Ministry of Justice).

Diamond, S.S. (1990) 'Revising Images of Public Punitiveness: Sentencing by Lay and Professional English Magistrates', 15 *Law and Social Inquiry*, 191.

Di Chiara, G. (2009) 'Scenari processuali per l'intervento di mediassone: una panoramice sulle' in G. Fiandaca and C. Visconti (eds) *Punire, mediare, reconciliari* (Turin: Giappichelli), 120–34.

Dignan, J., and Cavadino, M. (1996) 'Towards a Framework for Conceptualising and Evaluating Models of Criminal Justice from a Victim's Perspective', 4 *International Review of Victimology*, 153.

Doak, J. (2008) *Victims' Rights, Human Rights and Criminal Justice: Reconceiving the Role of Third Parties* (Oxford, Hart Publishing).

Doak, J., Henham, R. and Mitchell, B. (2009) 'Victims and the Sentencing Process: Developing Participatory Rights?', 29 *Legal Studies*, 651.

Dolcini, E. (1979) *La commisurazione della pena* (Padua: Cedam).

Dolinko, D. (1997) 'Retributivism, Consequentialism and the Intrinsic Goodness of Punishment', 16 *Law and Philosophy*, 507.

Donnelly, J. (2003) *Universal Human Rights in Theory and Practice* (Ithaca NY: Cornell University Press).

Douzinas, C. (1996) 'Justice and Human Rights in Postmodernity' in C. Gearty and A. Tomkins (eds) *Understanding Human Rights* (London: Mansell).

Drumbl, M.A. (2002) 'Sclerosis: Retributive Justice and the Rwandan Genocide', 2 *Punishment and Society*, 287.

——(2005) 'Collective Violence and Individual Punishment: The Criminality of Mass Atrocity', 99 *Northwestern University Law Review*, 539.

——(2007a) *Atrocity, Punishment, and International Law* (Cambridge: Cambridge University Press).

——(2007b) 'The Expressive Value of Prosecuting and Punishing Terrorists: Hamdan, the Geneva Conventions and International Criminal Law', 75 *George Washington Law Review*, 1165.

Duff, R.A. (1990) *Intention, Agency and Criminal Liability* (Oxford: Basil Blackwell).

——(1998) 'Desert and Penance' in A von Hirsch and A Ashworth (eds) *Principled Sentencing: Readings on Theory and Policy* (Oxford: Hart Publishing, 2nd ed.), 161.

——(2001) *Punishment, Communication and Community* (Oxford: Oxford University Press).

——(2003) 'Penance, Punishment and the Limits of Community', 5 *Punishment and Society*, 295.

Duff, R.A., and Garland, D. (1994) 'Introduction: Thinking about Punishment' in R.A. Duff and D. Garland (eds) *A Reader on Punishment* (Oxford: Oxford University Press).

Duff, R.A., Farmer, A., Marshall, S. and Tadros, V. (2004, 2006, 2007) *The Trial on Trial* (3 vols) (Oxford: Hart Publishing).

Durkheim, E. (1968) *The Division of Labour in Society* (New York, Free Press).

——(1982) trans. W.D. Halls, *The Rules of Sociological Method and Selected Texts on Sociology and its Method* (London: Macmillan).

——(1984) 'Two Laws of Penal Evolution' in S. Lukes and A. Scull (eds) *Durkheim and the Law* (Oxford: Basil Blackwell), 101.

Dworkin, R.M. (1977) *Taking Rights Seriously* (London: Duckworth).

Easton, S., and Piper, C. (2005) *Sentencing and Punishment: The Quest for Justice* (Oxford: Oxford University Press, 1st ed.).

——(2008) *Sentencing and Punishment: The Quest for Justice* (Oxford: Oxford University Press, 2nd ed.).

Eastwood, M. (2006) 'Issues within the Development of Incitement to Genocide' unpublished PhD thesis, University of Central Lancashire.

——(forthcoming) The Emergence of Incitement to Genocide within the Nuremberg Trial Process: The Case of Julius Streicher (Ceredigion: Edwin Mellen Press).

Edwards, I. (2001) 'Victim Participation in Sentencing: The Problem of Incoherence', 40 *Howard Journal of Criminal Justice*, 39.

——(2004) 'An Ambiguous Participant: The Crime Victim and Criminal Justice Decision-Making', 44 *British Journal of Criminology*, 967.

——(2009) 'The Evidential Quality of Victim Personal Statements and Family Impact Statements', 13 *International Journal of Evidence and Proof*, 293.

Elliot, C. (2001) *French Criminal Law* (Cullompton: Willan Publishing).

Emmerson, B., and Ashworth, A. (2001) *Human Rights and Criminal Justice* (London: Sweet & Maxwell, 1st ed.).

Emsley, C. (1996) *Crime and English Society 1750–1900* (London: Longman, 2nd ed.).

Engstrom, P. (2010) 'Human Rights: Effectiveness of International and Regional Mechanisms' in R.A. Denemark (ed.) *The International Studies Encyclopedia* (Oxford: Blackwell).

Erez, E. (1994) 'Victim Participation in Sentencing: And the Debate Goes on', 3 *International Review of Victimology*, 17.

——(1999) 'Who's Afraid of the Big Bad Victim? Victim Impact Statements as Victim Empowerment *and* Enhancement of Justice', *Criminal Law Review*, 545.

——(2004) 'Victim Voice, Impact Statements and Sentencing: Integrating Restorative Justice and Therapeutic Jurisprudence Principles in Adversarial Proceedings', 40 *Criminal Law Bulletin*, 483.

Erez, E., and Roeger, L. (1995) 'Crime Impact v Victim Impact: Victim Impact Statements in South Australia', 6 *Criminology Australia*, 3.

Erez, E., and Rogers, L. (1999) 'The Effects of Victim Impact Statements on Criminal Justice Outcomes and Processes: The Perspectives of Legal Professionals', 39 *British Journal of Criminology*, 216.

Erez, E., and Tontodonato, P. (1990) 'The Effect of Victim Participation in Sentencing on Sentence Outcome', 28 *Criminology*, 451.

Erez, E., *et al.* (1994) *Victim Impact Statements in South Australia: An Evaluation* (Adelaide: Office of Crime Statistics).

EurActiv (2009) 'Immigrant crime poisons Italy–Romania relations' 24 February http://www.euractiv.com/en/enlargement/immigrant-crime-poisons-italy-romania-relations/article-179703 (accessed 2009).

Ewald, U. (2006) 'Large Scale Victimisation and the Jurisprudence of the ICTY – Victimological Research Issues' in U. Ewald and K. Turković (eds) *Large-Scale Victimisation as a Potential Source of Terrorist Activities: Importance of Regaining Security in Post-Conflict Societies*, NATO Security Through Science Series, E: Human and Societal Dynamics, vol. 13 (Amsterdam: IOS Press), 171.

——(2008) '"Reason" and "Truth" in International Criminal Trials' in R. Haveman and A. Smeulers (eds) *Supranational Criminology: Towards a Criminology of International Crimes* (Antwerp: Intersentia).

Farmer, L. (2006) 'Tony Martin and the Nightbreakers: Criminal Law, Victims and the Power to Punish' in S. Armstrong and L. McAra (eds) *Perspectives on Punishment: The Contours of Control* (Oxford: Oxford University Press). 49.

Faugeron, C. (1991) 'Prisons in France: Stalemate or Evolution?' in D. van Zyl Smit and F. Dunkel (eds) *Imprisonment Today and Tomorrow: International Perspectives on Prisoners' Rights and Prison Conditions* (Deventer: Kluwer Law International, 1st ed.), 249.

Feinberg, J. (1971) *Doing and Deserving: Essays in the Theory of Responsibility* (Princeton NJ: Princeton University Press).

Feldman, D. (2005) 'Proportionality and Discrimination in Anti-Terrorism Legislation', 64 *Cambridge Law Journal*, 271.

Fenwick, H. (1997) 'Procedural Rights of Victims of Crime: Public or Private Ordering of the Criminal Justice Process', 60 *Modern Law Review*, 60.

Ferstman, C. (2002) 'The Reparations Regime of the International Criminal Court', 15 *Leiden Journal of International Law*, 667.

Fiandaca, G. (1994) 'Il comma terzo dell'art 27' in G. Branca and A. Pizzorusso (eds) *Commentario alla Costituzione* (Bologna: Zanichelli), 222.

Findlay, M. (2002) 'Internationalised Criminal Trial and Access to Justice', 2 *International Criminal Law Review*, 237.

——(2007) 'Terrorism and Relative Justice', 47 *Crime, Law and Social Change* 57.

——(2008) *Governing through Globalised Crime* (Cullompton: Willan Publishing).

——(2009) 'Activating a Victim Constituency in International Criminal Justice', 3 *International Journal of Transitional Justice*, 183.

——(2010b) 'Governing through Globalised Crime: Thoughts on the Transition from Terror' in R. Henham and M. Findlay (eds) *Exploring the Boundaries of International Criminal Justice* (Aldershot: Ashgate,), ch. 8.

Findlay, M., and Henham, R. (2005) *Transforming International Criminal Justice: Retributive And Restorative Justice in the Trial Process* (Cullompton: Willan Publishing).

——(2007) 'Integrating Theory and Method in the Comparative Contextual Analysis of Trial Process' in M. McConville and W.H. Chui (eds) *Research Methods for Law* (Edinburgh: Edinburgh University Press).

——(2010a) *Beyond Punishment: Achieving International Criminal Justice* (London: Palgrave Macmillan).

Finnis, J. (1980) *Natural Law and Natural Rights* (Oxford: Oxford University Press).

Fletcher, L.E., and Weinstein, H.M. (2002) 'Violence and Social Repair: Rethinking the Contribution of Justice to Reconciliation', 24 *Human Rights Quarterly*, 573.

Floud, J., and Young, W. (1981) *Dangerousness and Criminal Justice* (London: Heinemann).

Foucault, M. (1977) *Discipline and Punish: The Birth of the Prison* (Harmondsworth: Penguin).

——(1980) *Knowledge/Power* (London: Harvester Press).

Fournet, C. (2007) 'Reflection on the Separation of Powers: The Law of Genocide and the Symptomatic French Paradox' in R. Henham and P. Behrens (eds) *The Criminal Law of Genocide: International, Comparative and Contextual Aspects* (Aldershot: Ashgate,), ch. 17.

Frase, R.S. (1998) 'Comparative Criminal Justice Policy' in *Comparative Criminal Justice Systems: From Diversity to Rapprochment*, Proceedings of the International Conference for the 25th Anniversary of the International Institute of Higher Studies in Criminal Sciences, Syracuse, Italy, 16–20 December 1997, Nouvelles Etudes Penales, No. 17. International Association of Penal Law (Toulouse: Editions érès), 109.

——(2008) 'Sentencing and Comparative Law Theory', in J. Jackson, M. Langer and P. Tillers (eds) *Crime, Procedure and Evidence in a Comparative and International Context: Essays in Honour of Professor Mirjan Damaška* (Oxford: Hart Publishing).

Freccero, S.P. (1994) 'An Introduction to the New Italian Criminal Procedure', 21 *American Journal of Criminal Law*, 348.

Freedland, J. (2006) 'The *Sun* and John Reid are both right: these sentences do not fit the crime' *The Guardian*, 14 June 2006, http://www.guardian.co.uk/commentisfree/story/0,1796880,00.html (accessed 2010).

Freiberg, A., and Gelb, K. (2008) *Penal Populism, Sentencing Councils and Sentencing Policy* (Cullompton: Willan Publishing).

Frulli, M. (2001) 'Are Crimes against Humanity More Serious than War Crimes?', 12 *European Journal of International Law*, 329.

Fuller, L.L. (1969) *The Morality of Law* (New Haven: Yale University Press, 2nd ed.).

Gaeta, P., and Jessberger, F. (eds) (2006) 'Special Issue: Criminal Law Responses to Terrorism After September 11', 4/5 *Journal of International Criminal Justice*.

Gage Report (2008) *Sentencing Guidelines in England and Wales: An Evolutionary Approach* (London: Sentencing Commission Working Group).

Galabru, K. (2006) 'Reconciliation in International Criminal Justice: Lessons from Other Tribunals', *Open Society Justice Initiative*, 151.

Galo, E. (1995) 'The Penal System in France: From Correctionalism to Managerialism' in V. Ruggiero, M. Ryan and J. Sim (eds) *Western European Penal Systems: A Critical Anatomy* (London: Sage), 80.

Garfinkel, H. (1956) 'Conditions of Successful Degradation Ceremonies', 61 *American Journal of Sociology*, 420.

Garland, D. (1985) *Punishment and Welfare: A History of Penal Strategies* (Aldershot: Gower).

——(1990) *Punishment and Modern Society* (Oxford: Clarendon Press).

——(1996) 'The Limits of the Sovereign State: Strategies of Crime Control in Contemporary Society', 36 *British Journal of Criminology*, 445.

——(2001) *The Culture of Control: Crime and Social Order in Contemporary Society* (Oxford: Oxford University Press).

Gaynor, F. (2007) 'Ordinary Sentences for Extraordinary Crimes', 5 *Journal of International Criminal Justice*, 683.

Gelsthorpe, L. (2005) 'Back to Basics in Crime Control: Weaving in Women' in M. Matravers (ed.) *Managing Modernity: Politics and the Culture of Control* (Abingdon: Routledge).

——(2010) 'Working with Women Offenders in the Community: A View from England and Wales' in R. Sheehan *et al.* (eds) *Working with Women Offenders in the Community* (Cullompton: Willan Publishing).

Gelsthorpe, L., and Padfield, N. (eds) (2003) *Exercising Discretion: Decision-making in the Criminal Justice System and Beyond* (Cullompton: Willan Publishing).

Giddens, A. (1979) *Central Problems in Social Theory* (London, Macmillan).

——(1984) *The Constitution of Society: Outlines of a Theory of Structuration* (Cambridge: Polity Press).

Gillespie, A. (2006) Commentary on the Sweeney case, 156 *New Law Journal*, 1153.

Girling, E. (2006) 'European Identity, Penal Sensibilities and Communities of Sentiment' in S. Armstrong and L. McAra (eds.) *Perspectives on Punishment: The Contours of Control* (Oxford: Oxford University Press).

Gottfredson, M.R., and Hirschi, T. (1990) *A General Theory of Crime* (Stanford CA: Stanford University Press).

Grande, E. (2000) 'Italian Criminal Justice: Borrowing and Resistance', 48 *American Journal of Comparative Law*, 227.

——(2002) 'The Rehabilitative Ideal in Italian Criminal Justice', 2 *Global Jurist Topics*, 1.

Green, E. (1961) *Judicial Attitudes in Sentencing* (London: Macmillan).

Gregory, M. (2010) 'Reflection and Resistance: Probation Practice and the Ethics of Care', *British Journal of Social Work*, Advance Access published online on 22 March 2010: http://bjsw.oxfordjournals.org/cgi/content/abstract/bcq028v1 (accessed 2010).

Gross, H. (1979) *A Theory of Criminal Justice* (New York: Oxford University Press).

Guest, J. (1999) 'Aboriginal Legal Theory and Restorative Justice, Parts 1 and 2', Vols 1 and 2 *Justice as Healing* Native Law Center of Canada http://www.usask.ca/nativelaw/publications/jah/ (accessed 2008).

Habermas, J. (1987) trans. F.G. Lawrence, *The Philosophical Discourse of Modernity: Twelve Lectures* (Cambridge: Polity Press).

——(1996) trans. W. Relig, *Between Facts and Norms: Contributions to a Discourse Theory of Law and Democracy* (Cambridge: Polity Press).

Hall, M. (2009) *Victims of Crime: Policy and Practice in Criminal Justice* (Cullompton, Willan).

Hall, S. *et al.*, (1978) *Policing the Crisis: Mugging, the State and Law and Order* (London: Palgrave Macmillan).

Halliday, J. (2001) *Making Punishments Work: Report of a Review of the Sentencing Framework for England and Wales* (London: Home Office).

Harber, K., and Pennebaker, J. (1992) 'Overcoming Traumatic Memories' in S. Christianson (ed.), *The Handbook of Emotion and Memory: Research and Theory* (London: Lawrence Erlbaum Associates).

Hardt, M., and Negri, A. (2000) *Empire* (London: Harvard University Press).

Harman, G. (1999) 'XIV – Moral Philosophy Meets Social Psychology: Virtue Ethics and the Fundamental Attribution Error', 99 *Proceedings of the Aristotelian Society*, 315.

Hart, H.L.A. (1963) *Law, Liberty and Morality* (Stanford: Stanford University Press).

Hart, H.L.A. (1968) *Punishment and Responsibility: Essays in the Philosophy of Law* (Oxford: Oxford University Press).

Hawkins, K, (2002) *Law as Last Resort: Prosecution Decision-Making in a Regulatory Agency* (Oxford: Oxford University Press).

——(2003) 'Order, Rationality and Silence: Some Reflections on Criminal Justice Decision-Making' in L. Gelsthorpe and N. Padfield *Exercising Discretion: Decision-Making in the Criminal Justice System and Beyond* (Cullompton: Willan Publishing).

Haydon, D., and Scraton, P. (2000) '"Condemn a Little More; Understand a Little Less": The Political Context and Rights Implications of the Domestic and European Rulings in the Venables-Thompson Case', 27 *Journal of Law and Society*, 416.

Hedderman, C., and Gelsthorpe, L. (1997) *Understanding the Sentencing of Women*, Home Office Research Study 170 (London, Home Office Research and Statistics Directorate).

Henderson, J.Y. (1995) 'Exploring Justice as Healing', *Justice as Healing*, Native Law Center of Canada, http://www.usask.ca/nativelaw/publications/jah/1995/Exploring_Justice_Heal.pdf (accessed 2011).

Henham, R. (1990) *Sentencing Principles and Magistrates' Sentencing Behaviour* (Aldershot: Avebury).

——(1992) 'Evaluating the United States Federal Sentencing Guidelines', 21 *Anglo-American Law Review*, 399.

——(1994) 'Attorney-General's References and Sentencing Policy', *Criminal Law Review*, 499.

——(1996) *Criminal Justice and Sentencing Policy* (Aldershot: Dartmouth).

——(1997) 'Protective Sentences: Ethics, Rights and Sentencing Policy', 25 *International Journal of the Sociology of Law*, 45.

——(1998) 'Making Sense of the Crime (Sentences) Act 1997', *Modern Law Review*, 223.

——(1999a) 'Bargain Justice or Justice Denied? Sentence Discounts and the Criminal Process', 62 *Modern Law Review*, 515.

——(1999b) *Sentence Discounts and the Criminal Process* (Aldershot, Ashgate).

——(2000a) 'Problems of Theorizing Sentencing Research', 28 *International Journal of the Sociology of Law*, 15.

——(2000b) 'Sentencing Theory, Proportionality and Pragmatism' 28 *International Journal of the Sociology of Law* 239.

(2001) 'Theory and Contextual Analysis in Sentencing', 29 *International Journal of the Sociology of Law*, 253.

——(2003a) 'Some Issues for Sentencing in the International Criminal Court', 52 *International and Comparative Law Quarterly*, 81.

——(2003b) 'The Philosophical Foundations of International Sentencing', 1 *Journal of International Criminal Justice*. 64.

——(2004a) 'Conceptualising Access to Justice and Victims' Rights in International Sentencing', 13 *Social and Legal Studies*, 21.

——(2004b) 'Theorising the Penality of International Criminal Trials', 8 *Theoretical Criminology*, 429.

——(2004c) 'Some Reflections on the Role of Victims in the International Criminal Trial Process', 11 *International Review of Victimology*, 201.

——(2005a) 'Plea bargaining and the Legitimacy of International Trial Justice: Some Observations on the Dragan Nikolić Sentencing Judgement of the ICTY', 5 *International Criminal Law Review*, 601.

——(2005b) *Punishment and Process in International Criminal Trials* (Aldershot: Ashgate).

——(2007a) 'Developing Contextualised Rationales for Sentencing in International Criminal Trials: A Plea for Empirical Research', 5 *Journal of International Criminal Justice*, 757.

——(2007b) 'Theorising Law and Legitimacy in International Criminal Justice', 3 *International Journal of Law in Context*, 257.

——(2009a) Review of Wandall (2008), 49 *British Journal of Criminology*, 421.

——(2009b) 'Towards Restorative Sentencing in International Criminal Trials', 9 *International Criminal Law Review*, 809.

——(2010a) 'Punishment in Transition: Re-thinking the Role of Punishment and Sentencing for Transitional Justice' Paper presented at research seminar, Oxford Transitional Justice Research, Centre for Socio-Legal Studies, University of Oxford, February 2010, http://www.csls.ox.ac.uk/otjr.php?show=podcasts (accessed 2010).

Henham, R., and Drumbl, M. (2005) 'Plea Bargaining at the International Criminal Tribunal for the former Yugoslavia', 16 *Criminal Law Forum*, 49.

Henham, R., and Findlay, M. (2002) 'Criminal Justice Modelling and the Comparative Contextual Analysis of Trial Process', 2 *International Journal of Comparative Criminology*, 162.

Henham, R., and Mannozzi, G. (2003) 'Victim Participation and Sentencing in England and Italy: A Legal and Policy Analysis', 11 *European Journal of Crime, Criminal Law and Criminal Justice*, 278.

Herzog-Evans, M. (2009) 'French Post Custody Law (2000–2009): From Equitable Trial to the Religion of Control', 1 *European Journal of Probation*, 97.

Hickman, L., and Alexander, T.M. (eds) (1998) *The Essential Dewey* (Bloomington IN: Indiana University Press).

Hirschi, T. (1969) *Causes of Delinquency* (Berkeley CA: University of California Press, 3rd ed.).

Hodgson, J. (2000) 'Comparing Legal Cultures: The Comparativist as Participant Observer' in D. Nelken (ed.) *Contrasting Criminal Justice: Getting from Here to There* (Aldershot: Ashgate).

——(2001) 'The Police, the Prosecutor and the Juge d'Instruction: Judicial Supervision in France, Theory and Practice', 41 *British Journal of Criminology*, 342.

——(2002a) 'Constructing the pre-trial role of the defence in French criminal procedure: An adversarial outsider in an inquisitorial process?', 6 *International Journal of Evidence and Proof*, 1.

——(2002b) 'Hierarchy, Bureaucracy and Ideology in French Criminal Justice : Some Empirical Observations', 29 *Journal of Law And Society*, 227.

Hogarth, J. (1971) *Sentencing as a Human Process* (Toronto: Toronto University Press).

Home Office (2001) *Victim Personal Statements*, Circular 35/2001, 14 August.

——(2002) *Justice for All* CM 5563 (London: Stationery Office).

——(2004)'Spot Fines Extended In Crack Down On Petty Crime', Home Office Press Release 340/2004, 31 October http://press.homeoffice.gov.uk/press-releases/Spot_Fines_Extended_In_Crack_Dow?version=1 (accessed 2010).

——(2005) *Hearing the Relatives of Murder and Manslaughter Victims: Consultation Document* (London: Stationery Office).

——(2006) 'Making Sentencing Clearer: a consultation and a report by the Home Secretary, Lord Chancellor and Attorney-General', 9 November http://www.noms.homeoffice.gov.uk/news-publications-events/publications/consultations/Making_sentencing_clearer_consul?view=Binary (accessed 2006).

Hood, R.G. (1962) *Sentencing in Magistrates' Courts: A Study in Variations of Policy* (London: Stevens).

——(1972) *Sentencing the Motoring Offender* (London: Heinemann).

——(1992) *Race and Sentencing* (Oxford: Oxford University Press).

Hough, M., Jacobson, J. and Millie, A. (2003) *The Decision to Imprison: Sentencing and the Prison Population* (London, Prison Reform Trust).

Hough, M. *et al.* (2008) *Attitudes to the Sentencing Of Offences Involving Death by Driving* Research Report 5 (London: Sentencing Advisory Panel).

Hudson, B. (1993) *Penal Policy and Social Justice* (London: Macmillan).

——(1998) 'Doing Justice to Difference' in A. Ashworth and M. Wasik (eds) *Fundamentals of Sentencing Theory* (Oxford: Clarendon Press).

——(2003a) *Justice in the Risk Society: Challenging and Re-Affirming Justice in Late Modernity* (London: Sage).

——(2003b) *Understanding Justice: An Introduction to Ideas, Perspectives and Controversies in Modern Penal Theory* (Buckingham: Open University Press, 2nd ed.).

Hutchinson S (2006) 'Countering Catastrophic Criminology: Reform, Punishment and the Modern Liberal Compromise', 8 *Punishment and Society*, 443.

Hutton, N. (1995) 'Sentencing, Rationality and Computer Technology' 22 *Journal of Law and Society*, 549.

——(2006) 'Sentencing as a Social Practice' in S. Armstrong and L. McAra (eds) *Perspectives on Punishment: The Contours of Control* (Oxford: Oxford University Press).

——(2008) 'Institutional Mechanisms for Incorporating the Public' in A. Freiberg and K. Gelb (eds) *Penal Populism, Sentencing Councils and Sentencing Policy* (Cullompton: Willan Publishing).

ICTY Press and Information Office (1996) *Rule 61: The Voice of the Victims*, Information Memorandum 1.

Indemaur, D. (2008) 'Dealing the Public In: Challenges for a Transparent and Accountable Sentencing Policy' in A. Freiberg and K. Gelb (eds) *Penal Populism, Sentencing Councils and Sentencing Policy* (Cullompton: Willan Publishing).

Indermaur, D. and Hough, M. (2002) 'Strategies for Changing Public Attitudes to Punishment' in J. Roberts and M. Hough (eds) *Changing Attitudes to Punishment: Public Opinion, Crime and Justice* (Cullompton: Willan Publishing), ch. 11.

International Centre for Transitional Justice, (2006) 'Reconciliation' on the question of developing a 'Civil Trust Model of Reconciliation', http://www.ictj.org/en/index.html (accessed 2010).

Ipsos MORI (2003) 'Whom do we Trust: Neither Politicians nor Journalists!' 27 February at http://www.ipsos-mori.com/publications/rmw/whomdowetrust.shtml (accessed 2005).

Jackson, B.S. (1988) *Law, Fact and Narrative Coherence* (Liverpool: Deborah Charles).

Jackson, J. (2004) 'Experience and Expression: Social and Cultural Significance in the Fear of Crime', 44 *British Journal of Criminology*, 946.

——'Validating New Measures of the Fear of Crime' (2005) 8 *International Journal of Social Research Methodology* 297.

———(2009) 'Finding the Best Epistemic Fit for International Criminal Tribunals: Beyond the Adversarial-Inquisitorial Dichotomy', 7 *Journal of International Criminal Justice*, 17.

Jacobson, J., and Hough, M. (2010) *Unjust Deserts: Imprisonment For Public Protection* (London: Prison Reform Trust), http://www.prisonreformtrust.org.uk/uploads/documents/unjustdeserts.pdf (accessed 2010).

Johnstone, G. (2002) *Restorative Justice: Ideas, Values, Debates* (Cullompton: Willan Publishing).

Jung, H. (1997) 'Plea Bargaining and its Repercussions on the Theory of Criminal Procedure', 5 *European Journal of Crime, Criminal Law and Criminal Justice*, 112.

Keller, A. (2001) 'Punishment for Violations of International Criminal Law: An Analysis of Sentencing at the ICTY and ICTR', 12 *Indiana International and Comparative Law Review*, 52.

Keller, L.M. (2007) 'Seeking Justice at the International Criminal Court: Victims' Reparations', 29 *Thomas Jefferson Law Review*, 189.

Kenney, J. (2003) 'Gender Roles and Grief Cycles: Observations of Models of Grief and Coping in Homicide Survivors', 10 *International Review of Victimology*, 19.

King, M. (1978) 'A Status Passage Analysis of the Defendant's Progress through the Magistrates' Court', 2 *Law and Human Behaviour*, 167.

———(1993) 'The Truth about Autopoiesis', 20 *Journal of Law and Society*, 218.

Kirchengast, T. (2008) 'Sentencing Law and the "Emotional Catharsis" of Victim's Rights in NSW Homicide Cases', 30 *Sydney Law Review*, 615.

Kittichaisaree, K. (2001) *International Criminal Law* (Oxford: Oxford University Press) 227.

Kymlicka, W. (2002) *Contemporary Political Philosophy: An Introduction* (Oxford: Oxford University Press, 2nd ed.).

Lacey, N. (1987) 'Discretion and Due Process at the Post-Conviction Stage' in I.H. Dennis (ed.) *Criminal Law and Justice* (London: Sweet & Maxwell), 221.

———(1988) *State Punishment: Political Principles and Community Values* (London: Routledge).

———(1994) 'Government as Manager, Citizen as Consumer: The Case of the Criminal Justice Act 1991', 57 *Modern Law Review*, 534.

———(2008) *The Prisoners' Dilemma: Political Economy and Punishment in Contemporary Democracies*, The Hamlyn Lectures, 2007 (Cambridge: Cambridge University Press).

Langer, M.L. (2004) 'From Legal Transplants to Legal Translations: The Globalisation of Plea Bargaining and the Americanisation Thesis in Criminal Procedure', 45 *Harvard International Law Journal*, 1.

Lea, J. and Young, J., (1984) *What is to be Done about Law and Order? Crisis in the Nineties* (Harmondsworth: Penguin).

Leblois-Happe, J. (2000) 'De la transaction pénale à la composition pénale', 1 *JCP*, 198.

———(2003) 'Le libre choix de la peine par le juge: un principe défendu bec et ongles par la Chambre criminelle' *Droit pénal*, chronique 11.

———(2008) Personnalisation des Peines: Généralités. Semi-liberté. Placement à l'extérieur' LexisNexis.

Lelieur-Fischer, J. (2004) 'The Punishment of Serious Crimes in France' in U. Sieber (ed.) *The Punishment of Serious Crimes: A Comparative Analysis of Sentencing Law and Practice*, vol. 2: *Country Reports* (Freiburg im Breisgau: Max Planck Institute for Foreign and International Criminal Law).

Lemert, E.M. (1972) *Human Deviance, Social Problems and Social Control* (Englewood Cliffs NJ: Prentice Hall, 2nd ed.).

Liebling, A. (2010) 'Distinctions and Distinctiveness in the Work of Prison Officers: Legitimacy and Authority Revisited', Cambridge Institute of Criminology, 13th Annual Nigel Walker Lecture, May.

Lind, E.A., and Tyler, T.R. (1988) *The Social Psychology of Procedural Justice* (New York: Plenum Press).

Loader, I. (2006) 'Fall of the "Platonic Guardians": Liberalism, Criminology and Political Responses to Crime in England and Wales', 46 *British Journal of Criminology*, 561.

Loader, I., and Sparks, R. (2004) 'For a Historical Sociology of Crime Policy in England and Wales since 1968', 7 *Critical Review of International Social and Political Philosophy*, 5.

Louw, D.J. (1988) 'Ubuntu: An African Assessment of the Religious Other', Paper delivered at the 20th World Congress of Philosophers, August.

Lovegrove, A. (1989) *Judicial Decision-Making: Sentencing Policy and Numerical Guidance* (New York: Springer-Verlag).

——(1997) *The Framework of Judicial Sentencing: A Study in Legal Decision-Making* (Cambridge University Press: Cambridge).

McBarnet, D. (1981a) *Conviction: Law, the State and the Construction of Justice* (London: Palgrave Macmillan).

——(1981b) 'Magistrates' Courts and the Ideology of Justice', 8 *British Journal of Law and Society*, 181.

McCarthy, C. (2009) 'Reparations under the Rome Statute of the International Criminal Court and Reparative Justice Theory', 3 *International Journal of Transitional Justice*, 250.

McCoy, C. (1994) 'What We Say and What They Do: Prosecutors' and Judges' Sentencing Decisions at Guilty Plea versus Trial', Paper presented at the American Society of Criminology, Annual Meeting, New Orleans, November.

McCoy, C., and Henham, R. (2004) 'Guilty Plea Discounts in American and English Courts: An Empirical Description and Ethical Critique of the Trial Penalty' (unpublished paper).

McEvoy, K., and McGregor, L. (eds) (2008) *Transitional Justice from Below: Grassroots Activism and the Struggle for Change* (Oxford: Hart Publishing).

McGoldrick, D. (1999) 'The Permanent International Criminal Court: An End to the Culture of Impunity', *Criminal Law Review*, 644.

Mackie, J.L. (1982) 'Morality and the Retributive Emotions', 1 *Criminal Justice Ethics*, 3.

Makkai, T., and Braithwaite, J. (1996) 'Procedural Justice and Regulatory Compliance', 20 *Law and Human Behavior*, 83.

Mannozzi, G. (1996) *Razionalità e 'giustizia' nella commisurazione della pena: Il Just Desert Model e la riforma del sentencing nordamericano* (Padua: Cedam).

——(1999) 'Are Guided Sentencing and Plea Bargaining Incompatible? Perspectives of Reform in the Italian Legal System'. Paper presented at the Sentencing and Society International Conference, University of Strathclyde, June.

——(2000) 'Pena e riti differenziati: la crisi del modello "unitario" di commisurazione', *Rassegna penitenziaria e criminological*, 69.

——(2002) 'Are Guided Sentencing and Plea Bargaining Incompatible? Perspectives of Reform in the Italian Legal System' in C. Tata and N. Hutton (eds) *Sentencing and Society: International Perspectives* (Aldershot: Ashgate), ch. 6.

——(2003) 'Positioning Mediation in the Criminal Justice System: The Italian "Justice of the Peace"' in L. Walgrave (ed.) *Repositioning Restorative Justice* (Cullompton: Willan Publishing), ch. 16.

Masera, L. (2009) '"Terra brucciata" attorno al clandistino: tra misure penale simboliche e negazione reale dei diritti' in O. Mazza and F. Vigano (eds) *Il "pacchetto sicurezza"* (Turin: Giappichelli), 27–82.

Mathiesen, T. (1990) *Prison on Trial* (London: Sage).

——(2006) *Lex Vigilatoria: Towards a Control System Without a State?* in S. Armstrong and L. McAra (eds) *Perspectives on Punishment: The Contours of Control* (Oxford: Oxford University Press).

Matza, D. (1964) *Delinquency and Drift* (New York: John Wiley).

Mayhew, P., and van Kesteren, J. (2002) 'Cross-national Attitudes to Punishment' in J.V. Roberts and M. Hough (eds) *Changing Attitudes to Punishment: Public Opinion, Crime and Justice* (Cullompton: Willan Publishing) ch. 4.

Meierhenrich, J. (2006) 'A Question of Guilt', 19 *Ratio Juris*, 314.

Moore, M. (1993) 'Justifying Retributivism', *Israel Law Review*, 15.

Moretti, B. (2002) 'Sentencing Sexual Offenders in Italy: A Critical Analysis of the Law Governing Sex Crimes' Paper presented at the Second Sentencing and Society Conference, University of Strathclyde.

Morgan, R. (2002) 'The future according to Auld, 29 *Journal of Law and Society*, 308.

Morgan, R., and Russell, N. (2000) *The Judiciary in the Magistrates' Courts* (London: Lord Chancellor's Department).

Morris, N. (1994) '"Dangerousness' and Incapacitation' in R.A. Duff and D. Garland (eds) *A Reader on Punishment* (Oxford: Oxford University Press), 241.

Morris, N., and Tonry, M. (1990) *Between Prison and Probation: Intermediate Punishments in a Rational Sentencing System* (New York: Oxford University Press).

Mueller-Johnson, K., and Dhami, M.K. (2010) 'Effects of Offenders' Age and Health on Sentencing Decisions', 50 *Journal of Social Psychology*, 77.

Mulhall, S., and Swift, A. (1966) *Liberals & Communitarians* (Oxford, Blackwell, 2nd ed.).

Mythen, G., and Walklate, S. (2006) 'Criminology and Terrorism: Which Thesis? Risk Society or Governmentality?', 46 *British Journal of Criminology*, 379.

Nagel, S. (1962) 'Judicial Backgrounds and Criminal Cases', 53 *Journal of Criminal Law, Criminology and Police Science*, 333.

Nelken, D. (1998) 'Blinding Insights? The Limits of a Reflexive Sociology of Law', 25 *Journal of Law and Society*, 407.

——(2010) *Comparative Criminal Justice: Making Sense of Difference* (London: Sage).

Nelken, D, (ed.) (1997) *Comparing Legal Cultures* (Aldershot: Dartmouth).

——(2000) *Contrasting Criminal Justice: Getting from Here to There* (Aldershot: Ashgate).

Nobles, R., and Schiff, D. (1995) 'Miscarriages of Justice: A Systems Approach', 58 *Modern Law Review*, 299.

Norrie, A. (1995) *Crime, Reason and History: A Critical Introduction to Criminal Law* (London: Weidenfeld and Nicolson, 1st ed.).

——(1996a) 'From Law to Popular Justice: Beyond Antinomialism', 5 *Social and Legal Studies*, 383.

——(1996b) 'The Limits of Justice: Finding Fault in the Criminal Law', 59 *Modern Law Review*, 540.

——(2000) *Punishment, Responsibility and Justice* (Oxford: Oxford University Press).

——(2001) *Crime, Reason and History: A Critical Introduction to Criminal Law* (London: Butterworth, 2nd ed.).

——(2009) 'Citizenship, Authoritarianism and the Changing Shape of the Criminal Law' in B. McSherry, A. Norrie and S. Bronitt (eds) *Regulating Deviance: The Redirection of Criminalisation and the Futures of Criminal Law* (Oxford: Hart Publishing), ch. 2.

Oderberg, D.S. (2000) *Moral Theory: A Non-Consequentialist Approach* (Oxford: Blackwell).

Olusanya, O. (2005) *Sentencing War Crimes and Crimes Against Humanity under the International Criminal Tribunal for the Former Yugoslavia* (Groningen: Europa Law Publishing).

O'Malley, P. (1999) 'Volatile and Contradictory Punishment', 3 *Theoretical Criminology*, 175.

Owens, M.W. (1995) 'California's Three Strikes Law: Desperate Times Require Desperate Measures – But Will it Work?', 26 *Pacific Law Journal*, 881.

Packer, H. (1969) *The Limits of the Criminal Sanction* (Stanford: Stanford University Press).

Pakes, F. (2004) *Comparative Criminal Justice* (Cullompton: Willan Publishing, 1st ed.).

——(2010) *Comparative Criminal Justice* (Cullompton: Willan Publishing, 2nd ed.).

Parker, H., Sumner, M. and Jarvis, G. (1989) *Unmasking the Magistrates: The 'Custody Or Not' Decision in Sentencing Young Offenders* (Milton Keynes: Open University Press).

Pascoe-Watson, G., and Coles, J.(2006)'Out-rage at soft justice', *The Sun*, 14 June, http://www.thesun.co.uk/article/0,2006270459,00.html (accessed 2010).

Pavarini, M. (2001) 'Italy – the Politics of Punishment: The Death of Prison Reform in Italy' in D. van Zyl Smit and E. Dunkel (eds) *Imprisonment Today and Tomorrow: International Perspectives on Prisoners' Rights and Prison Conditions* (The Hague: Kluwer Law International, 2nd ed.), 400.

Perrodet, A. (2002a) 'The Public Prosecutor' in M. Delmas-Marty and J.R. Spencer (eds) *European Criminal Procedures* (Cambridge: Cambridge University Press), 409.

——(2002b) (rev. Ricci E) 'The Italian System' in M Delmas-Marty and JR Spencer (eds) *European Criminal Procedures* (Cambridge: Cambridge University Press), ch. 6.

Petrucci, C.J. (2002) 'Apology in the Criminal Justice Setting: Evidence for Including Apology as an Additional Component in the Legal System.', 4 *Behavioral Science and the Law*, 337.

Philips of Worth Matravers, Lord (2007) 'How Important is Punishment', The Howard League for Penal Reform, Cripps Lecture, 11 November 2007.

Picotti, L. (1998) *La mediazione nel sistema penale minorile* (Padua: Cedam).

Picotti, L., and Spangher, G. (2003) *Competenza penale del guidice di pace e "nuove" pene non detentive* (Milan: Giuffre).

Piercamillo, D., and Mannozzi, G. (2007) *La corruzione in Italia: Percezione social e controllo penale* (Rome: Editori Laterza).

Piper, C., and Easton, S. (2005) *Sentencing and Punishment: The Quest for Justice* (Oxford: Oxford University Press, 1st ed.).

Pizzi, W.T., and Marafioti, L. (1992) 'The New Italian Code of Criminal Procedure: The Difficulties of Building an Adversarial Trial System on a Civil Law Foundation', *Yale Journal of International Law*, 17.

Poole, T. (2005) 'Legitimacy, Rights and Judicial Review', 25 *Oxford Journal of Legal Studies*, 697.

Pradel, J. (1993) 'France' in C. Van Den Wyngaert *et al.* (eds) *Criminal Procedure Systems in the European Community* (London: Butterworth), 117.

——(2001) *Droit Pénal Général* (Paris: Cujas).

——(2008) *Manuel de Procédure Pénale* (Paris: Cujas).

Pratt, J. (1995) 'Dangerousness, Risk and Technologies of Power', 28 *Australian and New Zealand Journal of Criminology*, 3.

——(1998) 'Towards the "Decivilizing" of Punishment', 7 *Social and Legal Studies*, 487.

Radzinowicz, L. (1966) *Ideology and Crime* (London: Heineman).

Radzinowicz, L., and Hood, R. (1990) The Emergence of Penal Policy in Victorian and Edwardian England (Oxford: Clarendon Press).

Raine, J.W. (2000) 'Whither Local Justice?', 40 *Criminal Justice Matters*, 19.

——(2002) 'The Lay Magistracy after Auld: Safe as the Rock of Gibraltar?', 166 *Justice of the Peace*, 240.

——(2005) 'Courts, Sentencing and Justice in a Changing Political and Managerial Context', *Public Money and Management*, 291.

Rawls, J, (1973) *A Theory of Justice* (Oxford: Oxford University Press).

Raz, J. (1999) *Practical Reason and Norms* (Oxford: Oxford University Press).

——(2001) *Ethics in the Public Domain* (Oxford: Clarendon Press, rev. ed.).

Renout, H. (2009) *Droit Pénal Général* (Orléans: Paradigme, 13th ed.).

Retzinger, S., and Scheff, T. (1996) 'Strategy for Community Conferences: Emotions and Social Bonds' in B. Galaway and J. Hudson (eds) *Restorative Justice: International Perspectives* (Monsey NY: Criminal Justice Press).

Rex, S. (1998) 'A New Form of Rehabilitation?' in A. von Hirsch and A. Ashworth (eds) *Principled Sentencing: Readings on Theory and Policy* (Oxford, Hart Publishing, 2nd ed.).

——(2004) 'Punishment as Communication' in A. Bottoms, S. Rex and G. Robinson (eds.) *Alternatives to Prison: Options for an Insecure Society* (Cullompton: Willan Publishing).

——(2005) *Reforming Community Penalties* (Cullompton: Willan Publishing).

Rex, S., and Tonry, M. (eds) (2002) *Reform and Punishment: The Future of Sentencing* (Cullompton: Willan Publishing).

Risse-Kappen, T., Ropp, S.C., and Sikkink, K. (1999) *The Power of Human Rights: International Norms and Domestic Change* (Cambridge: Cambridge University Press).

Rizk, C., and Salle, G. (1998) 'La conduite en état alcoolique et sa répression' *Infostat justice*, déc. 1998, n. 52, 4.

Roberts, J.V. (2002) 'Alchemy in Sentencing: An Analysis of Sentencing Reform Proposals in England and Wales', 4 *Punishment and Society*, 425.

——(2008a) 'Punishing Persistence: Explaining the Enduring Appeal of the Recidivist Sentencing Premium', 48 *British Journal of Criminology*, 468.

——(2008b) *Punishing Persistent Offenders: Exploring Community and Offender Perspectives* (Oxford: Oxford University Press).

Roberts, J.V., and Erez, E. (2004) 'Communication in Sentencing: Exploring the Expressive Function of Victim Impact Statements', 10 *International Review of Victimology*, 223.

Roberts, J.V., and Hough, M. (2005) *Understanding Public Attitudes to Criminal Justice* (Maidenhead: Open University Press).

Roberts, J.V., and Hough, M. (eds) (2002) *Changing Attitudes to Punishment: Public Opinion, Crime and Justice* (Cullompton: Willan Publishing).

Roberts, P. (2002) 'On Method: The Ascent of Comparative Criminal Justice', 22 *Oxford Journal of Legal Studies*, 539.

——(2006) 'Theorising Procedural Traditions: Subjects, Objects and Values in Criminal Adjudication' in R.A. Duff, L. Farmer and S. Marshall (eds) *The Trial on Trial 2: Judgement and Calling to Account* (Oxford: Hart Publishing).

——(2008) 'Comparative Criminal Justice goes Global', 28 *Oxford Journal of Legal Studies*, 369.

Robertson, D. (1998) *Judicial Discretion in the House of Lords* (Oxford: Clarendon Press).

Robson, G. (2002) 'The Lay Magistracy: No Time for Complacency', 166 *Justice of the Peace*, 624.

Rogers, J. (2006) 'Restructuring the Exercise of Prosecutorial Discretion in England', 26 *Oxford Journal of Legal Studies*, 775.

Rogers, L.J., and Erez, E. (1999) 'The Contextuality of Objectivity in Sentencing among Legal Professionals in South Australia', 27 *International Journal of the Sociology of Law*, 267.

Rose, N. (2000) 'Government and Control', 40 *British Journal of Criminology*, 321.

Rottman, D., and Casey, P. (2000) 'Therapeutic Jurisprudence and the Emergence of Problem-Solving Courts', *National Institute of Justice Journal* 12.

Roxin, C. (1994) *Strafrecht, Allgemeiner Teil* (Munich: CH Beck).

Ruga Riva, C. (2009) 'Una nuova parola d'ordine: lotta senza quartiere contro l'illegalita diffusa' in O. Mazza and F. Vigano (eds) *Il "pacchetto sicurezza"* (Turin: Giappichelli), 131–51.

Ruggiero, V. (1998) 'The Country of Cesare Beccaria: The Myth of Rehabilitation in Italy' in R.P. Weiss and N. South (eds) *Comparing Prison Systems: Towards a Comparative and International Penology* (Amsterdam: Gordon & Breach), 207.

Russell, B. (1914) *Our Knowledge of the External World as a Field for Scientific Method in Philosophy* (London: Allen & Unwin).

Salas, D. (2002) 'The Role of the Judge' in M. Delmas-Marty and J.R. Spencer (eds) *European Criminal Procedures* (Cambridge: Cambridge University Press), 504.

Sandel, M. (1982) *Liberalism and the Limits of Justice* (Cambridge: Cambridge University Press).

Sanders, A. (2002a) 'Core Values, the Magistracy, and the Auld Report', 29 *Journal of Law and Society*, 324.

——(2002b) 'Victim Participation in an Exclusionary Criminal Justice System' in C. Hoyle and R. Young (eds) *New Visions of Crime Control* (Oxford: Hart Publishing).

Sanders, A. *et al.* (2001) 'Victim Impact Statements: Don't Work, Can't Work', *Criminal Law Review*, 447.

Sarre, R., and Wilson, D. (eds) (1998) *Sentencing and Indigenous Peoples* Proceedings of Roundtable convened by the Australian Institute of Criminology and the University of South Australia on 31 October 1997, Research and Public Policy Series No. 16 (Canberra: Australian Institute of Criminology).

Schabas, W. (1997) 'Sentencing and the International Tribunals: For a Human Rights Approach', *7 Duke Journal of International and Comparative Law*: 461, http://www.law.duke.edu/journals/djcil/articles/djcil7p461.htm (accessed 2003).

——(2006) *The UN International Criminal Tribunals: The Former Yugoslavia, Rwanda and Sierra Leone* (Cambridge: Cambridge University Press).

——(2007) *An Introduction to the International Criminal Court* (Cambridge: Cambridge University Press, 3rd ed.).

Scharf, M. (2004) 'Trading Justice for Efficiency: Plea Bargaining and International Tribunals', 2 *Journal of International Criminal Justice*, 1070.

Seiber, U. (2003) *ThePunishment of Serious Crimes: A Comparative Analysis of Sentencing Law and Practice*, vol. 1 *Expert Report*; vol. 2 *Country Reports* (Freiburg im Breisgau: Max Planck Institute for Foreign and International Criminal Law).

Sennett, R. (1980) *Authority* (New York: Knopf).

Sentencing Advisory Panel (2002) *Advice on Rape to the Court of Appeal*, 24 May, http://www.sentencing-guidelines.gov.uk/docs/rape.pdf (accessed 2002).

——(2010) *Advice to the Sentencing Guidelines Council: Overarching Principles of Sentencing* (London: Sentencing Advisory Panel), 11 March, http://www.sentencing-guidelines.gov.uk/docs/s_g_update_10_march/sgc_and_sap_annual_report_ 09_10.pdf (accessed 2010).

Sentencing Guidelines Council (2007) *Reduction in Sentence for a Guilty Plea*, Definitive Guideline, revised 2007, (London: Sentencing Guidelines Council).

——(2008) *Causing Death by Driving*, Definitive Guideline (London: Sentencing Guidelines Council).

Shearing, C. (2001) 'Punishment and the Changing Face of the Governance' 3 *Punishment and Society*, 203.

Shearing, C., and Johnston L. (2005) 'Justice in the Risk Society' 38 *Australian and New Zealand Journal of Criminology*, 25.

Sherman, L. (2003) 'Reason For Emotion: Reinventing Justice With Theories, Innovations, And Research, American Society Of Criminology 2002 Presidential Address, 41 *Criminology*, 1.

Shute, S. (1999) 'Who Passes Unduly Lenient Sentences? How Were They Listed: A Survey of Attorney-General's Reference Cases 1989–1997', *Criminal Law Review*, 603.

Simon, J. (2002) 'Governing through Crime Metaphors', 67 *Brooklyn Law Review*, 1035.

——(2007) *Governing Through Crime: How the War on Crime Transformed American Democracy and Created a Culture of Fear* (New York: Oxford University Press).

Sisti, L. (2007) 'Italy: Reporter's Notebook', *Global Integrity Report*, http://report.globalintegrity.org/Italy/2007/notebook (accessed 2010).

Skolnick, J.H. (1966) *Justice Without Trial* (New York: John Wiley).

Slack, J. (2009) 'Half a million criminals let off with just another caution' *Daily Mail* online, 7 November, http://www.dailymail.co.uk/news/article-1225844/Half-million-criminals-let-just-caution.html (accessed 2009).

Slapper, G.J., and Tombs, S. (1999) *Corporate Crime* (London: Addison Wesley Longman).

Sloane, R.D. (2007) 'The Expressive Capacity of International Punishment: The Limits of the National Law Analogy and the Potential of International Criminal Law', 43 *Stanford Journal of International Law*, 39; Paper Number 06–112, Columbia Law School, Public Law & Legal Theory Working Paper Group, http://ssrn.com/abstract=900641 (accessed 2010).

Smart, B. (1999) Facing Modernity: Ambivalence, Reflexivity and Morality (London: Sage).

Smith, A.B., and Blumberg, A.S. (1967) 'The Problem of Objectivity in Judicial Decision-Making', 46 *Social Forces* 96.

Sparks, R. (1996) 'Penal "Austerity": the Doctrine of Less Eligibility Reborn?' in R. Matthews and P. Francis (eds) *Prisons 2000* (London: Macmillan), 74.

——(2006) 'Ordinary Anxieties and States of Emergency: Satecraft and Spectatorship in the New Politics of Insecurity' in S. Armstrong and L. McAra (eds) *Perspectives on Punishment: The Contours of Control* (Oxford: Oxford University Press), 31.

Spencer, J.R. (2002) 'Evidence' in M. Delmas-Marty and J.R. Spencer (eds) *European Criminal Procedures* (Cambridge: Cambridge University Press), 620.

Stevens, R. (1999) 'A Loss of Innocence? Judicial Independence and the Separation of Powers', 19 *Oxford Journal of Legal Studies*, 365.

Sudnow, D. (1965) 'Normal Crimes: Sociological Features of the Penal Code in a Public Defender Office,' 12 *Social Problems*, 255.

Tallgren, I. (2002) 'The Sensibility and Sense of International Criminal Law', 13 *European Journal of International Law*, 561.

Tamanaha, B.Z. (1997) *Realistic Socio-Legal Theory* (Oxford: Clarendon Press).

——(2007) 'Understanding Legal Pluralism: Past to Present, Local to Global', St John's University School of Law, Legal Studies Research Paper Series, Paper No 07–0080, August, http://ssrn.com/abstract=1010105 (accessed 2009).

Tata, C. (1997) 'Conceptions and Representations of the Sentencing Decision Process', 24 *Journal of Law and Society*, 395.

——(2007) 'Sentencing as Craftwork and the Binary Epistemologies of the Discretionary Decision Process', 16 *Social and Legal Studies*, 425.

——(2010) 'A Sense of Justice: the Role of Pre-Sentence Reports in the Production and Disruption of Guilt and Guilty Pleas', 12 *Punishment & Society: The International Journal of Penology*, 239.

Taylor, R., Wasik, M. and Leng, R. (2004) *Blackstone's Guide to the Criminal Justice Act 2003* (Oxford, Oxford University Press).

Thomas, D.A. (1970) *Principles of Sentencing* (London: Heinemann, 1st ed.).

——(1979) *Principles of Sentencing* (London: Heinemann, 2nd ed.).

——(1982 as updated) *Current Sentencing Practice* (London: Sweet & Maxwell).

——(1989) Commentary at *Criminal Law Review*, 43.

Tonry, M. (1992) 'Selective Incapacitation: The Debate Over Its Ethics' in A. von Hirsch and A. Ashworth (eds) *Principled Sentencing* (Edinburgh: Edinburgh University Press, 1st ed.), 165.

——(1996) *Sentencing Matters* (New York: Oxford University Press).

——(2002) 'Setting Sentencing Policy Through Guidelines' in S. Rex and M. Tonry (eds) *Reform and Punishment: The Future of Sentencing* (Cullompton: Willan Publishing).

——(2004) *Punishment and Politics: Evidence and emulation in the making of English crime control policy* (Cullompton: Willan Publishing).

Tulkens, F. (2002) 'Negotiated Justice' in M. Delmas-Marty and J.R. Spencer (eds) *European Criminal Procedures* (Cambridge: Cambridge University Press), 641.

Twining, W. (1999) 'Narrative and Generalisations in Argumentation about Questions of Fact, 40 *South Texas Law Review*, 351.

Tyler, T.R. (2003) 'Procedural Justice, Legitimacy and the Effective Rule of Law', 30 *Crime and Justice*, 283.

——(2006) *Why People Obey the Law* (Princeton NJ: Princeton University Press).

Tyler, T.R. (ed.) (2008) *Legitimacy and Criminal Justice* (New York: Russell Sage Foundation).

Tyler, T.R. and Darley, J. (2000) ' Building a Law-Abiding Society: Taking Public Views about Morality and the Legitimacy of Legal Authorities into Account when Formulating Substantive Law', 28 *Hofstra Law Review*, 707.

United Nations (1997) *Reconceptualising Governance*, Management Development and Governance Division, Discussion Paper No 2 (New York: United Nations Development Programme).

van den Wyngaert, C., *et al.* (eds) (1993) *Criminal Procedure Systems in the European Community* (London: Butterworth).

van Dijk, J.J.M., van Kesteren, J.N. and Smit, P. (2008) *Criminal Victimisation in International Perspective: Key Findings from the 2004–2005 ICVS and EU ICS* (The Hague, Boom Legal Publishers).

van Zyl Smit, D. (2002) 'Punishment and Human Rights in International Criminal Justice' Inaugural lecture as Professor of Comparative and Penal Law, University of Nottingham, 30 January.

van Zyl Smit, D. and Ashworth, A. (2004) 'Disproportionate Sentences as Human Rights Violations', 67 *Modern Law Review*, 541.

Vassalli, G. (ed.) (1982) *Problemi generali di dirrito penale* (Milan: Giuffre).

Verrest, P. (2000) 'The French Public Prosecution Service', 3 *European Journal of Crime, Criminal Law and Criminal Justice*, 210.

Vogel, M.E. (1999) 'The Social Origins of Plea Bargaining: Conflict and the Law in the Process of State Formation, 1830–60', 33 *Law and Society Review*, 161.

Vogler, R, (2005) *A World View of Criminal Justice* (Aldershot: Ashgate).

Volqvartz, J. (2005) 'ICC Under Fire Over Uganda Probe', CNN, *Global Policy Forum*, 23 February, http://www.globalpolicy.org/intljustice/icc/2005/0223iccfire.htm (accessed 2008).

von Hirsch, A. (1976) *Doing Justice* (Boston MA: Northeastern University Press).

——(1993) *Censure and Sanctions* (Oxford: Clarendon Press).

——(1999) 'Punishment, Penance and the State' in M. Matravers (ed.) *Punishment and Political Theory* (Oxford: Hart Publishing), 69.

von Hirsch, A., and Ashworth, A. (2005) *Proportionate Sentencing: Exploring the Principles* (New York: Oxford University Press).

von Hirsch, A., Ashworth, A., and Shearing, C. (2003) 'Specifying Aims and Limits for Restorative Justice: A "Making-Amends" Model?' in A. von Hirsch *et al. Restorative Justice & Criminal Justice: Competing or Reconcilable Paradigms?* (Oxford: Hart Publishing) 21.

von Hirsch, A., and Roberts, J. (2002) 'Racial Disparity in Sentencing: Reflections on the Hood Study', 36 *Howard Journal of Criminal Justice*, 227.

Wacquant, L. (2009) *Prisons of Poverty* (Minneapolis MN: University of Minnesota Press).

Wald, P.M. (2003) 'General Radislav Krstić: A War Crimes Case Study', 16 *Georgetown Journal of Legal Ethics*, 445.

Waldman, E.A. (1998) *'The Evaluative–Facilitative Debate in Mediation: Applying the Lens of Therapeutic Jurisprudence*, 82 *Marquette Law Review*, 155.

Walker, N. (1972) *Sentencing in a Rational Society* (Harmondsworth: Penguin, rev. ed.).

——(1985) *Sentencing: Theory, Law and Practice* (London: Butterworth, 1st ed.).

Wandall, R.H. (2008) *Decisions to Imprison: Court Decision-Making Inside and Outside the Law* (Aldershot: Ashgate).

Wasik, M, (1998) *Emmins on Sentencing* (London: Blackstone Press).

Watson, T. (2010) 'Raoul Moat page reaction shows PM doesn't get social media' *The Guardian*, 15 July, http://www.guardian.co.uk/commentisfree/2010/jul/15/raoul-moat-facebook-tribute-cameron (accessed 2010).

Wexler, D.B., and Winick, B.J. (1996) *Law in a Therapeutic Key: Developments in Therapeutic Jurisprudence* (Durham NC: Carolina Academic Press).

Wexler, L.S. (1995) 'Reflections on the Trial of Vichy Collaborator Paul Touvier for Crimes against Humanity in France', 20 *Law and Social Inquiry*, 191.

——(1996) 'The Proposed International Criminal Court: an Appraisal', 29 *Cornell International Law Journal*, 665.

Wiener, M.J. (1994) *Reconstructing the Criminal: Culture, Law, and Policy in England 1830–1914* (Cambridge: Cambridge University Press).

Wiener, M.J. (ed.) (1984) *Crime and Punishment in England 1850–1922* (London and New York: Garland Publishing).

Wilkinson, P. (1989) 'Ethical Defences of Terrorism – Defending the Indefensible', 1 *Political Violence*, 7.

Wilson, R.A. (2001) *The Politics of Truth and Reconciliation in South Africa: Legitimizing the Post-Apartheid State* (Cambridge: Cambridge University Press).

Wood, D. (1998) 'Dangerous Offenders and the Morality of Protective Sentencing', *Criminal Law Review*, 424.

Woolf, H.K. (LJ) (1990) Prison Disturbances: Report of an Inquiry by the Rt Hon Lord Justice Woolf (London: HMSO).

Worrall, A. (2006) Review of Rex 2005, 46 *British Journal of Criminology*, 538.

Yazzie, R., and Zion, J. (1996) 'Navajo Restorative Justice: The Law of Equality and Justice' in B. Galaway and J. Hudson (eds) *Restorative Justice: International Perspectives* (Monsey NY: Criminal Justice Press).

Young, J. (1972) 'Mass Media, Drugs and Deviance' in P. Rock and M. McIntosh (eds) *Deviance and Social Control* (London: Tavistock).

Yue, M. (2002) 'Prosecutorial Discretion and Plea Bargaining in the United States, France, Germany, and Italy: A Comparative Perspective', 12 *International Criminal Law Review*, 2.

Zappala, S. (2003) *Human Rights in International Criminal Proceedings* (Oxford: Oxford University Press).

Zedner, L. (1994) 'Reparation and Retribution: Are they Reconcilable?', 57 *Modern Law Review*, 228.

——(1995) 'In Pursuit of the Vernacular: Comparing Law and Order Discourse in Britain and Germany', 4 *Social and Legal Studies*, 517.

——(2004) *Criminal Justice* (Oxford: Oxford University Press).

——(2005) 'Securing Liberty in the Face of Terror: Reflections from Criminal Justice', 32 *Journal of Law and Society*, 507.

Index

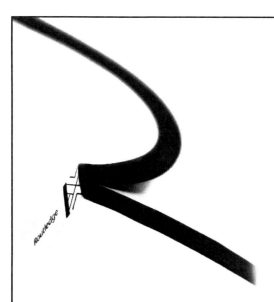